Nietzsche in American Literature and Thought

Nietzsche in American Literature and Thought

Edited by

Manfred Pütz

CAMDEN HOUSE

Published by Camden House, Inc.
Drawer 2025
Columbia, SC 29202 USA

The publisher and editor are grateful to Ullstein
Bilderdienst (Berlin) for the illustration appearing on the
jacket.

Printed on acid-free paper.
Binding materials are chosen for strength and
durability.

ISBN 1-57113-028-4

Library of Congress Cataloging-in-Publication Data

Nietzsche in American literature and thought / edited by Manfred Pütz.
   p.   cm. — (Studies in German literature, linguistics, and culture)
   Includes bibliographical references and index.
   ISBN 1-57113-028-4
   1. American literature—German influences. 2. Nietzsche,
Friedrich Wilhelm, 1844-1900—Influence. 3. German literature—
Appreciation—United States. 4. United States—Civilization—
German influences. 5. Philosophy, German—19th century.
6. Philosophy in literature. 7. Germany—In literature. 8.
Philosophy, American. I. Pütz, Manfred, 1938-   . II. Series:
Studies in German literature, linguistics, and culture (Unnumbered)
PS159.G3N49 1995
810.9 ' 351—dc20   95-9731
                                                CIP

Contents

Manfred Pütz

Nietzsche in America: An Introduction

"EVERY PHILOSOPHY ALSO *conceals* a philosophy; every opinion is also a hiding-place, every word also a mask," Nietzsche provocatively wrote towards the end of *Beyond Good and Evil* (1886), a book in which he had earlier voiced his conviction that

> the 'work', that of the artist or the philosopher, invents him who created it, is supposed to have created it; 'great men', as they are venerated, are bad little fictions invented afterwards; in the world of historical values false coinage *is the rule.*[1]

If one combines the two statements, which at first seem to be only loosely connected, into a more encompassing idea of the relationship between author, work, and audience, there could hardly be a more appropriate description of the interactive forces at work in the process of the American reception of Nietzsche from its very beginnings. For surely it was a marked feature of this reception, particularly in the early years, that most readers, commentators, and would-be exegetes were animated by the suspicion that behind Nietzsche's strange new philosophy lay the depth of another philosophy, replete with concealed intentions and effects, and that the public figure of the notorious author 'Nietzsche' somewhere encapsulated a 'true' Nietzsche whom it was advisable to bring to light in order to gain a full picture of the variably evil, beneficial, or whatever forces vested in the man behind the mask. One anonymous reviewer from the camp of early Nietzsche detractors formulated his suspicions quite bluntly when he called the enigmatic and shocking figure of Nietzsche, just arrived on the American scene, "A Philosophic Mr. Hyde."[2]

As a consequence of this situation, Americans who came into contact with the Nietzsche phenomenon indeed quickly set about to create the creator from his works, while at the same time they were busily re-creating these works in the light of what they believed to have identified in their preconceptions of the author. In a telling way, then, the American encounter with Nietzsche reveals itself, already in its earliest stages, as an engaged search for the 'real' Nietzsche, and was thus bent on discovering a 'new Nietzsche', or rather a whole array of new Nietzsches, not yet identified and/or appropriated by others, around every corner. What for many observers of the eventful history of Nietzsche reception appears to be a dominant tendency of various world-wide movements of the recent past, namely the discovery of ever-changing and ever-newer images of Nietzsche, can clearly be seen as the hallmark of American encounters with this philosopher from the very beginning.

In his extended critique of Jaspers's interpretation of Nietzsche, Walter Kaufmann has taken Jaspers to task for his all too facile concept of pervasive ambiguity in Nietzsche which, as Kaufmann holds in an ironic formula, must eventually lead to the maxim: "everybody is entitled to his own Nietzsche."[3] To be sure, we notice in retrospect and in reference to a more international picture of Nietzsche reception that Americans were not alone in intentionally or unintentionally following this maxim when they first encountered the works of this author who appeared to be enigma, oracle, tempter, and scapegoat all at the same time. To a certain extent, almost every national European culture that came into contact with Nietzsche followed this pattern and tended to invent its own welter of conflicting Nietzsche images by variously presenting, appropriating, praising, attacking, transforming, or simply ignoring parts and particles of his work in relation to selective topical issues and problems of its own time.[4] Thus Steven Aschheim has noted in his recent study of what he calls the Nietzsche legacy in Germany over the past hundred years that the history of Nietzsche's reception in Germany has been shaped by a multiplicity of interpretive impulses and refractions which "must be understood as a product of the dynamic interaction between the peculiar, multifaceted qualities of his thought and its appropriators,"[5] and, moreover, that this interaction can generally be seen as transcribing a "history of interested and selective paradigmatic representations."[6] With a similar thrust, Hays Steilberg argues, in his contribution to the present volume on Nietzsche's "First Steps in the New World," that "the early discussion of Nietzsche in America is from the outset a contest not only over the acceptability of Nietzsche's philosophy, but also over the ideological claim to the rights of interpretation."

However, where one finds striking similarities of reception, there are also bound to be differences and historical peculiarities, and I would like to turn to some of the latter in the context of the early dealings with Nietzsche in America. From the outset, the problem of translations, or what Americans were actually reading (or missing) when they dealt with Nietzsche, loomed large over the American scene. As later observers of this scene have noted, curiosities and co-incidences of major proportions at first abounded in respect to the project of providing America with reliable translations of Nietzsche's works.[7] One obvious and irritating curiosity was that during the first stages of reception most Americans interested in Nietzsche were not reading the author's works at all, but were rather forced to imbibe large portions of hearsay of the worst kind, stemming from a highly contaminated source. This source was Max Nordau's notorious book *Entartung*, which had appeared in English under the title *Degeneration* in 1895 (it made the best-seller list during the same year) and had thus preceded the publication of the first English translations of any of Nietzsche's works by a full year. Nordau's infamous book presented a raving denunciation of all modern art, literature, and thought as indications of a hopelessly degenerate European culture on its way to final catastrophe, and it had summarily claimed Nietzsche's writings as prime exhibits for the diagnosis of rapidly spreading madness and degeneracy. Consequently, most American readers intrigued by the Nietzsche problem (with the exception of very few intellectuals who were able to read him in the original) had a clear-cut but highly distorted image of 'Nietzsche' in their minds before they were ever granted access to his writings on an acceptable textual basis.

Moreover, when the first English translations actually appeared in 1896 in America, the Nietzsche canon was practically turned upside down in so far as some of Nietzsche's last works were published first (for instance, *Zarathustra*, *The Genealogy of Morals*, *Twilight of the Idols*, and *The Anti-Christ*), which had the unfortunate side effect that the picture of the author's complex and controversial interconnection and development of thought was distorted beyond recognition. Eventually, the whole project of a reliable English language edition of Nietzsche's *Complete Works* was marred by various financial and organizational problems, and consequently resulted — additionally burdened with problems of changing editors and publishers, as well as poor translations — in a decidedly less than satisfactory eighteen-volume edition (Levy edition) that was not finished until 1913, a time when the heated debate over 'Nietzsche' had already been going on for many years in America.

Yet it was within this field of tensions, partly created by imported and unverifiable stereotypes of Nietzsche against the background of the problematics of textual availability, that a first great wave of debates over Nietzsche took place which, according to all later commentators, marked the first important period of his presence and impact on the American scene. The period in question extended roughly from 1895 to 1914, and in the present volume the essay "First Steps in the New World" discusses its major features. Some veritable and durable Nietzsche legends and counter-legends, which occasionally make their influence still felt today, go back to this time of a free-for-all discussion, which often saw supporters and debunkers, admirers, enthusiasts, detractors, and self-declared disciples or exorcists of Nietzsche interlocked in a battle which knew no mercy or compromise. The dominant issues of what has been called the resulting "Nietzschean chiaroscuro" are, from today's perspective, surprisingly limited and recurrent since they almost exclusively centered on problems of ethics and morally informed politics at the expense of other dimensions in Nietzsche's thought, such as his metaphysics, epistemology, aesthetics, and critique of language, which in America as elsewhere seem to be almost without exception discoveries of the time after 1950. For the moment, the American scene overwhelmingly displayed the spectacle of crusaders and confessors from sharply divided camps battling it out over questions of Nietzsche's presumable influence on the scenario of an eternal fight of good versus evil, democratic versus anti-democratic principles, and traditional versus revisionist, as much as Christian versus anti-Christian values. Some of the provisional results open to inspection when the smoke temporarily cleared away after heavy ideological exchanges of fire were quite paradoxical as, for instance, in the case of the association of socialist and social Darwinian interpreters of Nietzsche, who both claimed him for their own causes and suddenly found themselves in the same camp of Nietzsche supporters and appropriators.

Of course, some of the drastically foregrounded issues of the first major wave of Nietzsche reception in America bore the stamp of genuinely American concerns. One of them aggressively addressed the question of Nietzsche's "Americanness," an issue that pointed to the problematics of whether the philosopher's ideas could either be seen as compatible or as totally incompatible with the whole framework of principles, tenets, and suppositions that supplied the basis for a genuinely "American creed" constitutive of the encompassing cultural and political practices of American society as such. Needless to say, the outcome of this debate was just as inconclusive as the results of the other controversies over the meaning and function of Nietzsche's ideas, since all camps involved drew their pro and con arguments from the very arsenal of fixed presuppositions and convictions which had already settled the question of Nietzsche's status as an accepted or rejected protagonist in the overall scenario. In view of this fact, Ludwig Marcuse's at once apodictic and puzzled verdict that Nietzsche for a long time figured in America as the "most un-American of all German thinkers"[8] does not make much sense, because it refers only to the adamant judgment of the habitual Nietzsche denunciators of the debate. However, what does make sense in this context is to recognize the seemingly irreconcilable opposition between early adherents and detractors of Nietzsche as a prefiguration of the various paradigmatic antagonisms, which time and again have been played out in the overall course of Nietzsche's reception in America, and which remain a conspicuous feature of the split American image of this philosopher until today (compare, for example, Allan Bloom's recent views on Nietzsche in *The Closing of the American Mind* (1987) to those of no less recent Nietzsche-inspired poststructuralist and deconstructive critics and theoreticians).

The literary figures, whose relationship to Nietzsche is analyzed in the first part of the present volume, were all witnesses, in varying degrees and senses of the word, to the first extensive period of Nietzsche's controversial appearance on the American stage. However, most of them were, and at the same time were not, part of the evolving scene of the highly polarized and vociferous Nietzsche debate of the time. Of course, H. L. Mencken was a direct participant in the proliferating discussions of Nietzsche, and he is widely regarded as the best-known American propagator, if not disciple, of the German philosopher at the beginning of the twentieth century. Mencken's multifaceted contributions to the debate regularly added fuel to the flames, and his book on *The Philosophy of Friedrich Nietzsche* (1908) is rightly considered as a landmark of the reception, interpretation, and propagation of Nietzschean ideas in America. Yet Mencken's case is also a special one, since his dealings with Nietzsche were rather borderline cases of an intricate mixture of literary, philosophical, and popular concerns, which finally made Mencken one of the most vociferous Nietzsche-inspired cultural critics of his time. With some of the other more literary-minded figures, whose relationship to Nietzsche is here evoked, the case was somewhat different. Jack London and Theodore Dreiser were demonstrably interested in and influenced by Nietzsche, but they never played a noticeable role in the raging public debates as sketched above. Instead, they turned what intrigued them in Nietzsche's philosophy (of which they had anything but a complete picture) into literature by weaving their reflections on certain Nietzschean ideas that fascinated them into the very texture of their novels. Finally, with William Dean Howells, Henry Adams, and Henry James, who are all treated here in the Nietzschean context, there is next to nothing of a direct influence of the German philosopher identifiable, and hence they would be poor subjects for a traditional influence study. However, as the contributions on these three authors demonstrate, there are abundant resources of conceptual, structural, and poetological configurations evident in their works, which warrant a detailed investigation of similarities and differences, of shared concerns and divergent sensibilities, in the light of a dialectical relationship between the absence and the presence of Nietzschean thought in their works.

During the next three decades, the debate over Nietzsche took a turn, in America as elsewhere, that was everything but congenial to subtle literary and/or philosophical dealings with his works. The time of the two world wars, as much as the period between them, saw a wave of radical politicizations of selective elements and aspects of Nietzsche's thought which, in retrospect, become recognizable as a direct function of those ideological battles on the grand scale that restricted any dialogue between the antagonistic parties involved to the point of a mutual extinction of opinions. During the first and the second world war alike, Nietzsche and Nietzschean ideas were hotly debated issues of the public discourse in America, but mostly in a form that saw both author and work vanish under a veritable avalanche of propaganda and counter-propaganda, and hardly left any room for an exchange of reasonable arguments beyond rigid political affiliation and ideological warfare.[9] Hence, even if Nietzsche was, to a certain extent, a spectacular presence in the public mind of these times, almost any non-political literary or philosophical approach to his works was branded as an intellectual aberration severely frowned upon by the American public at large.

Undeniably, however, there were American writers of the decades in question who, in varying degrees, can and must be seen in the Nietzschean context. From among those literary figures under some form of Nietzschean influence, the present volume selects O'Neill, Pound, Cummings, Eliot, Stevens, and Hemingway for detailed commentary. As in the case of the widely different literary influence stories concerning the prior generation of American writers, the term Nietzschean context demands further specification. In the case of O'Neill, an immediate influence by Nietzsche is undeniable; it extended from 1907, when O'Neill first discovered Nietzsche, to the very end of his career, and, for the most part, it worked like a spell on the young O'Neill and made Nietzsche his repeatedly confessed literary idol. In the exemplary cases of Ezra Pound and the other modernist poets here called upon, the Nietzschean influence was much more diffuse and differentiated, and it eventually constituted a complex of interactive forces rather reflecting a history of conflicting impulses, refractions, and tentative responses than the uniform story of straightforward influence along the lines of literary and intellectual heritage. Finally, in the case of the Hemingway-Nietzsche connection we are confronted by a relationship in which a direct influence perhaps cannot be substantiated at all, but the conceptual framework and the texture of some of Hemingway's works tell a different story.

If we have so far followed the lines of early popular and literary repercussions caused by Nietzsche's appearance on the American stage, it now remains to say something about the development of early American responses to Nietzsche in professional philosophical circles. The history of philosophical Nietzsche reception in a narrower sense forms yet another story which, in the present volume, is told in its major early stages in the essay "From Dolson to Kauf-

mann: Philosophical Nietzsche Reception in America, 1901–1950."
As is well known, Nietzsche was initially not taken seriously, often
not even regarded, as a 'real' philosopher by the overwhelming majority of those American thinkers (mostly representing the academic
establishment of their time) who had commonly agreed on a special
and restricted meaning of the terms *philosopher* and *philosophy*. This
being so, it cannot come as a surprise that dealing with Nietzsche as
a philosopher initially carried the stigma of an unreasonable enterprise with which academic philosophers of respectable standing were
reluctant to be associated. In a telling way, the leading American
philosophers of the turn of the century and after (William James,
Josiah Royce, George Santayana, John Dewey) all proved to be cases
in point in that they mostly bypassed Nietzsche as an important
philosophical subject and thus left the spadework of seriously dealing
with this outsider to what they considered minor and marginal figures of their trade. Those who did seriously, though not always favorably, deal with Nietzsche during the next decades consequently
came to the task from different quarters and were animated by different intentions, though the dominant topics of their philosophical
agenda displayed an almost uncanny uniformity. As Hays Steilberg
rightly emphasizes in his survey of the early philosophical scene, "the
question of morals or values in the light of Nietzsche's philosophy of
power has dominated almost every extensive American interpretation
of his thought within this time frame [the first fifty years]," which is
to say that the early philosophical discussions of Nietzsche mostly
duplicated the preoccupation with the narrow issues and concerns
familiar from the early popular reception.

Much of this changed dramatically when Walter Kaufmann published his epochal study *Nietzsche: Philosopher, Psychologist, Antichrist*
in 1950. Kaufmann's book became the pivotal work of the second
important period of Nietzsche reception in America — a wave of
topical dealings with the author that quickly gathered momentum
and seems to be reaching new peaks in our own time — in more respects than can even be mentioned here. It would not be an exag-
geration to say that many if not most kinds of Nietzsche scholarship
of the past four decades have been made possible, in one sense or
another, by Kaufmann's groundbreaking enterprise and by the simple fact that through his work, including his still valuable transla-

tions, Nietzsche has finally been established in America as an exceptionally important figure in the history of modern philosophy.

In the wake of Kaufmann's study — whether in continuation, modification or contradiction to it — another array of 'new Nietzsches' have made their appearance on the American scene. Among them we find Nietzsche the metaphysician (or, alternatively, the ultimate destroyer of metaphysics) next to Nietzsche the pre-Freudian proponent of an encompassing psychology of suspicion, and Nietzsche the proto-existentialist next door to Nietzsche the uncompromising critic of the pitfalls of language. Of the major stages of Nietzsche's further bewildering transformations after Kaufmann's near domination of the scene for almost twenty years, the present volume concentrates on several paradigmatic shifts of Nietzsche interpretation as embodied in important monographs by Arthur C. Danto (1965), Alexander Nehamas (1985), and Henry Staten (1990), and as characteristic of the extended preoccupations with Nietzsche in the works of Stanley Cavell and Richard Rorty. However, it should be noted that the scene of philosophical Nietzsche reception in America during the past twenty years is actually much more prolific and divergent than one can possibly hope to document in a single volume on the topic. Though it might be broadly justifiable to characterize, as Bernd Magnus has done in his essay on "Nietzsche Today," the divergent strands of Nietzsche interpretation in contemporary America as "analytical," "deconstructionist," and "reconstructionist,"[10] it is also obvious that any typological scheme of the above kind is bound to prove reductive in view of the accelerated output and divergency of the philosophical Nietzsche scholarship of recent years. In the eighties and early nineties alone, a virtual wave of philosophically-oriented books on Nietzsche has been published in America and it seems to defy all attempts at methodical classification. Among these books are challenging treatments of a multiplicity of philosophical aspects, as much as the overall structure, of Nietzsche's thought by recognized American Nietzsche scholars such as Bernd Magnus, Maudemarie Clark, Richard Schacht, and David Krell (to name only some important voices in the widening debate), but it seems still too early to venture an assessment of their actual impact on further developments in the ongoing philosophical interpretation of Nietzsche in America. In a certain way, it is even misleading to speak of a contemporary *American* Nietzsche reception at the given moment, because it is an obvious feature of this reception that it has merged, at least over the past two decades, with the European debate over Nietzsche to a point that a complex international dialogue can be seen taking shape (notice the world-wide reverberations of Heidegger's versus Derrida's readings of Nietzsche) which invalidates any clear demarcation lines between, say, French, German, English, and American concerns with Nietzsche's philosophy.

If this development of the past years effectively suspends attempts at clear external demarcations between various national complexes of the philosophical Nietzsche debate, a similar movement can be observed in the field of internal differentiation between allegedly divergent forms of discourse. In America as elsewhere, it is today, mostly due to poststructuralist influences, no longer possible to rely on clear-cut traditionalist distinctions between certain forms of discourse claimed and exclusively practiced by philosophers, literary critics/theoreticians, and writers of literature as such. Hence, in respect to Nietzsche as a topic and point of contention, neat divisions between allegedly "philosophical," "literary," "theoretical," and/or "popular" forms of reception have largely broken down. Obviously, many participants of the contemporary debate over Nietzsche are by profession literary critics, practicing their trade in departments other than the department of philosophy. Yet the issues they raise and the methodological approaches they pursue frequently merge with those of certain schools of philosophy and cultural history to the point where a host of formerly silenced aspects of Nietzsche's thought becomes the common reference point of an ever-widening discussion that no longer respects the traditional boundaries of established academic disciplines, in theory as much as in practice.[11] This phenomenon of an encompassing, non-compartmentalized discourse on Nietzsche, frequently labeled "postmodern" in want of a better term, becomes most obvious if one compares the conceptual agendas shared by recent literary critics and theoreticians on the one hand, and philosophers, cultural critics, and history-of-ideas scholars on the other. In this context, Bernd Magnus has recently offered, in a contribution on the problematics of "Nietzsche and Postmodern Criticism," the following scheme of seven central issues in Nietzsche's writings which, collectively, "may be thought of as elective affinities" shaping today's postmodern critical discourse in many direct or indirect ways:

These seven elective affinities . . . are, first, perspectivism; second, the diagnosis and critique of binarism, along with the metaphysics of presence; third, substituting genealogical narratives for ontology; fourth, diagnosing the power/knowledge connection, as well as the structures of ideological domination; fifth, erasing the boundaries between philosophy and literature; sixth, the disarticulation of the self; and seventh, the self-consuming, self-deconstructive character of Nietzsche's own discourse and categories.[12]

It is no coincidence that major parts of this very agenda form the backbone of a similar topical scheme which another critic sees governing the relationship between Nietzsche and the concerns of an important segment of contemporary American philosophy. In "Nietzsche's Prefiguration of Postmodern American Philosophy," Cornel West follows three crucial developments in the works of Quine, Goodman, Sellars, Kuhn, and Rorty (his somewhat idiosyncratic selection of postmodern American philosophers) which for him are clearly indicative of a Nietzschean heritage:

the move toward anti-realism or conventionalism in ontology; the move toward the demythologization of the Myth of the Given [Sellars] or anti-foundationalism in epistemology; and the move toward the detranscendentalization of the subject or the dismissal of the mind as a sphere of inquiry.[13]

Any such diagnosis of the shared concerns over the Nietzschean heritage in various disciplines is further corroborated by the obvious fact that the American Nietzsche reception of recent literary theory has largely taken shape under the direct influence of French poststructuralism, which itself was and is a protean movement beyond the confines of accepted compartmentalizations in intellectual matters. Hence, what today fascinates the representatives of certain schools of critical theory in America is largely identical to what fascinates poststructuralists across the board about Nietzsche, namely the newly discovered epistemological and radically anti-metaphysical, the more aesthetically than ethically-inclined Nietzsche, who, as proto-deconstructionist destroyer of all certainties, centers on perspectivism and the illusionary nature of truth, on rhetorics and the problematics of language, on the concealed anthropocentric and logocentric presuppositions of all world-views, and finally becomes a "linguistic pathologist" and "post-structuralist strategist of textual power,"[14] untiringly exposing all megalomaniac projects of final knowledge and meaning, though he himself remains entangled in repeating their patterns in self-reflexive gestures of endless ironic allegorizations.

It seems that on the recent literary scene in America adherents of poststructuralist rediscoveries and reinterpretations of Nietzsche have established a conspicuous platform in literary criticism and theory, while literature itself has largely withdrawn from dealing with Nietzsche and Nietzschean ideas. Except in a most general sense, hardly any presence or influence of Nietzsche can be substantiated in the works of contemporary American writers (with marginal exceptions such as Thomas Berger and Saul Bellow). As far as literature is concerned, the 'new Nietzsches' of variously postmodern, poststructuralist, and deconstructionist bent are simply a property of the literary critics and theoreticians, whose followers, however, not only recruit basic elements of their critical theories from Nietzsche but also display an uncompromising determination to project the Nietzschean context thus established into all literary works they encounter. Foremost among those American critics who, in one form or another, have claimed Nietzsche as one of the fountainheads for the radical reorientations of contemporary critical theory are perhaps the Yale critics (Harold Bloom, Paul de Man, Hillis Miller, Geoffrey Hartman) and their disciples. The present volume offers contributions on two of them, and our selection opts for Paul de Man, who is commonly regarded as the most eminent representative of French-inspired deconstruction in America, and Harold Bloom, who is considered to be an independent figure of truly American mold, but nevertheless stands, though defying direct associations with any particular school of present-day criticism, as a good example for the substantial influences of Nietzsche on the contemporary scene of critical theory in America.

"In America Nietzsche has been taken apart and put together again as was done in other parts of the world," Marcuse wrote more than forty years ago in his summary of the early stages of Nietzsche's reception in America.[15] In view of the immense flux of ongoing interpretations, diffusions, and appropriations of Nietzsche's thought, stimulating the rise and fall of many new Nietzsche legends and counter-legends in this country, the verdict is just as valid today as Paul Elmer More's observation from the year 1913: "if the number of books written about a subject is any proof of interest in it,

Nietzsche must have become the most popular of authors among Englishmen and Americans."[16] But what do we have today as survey attempts of the ever-growing complex of Nietzsche's challenging presence in America? There are three (unpublished) dissertations, one well-known book, and a handful of articles on the subject in question. The dissertations by LeRoy Kauffmann, Melvin Drimmer, and James Peter Cadello are, for the most part, conventional influence studies clearly limited in scope and methodological orientation, bringing the story of Nietzsche in America — variously seen from literary, historical, and philosophical angles — up to the twenties of our century.[17] The book referred to above is Patrick Bridgwater's often-quoted study *Nietzsche in Anglosaxony* (1972) which, as a path-breaking but now dated enterprise, dedicates some fifty pages to the discussion of Nietzsche's influence on some important American writers from the 1890s to the times of Eugene O'Neill and Wallace Stevens. The articles in question extend from early to quite recent contributions on the problem of Nietzsche in America, and they are all restricted to limited time periods and specific facets of the topic at hand.[18]

In comparison to such ventures, valuable as they might be in many respects, the present volume attempts to give a picture of Nietzsche's reception in America that is at once more inclusive and more detailed than the earlier attempts. It extends the period covered to our own day, and aims at a balanced mixture of methodologically diversified contributions, spanning from historical surveys of conspicuous periods and patterns of the Nietzsche debate, over detailed accounts of paradigmatic single cases of Nietzsche's literary and philosophical influence and/or appropriation, to critical revisions of the role of the "Nietzschean context" in relation to such American authors who are seldom seen in the light of this context. All of the essays included in this volume are original contributions which have not appeared before, and in the case of those essays which deal with a seemingly familiar subject of Nietzsche in America, new approaches to established topics have been developed.

What should also be noted is, of course, that the present volume is not dedicated to the impossible task of an all-inclusive documentation covering the bewildering varieties of Nietzsche's role, influence, and American reception during the past hundred years in their totality. In fact, the list of those American writers and thinkers with

Nietzsche affiliations not selected as specific targets of commentary here is probably longer than the list of those included. In some cases, the territory of prospective analyses has already been covered so thoroughly that new investigations did not seem to be warranted; in other cases, certain aspects of Nietzsche's presence in America did not prove weighty enough when coming under closer scrutiny. Furthermore, what is also not included as a topic of our volume is a subject that directly inverts questions about Nietzsche in American literature and thought by posing the problem of which influence, in turn, American writers and thinkers had on Nietzsche. The classical point of reference for such investigations would, of course, be the connection between Emerson and Nietzsche. But since Emerson's undeniable influence on Nietzsche, which has already attracted considerable critical attention,[19] would open a whole new field of concerns different from those in the given context, contributions on Nietzsche's view of Emerson (as much as on the topic of Nietzsche's general views on America) have been excluded.[20]

Finally, another feature of methodological orientation shared by most contributions to the present volume should be noted. Their point is not to defend an alleged definitive truth of Nietzsche's thought against an army of literary and philosophical descendants and pretenders over the past hundred years, who might or might not have understood and interpreted him in the correct sense. Nietzsche himself frequently voiced strong reservations about a possible canonization of his ideas which, he feared, would lose their force of provocation and power of regeneration in the very process of being turned into accepted and celebrated truths:

> Alas, and yet what *are* you, my written and painted thoughts! It is not long ago that you were still so many-coloured, young and malicious, so full of thorns and hidden spices you made me sneeze and laugh — and now? You have already taken off your novelty and some of you, I fear, are on the point of becoming truths: they already look so immortal, so pathetically righteous, so boring![21]

But if the one and undivided truth of Nietzsche's thought is not available to us, or rather is not meant to be easily available to us, then such an elusive 'truth' vanishes as a potential reference point for any enterprise that attempts to define processes of influence and reception in terms of the refraction of truth. Hence, what remains as a task for the study of Nietzsche's influence in America — embracing alleged readings and misreadings, imitations, modifications, and appropriations alike — is to follow lines of reception on their own terms of contextual occurrence and diversified direction, regardless of what the outcome of such an operation might be. The contributions to the present volume try to answer the challenges of this task by dealing, for the most part, with impulses, contexts, and consequences in the complex force field of Nietzsche's reception in America, instead of accentuating an overriding truth or veracity of matter. In doing so, they underline the exceptionally regenerative potential of what one critic has called Nietzsche's "legacy and its seemingly boundless capacity for renewal."[22] In their collective effort, they thus emphasize again the proliferations and divergencies of the Nietzschean heritage in America which, by their very existence, pay Nietzsche the compliment he believed to be strictly reserved for the 'true' philosophers and their ideals: "this shall be called greatness: the ability to be as manifold as whole, as vast as full."[23]

Notes

[1] *Beyond Good and Evil*, trans. R. J. Hollingdale (London/New York: Penguin, 1990), IX, sec. 289 and 269.

[2] Anonymous, "A Philosophic Mr. Hyde," *The Nation*, 62 (June 1896).

[3] Walter Kaufmann, "Jaspers' Relation to Nietzsche," *From Shakespeare to Existentialism* (Princeton: Princeton UP, 1980), p. 308.

[4] For documentations of the general tendency of early Nietzsche reception in various cultural contexts, see among others: Guy de Pourtalès, *Nietzsche en Italie* (Paris: Grasset, 1929); Geneviève Bianquis, *Nietzsche en France* (Paris: Alcan, 1929); Gonzalo Sobejano, *Nietzsche en España* (Madrid: Gredos, 1967); David S. Thatcher, *Nietzsche in England 1890–1914* (Toronto: Toronto UP, 1970); Patrick Bridgwater, *Nietzsche in Anglosaxony* (Leicester: Leicester UP, 1972); Bernice Glatzer Rosenthal (ed.), *Nietzsche in Russia* (Princeton: Princeton UP, 1986); Steven E. Aschheim, *The Nietzsche Legacy in Germany 1890–1990* (Berkeley/Los Angeles: U. of California Press, 1992).

[5] Aschheim, *Nietzsche Legacy*, p. 2.

[6] *Ibid.*, p. 314.

[7] For a short sketch of the situation, see Melvin Drimmer, "Nietzsche in American Thought, 1895–1925" (Diss. U. of Rochester, 1965), vol. I, pp. 80–81 and 106–09; cf. also Hays Steilberg's contribution to the present volume "First Steps in the New World."

[8] Ludwig Marcuse, "Nietzsche in America," *The South Atlantic Quarterly*, 50 (1951), 335.

[9] For a short discussion of Nietzsche's general reputation during the times in question, also referring to other reasons for his steadily diminishing importance during the twenties and thirties in America, see Melvin Drimmer, "Nietzsche in American Thought," vol. I, pp. 19–24.

[10] Bernd Magnus, "Nietzsche Today: A View from America," *International Studies in Philosophy*, 15, 2 (1983), 95–103. Though Magnus's survey was published in 1983, the tripartite scheme of classification is still valid for much of the Nietzsche reception in America after this date.

[11] As a consequence of this situation, we now see the first publications on Nietzsche in America which have been co-authored by scholars from various disciplines. For the most recent (and convincing) example of cooperation between representatives from philosophy, literary scholarship, and critical theory, see Bernd Magnus, Stanley Stewart, and Jean-Pierre Mileur, *Nietzsche's Case: Philosophy as/and Literature* (New York/London: Routledge, 1993).

[12] Bernd Magnus, "Nietzsche and Postmodern Criticism," *Nietzsche-Studien*, 18 (1989), 304–5.

[13] Cornel West, "Nietzsche's Prefiguration of Postmodern American Philosophy," in Daniel O'Hara (ed.), *Why Nietzsche Now?* (Bloomington: Indiana UP, 1985), p. 242.

[14] Daniel O'Hara, Preface to *Why Nietzsche Now?*, pp. vii-viii.

[15] Marcuse, "Nietzsche in America," p. 337.

[16] Quoted in Bridgwater, *Nietzsche in Anglosaxony*, p. 151.

[17] LeRoy C. Kauffmann, "The Influence of Friedrich Nietzsche on American Literature" (Diss. U. of Pennsylvania, 1963); Melvin Drimmer, "Nietzsche in American Thought, 1895–1925," 2 vols. (Diss. U. of Rochester, 1965); James Peter Cadello, "Nietzsche in America: The Spectrum of Perspectives, 1895–1925" (Diss. Purdue University, 1990).

[18] Gertrud von Petzold, "Nietzsche in englisch-amerikanischer Beurteilung bis zum Ausgange des Weltkrieges," *Anglia*, 53 (1929), 134–217; Benjamin De Casseres, *The Superman in America* (Seattle, 1929); Ludwig Marcuse, "Nietzsche in America," *The South Atlantic Quarterly*, 50 (1951), 330–39; Bernd Magnus, "Nietzsche Today: A View from America," *International Studies in Philosophy*, 15, 2 (1983), 95–103; John T. Wilcox, "Nietzsche's Epistemology: Recent American Discussions," *International Studies in Philosophy*, 15, 2 (1983), 67–77; Cornel West, "Nietzsche's Prefiguration of Postmodern American Philosophy," in Daniel O'Hara (ed.), *Why Nietzsche Now?* (Bloomington: Indiana UP, 1985), 241–69; Robert Ackermann, "Current American Thought on Nietzsche," in Sigrid Bauschinger *et al.* (eds.), *Nietzsche heute: Die Rezeption seines Werks nach 1968* (Bern/Stuttgart, 1988), 129–36; Bernd Magnus, "Nietzsche and Postmodern Criticism," *Nietzsche-Studien*, 18 (1989), 301–16; Wilfried van der Will, "Nietzsche in America: Fashion and Fascination," *History of European Ideas*, 11 (1989), 1015–23; Steven Taubeneck, "Nietzsche in North

America: Walter Kaufmann and After," Translator's Afterword to Ernst Behler, *Confrontations: Derrida/Heidegger/Nietzsche* (Stanford: Stanford UP, 1991), 159–77.

[19] See, for instance, Eduard Baumgarten, "Mitteilungen und Bemerkungen über den Einfluß Emersons auf Nietzsche," *Jahrbuch für Amerikastudien*, 1 (1956), 93–152 (also published as *Das Vorbild Emersons im Werk und Leben Nietzsches*, Heidelberg: Carl Winter, 1957); Stanley Hubbard, *Nietzsche und Emerson* (Basel, 1958). For more recent contributions, see Herwig Friedl, "Emerson and Nietzsche: 1862–1874," in Peter Freese (ed.), *Religion and Philosophy in the United States of America*, vol. I (Essen, 1987), 267–87, and George J. Stack, *Nietzsche and Emerson: An Elective Affinity* (Athens: Ohio UP, 1992).

[20] Under a different perspective, however, the Emerson-Nietzsche connection does play an important role in the present volume, but only in such contexts as in Olaf Hansen's essay on Stanley Cavell where recent American responses to Nietzsche are read from the vantage point of Nietzsche, in turn, reading Emerson. For the general question of Nietzsche's attitude towards America, see the opening pages of Marcuse's article "Nietzsche in America."

[21] *Beyond Good and Evil*, IX, sec. 296.

[22] Aschheim, *Nietzsche Legacy*, p. 314.

[23] *Beyond Good and Evil*, VI, sec. 212.

Hays Steilberg

First Steps in the New World: Early Popular Reception of Nietzsche in America

THIS MUCH IS generally remembered: over the antediluvian years of Nietzsche reception in America hung the clouds of misunderstanding. This is a useful bit of knowledge because it provides us with one explanation for the tidal wave of American criticism on Nietzsche that has been sweeping academe since 1950; confusion usually precipitates at least trickles of clarification in its wake, and once Walter Kaufmann opened the floodgates in that year, the surge was set loose. If the inclemency of early Nietzsche reception should, however, not descend to the level of mere legend, then we must, following academic etiquette, be a little more circumspect about inquiring into the nature and source of these early false conceptions. Just such an inquiry is the task at hand and I shall attempt to show what conditions influenced the course taken by the popular American discussion of Nietzsche around the turn of the century and what forms or, if one so will, tropes this discussion brought forth.

My investigation will concentrate on what I regard as pre-Menckenian tropes. H. L. Mencken's *The Philosophy of Friedrich Nietzsche* (1908) was the first significant and influential book of popular (and philosophical) American Nietzsche reception and signaled a shift in some areas of American interpretation (notably among certain essayists), yet here I wish to view what went before.[1] Thus, the gross of the material treated also comes mainly from journalistic publications. Some of the articles cited postdate the appearance of Mencken's monograph slightly, but the opinions they

represent all extend back to the earliest days of American Nietzsche
reception.

As a general model, a polarity of lionization on the one hand, and
vituperation on the other, holds true for the treatment of Nietzsche
in America (as well as in other places) from the 1890s up to the present day. A conflict has existed not only between supporters and detractors of Nietzsche's philosophy, but also between supporters
themselves as various "factions" have claimed to be in possession of
the one "true" interpretation. The firing line dividing Nietzsche's
admirers and detractors runs politically along the rift between anti-
democratic (including both "aristocratic" and socialist groups) and
democratic thought, and morally along that between ethical revision-
ists and traditionalists. Admirers again fall into the camps of conservative (primarily social Darwinian) and radical (socialist and
anarchist) thinkers. This pattern and these tropes, though first established around the turn of the century, persist in some forms to this
day. They form the foil against which Nietzsche's serious philosophical critics acted and still must act.

The general American attitude toward Nietzsche, to the extent
such a thing ever existed or exists, has thus retained certain consistent patterns, for instance in requiring an all-or-nothing choice between hate or love, fear or hope. Indifference has been the
exception. We shall directly take a closer look at what specific arguments fill out these patterns. First, I shall consider the external influences on American Nietzsche reception, then political and moral
themes of the overall discussion as well as internal American contextual influences and, lastly, tendentious characteristics of Nietzsche
reception that display how the philosopher was often appropriated as
opposed to being interpreted.

One must keep in mind that most of this popular discussion initially took place in the major newspapers and cultural journals of the
day such as *The Nation, The Living Age, The Monist, The North
American Review, The Bookman, The Open Court,* and others. With
the exception of Grace Neal Dolson's published version of her
Cornell dissertation of 1899,[2] an American monograph on Nietzsche
did not come on the scene until 1908 with the appearance of H.L.
Mencken's remarkable study. Another point to consider is that the
journalistic discussion of Nietzsche by and large bears the mien of
heated altercation. The two parties — Nietzsche supporters and op-

ponents — struggled with surprising vehemence to win enthusiasts for, or drive potential victims away from, Nietzsche. Very seldom does one encounter disinterested attempts to *interpret* Nietzsche because the motives of appropriation and polemicizing almost always came to bear on the issue of what Nietzsche means.

Nietzsche played a very visible role in the intellectual atmosphere of the crossover from the nineteenth to the twentieth century in America and the reception of his philosophy was influenced by the historic and cultural context of America at that time. But we must first consider what external circumstances prepared and preconditioned his arrival in the new world. Reception in the history of ideas never takes place in a vacuum and Nietzsche's case is no exception. The first source of Nietzsche interpretations was, of course, Germany (aside from Denmark, where Georg Brandes was working on the famous theory of "aristocratic radicalism"). Two German works in particular deserve our attention. First, for early Nietzsche aficionados, the hagiographic biography by Elisabeth Förster-Nietzsche was most significant.[3] It was she who popularized the image of her brother as a long-suffering, anachoretic hero, painfully ignored by the world of letters until after his collapse (which she likes to call a "stroke" caused by overwork). The modern icon of the austere alpine peripatetic, a philosophic gentleman of impeccable demeanor and taste, steadfast in the face of debilitating illness, always in search of the finest of men, as though straying through the dark alleys of Sils-Maria with lantern in hand, sprang from her scheming imagination. English translations of the two-volume biography were not available until 1912 and 1915,[4] respectively, but more memorable passages were often paraphrased in newspaper and magazine articles by German-reading authors, and her long introduction to the translation of *Thus Spake Zarathustra*[5] allowed English-bound readers access to at least the Nietzsche image if not the complete script of Elisabeth Förster-Nietzsche.

Elisabeth Förster-Nietzsche enjoyed the status of ultimate authority on her brother's life. One commentator maintained that it is "from the minute details given of her family by Madame Förster-Nietzsche [that] we owe our knowledge" of the real Nietzsche.[6] James Huneker, Nietzsche's most important popularizer before Mencken, painted a very favorable picture of *la* Nietzsche as "a good-looking intellectual lady, devoted to the memory of her brother and writing much about him."[7] The only thing one can credit Huneker with getting right is his remark on the profuseness of Elisabeth Förster-Nietzsche's writerly productivity. Even Mencken, by 1908 already skeptical of the accuracy she claimed for her accounts, admitted that she "was the only human being that ever saw him intimately, as a wife might have seen him."[8] Further German studies which peripherally figure into the picture of Nietzsche-supporters are Alois Riehl's *Friedrich Nietzsche: Der Künster und der Denker* (1897) and Raoul Richter's *Nietzsche: Sein Leben und Werk* (1903). These three works appear repeatedly as references in early American Nietzsche commentary.

Second, those who meant Nietzsche ill in America received even more useful assistance from another German writer who dedicated a long chapter of a much read study to the slandering of Nietzsche. Max Nordau's *Entartung* created a literary stir in Europe in 1892/93.[9] Dr. Nordau had set out to catalogue and denounce the phenomena of æstheticism, Wagnerism, and decadence in modern art and philosophy, for him all products of an increasingly degenerate culture, and his impassioned railing reached many an ear. So great was the interest in Nordau's incensed and at times almost inarticulate ravings, which Egon Friedell summarily shrugged off as "several hundred pages of uninterrupted abuse of all leading modern artists,"[10] that an English translation was ready for sale in 1895 under the title *Degeneration*.[11] I specifically mention the publication date not only to underscore the success of the book, but also to make clear that the English version of Nordau's tome reached America one year before any of Nietzsche's works were available in translation. The first volumes in English appeared in 1896. In America and England, Nordau thus had one up on a major target of his scorn. A sampling of this delicious vitriol will illustrate the general tenor of the anti-Baptist that Nordau played to Nietzsche's anti-Christ:

> From the first to the last page of Nietzsche's writings the careful reader seems to hear a madman, with flashing eyes, wild gestures, and foaming mouth, spouting forth deafening bombast . . . . So far as any meaning at all can be extracted from the endless stream of phrases, it shows, as its fundamental elements, a series of constantly reiterated delirious ideas, having their source in illusions of sense and diseased organic processes.[12]

The American intellectual community quickly caught on to Nordau's catchy melody. In early commentary, one repeatedly encounters recommendations of Nordau as suitable preparatory literature for the understanding of Nietzsche. One reviewer provides an exemplary bit of such fateful sanction when he concludes that "The proper preparation for the reader of Nietzsche is Nordau."[13] None other than William James reviewed the ponderous volume[14] for the *Psychological Review*, and Alfred Hake demonstrated heroic alacrity and righteous outrage by composing a 300-page reply to Nordau called *Regeneration*, the title of course being a cheeky riposte to that of the English translation of Nordau's book. Nicholas Murray Butler, dean of the department of philosophy at and later president of Columbia University as well as onetime Republican candidate for the vice presidency on the doomed Taft ticket (1912), praises Hake in a long introduction he contributed to the book, but unfortunately conflates Nordau with the very figures he lambasts, evincing a general loathing for the whole lot. That notwithstanding, as regards Nietzsche, Butler is most unequivocal: "To him who, with Nietzsche, is enthusiastic over the 'freely-roving, lusting beast of prey,' we cry: 'Get you gone from civilization!' . . . There is no place among us [in America] for the lusting beast of prey . . . ."[15] Recognizing the awareness in America of both the "Elizabethan" as well as the Nordauian Nietzsche is an important prerequisite for understanding the way the American image of Nietzsche developed. Sister and doctor together created a Janus-faced monster, an extreme antinomy of one Nietzsche, the deity, and another, the demon. One other major factor in the equation must, however, also not go unmentioned and this is the translation itself.

From the start, the English translation of Nietzsche was conceived of as a complete edition of the works based on the German original, the so-called *Großoktavausgabe*,[16] that was being supervised by the Nietzsche-Archiv in Weimar at the time. The magnitude of the project and the celerity with which editor and translators got under way stress once again the unusually broad popular attention showered on Nietzsche from the 1890s onward. This becomes especially clear in relation if, for instance, one considers the torpid progress with which English translations of Hegel's work were completed.

Two further tell-tale aspects of the Nietzsche translation will help us to understand the situation in America at the turn of the century more clearly. First, the initial editor, Alexander Tille (an expatriate German and instructor at the University of Glasgow), as well as his right hand man (and member of the team of translators) Thomas Common, were both staunch social Darwinians. Needless to say, their reading of Nietzsche was all but impartial. Tille still occasionally receives mention as the author of *Von Darwin bis Nietzsche: Ein Buch Entwicklungsethik*, in which he unfolds his ideal of "evolutionary idealism," a social Darwinian ethics based on a Nietzschean misreading. Although he authored no books like Tille, Common also had early inklings of the power of public relations and set about writing newspaper articles in which he put the brave new Nietzschean world of Darwinian ethics on display. Common was quite adamant that

> [Nietzsche's] philosophy can ... be best understood from the Darwinian point of view — indeed it forms the last and most important chapter of the Darwinian system. The most important distinction among animals is their fitness or unfitness for the conditions of existence, in fact, their superiority or inferiority. It is the same among human beings.[17]

Second, Tille very selectively chose those volumes of Nietzsche's works which should first appear in the edition. Thus, in 1896 the volumes 8, 10 and 11 of the planned edition were published containing the following texts written by Nietzsche in his final years: Vol. VIII - *Thus Spake Zarathustra*, Vol. X - *The Genealogy of Morals*, Vol. XI - *The Case of Wagner, Nietzsche contra Wagner, Twilight of the Idols, The Anti-Christ*. Moreover, up to the year 1909 these were the only texts translated and prepared for second and third printings (excepting the addition of another later work, *Beyond Good and Evil*, in 1907).[18] Tille's publisher, H. Henry and Co., folded, at which point the project was taken over by a new editor, Oscar Levy, and moved to a new publisher, T. N. Foulis. In America, Macmillan continued to present the edition as it appeared in England. What this all adds up to is that American (as well as English) readers immediately encountered Nietzsche at the pinnacle of his thought, with its startling intellectual experimentation and radical style, for which they were prepared mainly through second-hand (and, in part, second-rate) expositions.[19]

However, to interpret Nietzsche on the basis of superficial familiarity with the ultimate concepts of his philosophy such as will to
power, master and slave morality, the Antichrist, or the *Übermensch*
without any previous acquaintance with Nietzsche's earlier work is
risky business because it not only fosters rash conclusions, but also
restricts the aspects that enter into the discussion. The modes of interpretation to which Nietzsche was to be subjected crystallized
rather quickly. Nietzsche's readers relegated him early on to the
complimentary hemispheres of politics and morals. This concentration touches upon very important themes of Nietzsche's philosophy,
but also ignores the epistemological and ontological core of his
thought. Yet this outcome was more or less preprogrammed by the
combination of conditions under which Nietzsche's philosophy came
to the United States. At this point, we must ask which specific political and moral themes prevail in the discussion.

The concept of a natural order of rank among men appears recur-
rently in Nietzsche's thought, but especially comes to a fore in his
later works. Nietzsche goes far beyond the proposal of the artificial
equality of naturally unequal men before the law to suggest that the
very idea of "justice" is a privilege to be earned by the few. The consequences of such a position for the republican form of government
are obvious: Nietzsche makes no secret of his anti-democratic bias.
Nicholas Murray Butler formed his understanding of the political
implications of Nietzsche's thought under the influence of Hake and
Nordau and, in a manner typifying American resistance to Nietzsche,
retorted with a defense of the "plain people" of America, for in his
opinion

> They, and not a group or two of men and women in each of the
> capitals of Europe, are the real index to the degeneracy, or the
> contrary, of modern life. If democracy is to establish itself more
> widely and more efficiently as a form of government, it must rest
> upon the common sense of the plain people.[20]

Throughout Nietzsche's intellectual life, democracy appears to him
as "not merely a form assumed by political organization in decay but
also a form assumed by man in decay, that is to say in diminishment,
in process of becoming mediocre and losing his value . . . ."[21]
Straight away, then, Nietzsche challenges the body politic in America.

The order of rank also forces Nietzsche's readers to take one of the most vexing elements of his philosophy to task: this very question of the highest types. Logically, if Nietzsche proposes an inherent inequality among men, he must have some idea of what features constitute the highest types. Understandably, American critics immediately latched on to the *Übermensch* as Nietzsche's name for this greatest fulfillment of human potential. Just as quickly, the queries into the nature of the *Übermensch* were colored by the fascination of the age with all things eugenic. Once again, that Nietzsche reception should have taken this turn is hardly surprising. Even the reader who does not get particularly far in *Zarathustra* finds these incriminating lines in "Zarathustra's Prologue":

> *I teach you the Superman.* Man is something that should be overcome. What have you done to overcome him?
>
> All creatures hitherto have created something beyond themselves . . . What is the ape to men? A laughing-stock or a painful embarrassment. And just so shall man be to the Superman: a laughing-stock or a painful embarrassment.[22]

These words look like paraphrases to the early twentieth-century reader: man shall be like an ape compared to the *Übermensch* (evolution), and all creatures *create* things beyond themselves (breeding or "eugenics"). Darwin's *Descent of Man* had only just appeared in 1871, and eugenic research was flowering in America, for instance under the *American Breeder's Association*, founded in 1903, which changed its name to the *American Genetic Association* shortly thereafter. Madison Grant's inglorious *The Passing of the Great Race* would appear in 1916. Even Riehl supported this interpretation of the concept and stated that there could be "no doubt that in 'Zarathustra' the *Übermensch* stands for a new, 'stronger species' . . . to be bred from man."[23]

All this talk of anti-democratic sentiment and the planned breeding of supermen fed directly into the dispute on morals which occupied the minds of American Nietzscheans and anti-Nietzscheans. This concerned not only the desirability of breeding human beings, but also the consequences of refuting essential equality among them. All too often and for all too long Nietzsche's critique of morals has been rather exclusively viewed not as an attempt to lay bare the moralistic underpinnings of Western philosophy (the "translation of morality into the realm of metaphysics"[24]) or as a *de*scriptive examination of historical mores, but as the *pre*scriptive program for introducing new standards of social behavior which should behoove the production of *Übermenschen*. The upshot of this purported program has mostly been taken to mean the release of "higher men" from all restrictions which limit the free exercise of their wills (enter the will to power), first and foremost the release from the injunction to sympathy for or even consideration of their fellowmen.

II

Having thus clarified the themes which dominate the discussion of Nietzsche in America for much of the first half of our century, it now remains to examine how both Nietzsche's friends and foes responded to these ideas in order to present their case before the reading public. Many American Nietzscheans felt drawn to this notorious new philosophy precisely because of the radically anti-democratic stance taken by Nietzsche. The relation between the privileged or gifted individual and the group had long become a prevalent topic in reform politics. It is a constant of Nietzsche's thought that the "masses" deserve the attention of higher men only in a threefold regard: as inferior copies of great men, as an object of resistance to great men, and finally as the tools of great men; and otherwise "let the Devil and statistics take them!"[25] This, of course, appealed directly to a certain mood of aristocratic hero worship that had been cropping up repeatedly in the nineteenth century ever since the Napoleonic era. American hero cults have more often than not arisen around an ideal of nonconformism and "organic" personality as opposed to political might or courtly refinement. Much of Emerson's fame results from just this apotheosis of the self-creating individual. Thus Nietzsche is none too seldom portrayed by supporters, as here by John Warbeke, as a visionary whose clarion call bids us to flee the conformist tendencies of modern democracy:

> The whole tendency of our democratic times is to make men like one another, to look upon all men as equal, to keep all on the same level, and see to it that no man obtains predominating influence or expresses his genius. Thus Nietzsche was the arch-enemy of democratic institutions.[26]

This implies that those who conform with the spirit of democratic times lower themselves to the level of the "masses," who do not appear in a particularly advantageous light.

The early twentieth century produced two diametrically opposed images of the populace at large. One of these took the form of martyred working-class nobility or victimized destitution and was held high on the banners of the countless philanthropic movements of the age and even more effectively iconized in the socialist and progressivist/populist political canon. The outgrowth of such philanthropic and activist sentiment produced its own antithesis in the guise of anti-philanthropic elitism. Gilded Age dandies like Huneker (an open Stirnerite) and Edgar Saltus were idolized by "nonconforming" youths. In praise of the "neo-pagan" Nietzsche, Huneker scorned the "sentimentality of 'going to the people.' Brotherhood of man! Brotherhood of drudge and hypocrisy!"[27] So, for those resistant to this socially conscious liberation politics, Nietzsche appeared on the scene at an opportune time for using his name as the latest philosophical authority on the dangers of compulsory egalitarianism. "Give us such [Nietzschean] Supermen," was their reply to the demands of social conscience, "and let them assume their proper sphere as leaders. Such are, indeed, the only hope against rabble-democracy."[28] Even the pioneer sociologist Franklin Henry Giddings of Columbia University, the most prominent social Darwinian in America after William Graham Sumner, incorporated Nietzschean concepts into his *Democracy and Empire*, in which governmentally instituted charity comes under heavy fire.[29]

The era of social Darwinism also shared the general positivistic obsession of the times with statistics, prompting more draconian neo-Nietzscheans to support their arguments against any disturbance of the "natural" process of social selection with numerical, "scientific" evidence of "race deterioration" where welfare measures had been implemented. Thus, in the opinion of one advocate, it is through his criticism of democratic egalitarianism and Christian philanthropy that "Nietzsche . . . forced upon the attention of the world what is, after all, the most important of the questions of the future . . .": how to restore natural selection to its rightful place as the inherent weave of the social fabric.[30]

Just this denial of the need for solidarity and sympathy with one's fellowmen seriously roused the ire of Nietzsche's accusers. A general

acceptance of Nietzsche's thought would, in their version, produce
not a reduction of bland conformism, but an increase in violence and
social discord. The philosopher Paul Carus, editor of *The Open Court*
and *The Monist* as well as one of Nietzsche's most active early opponents in America, pulled out all the stops in his description of what
America under Nietzschean rule would look like:

> If the ethics of Nietzsche were accepted to-day as authoritative, and
> if people at large acted accordingly . . . the selfishness of mankind
> would manifest itself in all its nude bestiality. Passions would have
> full sway; lust, robbery, jealousy, murder, and revenge would in-
> crease and death in all forms of wild outbursts would reap a richer
> harvest than he ever did in the days of prehistoric savage life.[31]

This tableau has a specific point of reference. Nietzsche-followers
frequently referred to Nietzsche's philosophy of power and criticism
of morals as a (Rousseauian) attempt at a return to nature. In some
quarters, this vitalist picture of Nietzsche still persists to this day, although Nietzsche's repudiation of such an attitude is not at a loss for
clarity (see for instance the discussion of man's "nature" in aphorism
290 of *The Gay Science* or the excoriating rebuttal of Rousseau in
aphorism 48 from the section "Expeditions of an Untimely Man" in
Twilight of the Idols). Nietzsche considers the substratum of human
nature the "horrible original text *homo natura*" that is made admirable only through the conscious stylization of personality. That such
a "naturalist" interpretation prevailed in the early years of our century becomes understandable, however, if one takes into account the
oppressively moralistic atmosphere of temperance unions, ethical societies, and Comstock squads that is also part of this era. As Harry
Thurston Peck of *The Bookman* put it, "Ascetism, self-abnegation, a
colorless neutrality were . . . profoundly repugnant to Nietzsche's
strong vitality of temperament,"[32] and therein supposedly lay his
timeliness for American culture. Anti-Nietzscheans, however, read
this ostensive praise of the unfiltered and morally undaunted "natural
man" as a second fall, a mere atavism. This is where Carus gets his
aside about the "prehistoric savage."

The identification of a primitive, inarticulate urge in his philosophy to destroy everything held sacred by civilization characterizes the
opposition's half of the Nietzschean chiaroscuro. In a flight of stylistic fancy, the anti-Nietzschean faction adopted the epithet
"iconoclast" as a pithy description of their nemesis.[33] Nietzsche is for

them "the writer running amuck among the ideals of civilization, a veritable Mr. Hyde, ruthlessly trampling under foot the received standards of morality and religion, an *iconoclast*."[34] To lend credence and pull to this line of argumentation, Nietzsche's opponents also announced the existence of groups of imitation iconoclasts who intended to realize the apocalyptic visions of their master. The socialists and anarchists are the groups most frequently mentioned in this context. "Nietzsche has become a power with the masses . . . . He is their prophet and apostle,"[35] explains G. S. Patton; and Carus warns:

> His greatest admirers are anarchists, sometimes also socialists . . . Nietzsche's thought will prove veritable dynamite if it should happen to reach the masses of mankind, the disinherited, the uneducated, the proletariat, the Catilinary [sic] existences.[36]

This is a prime example of the vagaries of appropriation in the history of Nietzsche reception, since at one moment he was the enemy of the masses, and in the next he is their leader. We realize that this latter association packs a definite punch, though, if we recall that violence connected with anarchist activities was very present in the thoughts of Americans at the turn of the century. The Haymarket riot (1886) and other attacks were still relatively fresh in the national memory. Nordau also includes the rumor of a dangerous and politically active Nietzsche cult in his portrait.

Some socialists and anarchists did indeed identify with Nietzsche, or to be more precise, wished to employ Nietzsche as a philosophical standard-bearer for their own political purposes. The most infamous of all American anarchists, Emma Goldman, availed herself of Nietzschean exhortations in some of her essays and lectures, asserting that Nietzsche, "that giant mind," had a "vision of the *Uebermensch* [that] called for a state of society which will not give birth to a race of weaklings and slaves."[37] The socialist William English Walling (as well as a cast of others who cannot be treated here) frequently incorporated Nietzsche into his work. In general, though, both anarchists and socialists alike saw themselves forced to softpedal, downplay, or even deny Nietzsche's anti-egalitarian ideas in order to render him usable for their purposes. They imputed the intention of the production of a future "superrace" as Nietzsche's actual meaning behind the term *Übermensch*, which could, of course, be best achieved through anarchist or socialist political reform. Walling performs a giant (il-)logical somersault in maintaining:

> Because he [Nietzsche] came finally to admire certain caste sys-
> tems . . . it is sometimes supposed that he stood definitely for that
> sum of all reaction, caste. On the contrary, his whole philosophy
> was directed against caste, that is, until the very last of his writ-
> ings.[38]

Caste in one form or another intrigued Nietzsche from the onset of his career, but a socialist Nietzsche certainly could not admit of such a "reactionary" weakness without mortifying the leftist thinkers who were desirous of the propagandistic force of his reputation.

The anxiety of Nietzsche's defamers over the social disruption that would assuredly follow the popularization of Nietzschean thought goes hand in hand with their interpretation of Nietzsche's critique of moralism and Christianity. By dubbing himself the "Antichrist" or "anti-Christian," Nietzsche of course had already thrown a wild card into this exegetic poker game. His adversaries profited immensely from this direct opposition between the false prophet Nietzsche and the true Savior, Christ, who had warned of heretics to follow him. Charles Everett, dean of Harvard's divinity school, singled out Nietzsche's atheism as the foremost characteristic of his philosophy: "He is in the first place a hearty and thorough-going atheist. One of his favorite expressions is 'God is dead'."[39] Even more incriminating than the accusation of atheism was, however, the implication that Nietzsche was a theomaniac, in other words, that he suffered from the delusion of himself being God. This interpretation contains the double-edged insinuation that Nietzsche was not only blasphemous, but patently insane even before the outbreak of his final delirium. Nordau had, after all, adopted Hermann Türck's[40] phony reports that Nietzsche had written his works *between various stays* in mental institutions.[41] Once more, Nietzsche did not help matters by setting *Zarathustra* in a decidedly neo-evangelic framework and tone. And, admittedly, Zarathustra (commonly seen as Nietzsche's mouthpiece) states that if God existed, he (Zarathustra/Nietzsche) could hardly bear not to be a god himself. Moreover, Nietzsche wrote to Jacob Burckhardt in the final days before his collapse: "Dear professor, In the end I would much rather be a Basel professor than God; but I have not dared push my private egotism so far as to desist for its sake from the creation of the world" (Letter from January 6, 1889).[42] In the light of these words, indeed those of a madman, it seemed reasonable to conclude that

"Nietzsche, the atheist, deemed himself a God incarnate [and] developed all the symptoms of religious fanaticism."[43]

Nietzsche's American adjuvants frequently reacted to such accusations with meliorating gestures and highly selective quotations that made Nietzsche appear less menacing. Much of the defense of Nietzsche in the course of his American reception has sought refuge in various versions of a basically innocuous Nietzsche who, according to his sympathizers, has either been misunderstood or is simply difficult to interpret correctly because of his tendency toward "dramatic" language. Riehl tacks this course by admonishing his reader "not to take Nietzsche too literally"[44] when at his most radical, and American interpreters such as John Warbeke often followed suit with the concession that "In justice to Nietzsche . . . we must remember that as a radical thinker he sought constantly to emphasize his thoughts by striking presentation."[45] This is, however, evading the question instead of answering it. Nonetheless, some defenders claimed that Nietzsche's critique of Christianity was either "not to be taken literally" or to be seen only as a vendetta with Paul and not with Jesus himself. Others, such as Edwin Hardin, went so far as to posit the actual benefits of Nietzsche's critique for the church as a guideline for eliminating the outdated trappings of orthodoxy and asceticism, thereby granting Christianity a salutary opportunity to adapt itself to the demands of modern times:

> Nietzsche may justly be regarded as a sort of devil's advocate in the case of Christianity . . . his very hostility serves the stimulating purpose of compelling Christianity to reveal what merits it possesses . . . he is doing religion the wholesome service of shaking it . . . out of a slumber that may be as harmful as it is pleasant.[46]

Another tactic consisted in turning the tables on Nietzsche's enemies by interpreting the signs of "religious fanaticism" as proof of Nietzsche's actual deep and not un-Christian spirituality. Much of this stems from Elisabeth Förster-Nietzsche's highly stylized portrait of her brother as a latter-day Minervian hermit who also had "a true fondness for upright, pious Christians" and maintained a "tender love for the founder of Christianity" until the end of his days.[47]

In general, though, we must not overlook that Nietzsche's anti-Christian polemics are of lesser significance in comparison to his critique of Judeo-Christian morals as seen apart from questions of faith. The historical criticism of religion after the manner of Feuerbach and

Renan had already come to America[48] and it was by no means unheard of to declare the church expendable. The necessity of the basic
Judeo-Christian moral codex, though, was not widely considered
open to debate. This, for instance, is even a central point of William
James's thought on religion, who was less concerned with salvaging
the actual content of religious doctrine from the onslaught of empirical skepticism than with preserving the *effects* of religious doctrine
on the life of the believer. Religious people react to and act upon life
differently than the irreligious — this is a common social or pragmatic justification of a theistically grounded ethics. In complete ac-
cord with just this valuation, Charles Everett defines the real threat
of Nietzsche's philosophy with decidedly pragmatic clarity:

> Atheism under one form or another is no new thing . . . . But to
> deny the ideals of morality which have commanded the reverence if
> not the obedience of men for so many ages is something different.[49]

We can thus recognize the potential breakdown of the social order as
the most feared result of Nietzschean "immoralism." And yet, to
credit the work of one philosopher with such powers of devastation
is certainly ludicrous, whether coming from the mouth of Charles
Everett or Allan Bloom. Certainly, it is equally absurd to presume
that the church might rethink fundamental principles of its dogma
along Nietzschean lines in order to go with the times. If one also
considers that such disparate groups as socialists and social Darwinians both tried to claim Nietzsche's philosophical support for their
respective political platforms, it becomes all too apparent that interpretation frequently gives way to appropriation in the American debate on Nietzsche. Let us consider some of the more flagrantly
tendentious theses of both those who voice praise or who demand
denunciation in order to clarify just how irrelevant to the understanding of Nietzsche much of this bickering was.

Both supporters and detractors considered proving Nietzsche's
compatibility or incompatibility, respectively, with American culture
as one of their most important tasks. Those battling for compatibility
broached the topic by claiming either the inherent correspondence of
Nietzsche's thought with the American temper or the need for the
emendation of American culture by Nietzschean precept. With the
onset of Nietzscheanism in the United States, some new American
Nietzscheans began identifying their country as the culture destined
to bring forth the *Übermensch*. Even the anti-Nietzschean Paul Carus

conceded that "We Americans especially have faith in the coming kingdom of the overman, and our endeavor is concentrated in hastening his arrival."[50] In order to make the idea of an American *Übermensch* more palatable, supporters often searched for harbingers of the superhuman in the intellectual tradition of the new world. More than any others, Emerson and Whitman were identified as American forebears of Nietzsche. Already in 1896, W. Barry notes a 'correspondence' between the *overman* and the Emersonian *oversoul*:

> Mankind, he [Nietzsche] would say, has one supreme task, — not a moral duty, but a physiological necessity, — to produce the "overman". Does not Emerson talk of the "oversoul"?[51]

Another proponent of the 'Americanism of Nietzscheanism' groups Emerson and Nietzsche among the "most significant apostles of individualism"[52] in the nineteenth century, a brand of thought which for him reaches its zenith in America. Others wax poetic over the spiritual elective affinities between America's greatest bard and the philosopher-poet of *Zarathustra*. For Louise Collier Wilcox, Whitman and Nietzsche

> share the same grandiose egoism, the same courage to "sing myself," the same impatience with sick conscience, repentance and remorse, and finally, the same sense that as the individual acquires independence, freedom, and an expansive outlook he will become whole and well.[53]

This all serves, of course, to suggest that nothing could be more American than Nietzschean individualism. As stated, though, this conciliatory manner was not everyone's cup of tea. R. C. Schiedt bemoans the lack of American receptivity for Nietzsche's ideas and reasons that a Nietzschean transvaluation of American culture will be necessary before a proper understanding of such tragic philosophy appears on this side of the Atlantic.[54] Even the Whitmanesque Willcox toys with the idea that Nietzsche is foreign to the majority of Americans because he "abhorred commercialism, humanitarianism, facile optimism, any form of casual, easy-going light-heartedness."[55] Americans would have to learn a little more about the frightfully dour business of existence before their philosophical faculties would really be up to the challenge with which Nietzsche presented them.

For the opposition, Nietzsche was anything but all-American. It is precisely the absolute incongruence of Nietzschean thought with the

American temper that anti-Nietzscheans stressed as sufficient reason for abandoning the study of this 'pseudo-thinker'. Edwin Slosson maintains that it is "not likely that he will ever be much read in the United States. Nor is there any reason why he should be."[56] That sounds not indistinctly like an attempt on the part of the author to reassure both the reader and himself. One anonymous writer states: "Altogether it would be surprising if Nietzschian [sic] doctrine flourished in American soil . . . the Anglo-Saxon peoples have long learnt to reconcile liberty with order."[57] Here, a racial and nationalist note is struck that looms large in the rhetoric of resistance to Nietzsche before, during, and after the years of the World Wars. In a somewhat tongue-in-cheek manner that also contains a grain of true concern, Slosson identifies Nietzsche as part of an overall infiltration of America by German culture. "German philosophies," he quips, "are, like their plays and operas, shipped over to America when the Germans have got tired of them."[58] The attitude of slightly Germanophobic resentment that enters into the early discussion of Nietzsche also appears as the result of very disparate historical circumstances ranging from the identification of American anarchist groups with German immigrants (as was the case in the Haymarket riot) to the worldwide hegemony of German universities at this time (the serious Harvard student would not have thought of missing out on his *Wanderjahr* in Berlin, Göttingen, or Heidelberg) to the long-standing and nearly armed dispute between the United States and Germany over the Samoan Islands. Whatever the specific causes, Nietzsche was often derided as a "German" philosopher. Reactions included condescension — "That a German professor should aspire to a place in international literature is sufficiently surprising"[59] — and persiflage — "The German pedant [Nietzsche] . . . crawls on the earth and never knows the thrill that comes to the imaginative soul."[60] Various other flimsy criticisms are also brought against Nietzsche: that his work was unsystematic because he himself was muddle-headed; that he wrote in aphorisms because he was too impatient to sit down and think out his ideas (we have Nordau to thank for both of these); that he had no knowledge of exact sciences, plagiarized all his ideas from other thinkers, and otherwise brought mostly platitudes to paper, thus explaining his broad popularity with the philosophically unversed.

Most revealing are, however, the countless instances of appeals *ad hominem* to establish Nietzsche's unsuitability for serious readers. Almost all of Nietzsche's die-hard critics played endlessly upon his mental illness, taking the collapse as a direct sign of the infirmity of his philosophy. Again, Nordau provided many of these authors with rumors on the beginning and course of Nietzsche's illness as well as a psychological pseudo-analysis of Nietzsche in which Nordau pronounced him a clear-cut case of advanced sadism.[61] That makes it easy for American commentators to claim that Nietzsche "is supremely happy when he can rise on the dead and wounded bodies of the weak; this strengthens his feeling of cruelty."[62] Nietzsche's general "normalcy" is also regularly questioned.[63] Nietzsche's solitary, bookish, and "effeminate" childhood, the lack of a father in the house and the "priggish" manners of the "little pastor" also figure in the proto-Freudian nit-picking of his philosophy by spiteful Philistines. The discrepancy between the seemingly vitalistic ideal of the *Übermensch* and Nietzsche's own poor health also fueled the fires of hobby psychoanalysts who explained Nietzsche's philosophy as a form of projected compensation for the kind of hale and brawny life he was incapable of leading. Slosson views the whole of Nietzsche's thought as his "autobiography," yet "not of his actual, but of his dream life."[64] In the version designed by Nietzsche's admirers, on the other hand, his poor constitution and racking headaches transmute themselves into the insurmountable hurdles of fate which Nietzsche miraculously and heroically overcame, sacrificing himself for the sake of his work. The narcissistic and abnormal hypochondriac of Nietzsche's nemeses becomes the Promethean martyr of his disciples:

> We shall see Nietzsche [at the end of his mental life] . . . dignified, self-controlled, triumphant, in sickness and mental depression, and then our whole sympathy can go out to the stricken man, who makes such a noble fight with adverse circumstances.[65]

In this case as well, the source of the interpretation is to be sought outside American borders, for it was Elisabeth Förster-Nietzsche's panegyric which celebrated the martyrdom of the "lonely Nietzsche in the final days before his collapse," who had worked beyond the range of mortal powers, showing no concern for himself, given over to his fate because all friends who might have prevented the "stroke" that destroyed his mind had abandoned him.[66] Not only does

Nietzsche the man here obscure Nietzsche the thinker, the man himself does not even appear in a realistic light.

The realization that emerges from an examination of this fruitless dialectic is that the early discussion of Nietzsche in America is from the outset a contest not only over the acceptability of Nietzsche's philosophy, but also over the ideological claim to the rights of interpretation. Not only were supporters and detractors polarized, supporters were divided again amongst themselves. The dichotomy of Franklin Henry Giddings on one side of the argument and William English Walling or Emma Goldman on the other elucidates the desire of various factions within the ideological spectrum to employ Nietzsche's name for ulterior purposes. This pattern is particularly of interest because it does not fade away after a brief, heated debate, but persists for many years.

What the presence of these patterns evoked was a Nietzsche reception that tended to miss the thinker in whom it purported to be interested. The welter of debate all too frequently circumnavigates Nietzsche's ideas without ever actually centering in on them. When the dust settles, one can see that his philosophy itself has remained untouched. Where Nietzsche is viewed philosophically, the concentration is always upon politics and morals, making a social engineer out of Nietzsche instead of a (perhaps the ultimate?) metaphysician. As we have seen, the reasons why this early discourse on Nietzsche basically backfired are legion. Historical context, foreign influence, and political aspirations all acted upon the origin and development of Nietzsche reception in America and helped produce a tradition of misunderstanding that is still in the process of being dispelled. In the end, then, the truism with which we started has proven itself correct, but it is indeed useful to know the causes — at a later date they may even help us to view the second half of a century of American Nietzsche reception in new dimensions.

Notes

[1] H. L. Mencken, *The Philosophy of Friedrich Nietzsche* (Boston: Luce and Company, 1908).

[2] Grace Neal Dolson, *The Philosophy of Friedrich Nietzsche* (New York: Macmillan, 1901; previously Cornell dissertation, 1899, from which all citations here stem).

[3] Elisabeth Förster-Nietzsche, *Das Leben Friedrich Nietzsches*, 2 vols. (Leipzig: Naumann, 1895.)

[4] Elizabeth Förster-Nietzsche, *The Young Nietzsche*, trans. P. Cohn (London, 1912) and *The Life of Nietzsche*, vol. 2, *The Lonely Nietzsche*, trans. P. Cohn (New York, 1915).

[5] Elizabeth Förster-Nietzsche, "Introduction by Mrs. Förster-Nietzsche," *Thus Spake Zarathustra*, trans. Thomas Common (London: T.N. Foulis, 1909).

[6] W. Barry, "The Ideals of Anarchy," *Littel's Living Age*, 211 (1896), 618.

[7] James Huneker, *Steeplejack*, vol. 2 (New York: Scribner's, 1920), p. 224.

[8] H.L. Mencken, *The Philosophy of Friedrich Nietzsche*, p. 59.

[9] Max Nordau, *Entartung* (Berlin: Duncker, 1893).

[10] Egon Friedell, *Kulturgeschichte der Neuzeit*, 3 vols. (1927–1931; München: Beck [1 vol. ed.], 1989), p. 1415 (my translation).

[11] Max Nordau, *Degeneration*. Anon. translation (New York: Appleton, 1895).

[12] *Ibid.*, p. 416.

[13] Anonymous, "A Philosophic Mr. Hyde," *The Nation*, 62 (June, 1896), 459.

[14] William James, "Review of Max Nordau's 'Entartung'," *Psychological Review*, 2 (March, 1895), 294.

[15] Nicholas Murray Butler, "Introduction" to: Alfred Hake, *Regeneration. A Reply to Max Nordau* (New York: Putnam's, 1896), p. 243.

[16] Friedrich Nietzsche, *Werke*, 20 vol. (Leipzig: Naumann, 1894).

[17] Thomas Common, "Human Evolution According to Nietzsche," *Natural Science: A Monthly Review of Scientific Progress*, 10 (June, 1897), 394.

[18] A complete list of titles and dates for the English translations of Nietzsche's works up to 1930 can be found in the appendices of Melvin Drimmer's *Nietzsche in American Thought, 1895–1925* (Diss. U. of Rochester, 1965), pp. 724–26.

[19] Cf. the first chapter of David S. Thatcher's *Nietzsche in England 1890–1914* (Toronto: U. of Toronto P., 1970) for additional details on the history of the translation and the general state of Nietzsche reception in England.

[20] Butler, "Introduction," pp. xi-xii.

[21] Nietzsche, *Beyond Good and Evil*, trans. R. J. Hollingdale (1973; Middlesex: Penguin, 1981), p. 108.

[22] Nietzsche, *Thus Spoke Zarathustra*, trans. R. J. Hollingdale (1961; Middlesex: Penguin, 1982), pp. 41–42.

[23] Alois Riehl, *Friedrich Nietzsche. Der Künstler und der Denker* (Stuttgart, 1897), p. 124 (my translation).

[24] Nietzsche, *Ecce Homo*, trans. R. J. Hollingdale (1979; Middlesex: Penguin, 1982), p. 128.

[25] Nietzsche, *Untimely Meditations*, trans. R. J. Hollingdale (Cambridge: Cambridge UP, 1983), p. 113.

[26] John M. Warbeke, "Friedrich Nietzsche. Antichrist, Superman, and Pragmatist," *Harvard Theological Review*, 2 (July, 1909), 370–71.

[27] James Huneker, *The Pathos of Distance. A Book of a Thousand and One Moments* (New York: Scribner's, 1913), pp. 390–91.

[28] John M. Warbeke, "Friedrich Nietzsche," p. 381.

[29] Franklin Henry Giddings, *Democracy and Empire* (1900; New York: Books for Libraries Press, 1972).

[30] Edwin Slosson, "The Philosopher With the Hammer", *The Independent*, 65 (1908), 695.

[31] Paul Carus, "Immorality as a Philosophic Principle," *The Monist*, 9 (July, 1899), 613.

[32] Harry Thurston Peck, "A Mad Philosopher," *The Bookman*, 8 (1898), 29.

[33] "Iconoclast" was a generally popular term at the time, used frequently by Huneker and his ilk and also well known as the title of a radical periodical, *The Iconoclast*.

[34] Anonymous, "A Philosophic 'Mr. Hyde'," p. 460.

[35] George S. Patton, "Beyond Good and Evil," *The Princeton Theological Review*, 3 (July, 1908), 416.

[36] Paul Carus, "Immorality as a Philosophic Principle," p. 605.

[37] Emma Goldman, "Preface," *Anarchism and Other Essays* (1917; New York: Dover, 1969), p. 44.

[38] William English Walling, *The Larger Aspects of Socialism* (New York: Macmillan, 1913), p. 195.

[39] Charles Everett, "Beyond Good and Evil," *The New World*, 7 (1899), 686.

[40] Hermann Türck, *Friedrich Nietzsche und seine philosophischen Irrwege* (Dresden, 1891).

[41] Nordau, *Degeneration*, pp. 452–53.

[42] This famous epistle can be found among the letters translated in Walter Kaufmann's *The Portable Nietzsche*, trans. and edited by Walter Kaufmann (1959; New York: Viking, 1982), p. 685.

[43] Paul Carus, "Friedrich Nietzsche," *The Monist* (April, 1907), 235.

[44] Alois Riehl, *Friedrich Nietzsche. Der Künstler und der Denker*, p. 25.

[45] John M. Warbeke, "Friedrich Nietzsche," p. 374.

[46] Edwin Hardin, "Nietzsche's Service to Christianity," *The American Journal of Theology*, 18 (1914), 546–47.

[47] Elisabeth Förster-Nietzsche, *Das Leben Friedrich Nietzsches*, pp. 762, 765 (my translations).

[48] George Freeman Clarke's *Ten Great Religions* (1871) and Washington Gladden's *Who Wrote the Bible?* (1891) are prime early examples of this scholarly dismantling of religious rite and ritual.

[49] Charles Everett, "Beyond Good and Evil," p. 690.

[50] Paul Carus, "Immorality as a Philosophic Principle," p. 589.

[51] W. Barry, "The Ideals of Anarchy," *Littel's Living Age*, 211 (1896), 628.

[52] Lewis Smith, "Ibsen, Emerson and Nietzsche, the Individualists," *The Popular Science Monthly*, 78 (February, 1911), 147–48.

[53] Louise Collier Willcox, "Nietzsche: A Doctor for Sick Souls," *The North American Review*, 194 (1911), 766.

[54] R. C. Schiedt, "Nietzsche and the Great Problems of Modern Thought," *The Reformed Church Review*, 2 (April, 1912), 155.

[55] Willcox, "Nietzsche: A Doctor for Sick Souls," p. 766.

[56] Slosson, "The Philosopher With the Hammer," p. 697.

[57] Anonymous, "A Philosophic Mr. Hyde," p. 460.

[58] Slosson, "The Philosopher With the Hammer," p. 697.

[59] Anonymous, "A Philosophic Mr. Hyde," p. 459.

[60] Harry Peck, "A Mad Philosopher," p. 31.

[61] Nordau, *Degeneration*, pp. 450–51.

[62] Ernest Antrim and H. Goebel, "Friedrich Nietzsche's Uebermensch," *The Monist*, 9 (1908), 570.

[63] Cf. Paul Carus, "Friedrich Nietzsche," p. 236.

[64] Slosson, "The Philosopher With the Hammer," p. 693.

[65] M. D. Petre, "Studies on Friedrich Nietzsche," *The Catholic World*, 82 (1905), 325.

[66] Cf. Elisabeth Förster-Nietzsche, *Das Leben Friedrich Nietzsches*, pp. 892–93.

Julika Griem

The Poetics of History and Science in Nietzsche and Henry Adams

IN 1881, 36-YEAR-OLD Friedrich Nietzsche bought a typewriter and found himself stimulated by the regularity of mechanically produced letters. Eleven years later, at the age of 54, Henry Adams "solemnly and painfully learned to ride the bicycle."[1] Beyond these single heroic acts, intellectual and everyday life was changing with increasing rapidity. Inventions and discoveries like the telephone, the electric light bulb, the machine gun, the electromagnetic waves, the x-rays, and radium were creating new modes of perception, thought, and production and modifying the experience of time and space.

One year before the first telegraph would intensify transatlantic communication, the hysterically celebrated turn of the century saw Freud's *Interpretation of Dreams*, the formulation of quantum physics as well as modern genetics and, after twelve years of mental paralysis, the death of Nietzsche. At the same time Adams, who meanwhile had turned into an ironical observer of the "fin-de-siècle circus,"[2] "found himself lying in the Gallery of Machines at the Great Exposition of 1900, his historical neck broken by the sudden irruption of forces totally new" (*E,* 832). With his pilgrimage to the panoramic parades of progress the American historian, novelist, and man of letters represented exactly the intellectual type Nietzsche had attacked in his "Second Untimely Meditation": " . . . modern man who allows his artists in history to go on preparing a world exhibition for him . . . has become a strolling spectator and has arrived at a condition in which even great wars and revolutions are able to influence him for hardly more than a moment."[3] But Adams's attempt to measure historical force also put into practice a tenet Nietzsche had already suggested: "The press, the machine, the railway, the tele-graph are premises whose thousand-year conclusion no one has yet dared to draw" (*HH*, II, 278). Among the few scholars who have realized this common project at the bottom of Nietzsche's and Ad-ams's writings, Michael Lopez has pointed out that, following an Emersonian tradition, both men "were similarly committed to find-ing the 'scale of force' which could best explain to an energy-obsessed age the fundamental forces that set men and societies in motion."[4]

What has so far stood in the way of comparing Nietzsche's and Adams's "philosophies of force" is the simple fact that Adams's writings show hardly any traces of Nietzsche. This appears particu-larly curious because Adams visited Germany as early as 1858, since "the literary world then agreed that truth survived in Germany alone, and Carlyle, Matthew Arnold, Renan, Emerson, with scores of popular followers, taught the German faith" (*E*, 61). Ending up at a Berlin secondary school to study German, Adams became an assidu-ous reader of German philosophy — recurring names are Kant, He-gel, Schopenhauer, Hartmann, and Mach (*E*, 432). Nietzsche is only mentioned twice: in a rather general remark from the *Education of Henry Adams* (*E*, 485) and in a letter from 1911, although the Ger-man philosopher had by then become an important influence in American letters.[5]

Even though Nietzsche marks a curious blank in Adams's writ-ings, there are interesting parallels between the two men: they not only shared an early enthusiasm for Schopenhauer and music, but were also shocked by the stifling conditions of the Prussian educa-tional system and agreed on the striking contrast between American "restlessness" (*HH*, I, 285) and German inertia.[6] Moreover, Adams's insight that "the profoundest lessons are not the lessons of reason" but "sudden strains that permanently warp the mind" (*E*, 108) would have certainly been approved by the German philosopher, who "mistrusted all systematizers."[7]

Adams's comments on Germany are characterized by the slightly snobbish tone of the affluent heir of one of the most distinguished political dynasties in America. Adams could afford to operate in ironical distance from Puritan Boston without losing family protec-tion and important connections, and he could cultivate a cosmopoli-tan sense for the simultaneity of historical differences by lodging in some of the most privileged European and American locations. Nietzsche, like Kafka, knew America only from books. He traveled to escape German food and climate, but lack of financial resources and his poor health confined his traveling to Switzerland and Italy. Whereas Adams knew Europe, the South Seas, and Asia, Nietzsche was restricted to mental mobility: he became an "aeronaut of the spirit" (D, 575), trying to compensate for a Calvinistic upbringing and a petty bourgeois academic existence by mapping out the open frontiers of philosophical thinking.

The differences in background and lifestyle produced differences of tone and temperament which appear in inverse proportion to the biographical conditions of their lives. Whereas Nietzsche, cultivating an increasingly euphoric sense of mission, claimed nothing less than to "impregnate the past" and "to beget the future,"[8] Adams adopted an elegiac and darkly pessimistic pose:

> One learns to regard death and life as much the same thing when one lives more in the past than in the present. Indeed, when the present becomes positively repulsive, and the past alone seems real, I am not sure that death is the livelier reality of the two.[9]

Despite those different outlooks, however, Nietzsche's and Adams's intellectual strategies show surprising similarities. Both men's writings are eclectic, idiosyncratic, and speculative; both rejected the increasing academic professionalization towards the end of the nineteenth century and freely violated discursive rules and generic boundaries. While Nietzsche created a provokingly artistic philosophical style that polemically exploited scientific terminology and preached a radical historicizing of knowledge, Adams leaned towards a poetic historiographical style that did not shrink from philosophical questions and at the same time flirted with scientific objectivity. Even though a direct Nietzschean influence on Adams can hardly be discovered, there is still a common denominator in the diagnoses these two cultural critics and professional dilettantes addressed to the symptoms of their time:

> Like Nietzsche [Adams] had come to realize that the only justification for the world's existence had to be an aesthetic one. Like Nietzsche he was profoundly troubled by his own findings, recognizing only too well the consequences of his solutions to the world's dilemma.[10]

II

An important impulse in Nietzsche's and Adams's writings can be seen in what Hayden White has called "the burden of history": the sense of a widening chasm between life and letters, the feeling that an increasingly scientific and autonomous exploration of the past would destroy any authentic experience of the present.[11] One way in which both Nietzsche and Adams could observe the dominance of historicist consciousness was the failure to fulfill what they considered the tasks of education.[12] What both men had in mind was a kind of historical education that was not "wholly useless" (*E*, 302) but employed history "for the purpose of life" (*UM*, II, 1). However, the institutional reality Nietzsche and Adams experienced as students and as young professors in Basel and Harvard seemed to move into the opposite direction. While Nietzsche attacked historicism as "torture instrument" (*UM*, II, 7), as "disease" (*EH*, "The Untimely Ones," 1), and his teachers as "thinking-, writing-, and speaking-machines" (*UM*, II, 5), Adams suffered from "desultory and useless reading" (*E*, 60) and sarcastically concluded that "the education he had received bore little relation to the education he needed" (*E*, 53). The question was how to teach young men (young women were still mainly excluded from this enterprise) "to know how to learn" (*E*, 314) and to educate themselves in a universe that seemed to have denounced not only God but also the ideal of a sovereign, enlightened subject. An important reason for this demystification of the world was the publication of *The Origin of the Species* in 1859. Darwin's study was understood as an attack on the still common belief in the existence of a divine creator of cosmic order. After a short time, however, the book also demonstrated the unusually productive adoptability of Darwin's theory: its "extraordinary hermeneutical potential" and its "power to yield a great number of significant and various meanings"[13] provided a highly suggestive discursive formation that was apt to replace natural theology's divine telos by a new secular teleology of progress.

As for many young men of their generation, evolutionary theory was to become an important "Bildungserlebnis" for Nietzsche and Adams. Darwinism already occupied Nietzsche in the first two *Untimely Meditations*, which show "that the 'use' of history . . . is to gain self-knowledge and that the knowledge of the self he seeks with the aid of Schopenhauer becomes possible only on the basis of historical criticism."[14] Whereas the first meditation criticizes David Strauss's naively Darwinian good faith (*UM*, I, 7), the second attempts to unmask "overproud European's" evolutionary optimism as an enormous self-deception (*UM*, II, 9). Instead of following the linear conceptions of Darwinist historians, Nietzsche uses a quotation from the Austrian novelist Franz Grillparzer to illustrate a much more contingent sense of history:

> All human beings have at the same time their own individual necessity, so that millions of courses ran parallel beside one another in straight or crooked lines, frustrate or advance one another, strive forwards or backwards, and thus assume for one another the character of chance, and so, quite apart from the influence of the occurrences of nature, make it impossible to establish any all-embracing necessity prevailing throughout all events. (*UM*, II, 6)

This "anti-totalized, anti-teleological view of history"[15] does not simply reject all history but only criticizes the objective claims of historicism. By attacking "monumental" and "antiquarian" historiography, Nietzsche votes for a third ("critical") and radically historicized kind of historical thinking: " . . . the origin of historical culture . . . *must* itself be known historically, history *must* itself resolve the problem of history, knowledge *must* turn its sting against itself" (*UM*, II, 8).[16]

With his demand for a "*history of the origins* of feelings and valuations" (*GS*, 345) applying to all fields of knowledge, Nietzsche laid the foundation for the historical strategy he would later call "genealogy." In *On the Genealogy of Morals*, meant as a contribution to intensify the issues of *Beyond Good and Evil*, the attack on linearity and causality was put forward in a considerably sharper tone (*GM*, II, 12). One of the most controversial of Nietzsche's texts, the essay attempts "to debunk cherished values by demonstrating their contingency and ignoble origin."[17] Beside its polemical preoccupations, *Genealogy* concedes that even the genealogical 'method' can only be a temporary effort to "project 'meaning' into history" (*WP*, 1011): as the kind of historical philosophizing Nietzsche tries to practice, it can be nothing more than an "attempt to somehow describe the Heraclitean becoming and to abbreviate it in signs (to *translate* it, as it were, and to embalm it in a sort of semblance of being)."[18] Consequently, all historical description is an anthropomorphic construction that remains inevitably tied to the laws of language; it only provides chiffres for a "contiguous sign-chain of ever new interpretations and adaptions" (*GM*, II, 12), whereas the 'truth' of historical form "is fluid" and its "meaning is even more so" (*GM*, II, 12).

In *The Will to Power* the anti-teleological considerations of the earlier texts again meet with the anti-Darwinist strain of Nietzsche's thinking:

> Becoming must be explained without recourse to final intentions; becoming must appear justified at every moment . . . ; the present must absolutely not be justified by reference to a future, nor the past by reference to the present. (*WP*, 708)

Recent studies have emphasized Nietzsche's ambivalent attitude towards Darwinism.[19] While his aggressively Darwinian terminology often seems to advocate a more radical understanding of evolutionary theory, his "anti-Darwinist" objections predominantly aim at the moralizing impetus and implications of Darwin's and many of his followers' belief in an evolutionary effect of moral criteria (*WP*, 681). Another premise Nietzsche criticizes in this context is the Darwinists' concentration on environmental conditions:

> The influence of "external circumstances" is overestimated by Darwin to a ridiculous extent: the essential thing in the life process is precisely the tremendous shaping, form-creating force working from within which *utilizes* and *exploits* "external circumstances." (*WP*, 647)

Nietzsche, however, was not primarily interested in the unitary development of populations and species, but in the contingent inner life of individuals:

> . . . this mankind is not a whole: it is an inextricable multiplicity of ascending and descending life-processes — it does not have a youth followed by maturity and finally by old age; the strata are twisted and entwined together — and in a few millennia there may still be even younger types of man than we can show today. (*WP*, 339)

In an early draft Nietzsche tried to illustrate his discontinuous sense of history by referring to the keywords of "Lebenslauf" and "Lebensform."[20] His remarks on the necessity of destroying 'natural' chronological sequence and of finding meaning in ruptures and ecstatic moments of transition show that the genealogical approach radically individualizes and fragments the universalistic impetus of nineteenth-century historiography and evolutionary theory. Nietzsche refuses to subsume individual experience under objective laws and turns himself into the most prominent object of the genealogical method. The most curious results of this inversion can be observed in his autobiography, where he not only designates himself an "unbelievable atavism" and rejects any relation to his mother,[21] but also claims: "I am, to express it in the form of a riddle, already dead as my father, while as my mother I am still living and becoming old" (*EH*, I, 1). In this riddle, one of the most-commented passages in *Ecce Homo*, Nietzsche's anti-teleological genealogy presents itself with enigmatic precision.[22] In a series of paradoxical manipulations of his own genealogy the almost mad author characterizes his Dionysian messias as an evolutionary lapsus, portraying himself as a scientific riddle that would only be solved by the discovery of genetic mutation in the year of his death.

One of the masks Henry Adams has his autobiographical protagonist wear in the *Education* also presents him as a living proof against the validity of evolutionary theory. The chapter which narrates young Adams's first encounter with Darwinism in 1867 relates a curious encounter with an archaic dimension. Led by his interest in Charles Lyell's studies on the sequence of geological formations, he finds the "Wenlock Edge of time" (*E*, 229), a beautiful Walisian spot where historical sequences "became interchangeable":

> The Roman road was twin to the railroad; Uriconium was well worth Shrewsbury . . . . The shepherds of Caractacus or Offa, or the monks of Buildwas, had they approached where he lay in the grass, would have taken him only for another and tamer variety of Welsh thief . . . . One might mix up the terms of time as one liked, or stuff the present anywhere into the past, measuring time by Falstaff's Shrewsbury clock, without violent sense of wrong, as one could do it on the Pacific Ocean; but the triumph of all was to look south along the Edge to the abode of one's earliest ancestor and nearest relative, the ganoid fish, whose name, according to Professor Huxley, was *Pteraspis*, a cousin of the sturgeon, and whose kingdom, according to Sir Roderick Murchison, was called Silura. Life began and ended there. (*E*, 229)

This deep-sea fish was not what Adams had expected to find when he enthusiastically greeted Darwinism because it seemed to lead "to some great generalization which would finish one's clamor to be educated" (*E*, 224). The imaginative encounter with a witness of the earliest past left Adams in a mood of comic desperation: "He was conscious that, in geology as in theology, he could prove only Evolution that did not evolve; uniformity that was not uniform, and Selection that did not select" (*E*, 231). Asking himself why he could not trust evolutionary theory, Adams discovered psychology as a "new dark corner of education" (*E*, 231). Haunted by the premonition that his skepticism towards Darwinism would paralyze his action through a solipsist "pale cast of thought" (*E*, 232), Adams decided "to put psychology under lock and key" and "insisted on maintaining his absolute standards; on aiming at ultimate Unity":

> For the young men whose lives were cast in the generation between 1867 and 1900, Law should be Evolution from lower to higher, aggregation of the atom in the mass, concentration of multiplicity in unity, compulsion of anarchy in order; and he would force himself to follow wherever it led . . . . (*E*, 232)

But Adams's disillusioning "education as a Darwinian" went deeper than his manly resistance against the spirit of skepticism might suggest. As he happened to be acquainted with geologists Louis Agassiz and Clarence King, he was provided with fresh arguments against Darwinian uniformism and converted to the enemy's school of catastrophic change.[23] Looking back on his London years, Adams emphasizes the importance of this intellectual move in a rather catastrophic meditation:

> In 1900 he entered a far vaster universe, where all the old roads ran about in every direction, overrunning, dividing, subdividing, stopping abruptly, vanishing slowly, with side-paths that led nowhere, and sequences that could not be proved . . . . Evolution was becoming change of form broken by freaks of force, and warped at times by attractions affecting intelligence, twisted and tortured at other times by sheer violence, cosmic, chemical, solar supersensual, electrolytic — who knew what? — defying science, if not denying known law; and the wisest of men could but imitate the Church, and invoke a 'larger synthesis' to unify the anarchy again. (*E*, 400/401)

In its labyrinthine sense of disorientation this passage echoes the quotation from Grillparzer that Nietzsche had used to illustrate his genealogical concept of history. Adams's and Nietzsche's comments on history resemble each other not so much in their analyses but in their phenomenology of historical confusion. This also shows in their verbal depiction of historical and autobiographical time: both begin to prefer "differences of degree" to "opposites" (*HH*, II, 67), so that the remnants of Hegelian dialectics gradually dissolve into paradoxical inversions. In terms of the handling of time, a literary witness for both Adams and Nietzsche is Proust; often, seemingly stable oppositions suddenly appear as two sides of the same coin just like the two famous directions of Méséglise and Guermantes in the *Recherche du temps perdu*; with all three authors, history is no longer a chronological, linear process but a "hodge-podge of kaleidoscopic changes — something like clouds that gather and disperse at random."[24]

Some of the conclusions Nietzsche and Adams drew from their attempts to reform nineteenth-century historicism were at least as radical as the literary strategies of classical modernism. In claiming that "all historians speak of things which have never existed except in imagination" (*D*, 307) and that "the poetry is history" while "the facts are false" (*MSM*, 549), Adams and Nietzsche can be considered forerunners of the recent debate on the common discursive features of fiction and history. As a practical consequence, both authors were looking for a kind of stylistic *mimicry* to capture the labyrinthine realities of modern life.

Nietzsche's and Adams's literary attempts to reform the writing of history cannot be separated from their interest in other fields of knowledge and their keen sense for the intellectual sparks springing from a confrontation of different discourses. In both men's writings, images are often more reliable then theoretical terms. Concentrating on some of the metaphorical junctures of Nietzsche's and Adams's 'mental maps', the following considerations try to follow the crooked paths of both authors' excursions into scientific theory and terminology.

III

With the topic of science, the interpretation of Nietzsche and Adams is moving on particularly slippery ground. The writings of both authors confront their readers with something like a scientific turn. While *Human All Too Human* and the *Gay Science* discovered physics, physiology, and biology as a new "power-source" and "regulator" of philosophy (*HH*, I, 251), Adams recommended an

apparently strictly scientific theory of history in his "Letter to American Teachers" and the following essays, and already reflected on this
project in *Mont-Saint-Michel and Chartres* and his *Education*. There
has been much discussion about the compatibility of scientific, literary, and philosophical discourses.[25] Unfortunately, the question of
what and *how* Nietzsche and Adams read is often mixed up with the
question whether the scientific sources and theorems they referred to
have been 'properly' understood and 'adequately' used. In this context, it has often been held against both authors that they were vague
and highly selective in their handling of scientific terminologies.
Whereas Nietzsche from the beginning was extremely suspicious of
any claims to objectivity and mainly transferred scientific axioms
from their given contexts to his own idiosyncratic discourse, Adams
often complained that he did not know enough mathematics to follow scientific reasoning,[26] so that his only legitimation to "plaster
other people's standard text books together" was mere
"impertinence" (*E,* 401).[27]

Nietzsche's and Adams's writings are not so much serious efforts
in scientific terminology and methodology but more or less conscious "category mistakes" motivated by "an extraordinary sensitivity
to the *tone* of scientific theories."[28] Both were driven by a curiosity
that was decisively artistic and literary and tried to force multiple perspectives into new provoking coalitions. While Nietzsche followed a
"perspective" in which "things that had never before faced each
other are suddenly juxtaposed" (*EH,* IV, 1), Adams wrote to a
friend: "I like my Schopenhauer, and I like my Kelvin, — I like
metaphysics and I like physics, — but I don't much care to reconcile
them, though I enjoy making them fight."[29] With regard to
Nietzsche's and Adams's perspectivism there would be little hermeneutic value in judging their approaches to science according to the
strict rules of scientific discourse. As scientific authors in the narrowly
professional sense of the word both could but fail. From a less normative point of view, however, it is exactly this failure which offers a
chance to their readers; namely the possibility to witness their attempts to bridge the gap between the two worlds of science and the
humanities without abandoning their watchfulness against simplifying and ideological parallelizations of different ways of worldmaking.

Adams's excursions into the natural sciences are characterized by
a mixture of hope and skeptical irony:

Down through the years his marginalia have two characteristic themes: a querulous bafflement in the face of science's refusal to claim universality and finality for its theories, and . . . an emphatic delight . . . in any sign of uncertainty, confusion, or contradiction, admitted or manifested by a scientific writer.[30]

After his encounter with Darwinism had already brought Adams in dangerous proximity to epistemological solipsism, he was looking for other inspiring sources. He soon discovered the kinetic theory of gases as a "final synthesis of science" "which seemed to cover all motion in space, and to furnish the measure of time" (E, 431). Adams's euphoric mood echoes the enthusiasm which from the 1830s on had driven a number of scientists to explore the connection between magnetism, electricity, motion, heat, and light. Whereas the steam engine, the battery, and the dynamo were proving the practical convertibility of forces, it was soon agreed upon that in most physical processes the total sum of forces obviously remained constant.[31] When Thomson and Gait formulated the First Law of Thermodynamics as the Law of the Conservation of Force in 1862,[32] many scientists were still dreaming of a Spencerian universe of force which could be explored and described by a small number of universal laws.

Because of his highly general and metaphorical usage of the term *force*, Adams could turn the promising formula of the First Law of Thermodynamics into a kind of poetological program. For him, the conservation and the convertibility of energy provided an analogical principle apt to solve his problem of an adequate description of historical change. If, on an abstract level, all natural forces were *convertible*, then they would also be *translatable* into historical forces and, finally, into the historian's verbal images of those forces. From this point of view, the task of historiography suddenly appeared surprisingly simple: thermodynamics seemed to provide an instrument "to triangulate the future" (E, 423), and all Adams had to do was "to find and follow the force that attracts" (E, 478), to describe "its values, equivalents, conversions" (E, 389).

Since the middle of the century, though, things had become more complicated. When thermodynamic theory came up with its Second Law, the conflict between mechanics and the kinetic theory of gases (which already operated with atoms) could no longer be ignored. The crucial point puzzling even insiders was the question of

reversibility: whereas the First Law assumed reversibility of physical
and chemical processes, the Second Law claimed that

> although the absolute quantity of energy in the universe is con-
> stant, an increasing amount of it becomes unusable by man. En-
> tropy increases; the differentials between heat and energy levels,
> upon which our ability to do work depends, gradually and inevita-
> bly tend to equalize; change is irreversible.[33]

To the historian, "the matter of direction seemed vital" (*E,* 400). As
Kelvin's law of entropy and the dissipation of energy used equally
suggestive metaphors as Darwin's writings,[34] Adams fell into the
same trap as many of his contemporaries: he ignored the fact that the
Second Law did *not* apply to the closed systems which only Maxwell's Demon could prevent from entropic heat death,[35] so that the
earth suddenly seemed to move along an apocalyptic course, "like
that of a river falling into an ocean."[36] Adams's turn from the
"enthusiasm" fostered by the First Law to the "pessimism" nurtured
by the Second is hard to locate.[37] The Second Law's gloomy associations definitely dominate the "Letter to American Teachers" and
"The Rule of Phase Applied to History," but they can already be
glimpsed in the *Education's* narrative oscillating between the naively
optimistic protagonist and the ironically distanced narrator. A crucial
turning point can be found in the chapter "The Grammar of Science." In Karl Pearson's relativism, to which the title refers, Adams
discovered a further step within the gradual dissipation of epistemological certainty: while "to Kant, Truth was the essence of the 'I'; an
innate conviction; a categorical imperative; to Poincaré, it was a convenience; and to Karl Pearson, a medium of exchange" (*E,* 456).

The "Grammar of Science" taught Adams that there was no
"impersonal point" to measure history (*E,* 399), but only the human
mind to fall back upon; an inconspicuous lump of "gray matter"
which had not yet "revealed its mysterious mechanism" (*E,* 481):

> As far as one ventured to interpret actual science, the mind had
> thus far adjusted itself by an infinite series of infinitely delicate ad-
> justments forced on it by the infinite motion of an infinite chaos of
> motion; dragged at one moment into the unknowable and un-
> thinkable, then trying to scramble back within its senses and to bar
> the chaos out, but always assimilating bits of it, until at last, in
> 1900, a new avalanche of unknown forces had fallen on it, which
> required new mental powers to control. If this view was correct, the

mind could gain nothing by flight or by fight; it must merge in its supersensual multiverse, or succumb to it. (*E*, 461)

This passage at the end of "The Grammar of Science" marks an epistemological rupture in the text of the *Education*. It suggests that "the mind exists in a universe of its own creation" (*E*, 460) where subject and object, inside and outside, are no longer separated, and thus destroys one of the most important prerequisites of enlightened rationalism.

It is no accident that the disillusioning chapter on the relativistic "grammar of science" also mentions the discovery of radium. For Adams, Madame Curie had found a "metaphysical bomb" (*E*, 452) likely "to explode the scientific magazine, bringing thought, for the time, to a standstill" (*E*, 457). Throughout the text of the *Education*, radium is one element in a series of metaphors for the mind (*E*, 397). Compared to the unpredictable potential of radium, however, some of Adams's other scientific metaphors for the mind appear almost old-fashioned. While the dynamo and the magnet at least seem to create orderly lines of intellectual force (*E*, 397), radium, like the images of the comet and the cannonball (*E*, 489), produce the opposite effect of what Adams seemed to have in mind: they do not provide "a new centre" (*E*, 489) but function like mental explosions releasing an "avalanche of unknown forces" (*E*, 461).

Adams's technological images for the mind clearly illustrate this author's problems with his metaphors. On the one hand, he concedes that

> images are not arguments, rarely even lead to proof, but the mind craves them, and, of late more than ever, the keenest experimenters find twenty images better than one, especially if contradictory; since the human mind has already learned to deal in contradictions. (*E*, 489)

On the other hand, he observes that images are a dangerous compensation for a lack of mathematical knowledge — they are "phantoms" that, "once conceived," "become rapidly simple, and the lines of force present themselves as lines of attraction" (*E*, 427). Pearson and radium taught Adams that things were more complicated than just a matter of "translating rays into faith" (*E*, 383). He began to suspect that, like his own figures of thought, scientific terms, too, suggested order where chaos reigned; he realized that the scientific historian's images were not reliable labels of physical and metaphysical entities to uncover the structure of the world, but that they were arbitrary and temporary products of the mind with a sometimes surprising life of their own, proving that metaphors did not so much formulate "some similarity antecedently existing" but rather create it.[38]

Another of Adams's images for the mind at first sight seems to confirm the pragmatist insight that only "convenience was truth" (*E*, 457):

> For convenience as an image, the theory may liken man to a spider in its web, watching for chance prey. Forces of nature dance like flies before the net, and the spider pounces on them when it can; . . . The spider-mind acquires a faculty of memory, and, with it, a singular skill of analysis and synthesis, taking apart and putting together in different relations the meshes of its trap. (*E*, 474)[39]

Adams's "spider-mind" is busy organizing autobiographical and historical time. He "had to spin a new net" out of that "bundle of disconnected memories" other people called "identity" (*E*, 209), and he was looking for "a spool on which to wind the thread of history without breaking it" (*E*, 472), although history had long since ceased to be a "thread," but only presented itself as a "tangled skein" (*E*, 302). Science, in the *Education*, is also described as "tangled skein" out of which Adams was "idly pulling threads" "to see whether or why they aligned themselves" (*E*, 396).

It is at this point that the image of the spider meets "the child's magnet" and "Faraday's experiments and the invention of the dynamo" (*E*, 396/97). This conflation of images happens for more than accidental reasons. Since the dynamo contains a spool which organizes electromagnetic induction, both semantic fields merge in the idea of a "textual dynamo," which provided Adams, as N. Katherine Hayles has pointed out, with a "structure, a syntax and a paradigm" for the story of his life.[40] With the 'dynamic' spider's mind Adams seems to have found a principle that "defeats any static or linear conception of the narrative,"[41] but still spins the thread by which Adams's life could be turned into a text. But the imagery of an electromagnetic source of textual force remains ambivalent. After the discovery of radium had turned the dynamo into an almost prehistorical tool, the spider-mind's perceptive networks became labyrinths of forces which no longer offered any thread leading out.

The pessimistic undertones of the epistemological dilemma inherent in Adams's imagery are emphasized by a further semantic field shaping the text of the *Education*: the naturalist imagery of water. Considering himself a "bad sailor" who is "easily made sea-sick" in more than one sense,[42] the protagonist of the *Education* felt like an "ancient mariner" (*E,* 193) drifting through the "the dead-water of the fin-de-siècle" (*E,* 331). He saw himself as "flotsam" (*E,* 238) of "historical shipwreck" (*E,* 193), and his life appeared like a "succession of violent breaks or waves, with no base at all" (*E,* 312). The pessimistic undertone of Adams's water images undermines the *Education's* scientific enthusiasm. The motives of drifting and shipwreck anticipate and emphasize the disillusioning truth of "The Grammar of Science." Drifting like "a sensual raft in the midst of a supersensual chaos" (*E,* 452), the spider-mind's creative potential seems to have been swallowed by the dead ocean of epistemological entropy.

In his early essay "On Truth and Lie in an Extramoral Sense" Nietzsche attempts to uncover a covert metaphoricity of all language. To illustrate the genealogy of our theoretical terms he also uses the images of water and the spider:

> Here one can admire man as a powerful master architect who has succeeded in erecting an infinitely complicated dome of concepts upon a shifting foundation in the midst of flowing waters. However, in order to find a stable position on such a foundation the construction must be like a cobweb, delicate enough to be born by a wave, yet tight enough not to be destroyed by the least breeze of wind.[43]

But Nietzsche's spider imagery shows different connotations than Adams's use of the motif. While the latter's "spider-mind" is the ambiguous result of a process of epistemological disillusionment, Nietzsche from the beginning uses his notion of modern man, the "great cross spider at the node of the cosmic web" (*UM,* p. 108), as a weapon against metaphysical substantialism and as an allegory for one of the important premises of his thought (*D,* 117). For him, it seems to be a delightful insight that all our concepts are only a fragile "spider's web of purposes" which has to be destroyed to liberate authentic experience (*D,* 130).

The world-building potential of Adams's spider-mind seemed like a lost raft within an ocean of entropic chaos. Nietzsche's water imagery does not suggest shipwreck and stale water but adventure and an almost vitalist sense of becoming. Whenever the German philosopher talks about oceans, his imagination is obviously not yet strangled by the historical fact that these last frontiers were about to be closed:

> Would we *cross* the sea? Whither does this mighty longing draw us, this longing that is worth more to us than any pleasure? . . . Will it perhaps be said of us one day that we too, *steering westward, hoped to reach an India* — but that it was our fate to be wrecked against infinity? (*D*, 575)

Nietzsche's demands "Embark!" (*GS*, 289) and "We have to be conquerors" (*WP*, 219) celebrate the death of God as a liberating moment of departure.[44] In contrast to Adams, his water metaphors are not tainted by the thermodynamic pessimism which would become fashionable towards the turn of the century. Nietzsche often combines the image of the sea with metaphors of air. His "aeronauts of the spirit" (*D*, 575) are flying through the "bright, transparent, vigorous, electrified" and "*virile* air" of science: "In this severe and clear element they have their full strength; here they can fly. Why, then, go down into those muddy waters where one has to swim and wade and get one's wings dirty?" (*GS*, 293). Nietzsche's enthusiastic images of sailing and flying advocate a creative fusion of philosophy and science. The true philosophers must "turn to physics" (*GS*, 335), but they are also "brave birds which fly out into . . . the farthest distance" (*D*, 575), "adventurers and birds of passage," waking up "in the midst of the ocean of becoming" (*D*, 314).

Whereas Adams's ocean of entropic standstill designates a catastrophic finality of history, Nietzsche's "ocean of becoming" suggests a Heraclitean flux of all things. Using elements of Heraclitean philosophy of history in order to attack any kind of metaphysical essentialism, Nietzsche claims that all moral and religious entities are actually "rivers with a hundred tributaries and sources" (*HH*, I, 14), and notes that "everything is in flux: but *everything is also flooding forward*, and towards *one* goal" (*HH*, I, 107). Yet the direction of Nietzsche's stream of becoming is less clear than Adams's "river falling into an ocean." It cannot be grasped by any attempt to connect origins and ends; the "driving force" remains unintelligible, since it is not identical with the anthropomorphic illusion of a "directing force."[45]

For both Nietzsche and Adams, the problem of historical direction was rooted in the interplay of physical and psychological forces. To explore these forces, Nietzsche referred to the same thermodynamic subtext that organizes Adams's later writings. Numerous studies on Nietzsche's scientific sources have not only pointed to the logical flaws and unscientific generalizations of the German philosopher's meditations on force, but have also shown that he, too, stumbled over the specific heuristic premises of the First and Second Law of Thermodynamics.[46] Like Adams, Nietzsche was first attracted by the idea of the conservation of force.[47] The often-quoted final paragraph of *The Will to Power*, for instance, describes the world as a

> monster of energy, without beginning, without end; a firm, iron magnitude of force that does not grow bigger or smaller, that does not expend itself but only transforms itself; as a whole, of unalterable size, a household without expenses or losses, but likewise without increase or income . . . . (*WP*, 1067)

In the preceding paragraph, however, Nietzsche argues against the teleological implications of the Second Law, stating that Thomson's notion of an irreversible movement towards a "final state" cannot be reconciled with the idea of a reversible "circular movement that has already repeated itself infinitely often and plays its game *in infinitum*" (*WP*, 1066).

According to their temperaments, Adams and Nietzsche drew different conclusions from the thermodynamic confusion. Whereas Adams, in desperate need of historical direction, surrendered to the catastrophic determinism underlying the formulation of the Second Law, Nietzsche stuck to the First Law since it seemed to promise a regenerating whirlpool of powers:

> . . . a sea of forces flowing and rushing together, eternally changing, eternally flooding back, with tremendous years of recurrence, with an ebb and a flood of its forms; out of the simplest forms striving toward the most complex, out of the stillest, most rigid, coldest forms toward the hottest, . . . and then again returning home to the simple out of this abundance. (*WP*, 1067)

This thermodynamic meditation shows how the concepts of the will to power and its temporal equivalent, the eternal recurrence, emerge out of a "sea of forces." By returning to the image of the waves,[48] Nietzsche creates a historical and philosophical figure that fuses linear and circular processes, a movement of thought which would enable him to reject both mechanistic and teleological, deterministic and voluntaristic explanations.[49]

The relationship between "force" and "will" in Nietzsche's late writings is hard to grasp. While Adams attempted to translate "lines of will" into "lines of force" (*E*, 426) and desperately missed the subjective agency his operation had eliminated, Nietzsche advocated a modification of the scientific notion of force:

> The victorious concept "force," by means of which our physicists have created God and the world, still needs to be completed: an inner will must be ascribed to it, which I designate as "will to power".... one is obliged to understand all motion, all "appearances," all "laws," only as symptoms of an inner event and to employ man as an analogy to this end. (*WP*, 619)

Nietzsche's demand to psychologize the laws of mechanics and thermodynamics[50] follows the same argumentative pattern as his critique of Darwinism and atomism. He employs scientific terminology in order to desubstantialize traditional metaphysical entities, but at the same time he supports a radical 'humanization' of the allegedly objective categories of scientific thought.

While Adams in the end no longer cared whether a solipsistically atrophied mind was the playball or the center of a labyrinth of thermodynamic confusion, Nietzsche tried to open a creative terrain beyond the limitations of Cartesian rationalism. To mobilize individual forces *without* having to rely on an essentialist concept of the subject, he translated the macrostructures of thermodynamics into the microstructures of physiology. Whereas Adams had taken great care to erase all traces of bodily harm or pleasure from his writings, Nietzsche decided that the human body, not the cosmos, would become his 'connecting thread' through a labyrinth of force.[51] As a "political structure" of struggling "cells and tissues" (*WP*, 660) the body would provide a more concrete and sensual laboratory to study the human subject as "multiplicity" of forces.

During the second half of the nineteenth century, physiology was somehow in the air. Like many fin-de-siècle authors, Nietzsche adopted the fashionable naturalist pose of a 'vivisecteur' and consulted various theories of "degenerescence"[52] for his examination of European nihilism. When in 1888 he left *The Will to Power* to tackle the problem of *décadence* in the *Anti-Christ*, he also studied the

decadent styles of Wagner and Paul Bourget. Nietzsche's late reflections on a decadent "disgregation of will" also drew on thermodynamic and physiological sources,[53] and they show again that, unlike
Adams, Nietzsche was not interested in conjuring up universal de-
cline and degenerescence. For him, a deviating type might claim
leadership as an elected outsider, and nihilism was a transitory state
which could be used as a regenerative force.

Nietzsche's adoption of physiological theories is as ambivalent as
his comments on Darwinism and thermodynamics: it employs permanent change of perspectives and oscillates between positivist affirmation and a fundamental skepticism against the metaphorical
origins of scientific terms.[54] Finally, Nietzsche's notes on the decadent style led him back to his own beginnings without bringing him
full circle; they turned the mock-positivist plea for a "gay science"
into the idea of a "physiology of art" which in some points went
back to the early metaphysics of art.[55] But in contrast to the early
mystifications of the Dionysian, the double genitive of this formula
suggests a dynamic synthesis of science and art: it aims at a physiology of art that is at the same time artistic physiology, at an art of interpretation that combines Dionysian rapture with scientific lucidity
and no longer attacks the metaphoricity of scientific terminology but
uses it as creative potential.

IV

What makes Nietzsche and Adams fascinating reading is the fact
that both wrote from within a far-reaching crisis of representation.
Instead of creating unity from the "supersensual chaos" of fin-de-
siècle realities, human consciousness seemed to mimic the chaos
outside of it; the traditional boundaries between subject and object
were torn down, the distinction between theory and autobiography
seemed blurred. In dealing with fragmented selves in the midst of
historical discontinuity, Nietzsche's *Ecce Homo* and Adams's *Education* could only result in parodies of the genre. Both texts are curiously seismographic performances that play with masks and poses in
order to involve their readers in an ironical search for the true personality behind the text.

But the autobiographies also show that Nietzsche and Adams use
different ironical strategies to turn their lives into symptomatic

readings of their times. Thus, the final chapter of the *Education* finds the protagonist behind a club window "on the turmoil of Fifth Avenue," watching how "failure had become catastrophic":

> The outline of the city became frantic in this effort to explain something that defied meaning. Power seemed to have outgrown its servitude and to have asserted its freedom. The cylinder had exploded, and thrown great masses of stone and steam against the sky. The city had the air and movement of hysteria . . . . Prosperity never before imagined, power never yet wielded by man, speed never reached by anything but a meteor, had made the world irritable . . . , all the new forces, condensed into corporations, were demanding a new type of man . . . . (*E,* 498)

Seeking shelter from the democratic mob behind the club window, Adams shrank from the historical forces he had tried to examine. His final gesture aims at regaining ironical omniscience; it stabilizes the neat self-division between "manikin" and observer and reestablishes the epistemological boundary his narrative had temporarily broken through.

However, whereas Adams in the end defied historical change by seeking refuge in an interior republic of gentlemen of letters, Nietzsche, eager to represent the "new type of man," turned himself into a battlefield of the new forces. For him, too, "explosives taught most" (*E,* 342), but the German philosopher, unrestrained by the invention of radium, handled the dangerous material much more carelessly and playfully. Raving about the explosive potential of great men and the cathartic power of great explosions,[56] he exclaimed: "I am no man, I am dynamite!" (*EH,* "Why I Am a Destiny," 1). While Adams felt himself wasting away towards a final entropic state, Nietzsche cultivated a philosophy of excess that virtually blew him to pieces. Compared with the American's "dynamic theory of history," the German's explosive self-culture creates a much more radical sense of irony: it rejects any position of omniscience and leaves his readers to struggle with a plethora of fragments that radically deny any attempt of creating order and coherence.

As a final irony, Nietzsche's sense of excessive representation destroyed his ability to read the signs of his own times. His project to become his own "experiment and guinea-pig" (*GS,* 319) turned him into one of the most famous victims in the laboratory of intellectual history. Adams, more careful, had not used himself but rather a "manikin" to measure the forces of his time. His eighteenth-century precaution gained him time to watch the experiments of early modernism until he was sure they would lead to a finale that might be even less glorious than mad Nietzsche's embracing a horse on an Italian marketplace.

Notes

[1] Henry Adams, *The Education of Henry Adams*, ed. Ernest Samuels (Boston, 1961), p. 330; further references are to this edition (*E*) by page number in parentheses.

[2] See Harold Dean Cater, *Henry Adams and his Friends. A Collection of His Unpublished Letters* (New York, 1960), p. 290.

[3] Friedrich Nietzsche, "On the Uses and Disadvantages of History for Life," *Untimely Meditations*, trans. R. J. Hollingdale (Cambridge, 1983), p. 83. All further references to Nietzsche's works are to sections of the following editions: (*HH*) *Human, All Too Human*, trans. R. J. Hollingdale (Cambridge, 1986); (*GS*) *The Gay Science*, trans. Walter Kaufmann (New York, 1974); *(WP) The Will to Power*, trans. W. Kaufmann and R. J. Hollingdale (New York, 1967); (*GM*) *On the Genealogy of Morals*, trans. W. Kaufmann and R. J. Hollingdale (New York, 1967); (*EH) Ecce Homo*, trans. W. Kaufmann (New York, 1967).

[4] Cf. Michael Lopez, "Transcendental Failure: 'The Palace of Spiritual Power'," in Joel Porte (ed.), *Emerson: Prospect and Retrospect* (Cambridge/London, 1982), p. 124.

[5] In a letter from March 5th, 1911, Adams names Hartmann, "Nietsche" [sic] and Schopenhauer as representatives of an "excessively forcible school of pessimism" in Germany; see J. C. Levenson, Ernest Samuels *et al.*, *The Letters of Henry Adams, Vol. VI: 1906–1918* (Cambridge/London, 1988), p. 421. The reason for his general disinterest in Nietzsche could hardly have been a lack of opportunity: as early as 1875 Adams's assistant editor at the *North American Review* published a review of the "Second Untimely Consideration" in the same magazine; see Melvin Drimmer, *Nietzsche in American Thought, 1895–1925* (Diss. U. of Rochester, 1965), vol. I, pp. 59ff.

[6] Cf. *E*, 239 and *GS*, 329; *E*, 237 and *HH*, II, 287.

[7] *Twilight of the Idols* and *The Anti-Christ*, trans. R. J. Hollingdale (London, 1968), p. 26.

[8] Hartmut Schröter, *Historische Theorie und Geschichtliches Handeln* (Mittenwald, 1982), p. 208 (my translation).

[9] H. D. Cater, pp. 184f.

[10] Olaf Hansen, "Henry Adams: *Mont Saint Michel and Chartres*," *American Studies*, 28 (1983), 323.

[11] See Hayden White, "The Burden of History," *History and Theory*, 5 (1966), 111–34.

[12] Cf. *Human, All Too Human*, I, 242 and *Education*, 314.

[13] Cf. Gillian Beer, *Darwin's Plots* (London/Boston, 1983), p. 10.

[14] Catherine Zuckert, "Nature, History and the Self: Friedrich Nietzsche's Untimely Considerations," *Nietzsche-Studien*, 7 (1978), 55.

[15] Cf. John Pizer, "The Use and Abuse of 'Ursprung': On Foucault's Reading of Nietzsche," *Nietzsche-Studien*, 19 (1990), 477.

[16] Nietzsche's plea for a radical sense of history can also be found in *HH*, I, 292; *HH*, II, 1 and 17; *GS*, 337. Cf. also Karl Schlechta, *Der Fall Nietzsche* (München, 1958), pp. 42–70.

[17] Jeffrey Minson, *Genealogies of Morals: Nietzsche, Foucault, Donzelot and the Eccentricity of Ethics* (London, 1985), p. 7.

[18] Cf. Peter Heller, "Multiplicity and Unity in Nietzsche's Works and Thoughts on Thought," *German Quarterly*, 52 (1979), 335.

[19] Cf. Dieter Henke, "Nietzsches Darwinismuskritik aus der Sicht gegenwärtiger Evolutionsforschung," *Nietzsche-Studien*, 13 (1984), 189–210; Werner Stegmaier, "Darwin, Darwinismus, Nietzsche: Zum Problem der Evolution," *Nietzsche-Studien*, 16 (1987), 264–87.

[20] Bernhard Lypp, "Über drei verschiedene Arten Geschichte zu schreiben: Bemerkungen zur Logik historischen Diskurses im Hinblick auf Nietzsche," Reinhart Koselleck, Paul Widmer (eds.), *Niedergang: Studien zu einem Geschichtlichen Thema* (Stuttgart, 1980), p. 208.

[21] Nietzsche's attack on his mother does not appear in Kaufmann's translation; therefore see Giorgio Colli and Mazzino Montinari (eds.), *Kritische Gesamtausgabe (KSA)*, VI, 3, p. 266.

[22] Cf. Rodolphe Gasché, "Autobiography as Gestalt: Nietzsche's *Ecce Homo*," in Daniel O'Hara (ed.), *Why Nietzsche Now?* (Bloomington, 1985), pp. 271–90.

[23] William Jordy, *Henry Adams: Scientific Historian* (New Haven/London, 1952), pp. 172–200.

[24] Siegfried Kracauer, "Time and History," in Max Horkheimer (ed.), *Zeugnisse: Th. W. Adorno zum sechzigsten Geburtstag* (Frankfurt, 1963), p. 61.

[25] Pioneer work in the philological reconstruction of Adams's and Nietzsche's intellectual biographies has been done by Mazzino Montinari's project "Nietzsches Bibliothek" and by William Jordy. For Adams's scientific background I have greatly benefitted from Ronald E. Martin, *American Literature and the Universe of Force* (Durham, 1981) and N. Katherine Hayles, *Chaos Bound: Orderly Disorder in Contemporary Literature and Science* (Ithaca/London, 1990).

[26] Worthington Chauncey Ford (ed.), *The Letters of Henry Adams*, 2 vols. (Boston, 1938), vol. II, p. 519.

[27] *Ibid.*, p. 541.

[28] R. E. Martin, p. 106.

[29] Levenson/Samuels, *Letters*, VI, p. 272.

[30] R. E. Martin, p. 99.

[31] Cf. Martin, pp. 15–23.

[32] *Ibid.*, pp. 25–28.

[33] *Ibid.*, p. 28.

[34] Cf. N. K. Hayles, pp. 39ff.

[35] On Maxwell's Demon, cf. Hayles, pp. 42f.

[36] George Monteiro (ed), *The Correspondence of Henry James and Henry Adams: 1877–1914* (Baton Rouge, 1992), p. 77.

[37] R. E. Martin, p. 28.

[38] Cf. Max Black, *Models and Metaphors: Studies in Language and Philosophy* (Ithaca, 1962), p. 37.

[39] On the image of the spider, cf. John Carlos Rowe, *Henry Adams and Henry James: The Emergence of a Modern Consciousness* (Ithaca, 1976), p. 127; see also N. K. Hayles, pp. 79f.

[40] N. K. Hayles, p. 69.

[41] *Ibid.*, p. 68

[42] H. D. Cater, p. 111.

[43] "Über Wahrheit und Lüge im außermoralischen Sinne," in *KSA*, III, 2, p. 376 (my translation).

[44] Cf. also *GS*, 343: "At long last the horizon appears free to us again, even if it should not be bright; at long last our ships may venture out again, venture out to face any danger; all the daring of the lover of knowledge is permitted again; the sea, our sea, lies open again; perhaps there has never yet been such an "open sea."

[45] See *GS*, 360: "Is the "goal," the "purpose" not often enough a beautifying pretext, a self-deception of vanity after the event that does not want to acknowledge that the ship is *following* the current into which it has entered accidentally? that it "wills" to go that way *because it — must?* that it has a direction, to be sure, but — no helmsman at all?"

[46] Cf. Arthur Danto, *Nietzsche as Philosopher* (New York, 1965); Wolfgang Müller-Lauter, *Nietzsche: Seine Philosophie der Gegensätze und die Gegensätze seiner Philosophie* (Berlin/New York: de Gruyter, 1971); for a comprehensive summary of European and American contributions on the eternal recurrence, see Klaus Spiekermann, "Nietzsches Beweise für die Ewige Wiederkehr," *Nietzsche-Studien*, 17 (1988), 496–538.

[47] As Martin Bauer has shown, these passionate meditations on force can indeed be traced back to one of the more unknown and early 'discoverers' of the First Law of Thermodynamics: the German physicist and physician Julius R. Mayer, whose *Mechanik der Wärme* lead Nietzsche to conclude that the constant amount of total force required an endless movement of single forces. Only shortly after his study of this book Nietzsche found his idea of an eternal recurrence of limited possibilities confirmed by J. G. Vogt's attempt to prove the circularity of cosmic processes on a mechanistic basis. Cf. Martin Bauer, "Zur Genealogie von Nietzsches Kraftbegriff: Nietzsches Auseinandersetzung mit J. G. Vogt," *Nietzsche-Studien*, 13 (1984), 211–27.

[48] See *GS*, 310 (*"Will and wave"*).

[49] Wolfgang Müller-Lauter, "Der Organismus als innerer Kampf: Der Einfluß von Wilhelm Roux auf Friedrich Nietzsche," *Nietzsche-Studien*, 10/11 (1981/82), 205f.

[50] Cf. Robin Small, "Three Interpretations of Eternal Recurrence," *Dialogue*, 22 (1983), p. 92.

[51] On the "Leitfaden des Leibes," i.e. the evidence of the body, see also the preface to *GS*, 2 and *WP*, 489, 490, 518, 532, 659, 660. One important source of Nietzsche's physiological considerations was Wilhelm Roux's *Der Kampf der Theile im Organismus*. Cf. Müller-Lauter, "Der Organismus als innerer Kampf," pp. 192–221.

[52] A further physiological 'stimulus' Nietzsche followed were the writings of Charles Féré and Alexander Herzen, students of Jean Martin Charcot and Wilhelm Wundt. Cf. Bettina Wahrig-Schmidt, "'Irgendwie, jedenfalls physiologisch'," *Nietzsche-Studien*, 17 (1988), 435–64; Martin Stingelin, "'Moral und Physiologie'," in Bernhard Dotzler (ed.), *Technopathologien* (München, 1992), pp. 41–57.

[53] Cf. Werner Hamacher, "'Disgregation of the Will': Nietzsche on the Individual and Individuality," in Thomas C. Heller, Morton Sosna, David E. Wellbery (eds.), *Reconstructing Individualism: Autonomy, Individuality, and the Self in Western Thought* (Stanford, 1986), pp. 125f.

[54] Cf. Müller-Lauter, "Der Organismus als innerer Kampf," p. 196.

[55] The importance of the compilation "physiology of art," the last product of Nietzsche's physiological considerations, has only recently been emphasized by Mazzino Montinari during a research project in Berlin. The results of the seminar on the "physiology of art" were published in *Nietzsche-Studien*, 13 (1984).

[56] See, for instance, *GS*, 38; *TI*, "Expeditions of an Untimely Man," 44; *EH*, "The Untimely Ones," 3.

Jon-K Adams

Moral Opposition in Nietzsche and Howells

NIETZSCHE AND HOWELLS were almost exact contemporaries: they were born seven years apart, in 1844 and in 1837 respectively, and they wrote most of their crucial works in the 1880s. Although it is not likely that Nietzsche, before his collapse in 1889, had heard of Howells, Howells had definitely heard of Nietzsche by at least 1895, when he reviewed Max Nordau's *Degeneration.*[1] In his review, Howells does not mention Nietzsche's name but he indirectly defends him against Nordau, whom he calls cunning, dishonest, unscrupulous, and "very ignorant," and he implicitly includes Nietzsche among those he refers to as "some of the sublimest men who have ever lived."[2] But at the same time, it would be difficult to find two writers, contemporary in age, who were more different in career, thought, and temperament than these two. Howells's fortunes and reputation rose during the 1880s and 90s, at a time when Nietzsche's languished. Then as the American's prestige began to wane, the German's began to wax, until a reversal of their fortunes became complete and Nietzsche has come to eclipse Howells. Of course, it is not just Howells as a historical and literary figure that has been eclipsed but also, and more importantly, what he represents. In general terms of literary history, the opposition between Nietzsche and Howells is transcribed in the movement from the realism of the nineteenth century to the (post)modernism of the twentieth. More specifically, and especially in terms of their temperament, the opposition is founded in their attitudes towards society. Howells, however much he criticized society, placed a basic trust in it; Nietzsche, in contrast, distrusted society.[3]

The common ground that provides the basis for the opposition between Nietzsche and Howells is morality. Howells's battle for realism was a moral crusade because, as he said, "the finest effect of the 'beautiful' will be ethical and not aesthetic merely. Morality penetrates all things, it is the soul of all things."[4] At the same time, Nietzsche probed the logical and historical basis of morality in idealism and Christianity and worked toward a reversal in moral concepts. He claimed, for instance, "One's 'neighbour' praises selflessness because *he derives advantage from it!* . . . Herewith is indicated the fundamental contradiction of that morality which is precisely today held in such high esteem: the *motives* for this morality stand in antithesis to its *principle*."[5]

The concern for morality that Nietzsche and Howells share, the concern that makes their opposition possible, focuses on the belief in a better future. In Howells we see this belief documented in the utopian thought of *The Traveller from Altruria*. In Nietzsche we see it in the philosophical prophecy of *Thus Spoke Zarathustra*.[6] Just as Howells worked through his major realistic novels (*A Modern Instance*, *The Rise of Silas Lapham*, *A Hazard of New Fortunes*) to his Altrurian romance, so Nietzsche worked through his more nihilistic works (*Human, All Too Human*, *The Wanderer and his Shadow*, *Dawn*) to an encompassing philosophical prophecy. In both cases the earlier works represent penetrating critiques, in Howells's case a critique of American society and in Nietzsche's a critique of European thought. Having voiced these critiques, the next step that both writers took was also similar: the attempt to define a better future.

Utopian thought begins with the conception of a place that is distanced in either time or space. The underlying argument of utopianism is the claim that this distant place represents a better life. "Utopian thought is the product of dissatisfaction crossed with longing: dissatisfaction with the way things are today — any day; longing for the way things might be."[7] In *Thus Spoke Zarathustra* Nietzsche does not use the concept of utopian place; instead he uses a prophetic tradition that disdains this world and looks toward a better one. Yet his concept of the coming Superman maintains the three basic elements in the structure of utopian thought: a present time or place, a future time or distant place, and the transition from one to the other. Although this abstract model of utopian thought encompasses their beliefs in a better future, within the model itself

Nietzsche and Howells maintain an unresolved and unresolvable opposition.

This brings us to the main obstacle in a comparison of Nietzsche and Howells. Nietzsche not only transforms the prophetic tradition — beginning with the claim that God is dead — he also condemns the utilitarian and altruistic thought that informs Howells's utopian ideal, a condemnation that tends to preempt Howells's position. In a way, this makes Howells appear too weak a figure to place in direct opposition to Nietzsche. But Howells was aware of the prophetic tradition from Emerson, and through his critique of Emerson, Howells formulates the difference between himself and Nietzsche.[8] Writing in 1888, in a review of Cabot's *Memoir of Ralph Waldo Emerson*, Howells is full of praise for Emerson, arguing that "Emerson is still the foremost of all our seers, and will be so a hundred years hence" (130). But at the same time, Howells pinpoints the fundamental difference between himself and Emerson. About Emerson he held that "His sympathies perhaps lagged a little" and that "His indifference to consequences came partly from his impersonality; he was so much an idealization of the ordinary human being that his fears were attenuated, like his sympathies" (129).

It would be crass to claim that Howells's description of Emerson fits Nietzsche in every respect — it is not even certain that it fits Emerson that well — but in perceiving a lack of sympathy in Emerson, Howells also recognized what he could not accept in the prophetic tradition, namely its "extreme impersonality" (130). Thus, Howells takes up the utopian rather than the prophetic tradition, mainly, as we will see, because of such concepts as moral complicity, which he worked out in his novel *The Minister's Charge*. In the sermon on complicity, the minister of the novel's title says:

> No man . . . sinned or suffered to himself alone; his error and his pain darkened and afflicted men who never heard of his name. If a community was corrupt, if an age was immoral, it was not because of the vicious, but the virtuous who fancied themselves indifferent spectators.[9]

It is this contrast between Emersonian impersonality and Howellsian complicity that, like the relation between trust and society, specifies the complexion of the moral opposition between Nietzsche and Howells. In order to grasp this opposition in more detail, we need first to mark out Nietzsche's and Howells's position in relation to

the idea of a better future, and then we need to work through
Nietzsche's critique of morality and Howells's anticipation of that
critique.

II

At the beginning of *Thus Spoke Zarathustra*, Zarathustra comes
down from the mountain and presents a prophecy about the Superman. First he announces that *"God is Dead!"*[10] And then he says: *"I
teach you the Superman"* (*Z*, I, 3). It has been pointed out that
Nietzsche's description of the Superman is vague.[11] But just as the
Christian conception of heaven is vague, this vagueness about the
future is part of the prophetic tradition. More important, Nietzsche
emphasizes that the Superman represents a better future by using a
comparison: he says that just as man is to the ape, so shall the Superman be to man (*Z*, I, 3). One of Nietzsche's points about the
coming of the Superman is that major progress has been made. The
Superman, Zarathustra maintains, is the "meaning of the earth" and
he contrasts it with "superterrestrial hope" (*Z*, I, 3). This makes the
Superman an earthly replacement for the dead God, but it is also
more than just a replacement because, as Nietzsche makes clear, the
Superman is for him an attainable goal.

At the end of Howells's *A Traveller from Altruria*, the Altrurian
gives a lecture on his country to a large audience of Americans. Altruria is an economic and social utopia where the people as a whole
control the economic and political affairs of the state and where no
one works for another, but instead, everyone works for the benefit of
the whole: "Every one does his share of labor, and receives his share
of food, clothing and shelter, which is neither more nor less than
another's."[12] The moral basis for this economic and social equality
derives from utilitarianism, a principle, as J. S. Mill defines it, that
links morality to the happiness of the greatest number of people:

> The creed which accepts as the foundation of morals, Utility, or the
> Greatest Happiness Principle, holds that actions are right in pro-
> portion as they tend to promote happiness, wrong as they tend to
> produce the reverse of happiness.[13]

As Howells makes clear, happiness, and thus morality, depends on
economic and social equality. Howells even refers to utilitarianism in
his depiction of Altruria, for when the Altrurian describes the "ideal

great man" of his utopian country, he applies Mill's Greatest Happiness Principle: "I should say, speaking largely, that it was some man who had been able, for the time being, to give the greatest happiness to the greatest number" (119).[14]

The distance between the Superman as the "meaning of the earth" and Altruria as the "greatest happiness to the greatest number" can be calculated in Nietzsche's assessment of utilitarianism, which he refers to in a number of damaging ways, such as "fundamental contradiction" (*GS*, 21), "utility of the herd,"[15] "inherent psychological absurdity,"[16] and simply "naive."[17] Nietzsche's main attitude toward utilitarianism is one of contempt, which is most apparent in his characterization of the Ultimate Man, whom he calls "the most contemptible man" (*Z*, I, 5). Zarathustra mocks the Ultimate Man as the one who "discovered happiness" and then goes on to satirize the utopianism of his utilitarian society:

> They still work, for work is entertainment. But they take care the entertainment does not exhaust them.
>
> Nobody grows rich or poor any more: both are too much of a burden. Who still wants to rule? Who obey? Both are too much of a burden.
>
> No herdsman and one herd. Everyone wants the same thing, everyone is the same: whoever thinks otherwise goes voluntarily into the madhouse. (*Z*, I, 5)

Zarathustra contrasts the Ultimate Man with the Superman, and in doing so, he employs a reversal of values that begins with a rejection of society: "You solitaries of today, you who have seceded from society, you shall one day be a people: from you, who have chosen out yourselves, shall a chosen people spring — and from this chosen people, the Superman" (*Z*, I, "Of the Bestowing Virtue"). Here we see that man must withdraw from society, from the herd, in order to be transformed into the Superman.

But Howells anticipates this reversal of values by showing that his Utopia includes not only a development of society but also a development of the individual. First of all, when the Altrurian arrives in America, the narrator (who is himself an American) describes him as a new kind of man: "I had not the least trouble in identifying him, he was so unlike all the Americans who dismounted from the train with him" (7). But even more important, Howells emphasizes the change in human nature that takes place between America and Altruria. For example, in attempting to explain (and justify) American capitalism to the Altrurian, the narrator says: "I suppose that man likes to squeeze his brother man, when he gets him in his grip. That's human nature, you know" (83). The Altrurian responds with the rhetorical question, "Is it?" — but he does not pursue the topic of human nature at this point. Only later when he lectures on Altruria, he says:

> It used to be said, in the old times, that 'it was human nature' to shirk, and malinger and loaf, but we have found that it is no such thing. We have found that it is human nature to work cheerfully, willingly, eagerly, at the tasks which all share for the supply of the common necessities. In like manner we have found out that it is not human nature to hoard and grudge, but that when the fear, and even the imagination, of want is taken away, it is human nature to give and to help generously. We used to say, 'A man will lie, or a man will cheat in his own interest; that is human nature,' but that is no longer human nature with us, perhaps because no man has any interest to serve; he has only the interests of others to serve, while others serve his. It is in nowise possible for the individual to separate his good from the common good; he is prosperous and happy only as all the rest are so; and therefore it is not human nature with us for anyone to lie in wait to betray another or seize an advantage. (167)

This is not, of course, a direct answer to Nietzsche's contempt for utilitarianism — for which there is no answer — but while it was possible for an Emerson, or perhaps for a Thoreau, to withdraw from society, it was not possible for a Howells, mainly because he was more concerned with the individual in society than with the individual in isolation.

III

We have seen that Nietzsche uses satirical contempt in order to criticize the present state of man and morality. The direction of Nietzsche's criticism, as presented in the figure of the Ultimate Man, whom the herd prefers to the Superman, is that present morality is undesirable because more than anything else it undermines the possibility of higher moralities. In *Beyond Good and Evil* Nietzsche says, "*Morality is in Europe today herd-animal morality* — that is to say, as we understand the thing, only one kind of human morality beside which, before which, after which many other, above all *higher*, moralities are possible or ought to be possible" (*BGE*, 202). From Nietzsche's perspective, contemporary morality is not an objective to strive for or to defend but a limitation to overcome. The idea of herd morality is closely linked to Nietzsche's attitude toward democracy (herd society). In *On the Genealogy of Morals*, for example, he opposes "the mendacious slogan . . . 'supreme rights of the majority,'" which he associates with the French Revolution, to "the terrible and rapturous counterslogan 'supreme rights of the few,'" which he associates with Napoleon (*GM*, I, 16). In Nietzsche's genealogical analysis of morality, Napoleon is a modern representative of the "ideal of antiquity" in both its moral and political dimensions (*GM*, I, 16).

Howells's dissatisfaction with American morality takes a different direction, for he criticizes the inability of American society to attain well-marked moral goals; that is, where Nietzsche criticizes European society for abandoning the "ideal of antiquity" for democracy, Howells, in contrast, criticizes American society for not attaining the ideal of democracy. The problem, as Howells sees it, does not lie in the opposition between the individual and society, but between justice and law. Society recognizes justice in the form of altruism, which is to protect the weak against the exploitation of the strong. An American lawyer, who discusses this idea with the Altrurian, begins with the distinction between justice and law, and then goes on to say that "the prosperity of the weakest is the sacred charge and highest happiness of all the stronger. But the law has not recognized any such principle" (47). In other words, Howells diagnoses a gap between justice and law, that is, between what society says and what it does, and in this gap altruism fails because the strong are allowed to exploit the weak. This is the same gap that Howells had diagnosed earlier in his panoramic novel *A Hazard of New Fortunes*, where one of the characters says of American society that "Some one always has you by the throat, unless you have some one else in your *grip*."[18]

Like his rejection of utilitarianism, Nietzsche's rejection of altruism — which he refers to as "the most mendacious form of egoism" (*WP*, 62) — derives from his characterization of the opposition between the individual and society as a conflict between the strong and the weak. He argues that altruism raises the weak over the strong, which means the weak acquire "the right to help and to an equality of lot: these are prizes for the degenerate and underprivileged" (*WP*, 52). Nietzsche claims that altruism brings about a reversal in the relation between the strong and the weak, a reversal in which the strong are required to deny their own strength (*GM*, I, 13).

It is easy to overlook how radical Nietzsche's critique of altruism is, until we notice that he has a dramatically polarized conception of the strong and the weak. Not even when he uses extreme contrasts, such as the Superman and herd, does the radicalness of his conception become fully apparent. Only when we turn to a closer examination of Nietzsche's rhetoric do we begin to grasp that for him the strong and the weak represent two entirely different species. Nietzsche describes Napoleon, for example, as a "synthesis of the *inhuman* and *superhuman*" (*GM*, I, 16), leaving the merely human to refer to the weak, society, or the herd. This division of the strong and the weak into two separate species is even clearer when he characterizes the one as "lambs" and the other as "birds of prey":

> That lambs dislike great birds of prey does not seem strange: only it gives no ground for reproaching these birds of prey for bearing off little lambs. And if the lambs say among themselves: "these birds of prey are evil; and whoever is least like a bird of prey, but rather its opposite, a lamb — would he not be good?" there is not reason to find fault with this institution of an ideal . . . . (*GM*, I, 13)

On the surface, Nietzsche is simply arguing that there is a natural difference between species, but below the surface, he is characterizing not just weak and strong species of animals but also weak and strong humans. This association between animals and humans becomes unavoidable in his mocking criticism of altruism as "the belief that *the strong man is free* to be weak and the bird of prey to be a lamb" (*GM*, I, 13). Nietzsche's division of mankind into two different species is based, of course, on moral rather than biological grounds; however, his use of the concept *species* is more than, or at least not only, metaphorical. In *The Will to Power* he contrasts the "higher species" of man with its "lower species": The lower species, "herd" or "society," are those that vulgarize existence, while the higher species are those "whose inexhaustible fertility and power keep up the faith of man" (*WP*, 27).

Nietzsche's conception of the strong and the weak shifts the moral opposition between him and Howells to another level, where it is not a question of how we view the relation between the individual and society (or the Superman and the herd) but of how we view the human species as such. Howells, of course, views the problem of morality in America in terms of class rather than in terms of species; however, the very notion of projecting distinctions onto mankind is distasteful to him. In an essay on Matthew Arnold, Howells, rather than disputing Arnold's criticism that American life lacks distinction, embraces the idea of this lack as a "great advance on the lines of our fundamental principles" (141). Howells is careful not to trivialize the type of distinction that Arnold means, and so he goes on to characterize it in as positive terms as possible, terms that suggest a Nietzschean ideal:

> We do not mean the cheap and easy splendor of the vulgar aristocrat or plutocrat, but that far subtle effect in lives dedicated to aims above the common apprehension, and apart from the interests and objects of the mass of men; we mean the pride of great achievement in any sort, which in less fortunate conditions than ours betrays itself in the humiliation of meaner men. (144–45)

In Nietzsche such a distinction as "pride of great achievement" leads to the division of mankind into two species, but in Howells the very notion of such a distinction is rejected out of hand: "Our whole civilization, if we have a civilization of our own, is founded upon the conviction that any such distinction is unjust and deleterious" (141). The key word here is "conviction." Howells avoids claiming that it is truth or fact that makes such distinctions unjust; instead, he offers a moral interpretation. So although Nietzsche and Howells stand in opposition in terms of how they interpret morality, they both agree that it is a matter of interpretation: "There are no moral phenomena at all, but only a moral interpretation of phenomena" (*BGE*, 108).

IV

In utopian thought, the major problem is frequently not the depiction of a better future, though this tends to offer particular difficulties, but rather the depiction of the transition from the present to the future. In Nietzsche's *Thus Spoke Zarathustra* this transition is presented as a change in morality or "table of values." In the section called "Of the Thousand and One Goals" Zarathustra says that "A table of values hangs over every people. Behold, it is the table of its overcomings; behold, it is the voice of its will to power" (*Z*, I). Each people created its own values to give meaning to existence, and thus a change in creators means the birth of new values and the corresponding death of old ones. Nietzsche notes a change in this process of value formation when he says, "Peoples were the creators at first; only later were individuals creators" (*Z*, I, "Of the Thousand and One Goals"). The destruction of old values and the creation of new ones is the process that brings about the better future that Zarathustra envisions in the form of the Superman. And according to Zarathustra, the transition towards a better future has already begun because now individuals rather than peoples have become the creators of new values.

In terms of the transition to a better future, Howells's position follows a familiar pattern: it is not the individual that brings about the better future but those who Nietzsche calls the "degenerate and underprivileged" class. In Altruria this underprivileged class first voted the "plutocratic oligarchy" out of power, and then in a long process called the Evolution, developed Altruria into a utopian society. But in the course of Howells's novel, the transition to a better future is more complex than the history of Altruria because the Altrurian past represents the American present, so that when the Altrurian relates the history of his country, he describes at the same time the present conditions of America:

> But as before, there was alternately a glut and dearth of things, and it often happened that when starving men went ragged through the streets, the storehouses were piled full of rotting harvests that the farmers toiled from dawn till dusk to grow, and the warehouses fed the moth with the stuffs that the operative had woven his life into at his loom. Then followed, with a blind and mad succession, a time of famine, when money could not buy the superabundance that vanished, none knew how or why. (149)

The audience grows restless with this description of Altruria's past because, as an old farmer in the audience shouts: "When are you goin' to get to Altrury? We know all about Ameriky" (150). Yet by linking Altruria's past with America's present, Howells links Altruria's utopian present with America's future, and so the problem of the transition to a better future shifts from Altruria to America.

Nietzsche's critical analysis of the transition of society from one set of morals to another in *On the Genealogy of Morals* is crucial for an understanding of the opposition between Nietzsche and Howells. Nietzsche tells a story of how the present system of morals came about: the priests' caste, because of its *ressentiment* of the power and prestige of the nobles or aristocrats, revaluates morality from good and bad, which are based on the concepts of noble and common, to good and evil, which are based on the concepts of, for instance, pure and impure. This revaluation of values includes a reversal, for what was common, and thus bad, becomes good, and what was noble, and thus good, becomes evil (*GM*, 6–11). The basic narrative elements in this story are the priests and the nobles, who form the characters; resentment, which forms the motivation; and the reversal, which forms the change in events. As Nietzsche repeats this story, he brings it up to date with the French Revolution and Napoleon, and the most consistent feature in his repetitions is the motivation, that is, the resentment that the slaves feel towards the masters.

The way to oppose a story is to retell it, which is what Howells implicitly does in *A Traveller from Altruria*. Howells depicts contemporary America by using the same narrative elements that Nietzsche uses in his genealogical analysis, but now these elements are rearranged in terms of a transition from the present to the future. The American narrator sees Altruria as a reversal of America; for example, he says that the Altrurian's description of utopia "represented a wholly different state of things, the inversion of our own" (70). The fact that Altruria is accepted as a better society, placing America at a disadvantage, leads to resentment in the narrator. During his lecture on Altruria, the Altrurian remarks that it was impossible to be a gentleman under the competitive conditions of the past, "since a gentleman must think first of others, and these conditions *compelled* every man to think first of himself" (168). When it becomes clear that these competitive conditions apply to present-day America, the narrator feels "resentment" (168). The narrator's resentment becomes an element in the transition of American society to a better future, except that now it is motivated not by the desire for power and privilege, as in Nietzsche's analysis, but by a fear of its loss.

The main difference in Howells's version of the story is that there are three characters instead of only two and that the reversal comes not from the figures who feel resentment but from those who need to overcome it. The narrator in Howells's novel, and the cultivated class that he represents, feels resentment towards the Altrurian.

However, it is not the Altrurian who threatens the power and privilege of the narrator's class; instead, that threat comes from the third type of figure in Howells's version of the story, the working class, which must overcome the prestige of the cultivated class in order to strip it of its political and economic power. The point that Howells's story makes is that the better future is attained by the working class, the very class that in Nietzsche's moral world is simply part of the herd. And in the transition to the Howellsian Utopia, the individual is not pulled down to the level of the herd; instead, the man of the herd is pulled up to the level of the exceptional individual. Or in Howells's terms, the "normal man" becomes the "man of genius," and since the normal man becomes the man of genius, the man of genius becomes the normal man: "The artist, the man of genius, who worked from the love of his work became the normal man" (158). In Nietzsche's version of the story, the exceptional individual or man of genius does not, and probably cannot, rise out of the herd; that is why there are only two types of figures in his story, the strong and the weak. But in Howells's version of the story, three types of figures are required: the working class and the Altrurian — Nietzsche's herd and Superman — and also a cultivated class, which on the one hand feels resentment toward the Altrurian and on the other hand oppresses the working class. These two versions of the story, like two interpretations, form variants rather than contradictions. One story does not cancel the other out; it simply retells it.

If we now return to Howells's review of Cabot's biography of Emerson, it is possible to see how Howells's view of morality and mankind diverges from both Emerson's and Nietzsche's. In his review, Howells noted that Emerson "confesses to his diary that while he gets on well enough with Man, he finds it hard to meet men halfway or upon common ground" (130). The distinction between Man and men points to the source of the divergence between the prophetic and the utopian vision, and thus by extension, between Nietzsche and Howells. Zarathustra says that "My will clings to mankind, I bind myself to mankind with fetters, because I am drawn up to the Superman. That my hand may not quite lose its belief in firmness: that is why I live blindly among men, as if I did not recognize them" (Z, II, "Of Manly Prudence"). Zarathustra's distinction between mankind and men, and his desire not to recognize men but rather to cast his lot with mankind, is a verbal variation of the Emersonian distinction between Man and men. It is this very distinction that Howells finds so offensive, and as a result he follows his paraphrase of Emerson's diary entry with a comment that undermines it. After noting Emerson's belief in the crucial distinction between Man and men, Howells observes: "Now we are beginning to know that there is no such thing as Man, that there are only men" (130).

Notes

[1] Max Nordau, *Degeneration*, translated from the Second Edition of the German Work (1895; Lincoln: U of Nebraska P, 1993). For a discussion of Nietzsche and Nordau, see Hays Steilberg's "First Steps in the New World" in this volume.

[2] W. D. Howells, *W. D. Howells as Critic*, ed. Edwin H. Cady (London: Routledge, 1973), pp. 218–19. Unless otherwise noted, subsequent references to Howells's critical writings are from this edition and appear in the text.

[3] For example, Howells believed that man's "hopes rested in secular democracy" (Edwin H. Cady, *The Realist at War*, Syracuse: Syracuse UP, 1958, p. 146), but Nietzsche believed that society formed a barrier that "prevents man from realizing himself" (Walter Kaufmann, *Nietzsche*, Princeton: Princeton UP, 1974, p. 163).

[4] W. D. Howells, *Criticism and Fiction and Other Essays*, eds. Clara Marburg Kirk and Rudolf Kirk (New York: New York UP, 1959), p. 42.

[5] *The Gay Science*, trans. Walter Kaufmann (New York: Vintage, 1974), 21. Subsequent references to this translation appear in the text as *GS*. In citations to Nietzsche's works, Arabic numbers refer to sections, not to pages.

[6] See Kaufmann's description of Nietzsche as a prophet (*Nietzsche*, pp. 98–99).

[7] Robert C. Elliot, Introduction, *Looking Backward*, by Edward Bellamy (Boston: Houghton Mifflin, 1966), p. v.

[8] Throughout his study of the relation between Nietzsche and Emerson, Stack argues that "Nietzsche not only adopted the Olympian aristocratic tone of Emerson, but consciously molded and embellished his imaginative construct of the Übermensch out of materials he found dispersed in Emerson's fertile and seminal reflections on those he called 'exceptions'" (George J. Stack, *Nietzsche and Emerson*, Athens: Ohio UP, 1992, p. 8).

[9] W. D. Howells, *The Minister's Charge* (1887; Bloomington: Indiana UP, 1978), p. 341.

[10] *Thus Spoke Zarathustra*, trans. R. J. Hollingdale (London: Penguin, 1969), I, 2. Subsequent references to this translation appear in the text as *Z*.

[11] See, for example, Arthur C. Danto, *Nietzsche as Philosopher* (New York: Columbia UP, 1965), pp. 198–200.

[12] W. D. Howells, *A Traveller from Altruria* (1894; Bloomington: Indiana UP, 1968), p. 162. Subsequent references to this edition appear in the text.

[13] John Stuart Mill, *Utilitarianism, Liberty, and Representative Government* (London: Dent, 1944), p. 6.

[14] Pizer claims that the morality in *The Rise of Silas Lapham* (1885), especially as it is codified in Howells's expression "economy of pain," also derives from J. S. Mill's utilitarianism (Donald Pizer, "The Ethical Unity of *The Rise of Silas Lapham*," *American Literature* 32 (1960–61), 322–27.

[15] *Beyond Good and Evil*, trans. Walter Kaufmann (New York: Vintage, 1989), 201. Subsequent references to this translation appear in the text as *BGE*.

[16] *On the Genealogy of Morals*, trans. Walter Kaufmann (New York: Vintage, 1989), 3. Subsequent references to this translation appear in the text as *GM*.

[17] *The Will to Power*, trans. Walter Kaufmann and R. J. Hollingdale (New York: Vintage, 1968), 291. Subsequent references to this translation appear in the text as *WP*.

[18] W. D. Howells, *A Hazard of New Fortunes* (1890; Bloomington: Indiana UP, 1976), p. 436. Cf. Nietzsche's view of exploitation: "life itself is essentially appropriation, injury, overpowering of what is alien and weaker; suppression, hardness, imposition of one's own forms, incorporation and at least, at its mildest, exploitation — but why should one always use those words in which a slanderous intent has been imprinted for ages?" (*BGE*, 259).

Daniel T. O'Hara

Contagious Appearances: Nietzsche, Henry James, and the Critique of Fiction

A SENTENCE FROM Nietzsche's *Beyond Good and Evil* (1886) guides my thinking: "the 'work,' whether of the artist or the philosopher, invents the man who has created it, who is supposed to have created it."[1] As the entire passage makes clear, this ironic work of (self-)invention also arises in the cases of "the great statesman, the conqueror, the discoverer." All of these figures are invented and "disguised" by their "creations, often beyond recognition." Consequently, for "the crowd," coming after the work in question succeeds, the creator is recreated in turn by the crowd according to the venerable myth of genius or the great man as its own piece of "wretched minor fiction" (*BGE*, IX, 269). So powerful is this aesthetic illusion of the successful work, so contagious is it, that it serves as the rule of the "counterfeit" constituting "the world of historical values." It serves, for a central example, as the model of misunderstanding inspiring the social production of a culture's ultimate values as "gods": "And who knows whether what happened in all great cases so far was not always the same: that the crowd adored a god — and that the 'god' was merely a poor sacrificial animal" (*BGE*, IX, 269) expiating the guilt of the tribe with respect to its ancestors.[2]

I take Nietzsche's complex speculation to be the following: Insofar as a 'work' of statesmanship forming a people into a nation, a 'work' of conquering gaining the materials for the formation of a people, a 'work' of discovery opening a new field of reality to explore, a 'work' of art or philosophy producing a new aesthetic or rational order achieves "success" with "the crowd," this success retroactively creates, via a process of contagion, the standard image of its creator, and so disguises the creator's own invented image for his condition, which is one of radical contingency, risk, and suffering. Just as the growing numbers of disciples of a new and spreading religion progressively see in their pathetic scapegoat founder and in his words more and more of the lineaments of divinity, so, too, in these other cases "the crowd" misreads them.

Nietzsche's point is even more radical, however, than this statement may make it sound. For, as I see it, he is saying that the ontological condition for the production of any identity involves a foundational contingency of cultural work. At least two different, perhaps conflicting images of identity arise as productions or inventions: the creator's and the crowd's. Both are "works" disclosing and disguising, but according to different sets of values, one singular, the other common, the wholly conditional nature of any identity. The truth of a work, individual or collective, is in case after case a contest of images, a contagion of masks, a work itself of fiction.[3]

All forms of morality, whether of aristocratic or democratic kinds, would rationalize this radical contingency or contagious fictionality of identity, individual and cultural, according to different metafictional "tables of the law," different hierarchies of value.[4] As we know, in his later work from *Beyond Good and Evil* (1886), through *On the Genealogy of Morals* (1887), to *The Twilight of the Idols* and *The Anti-Christ* (both 1888) Nietzsche attempts to distinguish from "a supramoral" perspective the virtues and vices of aristocratic (or "master") and democratic (or "slave") moralities (*BGE*, IX, 260). Thanks to the Greco-Roman and Christian legacies, as Nietzsche argues in *Ecce Homo* (1889), all modern individuals and cultures are complex mixtures of both kinds of moralities or metafictional measures for regulating the pandemic contagion of fictionality or aesthetic illusion.[5] For Nietzsche, of course, the most interesting and promising cases, like himself, are beings composed by and as a sharply staged contest, a repeatedly improvised drama, of antithetical virtues and vices, the dangerous game or play of the divided soul, what we now call the split self or, more formally, the multiple subject positions of human agency.[6] I'm not concerned here either to follow or to dispute Nietzsche's critique of moralities, which is really a critique of the metafictional measures of human cultures. Instead, I just want to note that, for him, regardless of kind, morality per se seeks to rationalize and disguise the radical contingency and fictionality of any form of identity. Concealing the "work" nature of any identity formation with a unifying image or name makes possible all politics of identity.[7] What I'm calling, in connection with Henry James's theory and practice, the critique of fiction refers to this recognition of the fictional limits of identity, and the pragmatic ethical consequences of such recognition for the modern novelist, about which more later.[8]

As an implicit commentary on Nietzsche's nominalistic analysis of identity formations, Heidegger's remarks from "The Origin of the Work of Art" (1934–36) on the agonistic "play of beings" make for an interesting and important elaboration.[9] For they make the work of producing aesthetic illusion no longer simply a matter of subjective imaginative agency and cultural influences; they make this work of contagious appearances a matter of formal relations in the larger process of concealment and disclosure that defines, for Heidegger, Being's ambiguous coming (in) to the appearance of truth in the case of each being or entity, including especially that of "Dasein" or human being (there).[10] I cite the passage in full because of its provocatively useful difficulty:

> One being places itself in front of another being, the one helps to hide the other, the former obscures the latter, few obstruct many, one denies all. Here concealment is not simple refusal. Rather, a being appears, but it presents itself as other than it is. This concealment is dissembling. If one being did not simulate another, we could not make mistakes or act mistakenly in regard to beings; we could not go astray and transgress, and especially could never overreach ourselves. That a being should be able to deceive as semblance is the condition for our being able to be deceived, not conversely. Concealment can be a refusal or merely a dissembling. We are never fully certain whether it is the one or the other. Concealment conceals and dissembles itself. This means: the open place in the midst of Being, the clearing [of Being], is never a rigid stage with a permanently raised curtain on which the play of beings runs its course. Rather, the clearing happens as this double concealment [of refusal and dissembling] (OWA, 54).

As exemplified best, perhaps, by the Heisenberg principle of indeterminacy in sub-atomic physics, there is a constitutional inaccessibility of entities, what Heidegger sees as a protective dissembling on the ontological level that produces aesthetic semblance, which makes for epistemological errancy and moral transgression, for what feels like an entity's refusal to fully appear and to still conceal itself from our view.

Each entity, that is, appears masked as it is. This openly masked appearance makes each entity ambiguous — both itself and other than itself. It is like the way an itinerant actor improvises a role on a provisional country stage, appearing both as the person the actor is and as the other, the momentary persona, the improvised speech exhibits. Or, perhaps a better analogy may be, because it's one that dispenses with the idea of convention virtually altogether, at least in any sense of stylized and predictable rule, it is like the way Robin Williams appears during a television interview. The improvised personae are indeed contagious appearances that conceal as much as they reveal. I like to think of each being, as Heidegger here presents them, in this light, as such an unpredictable repertoire of improvised figures making their appearances against the background of Being's openly concealing masked revelation of any identity formation's radically contingent fictionality. Custom, convention, culture — as exemplified and elaborated in and as morality — attempt to perform a single coherent politics of identity in systematic efforts to stabilize, regularize, and normalize — to make comprehensively predictable — a nonetheless selective range of permitted roles beings may now assume in accordance with some centralized ideal. In this moralizing context, beings bring Being to questionable light without question. Nevertheless, as Heidegger's remarks show, each entity is a working of fiction in not only Nietzsche's senses of "individual" and "social" production (or revisionary invention), but in an ontological sense, as well. In short, any phenomenon defined by a name is, however disguised by custom, a conflicted fictional construction produced in each moment according to one or another improvised design made available (but not necessary) by the diverse contests of cultural existence. Agency, then, can never in principle be restricted and localized, only as a pragmatic matter of perspective and as a way of speaking that "forget themselves," as it were.

Foucault, in the end, has the clearest sense of what this radically contingent fictionality conditions for the modern writer. In a September 1983 interview, nine months before his death, he comments on "the obscure desire of a person who writes" in a way that concretizes the Nietzschean-Heideggerian problematic of fiction.[11]

One writes to become someone other than who one is . . . . There is an attempt at modifying one's way of being through the act of writing . . . . Therefore, I believe that it is better to try to understand that someone who is a writer is not simply doing his work in his books, in what he publishes, but that his major work is, in the end, himself in the process of writing his books. The private life of an individual, his sexual preferences, and his work are interrelated not because his work translates his sexual life, but because the work includes the whole life as well as the text. The work is more than the work: the subject who is writing is part of the work (*IWMF*, 182, 184).

The work the writer writes is only the publicly visible and conventionally accepted work, when the entire existence of the writer is itself a work, a project, which incorporates the "life" and the "work" in the ordinary senses of those terms. As Nietzsche puts it, the work in the extended sense creates the person, and as Heidegger elaborates this point, any being is like that of the writer or the creator in that it openly works to produce a protective semblance of itself as it discloses this truth of Being. Foucault's critical understanding of his own "project" (in a Sartrean sense) grounds this Nietzschean-Heideggerian critical ontology of fiction in modern cultural contests of subjectivity and sexuality, a grounding that provides me with a general horizon for my subsequent remarks on Henry James.

But first the central question of this essay: given Nietzsche's Dionysian and Heidegger's hermeneutic sublimes, it could be argued that "contagious appearances" arise from the "works" of "fiction" of all beings as such and that finding some way to oversee and regulate, to supervise and discipline, this pandemic fictionality would indeed be the order of the day — an order of things Foucault spent his life detailing and exposing as fictional in his avowedly "critical fictions."[12] In the light of the spread of "contagious appearances" as the ontological, epistemological, political, and moral conditions of radical contingency, a "state" culture via morality historically tries to control and conventionalize, how does a supposed "master" of reflexive fiction conceive of his "work"?[13]

My text for answering this question is the Preface to *The Golden Bowl*. James originally published his last completed novel in 1904 and then minimally revised it, as one would expect, for inclusion five years later in The New York Edition of the *Collected Works* (1907–1909).[14] I choose this final Preface because James uses it as the occa-

sion to speak generally about aesthetic representation in some of its
different modes. Specifically, he speaks first about his narrative
"system" (*AN*, 331) of restricted point of view, next about the critical distinction between traditional fictional and modern photographic art, then about the surprising agon of self-revision — its
dramatic acts, scenes, and different agents of "re-representation"
(*AN*, 335) and "re-appropriation" (*AN*, 336) — and finally, he
speaks, in a visionary vein, about the responsible pleasures of being a
writer. I find these four aspects of aesthetic representation interesting
in their combination.

James concludes the Preface with what I would call an American
version of "the writer's faith," a post-romantic credo in the Wordsworthian mold. Our acts of writing, James affirms, are not merely
private and purely contingent, like our ordinary everyday acts, whose
reality and consequences may become unremembered or may remain
nameless. Instead, like our unique acts of kindness and love, but
more certainly and securely so because they are inscribed accounts,
our acts of writing are necessary links in what James envisions as "the
whole chain of relation and responsibility" constituting society. And
because each act of writing is also necessarily a matter of selection, it
is an act of judgment, as well. Writing, in James's ethical imagination, is thereby "conduct with a vengeance, since it is conduct minutely and publicly attested" (*AN*, 348). Both Emerson and
Habermas could live with that. Perversely enough, perhaps, James
finds this morally constraining condition also, as a Nietzsche or Foucault might suggest, vigorously and dialectically empowering. Holding oneself "accountable" to oneself as a model for becoming
responsible to others, in the repeated act of writing, makes up, for
James, precisely his writing's "exquisite law" and paradoxically duti-
ful "joy," or what he terms his writing's "one sovereign truth" (*AN*,
348). This holding oneself "accountable" to oneself is James's
"work."

As we'll see shortly, and could see even better if I had more space
to show it in detail, this "one sovereign truth" of his writing both
informs and arises from the writer's radical dispersion among what
we now so cumbersomely call multiple subject positions, including
some of a vaguely religious, liberally mythical, and even socially mystical inflection. It is as if the writer, in the writing, makes up in
miniature a society of different discursive subjects, or as James might

better phrase it, a society of imaginative souls. The writer's "one sovereign truth," in other words, is to become, in the writing, a community of diverse constituent "parts," in several strong senses of the word, whether we choose to "Bakhtinianize" this Jamesian vision or not. However well we may believe James puts this vision into practice, in any particular case, it is nonetheless a novel idea, I believe, in principle, as James works it out.

Ironically enough, at the very time James's Preface to *The Golden Bowl* solicits full attention to all these facets of aesthetic representation, he already knows that his and Scribners's gamble on the new and expensive twenty-four volume edition of his collected works is failing to recapture the general public's interest which his increasingly difficult style had lost, and it is even selling poorly among literary intellectuals, particularly in America, and more poignantly, particularly in New York.[15] In this ironic context, I find its combination and treatment of topics, all concerning aesthetic representation, irresistible. For the strain running through and connecting what James has to say on point of view, on fiction versus photography, on revisionism, and on a writer's strangely joyful accountability to the public, composes a vision of judgment just too interesting to ignore. And this topic, the practice of aesthetic judgment, then and now, in relation to perspectivism, to traditional literary versus modern technologies of representation, to the radically split subject of revisionary agency, and to art's sublime power to teach delight in its beauty — aesthetic judgment in these contexts does indeed sound the complex theme of my current work in progress, which is intended in large part, as a critique of fiction.[16] But clearly, given the constraints of this essay, I won't be able to compare James on judgment with Kant or Lyotard. In fact, I won't be able to discuss all four sections of the Preface in the kind of detail they deserve. I won't even be able to speculate on why this four-part structure starts to multiply abysmally in a variety of ways. I must focus my remarks instead on the Preface's first and fourth sections, with a few glances at other passages, since these sections, given the Nietzschean-Heideggerian framework, are immediately germane to my purposes.

Let me add, still largely as preface to this Preface, that contrary to expectations, there is nothing in James's critical discrimination of fictional and photographic arts, or in his belief in a writer's simultaneous responsibility to the work and the public, which betrays even a hint of genteel squeamishness or reactionary snobby hostility toward the modern.[17] In fact, from what he does say about how Alvin Langdon Coburn's photographs work so well, as frontispieces for the New York Edition volumes, to illustrate the general idea of the sort of thing his original fictional images particularize, as if Plato and Aristotle joined hands over this harmonious accomplishment, I suspect that James would welcome two recent developments, regarding him and his work, in the popular culture industry. I refer, first of all, to Merchant and Ivory's latest deal, with Touchstone Pictures, to film *The Portrait of A Lady.* I can see it now: Jeremy Irons will play Gilbert Osmond, Emma Thompson will play Madame Merle, Christopher Reeve will play Caspar Goodwood, Sir Anthony Hopkins and Daniel Day Lewis will play, respectively, father and son Touchetts, and, in a casting coup, now that she has Edith Wharton under her belt, Michelle Pfeiffer, the Cat Woman, will play the lead, Isabel Archer, the all-American imaginative girl with the whiplash tongue, who is to become a "lady" in the end. The second development I think James would also find amusing. Carol De Chellis Hill's recent novel, a feminist romantic thriller, *Henry James' Midnight Song*, casts him and Sigmund Freud, among others, as both protagonists and potential psychopathic serial killers of the women of Vienna. The novel has been critically well-received, apparently being worthy of favorable comparison with the postmodern likes of *Ragtime*, *Flaubert's Parrot*, and *Possession.* There is so much play with point of view here that the novel is, perhaps, really more akin to Kierkegaard's pseudononymous authorship, with its panoply of editors, narrators, and ironic reflexiveness so prophetic of metafictional experiments.[18] In any event, I also suspect, from what James has to say in the Preface to *The Golden Bowl* about authorial or imaginative agency — it being necessarily split into functions he figures as "the historian" (*AN*, 341), "the docile reader" (*AN*, 336), and "the revisionist" (*AN*, 342), each of which figures comes in two avatars at least — James would also recognize himself in many poststructuralist theories of the subject, including the latest Lacanian one from Slavoj Zizek's *Tarrying With the Negative: Kant, Hegel, and the Critique of Ideology.*[19] In the end, however, I think, as does Martha Nussbaum in *Love's Knowledge: Essays on Philosophy and Literature*, that James would still want to hold out for the Aristotelian particularity of the representative ethical subject against either any new historicist reduction of the subject to an epiphenomenal relay of political power machinery or any revisionary psychoanalytic reduction of the subject to the specular grandiosity of pure narcissism.[20] However all that may be, now, at last, we can turn to some more details of the Preface to *The Golden Bowl.*

In the Preface's first part, James reminds us that his "system" of fictional narration is that of restricted point of view (*AN,* 331); this is a third-person account of things generally limited to one center of consciousness, or, in some cases, to one of several at a time. He then explains how things work in *The Golden Bowl.* Each of its two volumes, titled, respectively, "The Prince" and "The Princess," are intended to exhibit everything from, first, poor Prince Amerigo's point of view, to that of his rich American wife, now Princess Maggie (née Verver). But James notes the apparent breaks in his intended design, the large role assigned to the Assinghams, particularly Fanny Assingham, James's ficelle. Her husband, the ex-Colonel, is less immediately important. I'll come back to all this.

For the moment, I'm more interested in how James opens his discussion of point of view by generally distinguishing between "the muffled majesty" of a sovereign but "irresponsible authorship" (*AN,* 328), which assumes that omniscience should "reign" in the novel with respect to character, and his own innovative method of characterization: "I get down into the arena and do my best to live and breathe and rub shoulders and converse with the persons engaged in the struggle that provides for the others in the circling tiers the entertainment of the great game [of life]." And yet, as James admits, he practices, as best he can, "invisibility." "There is," as he says, "no other participant, of course, than each of the real, the deeply involved and immersed and more or less bleeding participants" (*AN,* 328). This means, I take it, that the James narrator effaces himself and plays the role of the imaginative and compassionate, ideally discrete reporter, the mimic register, of his central characters' own accounts of and perspectives on their conflicts in the great game of the arena. James is not, however, a "real" participant, because he is no broadly self-dramatizing and fully imagined narrator. When such a figure does appear, especially in the tales, we know immediately that it is not our man James, but "just" another character. In an openly fictional world, the fully imagined constitutes what is "real." Yet James is also never a purely distanced spectator, despite his fascination with the spectatorial type and the acquisitive or lustful eye of the collector. He is no Olympian connoisseur. Neither is he, clearly, a gladiator or martyr, decadent Epicure or an omnipotent Emperor. Rather, as he says later, James is "the historian" of what I would call, after Nietzsche's insights into culture, James's genteel combatants' savage civilities (*AN*, 341). Although it is a traditional figure for the novelist, "the historian," as James conceives of and critically practices this spectral role, is more like what we would now call "a ghost writer" for some celebrity's reflections on life, only James is the *particular* ghost writer for his own imagined creations' embodied perspectives, ever-ready to suggest by just the right word in one of their own mouths an appropriate (self-) condemnation.

A climactic scene in *The Golden Bowl* exemplifies this Jamesian practice of judgment quite nicely. When Princess Maggie and Charlotte Stant Verver, her best friend and new step-mother, meet in the garden directly outside the long windows of the room where the rest of the gathering are playing cards, we anticipate a conventionally melodramatic "scene" of confrontation over the question of Charlotte's apparent affair with Maggie's husband, Prince Amerigo.[21] Instead, we get a freely improvised "turn" on such a scene. When questioned directly on the matter, Maggie responds deftly, in a manner that conceals as much as it may reveal: "'I accuse you — I accuse you of nothing'," Maggie hesitatingly disclaims with shifting tonal balances of stress and inflection (*GB*, 498). "'Ah, that's lucky!'" Charlotte sighs in her (self-) betraying turn. The narrator's comment at this point is a telling mimicry of Maggie's characteristic mode of discourse: "It was only a question of not by a hair's breadth deflecting into the truth" (*GB*, 498). Figured previously as "a willing scapegoat" (*GB*, 487) ready to re-set shattered relations formally aright, standing in her garden of agony now in full view of the assembling "crowd" of her husband, her father, and her friends, the Assinghams, Maggie seals Charlotte's fatal misunderstanding and her own policy of winning back her husband by subtle arts of saving appearances, rather than by crude confrontations, with a kiss that Maggie herself permits Charlotte to give her. This most ironic Judas "kiss-off" scene — its sexual revisionism is transgressive — revaluates the value of its traditional biblical paradigm by espousing how a lie, a fiction, must necessarily underlie even the willing scapegoat's self-understanding and public identity. For Maggie's exemplarily protective dissemblance, which throws Charlotte into errant ignorance, is a strategic, contingently improvised, and (self-) betraying work, even as it formally indicts social relations at large ("I accuse *you* of nothing," my emphasis) for her particular condition, and exhibits Maggie's wise "passivity" as an exemplary release of imaginative power due to this surprising finale's "high publicity" (*GB*, 499), which helps to convince all that things are going to be in order once again — Maggie's greatest work of fiction? A contagious visionary quality of self-conscious bewilderment haunts this entire scene, a scene which each participant-observer reads as (s)he will(s), even as every entity in the scene works to disclose the world's dissemblance.

We can see more precisely what all this means when James now turns to explain carefully the apparent breaks in his systemically restricted point of view in *The Golden Bowl* (*AN*, 331). He notes, rightly, that, as I've already mentioned, the Assinghams, especially Fanny, assume throughout the novel the position of important albeit less than major centers of consciousness, even though James also still maintains that, as intended, the Prince and Princess do indeed preside as the informing consciousnesses of their respectively titled volumes. James accounts for this Assingham contingency — he hadn't originally planned on such a full role for his ficelle, Fanny, for example — by saying that what she or her husband or, for that matter, any of the other characters perceive and respond to is primarily exhibited in light of and colored by the consciousness of the Prince or Princess. How everyone else — other characters, readers, the author himself — perceive when reading themselves in(to) the novel depends on how this royal pair's exhibitions inspire all of these others to see and feel. It is as if the Prince and the Princess participate in the author's imaginative power, share narrative sovereignty with him, once he creates them and releases them to the singular case of their textual fates. They clearly stimulate in the other characters what an author stimulates in a reader: viz., a "contagious hallucination," a visionary phantasmagoria, an aesthetic "semblance" (*AN*, 332). As James spells it out, a fortuitous creative "contagion" shapes the imaginative responses of author, narrator, central character, other characters, and readers, more or less alike. Both Nietzsche's Dionysian and Heidegger's ontological sublimes bear a strong family resemblance to James's vision here.

James's is, however, a curiously democratic aesthetic, an American or Emersonian conception of the sublime, which is yet not a case of mass hysteria à la Whitman, since author and reader, and the more intelligent of James's reflective characters recognize and judge the fictional quality of what they perceive. This is one reason why his characters comment so often on how beautiful this or that appears to be. Ideally, James concludes, readers complete their productive experience of reading only when they put into some medium of their own, in their own words, their sense of what they have read. This contagious emanation of creativity for which the image of the golden chain is most apt, explains why James believes that his narrative "system" of restricted point of view remains significantly intact in *The Golden Bowl*. The Assinghams can't help but become in turn creative as they respond to the genius of the Prince and the Princess, any more than we can't help but become in our turn creative vis-à-vis them, or James can't help himself but become in his turn creative vis-à-vis his own imaginative productions as he originally envisions and performs them or even now as he re-reads them. This curious poetics of sovereignty — a democratically aesthetic sovereignty — also explains, I believe, why James thinks he can become an invisibly moving and dispersed, spectral presence in the arena of life's great game, and so do something different in the novel genre from anything Thackeray and George Eliot have already done. That is, James, in the writing, is the stage for the provisionally improvised performances by characters, narrator, author, and reader of a democratically saving immanence, whether Neo-Platonic or Christian or Hegelian or Dionysian in origin. For, if the creative power of imaginative innovation contagiously disseminates itself among characters and readers, so that they, too, become authorial, then, by the logic of the contagion figure which, whether madness or disease or eros is thought of, swings potentially in all ways at once, James also must become creaturely, just as Foucault's earlier remarks suggest.

Two figures — "the poet" and "the god" — dominate the Preface's fourth and final, most religious-sounding, myth-laden, and also ethically responsible part. These figures follow a whole series of others — "the historian," "the docile reader," "the revisionist," "Scott," "Balzac" and so on, which represent one after another aspects of imaginative agency. For James, as we've seen, "the poet" is like the rhapsode in Plato's *Ion*. "The poet" is the archetypal title for the creative responsiveness which works, via whatever genre, to inspire by sublime contagion in readers their own species of imaginative production (*AN*, 332 and 341). So great can be "the poet's" work of responsive performance to the impersonal creative power flowing through him or her that it can even lure or seduce the ultimate figure, "the god," to descend so as to inhabit the created form, whatever it may be: lyric poem, drama, novel. The particular age's version of "the poet" thus plays, whatever the poet's gender or sexual orientation, the muse to "the god" — whether in the mode of visionary madman or madwoman, popular playwright, or prose master. "The poet" in this generic perspective projects and produces the age's own unique shrine to house "the god." "The god" is the figure, then, for the mysterious, impersonal, indeed anonymous and so pre-Oedipal and "pre-gendered" but not asexual, purely contingent power of imaginative agency. No one individual can possess this power, but any one self or part of self may participate in it to one degree or other, depending, as Longinus might say, on the quality of the response. James sees this quality arise from the often bewildering fiction of (self-)judgment, which is inspired by this power's contagious emanations of aesthetic semblance. Lambert Strether's nobly pyrrhic career of judgment in *The Ambassadors* is just one ironic case in point. Even material objects, via their shining appearances, can become creative entities, as with the golden bowl that entitles its novel (*AN*, 342). Heidegger would not be surprised.

I could speculate on the sources for James's vision of judgment in this Preface. Romantic, occult, transcendental resonances resound. More precisely, I hear echoes of Wordsworthian pantheism, the Emersonian and Swedenborgian notions of James's father, James's own sublime reflections on Shakespeare's, Balzac's, and Milton's practices of beauty. For one example, the pervasive light imagery in the Preface reflects this last inflection, especially in the familiar Miltonic epithet, "the fields of light" (*AN*, 341). Appropriately enough, James uses this epithet to conclude his identification of the best poetry with the best prose, precisely in their vital rhythmical rightness for articulation by a living voice. There is also, of course, the Biblical and Blakean allusions of the novel's title.[22] But, for this occasion, I just want to note how all these possible resonances contribute to the broadly religious, liberally mythical, and democratically mystical rhetoric of imaginative ethical agency in the final Preface. James, in reviewing the whole of the New York Edition of the *Collected Works*, finds that it is good.

It is, as I have called it, the writer's faith that, I believe, accounts for James's radical differences from other writers of his time and ours, and so makes him possible, indeed necessary, for us today. I still find it extraordinary and exhilarating, for one major example, that James can speak of all these personae, masks, figures, subject-positions — all these disseminated selves or contagious emanations — both pleasurably and as forming "the whole chain of relation and responsibility" of society, what he characterizes, after Emerson and Arnold, as if it were society's defining and indeed constitutive trait, "conduct with a vengeance," that is, "conduct minutely and publicly attested" in and through writing (*AN*, 348). Neither Heidegger, nor Foucault, exhibit such an attitude, although Nietzsche, of course, often does, but he lacks James's democratic sense of creativity. James, in other words, is not only radically different from others of his time, neither reductive ideologue, nor genteel aesthete; he is, I dare suggest, still very different, perhaps more different than we can know, even as we recognize our concerns and our precursors' concerns in him, precisely from us. If so, as we can perhaps yet say without offense, *vive la différence!*[23]

Notes

[1] *Beyond Good and Evil*, trans. Walter Kaufmann (New York: Vintage, 1966), IX, 269. All citations from this work will be given in parentheses in the text, referring to parts and sections of *BGE*.

[2] For an excellent overview of Nietzsche's philosophy, see the entry on Nietzsche by Alexander Nehamas in Michael Groden and Martin Kreiswirth (eds.), *The Johns Hopkins Guide to Literary Theory and Criticism* (Baltimore: Johns Hopkins UP, 1994), pp. 545–48.

[3] I here follow Richard Rorty's general line of argument in *Contingency, Irony, and Solidarity* (Cambridge: Cambridge UP, 1989).

[4] For more on this topic, see my "The Prophet of Our Laughter: Or Nietzsche As — Educator?," in Daniel T. O'Hara (ed.), *Why Nietzsche Now?* (Bloomington: Indiana UP, 1985), pp. 1–19.

[5] I'm using "metafictional" to refer to those invented and problematic limits, critical and speculative in nature, used to attempt to order and contain the forms of representation. On this often quixotic attempt, see Susan Stewart, *Crimes of Writing* (New York: Oxford UP, 1991). See also Nietzsche, *The Birth of Trag-*

edy, trans. Walter Kaufmann (New York: Vintage, 1967), pp. 61–67; cf. also my discussion of Foucault's "What is An Author?," in *Radical Parody* (cited below).

6 For the best argument for this being, ironically enough, the general condition of the human psyche, see Richard Rorty, "Freud and Moral Reflection," in *Essays on Heidegger and Others, Philosophical Papers*, Vol. 2 (Cambridge: Cambridge UP, 1991), pp. 143–63.

7 For a candid statement of this position, see Stanley Fish, *There's No Such Thing As Free Speech . . . And It's A Good Thing, Too* (New York: Oxford UP, 1993), especially the Appendix "Fish Tales: A Conversation With 'The Contemporary Sophist'," pp. 281–307.

8 For more on this topic, see my "Becoming Other: The Conscience of the Reader in Late James," in Jonathan Arac and Donald E. Pease (eds.), *Re-Figuring U.S. Nationalisms* (Minneapolis: U. of Minnesota P., 1994).

9 All citations from this work come from *Poetry, Language, Thought*, trans. Albert Hofstadter (New York: Harper and Row, 1971), pp. 15–87, and they will be given in the text. For an excellent overview of Heidegger's work, especially his later work after *Being and Time* (1927), in the context of the recent controversy over his Nazi affiliations, see the entry on Heidegger by Gerald L. Bruns in *The Johns Hopkins Guide to Literary Theory and Criticism*, pp. 373–75.

10 I have been influenced in my reading of this work by the arguments in Gerald L. Bruns, *Heidegger's Estrangements: Language, Truth, and Poetry* (New Haven/London: Yale UP, 1989), pp. 27–51. Although Heidegger criticizes seeing everything solely in terms of the form and content model of art, the artwork, seen as the working of Being into the emergence of a world of beings, is key in his later philosophy. See, for example, the 1941 lecture series *Basic Concepts*, trans. Gary E. Aylesworth (Bloomington: Indiana UP, 1993), pp. 99–101. As Fred Dallmayr remarks in *The Other Heidegger* (Ithaca: Cornell UP, 1993), for Heidegger (as for Nietzsche, Foucault, and James), "it is the artwork that constitutes its maker as an artist" (p. 18).

11 All citations from this work come from "Postscript: An Interview With Michel Foucault," in Michel Foucault, *Death and the Labyrinth: The World of Raymond Roussel*, trans. Charles Ruas (Berkeley/Los Angeles: U. of California P., 1986), pp. 169–86. For more on this topic in relation to Foucault, see my *Radical Parody: American Culture and Critical Agency After Foucault* (New York: Columbia UP, 1992); cf. also my forthcoming essay "Why Foucault No Longer Matters," in Ricardo Miguel Alfonso and Silvia Caporale Bizzini (eds.), *Reconstructing Foucault* (Binghamton: SUNY/Binghamton P., 1994).

12 As quoted in James Miller, *The Passion of Michel Foucault* (New York: Simon and Schuster, 1993), pp. 130, 211. For a full discussion of this topic, especially as it relates to Foucault's idea of how modern society attempts to supervise and discipline the fictionality of all discourse, see my *Radical Parody*, pp. 37–95.

13 For a critique of James as "master," see my "Becoming Other: The Conscience of the Reader in Late James," in Arac and Pease, *Re-Figuring U.S. Nationalisms*.

[14] Henry James, *The Art of the Novel*, Introduction by R. P. Blackmur, Foreword by R. W. B. Lewis, Fiftieth Anniversary Edition (Boston: Northeastern UP, 1984). This volume collects all of the Prefaces to the original twenty-four volumes of the New York Edition of the *Collected Works*. The volume of Prefaces was first published in 1934 by Scribners. All citations from *The Art of the Novel* will be given in my text.

[15] See Philip Horne, *Henry James and Revision: The New York Edition* (Clarendon: Oxford UP, 1990); cf. also as a useful introduction Horne's "Writing and Rewriting in Henry James," *Journal of American Studies*, 23, 3 (1989), 357–74.

[16] See my "The Quality of Judgment," forthcoming in *Review*, 16, 1 (1994). Here I spell out James's relations to Foucault's later ethics of self-stylization and sexuality.

[17] For a similar view, see Ross Posnock, *The Trial of Curiosity: Henry James, William James, and the Challenge of Modernity* (New York: Oxford UP, 1992).

[18] See Carol De Chellis Hill, *Henry James' Midnight Song* (New York: Poseidon/Simon and Schuster, 1993).

[19] Slavoj Zizek, *Tarrying With the Negative: Kant, Hegel, and the Critique of Ideology* (Durham: Duke UP, 1993).

[20] Martha Nussbaum, *Love's Knowledge: Essays on Philosophy and Literature* (New York: Oxford UP, 1990). For Kant on aesthetic judgment and ethics, see Paul Guyer, *Kant and the Experience of Freedom: Essays on Aesthetics and Morality* (Cambridge: Cambridge UP, 1993).

[21] All citations, which will be given in the text, come from Henry James, *The Golden Bowl* (New York/London: Penguin Books, 1985).

[22] See *Ecclesiastes* 12.6 and 7: "Or ever the silver cord be loosed / Or the golden bowl be broken, / Or the pitcher be broken at the fountain, / Or the wheel broken at the cistern. / Then shall the dust return to the earth as it was"; cf. also William Blake, "The Book of Thel": "Can wisdom be kept in a silver rod, / Or love in a golden Bowl." For these references, and others, see Robert L. Gale, *A Henry James Encyclopedia* (New York: Greenwood Press, 1989), p. 264.

[23] Surprisingly, the number of comparative studies of Nietzsche and Henry James is not great. The most important is Stephen Donadio, *Nietzsche, Henry James, and the Artistic Will* (New York: Oxford UP, 1978). For a strong critique of this work, see Jonathan Arac, *Critical Genealogies: Historical Situations For Postmodern Literary Studies* (New York: Columbia UP, 1987), pp. 239–48. For a Nietzschean-style deconstructive genealogy of James's academic reception, see John Carlos Rowe, *The Theoretical Dimensions of Henry James* (Madison: U. of Wisconsin P., 1984). The recent work of Henry McDonald is most promising in forging connections between Nietzsche and James. Cf. "Henry James as Nietzschean: The Dark Side of the Aesthetic," *Partisan Review*, 56, 3 (1989), 391–405; "Nietzsche Contra Derrida," *The Henry James Review*, 11, 2 (1990),

133–48; and forthcoming in *Boundary 2*, "Power and the Jamesian Narrator: A Nietzschean Reading of *The Wings of the Dove*." I disagree with McDonald's reading of the Jamesian narrator — I find the latter to suffer the contagion of imaginative agency as much as characters and readers do — and I disagree with his equation of Milly Theale with Nietzsche's idea of master morality and Kate Croy with his idea of slave morality. See my "Becoming Other: The Conscience of the Reader in Late James" in Arac and Pease, and, of course, my argument here. Despite this disagreement, McDonald's work on Nietzsche and James is the most promising since the work of Donadio and Rowe. Finally, for a very different view of the general question of aesthetic representation, fictionality, and moral and political strategies to contain the excesses of art, see the two books by Philippe Lacoue-Labarthe: *Typography: Mimesis, Philosophy, Politics*, ed. and trans. Christopher Funsk (Cambridge: Harvard UP, 1989) and *Heidegger, Art, and Politics: The Fiction of the Political*, trans. Chris Turner (Oxford: Basil Blackwell, 1990).

Manfred Stassen

Nietzsky vs. the Booboisie: H. L. Mencken's Uses and Abuses of Nietzsche

CONVENTIONAL WISDOM ATTRIBUTES to H. L. Mencken the merit of having initiated and sustained, over quite a period of time, the American reading public's interest in, and fascination with, Nietzsche. There is ample evidence that this was indeed the case.[1] True enough, the earlier circle around James Huneker may have been the first to cultivate an avant-garde image of the German philosopher, and George Bernard Shaw's *Man and Superman* (1903) may initially have introduced Nietzsche to another circle of *aficionados* of "radical" modern European thought. But it was not until the publication of Mencken's monograph *The Philosophy of Friedrich Nietzsche* in 1908 that a broader spectrum of the American public became aware of Nietzsche.

Upon closer investigation, however, it appears that what Americans of the time actually became aware of was rather Mencken himself and his idiosyncratic uses and abuses of Nietzsche as a veritable cult figure. There is by now a broad consensus among Mencken critics and biographers[2] that by the time Mencken had completed his education he was a closed system, a monad with a very small window to the intellectual world around him. Mencken would only perceive what matched his own attitudes, only appreciate what struck an inner cord in him, and only disseminate what he identified as his own. This situation renders any discourse of Nietzschean influences on Mencken somewhat inappropriate. Of course, it is possible to establish impressive inventories of Nietzschean stock in Mencken's vast literary and journalistic storage house, and this task has indeed been successfully undertaken in the four decades since his death.[3] It is also true that some of Mencken's later works obviously take their cue, in form and in content, from his earlier monograph on Nietzsche.[4] But much of what the American critic and journalist wrote took shape as a self-referential system of quotes that saw Mencken appropriating bits and pieces from Nietzsche. In this respect, what might have started out as Mencken's pursuit of an elective affinity with a provocative genius of a country to which Mencken traced his ethnic roots — his forebears where distant relatives of Otto von Bismarck — soon turned into a *selective* affinity with the stance, the style, and the salient subject matters of the controversial German philosopher.

It it impossible, and by now futile, to speculate on what would have become of Mencken's visceral appropriation and vituperous defence of some of Nietzsche's principal doctrines if the two world wars had not intervened. As it stands, Nietzsche's philosophy, as seen through the lenses of some of his early American interpreters, was to a large extent deemed responsible for the outbreak of these wars. The anti-democratic spin that Mencken gave to his interpretation of Nietzsche did not exactly help in this situation, since it increased the plausibility of the charges that German political and military leaders had taken their cues from Nietzsche. At least, this interpretation of Nietzsche's influence on rampant German nationalism and aggressiveness was a chance too good to pass up by the American homefront ideologists. Mencken's popularizing and propagandistic treatment of Nietzsche's philosophy, as much as his militancy in defending "the cause" — in addition to his overt sympathies with the German war effort in World War I, and his relative silence on the issues of World War II — did nothing to stem the tide of anti-German sentiments in America that centered on Nietzsche as the arch-villain. On the contrary, Mencken as the standard-bearer of Nietzsche in thought and practice may very well have prevented an unbiased American reception of Nietzsche during his own day. To gain and sustain popularity in a country most of whose people he despised and relentlessly vilified, was always a risky and unsure business for Mencken. Hence it is understandable that the eventual popular backlash to Mencken's vociferous iconoclasm associated with Nietzsche unleashed its wrath on the American messenger and his German oracle alike.

II

As far as elective affinities between the two men were concerned, Van Wyck Brooks, who knew so much about Mencken, points to some of the more obvious parallels in their lives and modes of self-interpretation:

> Had not Nietzsche regarded himself as a Polish grandee set down among German shopkeepers by an unkind fate? Just so Mencken saw himself as a sort of German Junker whose lot it was to live with American peasants. As Nietzsche had constantly pointed out "what the Germans lack," so Mencken set out to "transvalue" American values, — another Dionysus in a pallidly Apollonian world, a hierophant of idol-smashing and "natural selection."[5]

Mencken's sympathy for Nietzsche arose from his own resentment against the American bourgeoisie of which, alas, he was unequivocally a part. Perhaps more than anything else, this accounts for the vitriolic language in which Mencken launched his attacks on his own kind. His ancestors had left Germany for fear that the anti-aristocratic, pro-democratic revolution of 1848 might actually succeed, and they had ended up in an even more democratic United States. Mencken's attitude towards his father's cigar-manufacturing business in Baltimore was comparable to the attitude of some of Henry James's heroes quarrelling with their fathers' enterprises in Schenectady. His education in a German school had kept him in early touch with the culture of his origin, as much as it constantly kept him apart from that of his American habitat. In Mencken's case, the self-hatred of the typical displaced person needed a foil and a medium through which he could secrete his venom and attack his innocent victims who, at first, did not know what hit them. Mencken found this medium, against considerable odds, in Nietzsche's philosophy. Nietzsche was still a relatively unknown author in 1906/08 for most Americans, yet those who knew of him were in awe of his controversial reputation. Nietzsche's alleged greatness thus lent stature to his American interpreter Mencken, while at the same time the allegiance with him put a critical distance between Mencken and his American countrymen, whom he accused of nearly everything that his idol Nietzsche despised.

Mencken had already made a reputation for himself in America as a flamboyant journalist. Though a brilliant critic, he had curiously little flair for the visual arts, even less appreciation for poetry and, for that matter, philosophy. The study of Greek tragedy, which had been the starting point of Nietzsche's spectacular career — and to which he wanted to return, as he confided to Jacob Burckhardt in a rare moment of lucidity during his later madness — was merely "an unparalleled bore" for Mencken.[6] And of philosophers, especially the despised metaphysicians, he had this to say, in a series aptly called "Prejudices":

> Since the dawn of time they have been trying to get order and method into the thinking of Homo Sapiens — and Homo Sapiens, when he thinks at all, is still a brother to the lowly ass (Equus Africanus), even to the ears and the bray. I include the philosophers themselves, unanimously and especially . . . . What man in human history ever wrote worse than Kant? Was it, perhaps, Hegel?[7]

While in the same passage Mencken exempts Nietzsche from his sweeping indictments — on grounds of his being a poet rather than a philosopher — he has nothing to say about Nietzsche's poetry in the course of his entire dealings with him. Thirty-five years after Mencken's death, the vaults of the Enoch Pratt Library in Baltimore were opened to scholars, who now have access to both his *Diary* and all four volumes of his autobiography, *My Life as Author and Editor*. Both works are remarkably silent about the allegedly overwhelming influence Nietzsche had on Mencken. In the *Diary*, which covers, roughly, the years from 1930 to 1948, one might have expected some reminiscences of note to Mencken's lifetime infatuation with Nietzsche. Yet there are altogether only two references to the German philosopher, one entirely trivial, and the other to the 100th anniversary of Nietzsche's birthday in 1944. The second document, Mencken's autobiography, spans a period of almost a quarter of a century, including the crucial years of his flirtation with Nietzsche from 1896 to the mid-twenties. The author records numerous literary, philosophical, academic, and other luminaries who had a formative influence on him: Nietzsche, conspicuously, is not among them. In fact, Mencken mentions Nietzsche only in a small number of instances in his autobiography, usually in quotations or references from unfavorable American reviews on Nietzsche's writings. Instead, he tells us at length about his early infatuation with Kipling and about the invaluable contribution that Thomas Huxley made to the formation of his own style, as well as the influences of Darwin and Spencer on his "Weltanschauung." In regard to such sources, then, we are left in the dark as to what may have aroused Mencken's interest in Nietzsche to the point of devoting an entire monograph to him, translating one of Nietzsche's works, *The Antichrist*, in its entirety, and compiling *The Gist of Nietzsche* (1910), an anthology of aphorisms, quotes, and famous (or by then infamous) pronouncements of the German sage on altogether twenty-three topics ranging from "Art," "Beauty," and "Christianity," via "Jews," "Morality," and "Progress," to "Superman," "Weakness," and "Women."

The longest passage on Nietzsche recorded in the autobiography concerns the famous "Nietzsky" episode during World War I. Seen in historical context, Mencken wrote his autobiography in the early days of the Cold War — he was forced to abandon the project when he suffered a stroke in 1948 — and he clearly anticipates the paranoid chauvinism of the coming McCarthy era. This explains the derisive references to the American Protective League of the inter-war years as a kind of forerunner to the House Un-American Activities Committee. From the slim remainder of Mencken's account on the notoriety of Nietzsche in America, it becomes clear that many others — such as the translators Levy and Ludovici, the critic Huneker and his circle, the novelists Dreiser and London — had either propagated, assimilated, or distorted Nietzsche earlier than Mencken did, or simultaneously with him, or long after his monograph had been forgotten. Of course, Mencken's relative silence about his relationship to Nietzsche could also be interpreted as being quite revealing and to the point. Mencken, it could be argued, was too vain to acknowledge any large-scale influence by others, or, more plausibly, he had completely suppressed the insight that, in his case, writing about Nietzsche meant nothing else but writing about himself. Mencken's propagation of Nietzsche did not teach Americans much about this author; it rather acquainted them with an American "Ersatz" Nietzsche in the person of Mencken whose Teutonic origins and sympathies became all too obvious in the process.

III

The more interesting question, consequently, is what his penchant for Nietzsche tells us about Mencken himself. For the most part, there were three aspects of Nietzsche's thought that struck a cord with Mencken. First, there was the dialectic between destruction (of the old Order) and affirmation (of the new Life), which was transformed into the positive force of an iconoclasm that took no prisoners. For Mencken, this attitude was clearly a matter of intellectual pose: arrogant, cruel, uncompromising, but courageous. It was an attitude that reminded him of Ibsen (whose iconoclasm had optimistic overtones) and Shaw (who had compromised his iconoclasm by associating it with socialism). Second, there was the force of Nietzsche's language, the "evangelical fervor" of his style.[8] Mencken's quote from Nietzsche's *Ecce Homo* (II, 4) is revealing in this regard:

> People will say some day that Heine and I were the greatest artists, by far, that ever wrote in German, and that we left the best any mere German could do an incalculable distance behind us.[9]

Mencken's assumption was that what the Pole Nietzsche and the Jew Heine, both no "mere Germans" and both with a strong bias for anything French, could do for Germany in the nineteenth century, he could do, in the footsteps of Thomas Huxley, for American literature in the first half of the twentieth century. Third, Mencken found in Nietzsche a peculiar assortment of views, doctrines, and strong opinions that somehow seemed to form a coherent body of ideas, among them the relativity of all accepted truths and values; the ontological and political preeminence of the (higher) individual over the collective; the superiority of an "aristocracy of efficiency" over any democratic rule; the castigation of the nefarious influence of Christianity on human history; the celebrated inevitable and ineradicable inferiority of the so-called "unfit"; and, mistakenly attributed to Nietzsche, the pervasive law of "natural selection." This was, in fact, the "Gist of Nietzsche" that seemed to fit Mencken's mold, and this was the Nietzsche he set out to popularize and to propagate. As one critic put it: "Mencken had in fact made up his mind about Nietzsche even before beginning the study . . . . Mencken made Nietzsche over into his own image."[10]

Other motives of a more mundane nature added fuel to Mencken's zest for becoming Nietzsche's spokesman in America. Mencken's earlier book on Shaw had been a great success in America and England. His publisher understandably wanted to repeat the performance with a book on Nietzsche. It is to Mencken's credit that he put up some resistance against this popular spirit of commercial expediency. The result of the ensuing tug of war between the author and his publisher was a compromise between a merely popular version of Nietzsche and an intellectually serious, scholarly respectable interpretation. However, due to Mencken's competitive and combative spirit, it was still going to be a book for the market place of ideas, for the controversies in the *feuilleton* of the journals for which the author and his friends wrote, and less a contribution to the war of academic footnotes.

Popularization meant cutting the towering philosopher Nietzsche down to size, linking his ideas to those currently held, or deemed most provocative, and looking at the controversies of the day in a fresh, exotic light. Mencken quoted extensively from Nietzsche, using wherever possible American examples in order to illustrate a given point. He also invariably used his own translations of Nietzsche's works, not so much for reasons of aesthetic coherence, but rather because the few existing translations, mostly by Levy and Ludovici, were totally inadequate in his view. The early reactions to Mencken's work on Nietzsche give evidence of his initial success. Most reviewers praise the book as a lucid, down-to-earth exposition of the doctrines of a difficult thinker, and most agree that the American intelligentsia somehow needed exposure to such a new if radical voice in order to shake them out of their complacency.

However, propagating new ideas meant, in Mencken's case, not only simplifying and shocking, but also proselytizing. Here was a new doctrine Americans had better become acquainted with in order to organize their own body politic differently in the interest of their survival and aspired hegemony in the twentieth century. The Nietzsche that Mencken understood and wanted his fellow countrymen to understand was, to overstate the case slightly, a German Darwin minus the burden of scientific argument, yet with the benefit of the grander vision and, not unimportant for an *homme de lettres*, with the better style. The key to Mencken's reading of Nietzsche became the link between the ideas of the "unfit" and the "aristocracy of efficiency." The "unfit," in Mencken's view, were a biological given, whereas the envisioned "aristocracy" was the necessary *telos* of human history, if the survival of the species, even against its own doings and inclinations, was to be achieved as a genuine task for the new breed of Dionysian politicians. It seems that for Mencken everything followed from here. Since it was presumably impossible to combat biological givens, any attempt at removing the conditions that led to the existence of the class (or caste) of the "unfit" — such as the elaborate programs of Marx and revolutionary socialism demanded — was *a priori* futile. Even worse than such programs were attempts at ameliorating the condition of the "unfit" — such as in the campaigns of Christianity and democratic socialism — since they had a tendency to drain away the resources and the energy that allowed the fit, especially the fittest, to thrive. The worst, in Mencken's understanding, were the ideological underpinnings of these attempts in the name of God-given truth and universal values, such as sympathy, pity, and altruism. Only if the fit(test) few were allowed to progress unhampered would an "aristocracy of efficiency" finally be achieved. In order to bring this about, it required the activation and celebration of an all-powerful "Will to Life" that was never found in the many, hardly ever in the reigning bourgeoisie, and not even in the aristocracy of birth. The members of Mencken's envisioned new aristocracy were, therefore, not the "buccaneers of finance" or the "captains of industry" whom his close friend Theodore Dreiser had celebrated in his novels, but rather the Bismarcks and Napoleons, the Pasteurs and Darwins, the Machiavellis and the Nietzsches, and, of course, the Menckens of this world.

Mencken simply longed for an America different from the one he lived in. He wanted to redress history and to overcome the influence of the French Enlightenment and Rousseau on the American ideal of democracy, radically replacing it by a politics of strength which, in the years before World War I, he saw manifested in German thought and action. In linking, for instance, Theodore Roosevelt ("Roosevelt Major") to Nietzsche, Mencken sought to Americanize the political implications of Nietzsche's ideas:

> In all things fundamental the Rooseveltian philosophy and the Nietzschean philosophy are identical . . . . It is inconceivable that Mr. Roosevelt should have formulated his present confession of faith independently of Nietzsche.[11]

According to Mencken's view of political Washington and the ruling American elite, expressed in a myriad of articles in the *Baltimore Sun*, it was actually quite conceivable that Roosevelt had never read or understood Nietzsche. Mencken simply needed a towering public hero of the American scene to rank with Bismarck and Napoleon in the Nietzschean Olympus of Dionysian politicians in order to justify his optimism about a future heroic turn of events in the history of the West. Any language that evoked a "doctrine of the strenuous life" and of asceticism as prerequisites for "the splendid ultimate triumph," as Roosevelt had emphasized in his famous speech on "The Strenuous Life" in 1899,[12] was suggestive enough for Mencken to construe a link that suited his political agenda.

The propagandistic element in Mencken's exposition of Nietzsche's views is furthermore underscored by the rhetorical presentation of his arguments. Mencken frequently introduces a subject by using such formulas as "it is apparent, on brief reflection," or "as everyone who has given a moment's thought to the subject well knows," thus postulating universal agreement precisely without inviting "a moment's thought" or a "brief reflection." With the help of this strategy, Mencken the propagandist attempted to silence a good deal of the initial outrage over his arguments and underscored the rational, in contrast to the prejudicial, element of his thinking. The strategy is used fairly consistently throughout Mencken's diatribes, and it also plays an important role when he either wanted to agree emphatically with Nietzsche or, inversely, when he saw himself forced to disagree with his prime witness and, consequently, had to bend Nietzsche's arguments in order to make them fit a Menckonian agenda. Consider the following two complementary examples. In the one case, it is Nietzsche's doctrine of the existence of three natural castes of men that stands at issue. Having quoted Nietzsche approvingly on the distinction between these natural classes of men, and having reinforced his approval by adding, "Empirical evidence has more than once proven its truth," Mencken feels compelled to continue with great flourish:

> It is apparent, on brief reflection, that the negro, no matter how much he is educated, must remain, as a race, in a condition of subservience; that he must remain the inferior of the stronger and more intelligent white man so long as he retains racial differentiation.[13]

In the other case, Mencken elaborates with the help of Nietzsche on the topic of "The Jews." Quoting from Nietzsche's *Daybreak*, "The Jews . . . will either become the masters of Europe or lose Europe, as they once lost Egypt," Mencken appends this quite uncalled-for addendum:

> For the Jewish slave-morality which prevails in the western world today, under the label of Christianity, Nietzsche had . . . the most violent aversion and contempt, but he saw very clearly that this same morality admirably served and fitted the Jews themselves.[14]

Earlier Mencken had refuted this very idea, when he had contradicted Nietzsche in the name of common sense and plausibility:

> In a word, the Jews detested the slave-morality which circumstances thrust upon them, and got their revenge by foisting it . . . upon their masters. It is obvious that this idea is sheer lunacy. That the Jews ever realized the degenerating effect of their own slave-morality is unlikely, and that they should take council together and plan such an elaborate and complicated revenge, is impossible.[15]

Whatever the intrinsic merits of Nietzsche's theory or Mencken's refutation of it may be in the given case, the latter passage clearly shows that Mencken's predisposition on any particular issue easily overrode his allegedly firm allegiance to Nietzsche when it came to a clash. In the given case, Mencken's own blind spot did not allow him to see Nietzsche's *anti*-anti-semitism; in fact, his analysis squarely draws Nietzsche into the anti-semitic camp.

Quite generally, where Mencken differs, he distorts, and where he does not understand, he ridicules. A case in point is his account of Nietzsche's belief in eternal recurrence, "the most hopeless idea, perhaps, ever formulated by man."[16] Arguably one of the centerpieces of Nietzsche's philosophy, the idea is treated by Mencken with utmost derision. While he acknowledges, quite irrelevantly but with praise, the origins of the idea with the Pythagoreans, he can only sum it up by taking recourse to an uncharacteristically unsophisticated anecdote :

> This concerns a joker who goes to an inn, eats his fill and then says to the innkeeper: "You and I will be here again in a million years: let me pay you then." "Very well," replies the quick-witted innkeeper, "but first pay me for the beefsteak you ate the last time you were here — a million years ago."[17]

In view of such evidence, we have to conclude that Nietzschean concepts such as eternal recurrence were clearly beyond Mencken's philosophical grasp. As a good journalist, he reported on them, but only in order to show that mystical and metaphysical residues existed even in the most clear-headed and iconoclastic of European thinkers, though, of course, to the new iconoclasts like himself they were mere jokes.

IV

In an entry to his *Diary*, Mencken wrote on October 15, 1944:

Today is the one hundredth anniversary of the birth of Friedrich Wilhelm Nietzsche. If it is noted anywhere in America it will be on the ground that Nietzsche was a wicked fellow and the inventor of all the deviltries of Hitler. I can see little hope for this great Christian country. It has been going downhill steadily throughout my time, and its pace of late has been fast accelerating.[18]

There can be little doubt that Mencken deeply regretted what he considered the wrong development America had taken during his lifetime and that he saw himself, almost from the beginning of his career, as a Nietzsche-inspired prophet of coming national disasters which he wanted to prevent. Yet if we believe that Mencken chose Nietzsche as an ally and a guiding star in his pursuit of the self-assigned task to change the course of American history, though in doing so his interpretation of Nietzsche became "not only arbitrary but superficial,"[19] the question that must be asked is how successful Mencken was in his reformatory work and what actual impact he had on the American intellectuals of his day. The answer, as might be expected, is rather mixed.

Before and immediately after World War I, Mencken, in his adopted Nietzschean stance, was the standard-bearer of the restless youth of America. In his own assessment, corroborated by most of his critics, he found himself in the position of having become the symbol figure of a widespread revolt among young intellectuals against anything that suggested old American certainties and values. Mencken was occasionally embarrassed by his following; he feared that he was receiving their accolades for the wrong reasons — and he was probably right. But, nevertheless, a serious debate over Nietzsche in America was made possible by his monograph and his other contributions on this highly controversial and alien figure. The debate was relatively limited in scope and in participants, esoteric in character, and for the most part without tangible results, but at least it took place.

During World War I, the situation was somewhat different. The popularizer and propagandist Mencken then found his match in certain American home-front ideologists who fought him with his own weapons. The popular reaction to Mencken's championing of Nietzschean causes was to accuse, in turn, the German philosopher of being a raving propagandist of everything imaginable in the arsenal of American stereotypes and prejudices about Germany and the Germans. Mencken managed to achieve that his idol was held responsible for fostering a rampant German superiority complex, with the whole German war machine in its service. Mencken's strong politicization of Nietzsche's message and his concomitant broadside attacks on American values left those who had never read anything by Nietzsche little choice but to arrive at a misunderstanding of some magnitude. Mencken's assessment of Germany's leadership at the dawn of World War I did not improve matters:

> The aristocracy of birth and vested rights has given place to a new aristocracy of genuine skill, and Germany has become a true democracy in the Greek sense. That is to say, the old nobility has taken a back seat and the empire is now governed by an oligarchy of its best men.[20]

In the light of such pronouncements, it was not surprising that the paranoia endemic to the political right in America put its specific spin on Mencken's assessments, and anti-German sentiments in his predominantly "German" home town of Baltimore added a local flavor of overzealous immigrants rushing to the defence of their host country. As a result, a ruthless campaign against Mencken temporarily cost him his job at the *Baltimore Sun*. In this context, what offended Mencken's pride was not so much the relative silence of the few intellectuals he respected, but rather the popular and vicious reactions of such groups as the Allied Cause and other patriotic organizations such as the American Protective League, the governmental Committee on Public Information, and the private National Security League. In practically all of his publications — particularly in the Introduction to his own translation of Nietzsche's *Antichrist*, in the *Smart Set* papers of 1915, and in his autobiography — whenever Mencken refers to Nietzsche at all, he dwells at some length on the so-called "Nietzsky" episode of this time:

> On the strength of the fact that I had published a book on Nietzsche in 1906 [sic], six years after his death, I was called upon

by agents of the Department of Justice, elaborately outfitted with badges, to meet the charge that I was an intimate associate and agent of the "German monster, Nietzsky."[21]

While Mencken's innate arrogance and anti-authoritarian stance made him largely immune against such rather silly attempts at intimidation by a vengeful government agency, other reactions by the inevitable ideological soldiers, who man the literary and journalistic trenches in times of war, provoked him to some of his most vitriolic prose:

> Of the late Professor Friedrich Wilhelm Nietzsche . . . one hears a lot of startling gabble in these days of war, chiefly from the larynxes of freshwater college professors, prima donna preachers, English novelists, newspaper editorial writers, Chautauqua yap-yankers and other such hawkers of piffle.[22]

After Mencken had ostentatiously visited the war front on the German side in 1916/17, public attacks on him escalated, and vigilante efforts of the American Protective League, as well as other organizations, made him fear for his safety:

> Early in March, 1918 . . . the A.P.L. had received an anonymous complaint against me . . . . It was a half literate document denouncing me as "a friend of Nitzky, the German monster" . . . who had by now become a really horrendous bugaboo to all 100 % Americans.[23]

The average American, if he knew of Mencken's existence, never forgave him for having been on the wrong side in the war, and certainly not for attacking the esteemed winner of that war, President (of Princeton and of the United States) Woodrow Wilson, from a vantage point of pro-German sympathies. After all, it was well remembered that Mencken had written:

> . . . for the university president who prohibited the teaching of the enemy language in his learned grove, heaved the works of Goethe out of the university library . . . for this giant of loyal endeavor let no 100 per cent American speak of anything less than the grand cross of the order.[24]

During the Depression, Mencken's earlier political interpretation of Nietzsche that had led him to equate the philosopher with Theodore Roosevelt, was perhaps only partially but significantly responsible for his eclipse — and that of Nietzsche — in the American public consciousness. As much as "Roosevelt I" had been his hope for the advent of Dionysian politics in the New World, "Roosevelt II," whom he sarcastically referred to as "Dr. F. D. Roosevelt," became his new pet target since he saw in him socialism incarnate. Mencken had simply no antenna for registering the changing political mood in America. Melvin Drimmer has accurately summed up the downward trajectory of Nietzsche's "agent," and concomitantly that of his idol, in America:

> Since much of Nietzsche's impact upon American intellectuals depended on their alienation from American society, their reconciliation with America resulted in a corresponding loss of interest in Nietzsche's criticism and answers.
>
> Only H. L. Mencken and Benjamin De Casseres remained to preach an arch-individualism to an audience concerned with larger economic and political questions, and by 1935 both spokesmen found themselves estranged from an American audience.[25]

While Mencken later valiantly refused to equate Hitler with the elitist Nietzschean superman — as American and British counter-intelligence units were so fond of doing — he nevertheless lacked the political instinct of distinguishing between the various targets of his attack:

> ... Mencken retreated into provincial Baltimore to work on his autobiography. Unable to differentiate between a Roosevelt and a Hitler, between a Babbitt and a storm trooper, between a bourgeois society leaning towards reform and a bourgeois society becoming totalitarian, Nietzsche's teachings reached a dead end in the hands of Mencken . . . .[26]

Perhaps Van Wyck Brooks found the best formula to sum up the rapidly waning appeal of Mencken's interpretation of Nietzsche, as well as Mencken's lifelong fight against what he liked to call the American booboisie: "Time broke the lance of the 'literary uhlan,' as the German-American societies had called him, and the critic who had said, 'Most of the men I respect are foreigners,' ceased to be a spokesman for the 'mongrel and inferior' Yankees."[27]

V

In what may have been the last relatively lucid moments before his madness, Nietzsche had asked for the formation of a "Party of

Life." He wanted several million people to be on hand when he would lead humanity into the dawn of a new Dionysian age of politics. The leaders at the helm of this party were to be recruited from two classes of people: the officers of the armies of Europe, and the representatives of world-wide Jewish capital. Obviously, the military brass and the bankers represented for the Nietzsche of the last phase the will to power.[28] Mencken did not know of his ideological mentor's late hidden agenda. But while he would not have agreed with his choice of the "chosen Dionysians," he shared the delusion that a philosophical program such as Nietzsche's could easily be transferred to the concrete political arena. Mencken's vision of a new and envigorated America through Theodore Roosevelt's radical program is one of the not so rare misunderstandings in history between intellectuals and politicians. Mencken believed to have identified in "Roosevelt Major" the incarnation of the Dionysian principle in politics, which ignores the superficial cravings of the masses and follows the great design in spite of them, knowing that all this will benefit future generations. Less than three decades later, out of a similarly anti-democratic motivation, Heidegger would fall into an analogous trap with regard to Hitler, crediting him with bringing about the advent of a new unfolding of Being. The difference is that Mencken's error was, for all intents and purposes, due to his personal idiosyncracies, and thus rather private and ultimately inconsequential. Heidegger's error, in contrast, was shared by a good many German intellectuals, and hence — anything but harmless — of immeasurably more sinister consequences.

Writing from a German perspective and after a long period of exile in America, Ludwig Marcuse, in his study *Amerikanisches Philosophieren*, acknowledges Mencken's contribution to the early American reception of Nietzsche as a dedicated anti-philistine, a view that was shared by a small circle of like-minded intellectuals of Mencken's immediate entourage. Marcuse deplores, however, that in the course of two world wars this group under Mencken's leadership was unable to prevent the degeneration of Nietzsche's image to that of the creator of the "blond beast" and to that of the ideological forerunner of both, Wilhelm II and Hitler. According to Marcuse, a more genuinely philosophical and therefore more congenial mediator for Nietzsche in America would have been William James. Unfortunately, however, this connection never came about:

Nietzsche did not live to become familiar with Pragmatism which, in his set of aphorisms entitled "Theory and Practice," he had to some extent prefigured; and James did not live long enough to become part of the American debate on Nietzsche that was launched by Mencken's monograph only shortly before World War I.[29]

The American Nietzsche of today no longer resembles at all the portrait that Mencken drew of him throughout the better part of his career as a critic and journalist. Whereas it is Mencken's merit to have introduced Nietzsche to an American audience as a serious and catalytic thinker, who represented a different German tradition of philosophy than that of Kant, Hegel, and Marx, the new American Nietzsche of today decidedly speaks with a French accent. As is well known, French deconstructionists and postmodernists, who themselves have rediscovered Nietzsche via Heidegger, have caught the American intellectuals' interest as far as Nietzsche is concerned. Perhaps it will take a new Mencken, preferably with a less egocentric and propagandistic anti-American agenda of his own, to rediscover, one day, yet another "new" Nietzsche for America.

Notes

[1] On the importance of Mencken for the introduction of Nietzsche to America, see among others: Patrick Bridgwater, *Nietzsche in Anglosaxony* (Leicester: Leicester UP, 1972); LeRoy C. Kauffmann, "The Influence of Friedrich Nietzsche on American Literature" (Diss. U. of Pennsylvania, 1963); Melvin Drimmer, "Nietzsche in American Thought, 1895–1925," 2 vols. (Diss. U. of Rochester, 1965); Chenliang Sheng, "Nietzsche's Superman Americanized: On Dreiser's *The Financier*" (Diss. U. of Maryland, 1989); Ludwig Marcuse, "Nietzsche in America," *The South Atlantic Quarterly*, 50 (1951), 330–39.

[2] For biographical information on Mencken, see in particular Carl Bode, *Mencken* (1969; rpt. Baltimore: Johns Hopkins UP, 1986); Vincent Fitzpatrick, *H. L. Mencken* (New York: Continuum, 1989); Edgar Kemler, *The Irreverent Mr. Mencken* (Boston: Little, Brown and Comp., 1950); William Manchester, *Disturber of the Peace: The Life of H. L. Mencken* (1950; rpt. Amherst: U. of Massachusetts Press, 1986); Douglas C. Stenerson, *H.L. Mencken: Iconoclast from Baltimore* (Chicago/London: U. of Chicago Press, 1971).

[3] In addition to the works listed in note 1, consult Edward Stone, "H. L. Mencken's Debt to Friedrich Nietzsche" (M.A. Thesis U. of Texas, 1937).

[4] See, for instance, Mencken's *In Defense of Women* (1918), *Notes on Democracy* (1926), *Treatise on the Gods* (1930), and *Treatise on Right and Wrong* (1934).

[5] Van Wyck Brooks, "Mencken in Baltimore," in Douglas C. Stenerson (ed.), *Critical Essays on H. L. Mencken* (Boston: G. K. Hall, 1987), p. 166.

[6] See Van Wyck Brooks, p. 120.

[7] Mencken, *Prejudices: Sixth Series* (New York: A. Knopf, 1927).

[8] Bode, *Mencken*, p. 83.

[9] Mencken, *The Philosophy of Friedrich Nietzsche* (1908; rpt. Port Washington: Kennikat Press, 1967), pp. 265–66.

[10] Drimmer, *Nietzsche in American Thought*, vol. I, p. 157.

[11] Quoted from Bridgwater, *Nietzsche in Anglosaxony*, p. 161.

[12] See Theodore Roosevelt, *The Strenuous Life: Essays and Addresses* (New York: Century, 1902), p. 1.

[13] Mencken, *Philosophy of Nietzsche*, p. 167.

[14] *Ibid.*, p. 237.

[15] *Ibid.*, p. 145.

[16] *Ibid.*, p. 260.

[17] *Ibid.*, p. 120.

[18] *The Diary of H. L. Mencken*, ed. Charles A. Fecher (New York: Knopf, 1990), p. 333.

[19] Bode, *Mencken*, p. 83.

[20] Mencken in a letter to Ellery Sedgwick on September 1, 1914. Quoted from Drimmer, *Nietzsche in American Thought*, pp. 167–68.

[21] See Mencken's "Introduction" to his translation of Nietzsche's *The Antichrist* (Torrance, CA: Noontide Press, 1923), p. 15.

[22] See *H. L. Mencken's "Smart Set" Criticism*, ed. William H. Nolte (Ithaca, NY: Cornell UP, 1968), p. 194.

[23] Mencken, *My Life as Author and Editor*, ed. Jonathan Yardley (New York: Knopf, 1993), pp. 90–91.

[24] Mencken in *The New Republic*, quoted from Carl Bode, *Mencken*, p. 129.

[25] Drimmer, *Nietzsche in American Thought*, vol. I, p. 24.

[26] *Ibid.*

[27] Van Wyck Brooks, "Mencken in Baltimore," p. 121.

[28] Cf. Ernst Nolte's discussion of Nietzsche's "Wahnsinnszettel" in "Ein Ende und ein Anfang," *Frankfurter Allgemeine Zeitung* (January 7, 1989).

[29] Ludwig Marcuse, *Amerikanisches Philosophieren: Pragmatisten, Polytheisten, Tragiker* (Hamburg: Rowohlt, 1959), p. 58 (my translation).

Gerd Hurm

Of Wolves and Lambs: Jack London's and Nietzsche's Discourses of Nature

> Friedrich Nietzsche, the mad philosopher
> of the nineteenth century of the Christian
> Era, who caught wild glimpses of truth,
> but who before he was done, reasoned
> himself around the great circle of human
> thought and off into madness. (*IH*, 7)[1]

WITH ITS APPARENT crudity of judgment, Jack London's characterization of Nietzsche in *The Iron Heel* seems to verify a persistent prejudice in London scholarship. As the oft-told story goes, the autodidactic American adventure-writer failed to understand and do justice to the complexities and subtleties of the German philosopher's essentially spiritual ideals. Yet the epigraph from London may well be used to illustrate the contrary, highlighting some of the difficulties in criticism in dealing with an intricate case of intertextuality. Since it was London who introduced many of Nietzsche's ideas to American literature, a differentiated assessment seems particularly relevant.[2]

Two facets of the opening quotation may be singled out for exemplary comment. Its explicit antipathy challenges the host of readings which have asserted London's conformity with Nietzschean positions. Throughout his career, the novelist tried in vain to repudiate affirmative interpretations that disregarded his criticism. A note written shortly before his death testifies to London's preoccupation with this misunderstanding: "Socialist biography. *Martin Eden* and *Sea-Wolf*, attacks on Nietzschean philosophy, which even the socialists missed the point of."[3] Also, the resumé, which conveys the opinion of *The Iron Heel's* fictive editor, presents but one of several perspectives on Nietzsche in the text. The novel's hero, for instance, concomitantly receives praise as "a superman, a blond beast such as Nietzsche has described" (*IH, 7*).[4]

Exemplifying Nietzsche's central tenet of perspectivism, the opening statement's ultimate relational character thus can be used to shed light on the broader dilemma that confronts students of London's Nietzsche reception: if there is but a diversity of interpretations, yet no definitive version of Nietzsche's pluralist philosophy, neither London nor his critics can claim to possess a privileged access to an authentic, original meaning. Hence, possibly, the customary accusations concerning London's alleged misrepresentation of Nietzsche may signify only divergent, if equally justified interpretations. The emphasis in the following discussion will then have to be as much on the mode of the ineluctable bias as on the validity and consistency of London's specific perspective. The foremost aim of the essay will therefore be to assess the difference, but also the noticeable affinity in the two authors' basic assumptions. From this perspective, it can be shown that a kindred discourse of nature guided London's reception and fuelled his ambivalent fascination with Nietzsche's concept of the "blond beast" (*GM*, 40).[5]

Since it was London's and Nietzsche's fictional and philosophical attacks on bourgeois society and Christian morality that helped to challenge traditional formulae and helped to launch such dominant modern and postmodern paradigms as naturalism and deconstruction, it seems most fruitful from today's vantage point to tone down a discussion of the validity of their criticism in favor of an analysis of the degree to which their proposed solutions were yet a product of the very nineteenth-century modes of thought that they tried to overcome. Indeed, in their general adherence to evolutionary theory, and thus to the privileged male-dominated discourse of nature in the last century, the central discursive scheme of both men appears more deeply entrenched in biased biological concepts of gender and race than is often granted.

II

In the record of Jack London's relation to Nietzsche, the date of the initial acquaintance and the degree of concurrence in opinion were for a long time the two most contested issues.[6] It is now common knowledge that London was familiar with Nietzsche's ideas from the beginning of his career and that his attitude towards the German philosopher was a thoroughly ambivalent, if unrelentingly critical one.[7] The date of initial acquaintance remained uncertain for so long because two distinct reception phases were blurred: London first encountered Nietzsche's philosophy through a primarily oral discourse, and only years later turned to his books. In 1898/99, London became acquainted with Nietzschean thought through the John Ruskin Club, a socialist debating circle in San Francisco that was presided over by the intellectual, and later London mentor, Frank Strawn-Hamilton.[8] This early socialist reception of Nietzsche's ideas provided the basis for London's second study of the philosopher's works in 1904: the renewed fascination then created the impression that he had encountered Nietzschean ideas for the first time. Judging from the evidence in London's writings, however, this later reception did not substantially alter the general trend of his original assessment. Another indication of continuity is the unchanged preference for certain texts as prime sources for Nietzsche's philosophy.

Throughout London's writings, his chief references mostly concern Nietzsche's *On the Genealogy of Morals* and its complex concept of the "blond beast." London was fascinated by the *Genealogy*: it ranks first on his list of Nietzsche books in 1904 and he also recommended it as an introductory text to his wife Charmian. Likewise, the term "blond beast" is his first literal allusion to Nietzsche in the politically fundamental essay "How I Became a Socialist." In addition, the concept finds application in *The Call of the Wild* and *The Sea-Wolf*, and is explicitly used to exemplify Nietzschean tenets in *The Iron Heel* and *Martin Eden*.

By focusing on the "blond beast," a term that seems as simple as it is complex and thus was predestined to become one of the most current and misunderstood Nietzschean coinages, London provided fuel for the widely held prejudice that he only knew Nietzsche through superficial slogans without grasping their theoretical underpinnings. Yet, in emphasizing a facet that was linked to the larger "naturalistic" discourse in the *Genealogy*, London only followed the dominant trend among turn-of-the-century scholars who accentuated Nietzsche's indebtedness to the Darwinian paradigm and generally read him as a "philosopher of evolution."[9]

While interpretations which highlighted an anti-Darwinian thrust in Nietzsche's philosophy have since dominated the field in the twentieth century, recent research has brought a differentiated validation of the early Darwinistic assessments. Theodore R. Schatzki, for instance, asserts that "in order to account for the centrality of power in his writings, it is necessary to acknowledge the tremendous influence exerted in the second half of the nineteenth century by the biological, evolutionary notion of a 'struggle for existence'."[10] Moreover, Detlef Brennecke's detailed research on the origins of the "blond beast" concept has indicated that Nietzsche consciously created a symbol with naturalist implications for his *Übermensch*.[11]

Exactly this constitutive link between the blond beast and the superman, however, has been frequently cited as evidence for the novelist's misunderstanding of Nietzsche's philosophy.[12] London was accused of mere biographical projections or plain biological reductionism when combining the two concepts. Even such differentiated accounts as the ones by Patrick Bridgwater and Katherine M. Littell follow this pattern. Bridgwater, for instance, held that London, captivated by Nietzsche "on an irrational level," was guided by a "popular misconception" of the "Übermensch," turning the essentially spiritual figure into "a merely biological Superman."[13]

Katherine M. Littell, whose accomplishment it was to establish the depth and variety of London's knowledge of Nietzsche, also singles out the "blond beast" as the prime example for the "more superficial" of the three Nietzsche strands in London's writings. It is in London's application of the "blond beast" concept, she claims, that one may find a "total distortion" of Nietzschean thought. Littell bases her arguments on Walter Kaufmann's interpretation of Nietzsche, a version that was "almost completely dominant in America" when her article appeared, but which has since been challenged and is now found no longer to be wholly "consistent with the Nietzschean texts."[14] Kaufmann, who saw in Nietzsche a proponent of the ascetic ideal, played down the pervasiveness of the Darwinian paradigm in his philosophy; for him, the naturalistic strand belonged to the Nietzsche legend in which the *Übermensch* was misrepresented as a "Darwinistic Superman."[15] To legitimize such a specific view of Nietzsche, certain works within the canon had to be marginalized. Thus the *Genealogy*, London's central text, becomes less than trustworthy for Littell as "Nietzsche's last work before his insanity," providing only a "somewhat distorted statement of Nietzsche's ideas." In like manner, she holds that London "falsely attributes to Nietzsche enthusiastic approval of the 'blonde Bestie'" and argues that a close link between the blond beast and the superman is wrong, since it represents "the exact opposite in Nietzsche's theoretical conceptualizations."[16]

The disclosure of a bias in such reception studies does not render London's reading of Nietzsche by itself any more accurate or valid. It indicates, however, that the question of London's relation to Nietzsche needs to be examined critically and in full acknowledgment of the reductionism involved in privileging a particular perspective. The denigration of London's interpretation of Nietzsche has frequently been founded on such partisan grounds.[17]

To lay bare the basis for the evaluation in this study, the concept of the "blond beast" as created by Nietzsche and as appropriated by London will have to be analyzed carefully. A closer look at Nietzsche's *Genealogy* becomes indispensable because it is the book that introduced and developed the concept most fully. Moreover, Maudemarie Clark has pointed out that the *Genealogy* holds paramount significance for Nietzsche's philosophy as a whole since it contains a critique of the earlier denial of truth. Its focus on values effectively represents the central strand of Nietzsche's contribution to modern thought: "Nietzsche's ultimate importance is connected to what he has to say about values, especially to the challenge he offers to received values."[18] The concept of the "blond beast," then, in its rootedness in the *Genealogy*, may be considered to represent one of those crucial Ariadne threads that are indispensable as guidance in leading through the Dionysian multiplicity of perspectives in Nietzsche's textual labyrinth.[19] And it was this thread that London used to unravel the Nietzschean pattern.[20]

III

In his examination of the literary and political genealogy of the "blonde Bestie," Detlef Brennecke shows that the term's syncretism of man and animal was constitutive for its serving as a symbol of the *Übermensch*. In typically Nietzschean manner, the concept combines a set of contrary associations. Its blondness refers to the lion and thus alludes to genuine predatory strength, but also connotes the lion's function as a traditional feudal emblem. Its blondness further suggests the barbarian, specifically the primitive Teuton as conceived by classical sources. Within the discourse on race in the nineteenth century, however, blondness came to signify Aryan superiority. In both instances, then, for man and animal, regression and inferiority as well as progress and superiority are intricately related. Brennecke discerns the same admixture in the *Nachlaß* where Nietzsche alludes to the future higher types as the "new barbarians," who fuse physical with intellectual power. Nietzsche defines these new blond beasts, the true embodiments of his will to power, as Promethean figures.[21]

Against its surface simplicity, the concept of the "blond beast" is highly complex and congenially represents Nietzsche's equally intricate investigation of the origins of values in the *Genealogy*. Its arguments are similarly proposed in a complicated set of paradoxes that link Nietzsche's poetic acuity and aphoristic suggestiveness with the "essential vagueness" and unsystematic mode of his writings.[22]

The "naturalistic" conception of nature that Theodore R. Schatzki posits at the core of Nietzsche's philosophy also grounds the proceeding in the *Genealogy*: its search for new value judgments finds its foremost justification in overcoming the morals that inform the unhealthy, degenerating tendencies of nineteenth-century Christian asceticism. Nietzsche's philosophy proposes a regeneration by suggesting a life according to nature or, as Zarathustra admonishes, by remaining "faithful to the earth" (*ZA*, 42).[23] When examined critically, however, Nietzsche's concept of nature reveals a crucial contradiction. He claims to represent nature truthfully as a world of experience untainted by moral concepts, yet in his descriptions he relies on an evaluative evolutionary scale that limits the diverse forms of nature to signify almost exclusively violence, struggle, and domination.[24]

Against the claim that "the world is so is simply fact, in itself neither good nor bad, and a naturalistic viewpoint dictates that it be accepted as such,"[25] Nietzsche's image of nature is markedly shaped by androcentric preconceptions. He superimposes a hierarchical structure on the various modes of existence and redefines natural diversity to signify high and low, superior and inferior, progressive and regressive forms in the development of life. In addition, Nietzsche's concept of animal life as the will to and struggle for power also projects the *bellum omnium contra omnes* of industrial capitalism onto nature.

The discourse of nature in the *Genealogy* generally mirrors such a conflicting design. Nietzsche transfers biological patterns to the realm of morals and conceives of the development of value judgments as a battle between a master and a slave morality: "'Good and evil' have been engaged in a fearful struggle on earth for thousands of years" (*GM*, 52). For Nietzsche, the master morality contains the positive ideal which will prove helpful in the transvaluation of values. Its noblemen freely and actively create values out of themselves in full consciousness of their innate superiority (*GM*, 26). In contrast, the slave morality embodies the evil resentment of the physically weak and unhealthy (*GM*, 32). In a dialectic move, Nietzsche argues that in the course of history the mass of the lowly and degenerate proved victorious and that through them the life-denying, ascetic ideal came to dominate. If the forces of resentment are thus responsible for the creation of culture and for man's having become "an interesting animal" (*GM*, 33), they are also blamed for inducing the bad conscience, furthering oppressive instincts, and giving man an "evil" soul (*GM*, 33). The "instruments of culture" represent the "*regression* of mankind" (*GM*, 43) and are a "disgrace to man and rather an accusation and counterargument against 'culture' in general" (*GM*, 43).

Following Darwin's non-teleological thrust, Nietzsche, too, shows that evolution does not necessarily help the fittest to survive.[26] At the same time, he reaffirms the basic poles of an evolutionary teleology by arguing that it is the distinction of higher types to serve as "a genuine battleground" (*GM*, 52) for the continuing struggle of the two moralities. Nietzsche thus reasserts the validity of the distinctions between progress and regression, high and low, superior and inferior. It is here that true nature, as confirmed by the higher types, is enhanced as a spiritual ideal. Yet the *Genealogy* does not elaborate further on its contents: there is, as Arthur C. Danto has generally criticized, an "indefiniteness and vagueness"[27] about Nietzsche's positive values.

Indicatively, in the most explicit definition of the perfect aristocrat's "typical character trait," all Nietzsche has to say is that he "signifies one who *is*, who possesses reality, who is actual, who is true" (*GM*, 29).[28] Since the more whole human beings are the "more whole beasts" (*BGE*, 257) for Nietzsche, the blond beasts in the *Genealogy* assume an exemplary quality. Their model of grounding values will prove also helpful to future higher types, as Nietzsche explains in a section of the *Nachlaß*: "I point at something new: certainly, for a . . . democratic state there is the danger of the barbarian, but one usually searches for them in the lower regions. There is also a *different kind of barbarian*, descending from the top: conquering and dominating types who are looking for matter that they may mold."[29]

The term "blond beast" is characteristically introduced in the *Genealogy* at a point where Nietzsche argues the necessity of the good men's reinvigoration through an atavistic return to nature:

> One cannot fail to see at the bottom of all these noble races the beast of prey, the splendid *blond beast* prowling about avidly in search of spoil and victory; this hidden core needs to erupt from time to time, the animal has to get out again and go back to the wilderness . . . . (*GM*, 40f)

Elsewhere, too, strength and an overflowing physicality form the basis for the noble types. They are the "rounded men replete with energy and therefore *necessarily* active" (*GM*, 38) and their knightly-aristocratic value judgments presuppose "a powerful physicality, a flourishing, abundant, even overflowing health, together with that which serves to preserve it: war, adventure, hunting, dancing, war games, and in general all that involves vigorous, free, joyful activity" (*GM*, 33). Their urge for domination and destruction is justified with the necessity that exists in the animal realm:

> That lambs dislike great birds of prey does not seem strange: only it gives no ground for reproaching these birds of prey for bearing off little lambs. And if the lambs say among themselves: "these birds of prey are evil; and whoever is least like a bird of prey, but rather its opposite, a lamb — would he not be good?" there is no reason to

find fault with this institution of an ideal, except perhaps that the birds of prey might view it a little ironically and say: "we don't dislike them at all, these good little lambs; we even love them: nothing is more tasty than tender lamb." (*GM*, 45)

Consequently, one cannot demand of strength that "it should not express itself as strength, that it should *not* be a desire to overcome, a desire to throw down, a desire to become master, a thirst for enemies and resistances and triumphs" (*GM*, 45). For Nietzsche, this "is just as absurd as to demand of weakness that it should express itself as strength" (*GM*, 45). The roles of master and slave are determined by disinterested natural laws. The life that is "will to power" cannot be denied or changed. Yet the forces of resentment "maintain no belief more ardently than the belief that *the strong man is free* to be weak and the bird of prey to be a lamb — for thus they gain the right to make the bird of prey *accountable* for being a bird of prey" (*GM*, 45). The symbol of the "blond beast" in the *Genealogy* thus signifies a strategy to ground values in instinctual urges and physiological endowments. Overall, it embodies Nietzsche's paradigm of a progressive regression, of an atavistic ascent that returns in its most abstract form in the concept of an eternal recurrence in which the end is the beginning and the lowest the highest.[30] Clearly, the naturalist reading of the "blond beast" is at the opposite end of Kaufmann's interpretation of the concept. From this perspective, it is not primarily a symbol for the low "unsublimated animal passion" that man needs to overcome.[31]

The *Genealogy* is thoroughly embedded in a naturalistic discourse of nature. Granted, Nietzsche redefined the biologist paradigm to suit his particular purposes, even to the degree of fusing strands from the antipodes Darwin and Lamarck.[32] Yet he did not depart from the evolutionary paradigm in principle.[33] His philosophy privileges a view of nature that exclusively emphasizes competition over cooperation and that primarily focuses on hierarchical over non-hierarchical patterns of organization in nature. Not surprisingly, Nietzsche selects the idiosyncratic behavior of birds of prey in the *Genealogy* to make his general claim about the animating force in nature's becoming. It is then not his knowledge of beasts of prey that could be challenged, but the fact that his view generalizes one specific trait to represent an open totality of diverse forms of life.

IV

The discourse of nature in the *Genealogy* could not but strike a chord of recognition in Jack London. Nietzsche's teachings confirmed the ideas London had gained by studying Darwin, Spencer, Huxley, and other evolutionists. From the beginning, however, London also took a critical stance towards Nietzsche's philosophy as a whole. He told a friend, "Personally I like Nietzsche tremendously, but I cannot go all the way with him."[34]

Due to London's split attitude, partly accepting, partly rejecting Nietzsche's philosophy, it is difficult to assess his presentation of the philosopher's ideas properly. Also, London as novelist is not primarily interested in a comprehensive refutation of Nietzsche's philosophical system, but in creatively appropriating ideas that suit his fictional projects. London's approach is most concisely captured in a response to Strawn-Hamilton, who accused him of misrepresenting Nietzsche: "Where Nietzsche travels my road, he's a good companion. Where I would have to turn around because of him, I simply do not. I go on and leave him behind."[35] Two distinct patterns recur in London's use of Nietzsche. First, he fully sides with Nietzsche's criticism of life-denying and hypocritical bourgeois morals and he adopts his pattern of a progressive regression as a strategy to ground new values. Second, he criticizes Nietzsche for assuming an individualistic "will to power" as the fundamental animating force in nature in contrast to his own belief that the evolutionary development was towards altruism, cooperation, and collectivism.[36] The first two texts that deal with Nietzsche's ideas, *The Call of the Wild* and "How I Became a Socialist," develop this paradigmatic response. They prefigure later treatments in *The Sea-Wolf*, *The Iron Heel*, and *Martin Eden*.

In describing an atavistic process of education, London's *The Call of the Wild* takes its central theme from Nietzsche's *Genealogy*. In enemy territory, Nietzsche explains,

> . . . they [the good men] savor a freedom from all social constraints, they compensate themselves in the wilderness for the tension engendered by protracted confinement and enclosure within the peace of society, they go back to the innocent conscience of the beast of prey, as triumphant monsters who perhaps emerge from a disgusting procession of murder, arson, rape, and torture, exhila-

rated and undisturbed of soul, as if it were no more than a student's's prank, convinced that they have provided the poets with a lot more material for song and praise. (*GM*, 40)

The Call of the Wild successfully translates the constitutive Nietzschean syncretism between man and animal into fictional form: the dog story combines the realism in figures and setting with the anthropomorphic and didactic tendencies of a beast fable. While generally praising the story's pathbreaking naturalism, critics also noted that the dogs are conceived as "men dressed in furs."[37]

The narrative presents the necessity to go back to more natural forms of life through a series of geographical, cultural, and moral dislocations. The story significantly opens with an aesthetic dislocation: "Buck did not read the newspaper, or he would have known that trouble was brewing, not alone for himself, but for every tidewater dog, strong of muscle and with warm, long hair, from Puget Sound to San Diego" (*CW*, 9). The initial uncertainty and ambiguity whether Buck is man or animal, disrupts conventionalized forms of perception in a manner not unlike Kafka's introduction of the beetle Gregor Samsa in his "Metamorphosis." London, however, uses his ploy to identify readers more closely with the perspective of his dog figure and to throw light on the limited possibilities of domesticating a wild species. Yet the underlying link with human capacities also heightens the readers' interest in Buck's subsequent re-education.[38]

The second dislocation in *The Call of the Wild* is both geographical and cultural: Buck has to learn to survive in a hostile environment. At the outset, the Southland Buck is depicted as a pampered ruler who lives the life of "a sated aristocrat" (*CW*, 10). Buck's forced relocation, however, unearths his original instincts. He regains his true aristocratic stature by proving his superiority under wilderness conditions. The most significant dislocation is then a moral one: Buck has to learn that in the Northland "the law of club and fang" (*CW*, 19) rules relentlessly. Against the Spencerian evolutionary ascent thesis, the narrative symbolically projects a successful progressive regression.[39] Buck's genuine cleverness, the awakening of the "primordial beast" (*CW*, 27) in him, and generally his qualities as a superdog make him represent symbolically the atavistic path for future higher types.

Ultimately, however, *The Call of the Wild* reveals a telling departure from Nietzsche's design when the story proceeds beyond the stage at which Buck becomes a dominating overdog. His learning process also encompasses the experience of companionship and love in his days with John Thornton. Eventually, he reaches his highest destination:

> When the long winter nights come on and the wolves follow their meat into the lower valleys, he may be seen running at the head of the pack through the pale moonlight or glimmering borealis, leaping gigantic above his fellows, his great throat a-bellow as he sings a song of the pack. (*CW*, 87)

Buck's true nobility thus finds its congenial expression in and through the collective. In London's typically idiosyncratic manner, the proto-socialist tale fuses Marx and Spencer in order to transcend Nietzsche. Not individualism, but cooperation, altruism, and collectivism constitute the root and goal of evolution for London.[40]

"How I Became a Socialist" adds another dimension to the pattern developed in the dog story. Like the *Genealogy* and *The Call of the Wild*, the essay focuses on the process of an education in the form of London's retrospective account of his conversion from individualism to socialism.[41] London is a rampant Nietzschean egoist in the beginning: he conceives of himself as one of "Nature's strong-armed noblemen," loves to lead a "life in the open," and sings "the paen of the strong" (*HS*, 363) with all his heart. Like Nietzsche's noble types, he is not crippled by a morality of pity in his adventurous forays: "I could see myself only raging through life without end like one of Nietzsche's *blond beasts*, lustfully roving and conquering by sheer superiority and strength" (*HS*, 363).

As in Buck's case, a crucial geographic dislocation initiates the conversion. A "new *blond-beast* adventure" has London move from the "open West" to the "congested labor centres of the East," only to find himself looking on life "from a new and totally different angle" (*HS*, 363f.). Nietzschean individualism falters under the changed conditions of modernity:

> I found there [in the East] all sorts of men, many of whom had once been as good as myself and just as *blond-beastly*; sailor-men, soldier-men, labor-men, all wrenched and distorted and twisted out of shape by toil and hardship and accident, and cast adrift by their masters like so many old horses. (*HS*, 364)

The date and circumstance of London's autobiographical experiences add further importance to his narrative of conversion. It was the severe economic crisis of 1893/94 that produced Jacob Coxey's industrial army and that made London and others want to join Coxey's Western contingent in its eastward trek. In a sense, London creates the collective march as his symbol for the vanishing of the frontier that the Census Bureau had officially announced closed in 1890 and that Frederick Jackson Turner had lifted to the status of a national myth in his 1893 Columbian Exposition lecture. Moreover, with the replacement of the "open West" by the "Social Pit" (*HS*, 364) of the East, the very American wilderness is obliterated that had rendered Emerson's philosophy of nature such an important influence on Nietzsche's thought. London's challenge to Emerson's Oversoul and to Nietzsche's Overman thus occurs at the very historical moment when the conditions that had originally nurtured these individualist philosophies ceased to exist.

London's criticism of Nietzsche in "How I Became a Socialist" is twofold. Far from being "very natural," the "rampant individualism" (*HS*, 362) proves inappropriate in modernity. On another occasion, London asserted that "the superman is anti-social in his tendencies, and in these days of our complex society and sociology he cannot be successful in his hostile aloofness."[42] Next, the essay challenges Nietzsche's conservative anthropology of natural masters and slaves. For London, the hierarchy is not unalterably given by birth, but springs from historical and economic conditions.

In *The Sea-Wolf*, London's creative dialogue with Nietzsche finds its most elaborate form.[43] Resuming the above patterns, the novel assigns the various philosophical strands to different figures in the narrative. Critics who identify the Nietzschean element solely with Wolf Larsen — be it as an accurate portrait, be it as a caricaturist misconception — miss the underlying design. *The Sea-Wolf*, too, projects an educational process that develops in a series of dislocations. Like Buck, Humphrey Van Weyden, a complacent "temperamental idealist" (*SW*, 74), finds himself thrown into the hostile environment on Wolf Larsen's *Ghost*.[44] The wreck of the "new ferry-steamer" in the beginning of *The Sea-Wolf* foregrounds the Nietzschean theme of the fragility of the modern world. The collision of ships robs Van Weyden of several certainties: his habitualized ferry trip on "a safe craft" (*SW*, 1) results in disaster and gives his life a totally new direction; the accident shatters his belief in the accuracy of science whose workings formerly seemed "as simple as ABC" (*SW*, 2), and the fear of the drowning women who scream "like rats in a trap" (*SW*, 6) discloses to him the true core of civilized sublimity.

The collision has Van Weyden symbolically undergo death and rebirth: after the accident "a blankness intervened" and he finds himself "swinging in a mighty rhythm through orbit vastness" (*SW*, 10). He then regains consciousness on "a little floating world" that represents a primordial microcosm devoid of morals: "Force, nothing but force, obtained on this brute-ship. Moral suasion was a thing unknown" (*SW*, 40). The voyage closely follows Nietzsche's sea and ship imagery for the "long sickness" that accompanies the transvaluation of values. The *Ghost*, too, is a "ship far removed from the security of land, tossed about on stormy and unchartered seas."[45] Its miniature world is dominated by Wolf Larsen, a "great big beast": "He was a magnificent atavism, a man so primitive that he was of the type that came into the world before the development of moral nature" (*SW*, 87). London turns Larsen into a Promethean barbarian, who holds "the schooner to the course of his will, himself an earthgod, dominating the storm, flinging its descending waters from him and riding it to his own ends" (*SW*, 148).

Van Weyden's education on the *Ghost* reenacts the *Genealogy's* central conflict between altruism and egoism. In Larsen's violent and physical repudiations of the morality of pity, Weyden encounters a heretofore unknown "world of the real" (*SW*, 138). In laying bare the bestial instincts in man, the experiences surpass Charley Furuseth's mere "brutality of the intellect" (*SW*, 106) and hence the very attitude identified with the "be-pillowed" (*SW*, 38) Nietzschean intellectual who is said to lie at the "cause of it all" (*SW*, 1). The idealist Van Weyden thus first is regenerated through the primitive "carnival of brutality" aboard the *Ghost*, but eventually manages to dominate this world. His transvalued ideals prove superior to the meaningless Nietzscheanism of Larsen:

> Why is it that you have not done great things in this world? With the power that is yours you might have risen to any height. Unpossessed of moral instinct, you might have mastered the world .... And yet here you are at the top of your life ... living an obscure and sordid existence .... Why have you not done something? (*SW*, 87f.)

London's rejection of Nietzsche's individualism also surfaces on another level. In depicting Larsen's decay in the form of progressive
paralysis, London selects "the supposed cause and symptoms of the
collapse of Friedrich Nietzsche."[46] On the whole, London's response
remains ambiguous. Although altruism wins in the end, the
"survivors survive only in terms of Larsen's ethics."[47]

The novel's oft-criticized second half provides the ultimate
touches in Van Weyden's progressive regression. With the appearance of Maud Brewster, the narrative's representation of the regenerating power of love, Van Weyden is fully transformed. Her
presence causes the effeminate "Sissy" Van Weyden, who initially
"behaves like a woman" (SW, 6), to assume his natural role: "I shall
never forget, in that moment, how insistently conscious I became of
my manhood. The primitive deeps of my nature stirred. I felt myself
masculine, the protector of the weak, the fighting male" (SW, 255).
For many critics, the second part fails because the love relationship
between Humphrey Van Weyden and Maud Brewster seems super-
imposed and hollow. In a sense, the next novels continue to show
similar problems in London's attempts to challenge Nietzsche's individualism with believable alternatives and in artistically viable
forms.

The Iron Heel and Martin Eden are variations on the above dia-
logues with Nietzschean themes. The Iron Heel recasts the Genealogy's struggle between altruism and egoism in the form of a utopian
novel. Its hero Ernest Everhard, whose telling name indicates his
closeness to Nietzsche's will to power, successfully fights an oligarchy
of industrialists. He is a Nietzschean character with a difference,
however, since he is also "aflame with democracy" (IH, 7). His
movement will eventually succeed in the future, leaving behind
Nietzsche's antediluvian positions. Yet, the world depicted in the
novel is so bleak that the narrative's dystopian despair overshadows
by far the socialist optimism provided by the fictive editor's annota-
tions.

Martin Eden records a further stage in London's political disillusionment. In the novel, both the Nietzschean individualist Eden and
the socialist poet Brissenden signal despair and defeat by committing
suicide. Nietzsche's stance again is partly celebrated:

Nietzsche was right . . . . The world belongs to the strong — to the
strong who are noble as well and who do not wallow in the swine-

trough of trade and exchange. The world belongs to the great
blond beasts, to the non-compromisers, to the yes-sayers. (*ME*,
322)

Ultimately, however, Martin Eden fails, as London explained,
"because he was an individualist . . . of the extreme Nietzschean
type. I live because I am a socialist and have a social consciousness."[48]

London's reaction to Nietzsche in his fiction is thus an ambiva-
lently complex one. Judging from the above evidence, there can be
no definitive answer to the accuracy of London's appropriation of
Nietzschean thought. His interpretation of the "blond beast," however, clearly is in tune with a dominant line of argumentation in
Nietzsche's philosophy and cannot be downgraded as "one-sided
and incomplete."[49] But since his intentions also are to challenge
Nietzschean ideas in his novels, London at times presents details in
partisan fashion and plays down possible justifications for what he
sees as Nietzsche's individualist ethics. From today's perspective,
more important than the question of the ultimate coherence of London's reception is an examination of the mutual bias in the two
authors' decidedly masculinist representations of nature and the relevance of such a partial assessment for their criticisms of modern society.

V

The androcentric slant in Nietzsche's and London's writings does
not come as a great surprise and indeed has repeatedly been noted.
Both writers resume the bias of the Darwinistic paradigm that Carolyn Merchant has characterized most succinctly:

> In the nineteenth century, Darwinian theory was found to hold
> social implications for women. Variability, the basis for evolutionary
> progress, was correlated with a greater spread of physical and men-
> tal variations in males. Scientists compared male and female cranial
> sizes and brain parts in the effort to demonstrate the existence of
> sexual differences that would explain female intellectual inferiority
> and emotional temperament. Women's reproductive function re-
> quired that more energy be directed toward pregnancy and ma-
> ternity, hence less was available for the higher functions associated
> with learning and reasoning. The 'adventurous sperm' and the
> 'passive ovum' continued to serve as reproductive metaphors.[50]

Nietzsche uses similarly loaded oppositions, assigning activity and passivity, competition and cooperation, primary and secondary status to man and woman. Nietzsche's "blond beast," for example, clearly privileges 'Man the Hunter' over 'Woman the Gatherer' as a creator of values. In this, he closely follows the traditional dichotomy of culture and nature that Sherry Ortner describes for patriarchal societies.[51] Nietzsche's apparent elevation of women in the metaphor of the vita femina occurs within this context. Indeed, in comparison with men, women's nature shows in their "instinct for a secondary role" (*BGE*, 89).[52] By privileging active, competitive, and aggressive forms of life, women are devalued by their very passivity: "Woman wants to be taken and accepted as a possession, wants to be absorbed into the concept of possession, possessed" (*GS*, 363). The feminist project of emancipation must fail since it de-naturalizes woman; consequently, Nietzsche condemns the suffragettes' fight for equal rights "as a symptom of sickness" (*EH*, 76). Women best fulfill their assigned natural roles by focusing on reproduction. In Greek civilization, Nietzsche claims, "women had no other task than to bring forth handsome, powerful bodies in which the character of the father lived on as uninterruptedly as possible" (*HH*, 122).

Those forms of nature that are not in tune with Nietzsche's masculinist "will to power" are marginalized. Ultimately, the deprecation of women results in their exclusion from the processes that generate cultural values. Women are virtually absent in the *Genealogy*, and the creation of meaning is described as a "Herr-werden," a "becoming master" (*GM*, 77). In a way, Nietzsche's autonomous noblemen but follow the old patriarchal pattern in which "men have been free to imagine themselves as self-defining only because women held the intimate social world together."[53] Moreover, as Jorgen Kjaer has pointed out, parts of Nietzsche's philosophy contain an attempt to replace female reproduction with the generative principle of eternal recurrence.[54]

Jack London resumes the androcentric discourses of Darwin, Spencer, and Nietzsche without substantial alterations. For him, too, there is a higher law that denies women the right to vote.[55] Although London develops a concept of "new womanhood," in which an active female mate acquires all the qualities of the male model, the emancipated woman primarily serves to procreate and perpetuate the superior racial stock of the group.[56]

Since both men's discourses of nature stress bio-physiological criteria, it is not surprising that the concept of race assumes paramount significance for them to explain social cohesion and cultural training. Yet, as Henry Louis Gates has pointed out, race "as a meaningful criterion within the biological sciences, has long been recognized to be a fiction."[57] Clearly, Nietzsche's concept of the "blond beast" is related to such biological misnomers and metaphors of his day.[58] His philosophy incorporates physiological theories and provocatively attributes importance to racial features: the *Genealogy* contains a host of arguments concerning blood or the shape and size of skulls (*GM*, 30).[59]

Again, London does not find fault with this subtext in Nietzsche's thinking. Rather, he repeatedly espouses Anglo-Saxon racial supremacy. Indeed, his concept of socialism is closely tied to such chauvinistic notions: "Socialism is not an ideal system, devised by man for the happiness of all life; nor for the happiness of all men; but it is devised for the happiness of certain kindred races."[60]

To assess the above positions on race and gender properly, the statements clearly should be set in relation to their historical context. Conversely, their extreme androcentric leanings should be kept in mind when assessing London's and Nietzsche's views and their significance for modernity. In recent years, both authors have again been linked to updated biologist models. London was seen as a literary precursor of E. O. Wilson's sociobiology and Nietzsche was claimed both as a part sociobiologist and as an anticipator of a constructivist and cybernetic view of nature.[61]

It is important to note for assessments of the new Nietzsche that there is a striking parallel in his arguments about nature and language. Nietzsche's creatively 'contagious' impulse for postmodern thought largely stems from his central idea that notions of order or essence are fallacies engendered by the structure of our language that suggests stability where there is none. Atoms, subjects, and moral concepts are all subjective, interested projections rather than definitive entities or timeless principles. Nietzsche's own discourse, however, falls victim to a similar linguistic fallacy.[62] He himself deduces his denial of truth from the structure of language: his "overarching metaphor"[63] is that the world is an open text to be interpreted endlessly. He thus suggests a metaphysical instability that is disproved by his own proceeding. George J. Stack, for instance, argues convincingly that evidence from biological science is one of the primary sources for Nietzsche's belief in the perspectival optics of life.[64] His reliance on a stable, science-based "will to power" that aspires, in Richard Rorty's words, to get "beyond all perspectives,"[65] may be used as a further proof that any philosophical system, even one that assumes a Heraclitean form of eternal becoming, inevitably needs certain fixed points of reference. Nietzsche's "will to power," as an organic urge to conquer and master, is based on remnants of metaphysical assumptions in evolutionary theory. In mystifying crucial tenets as natural, Nietzsche asserts an essentialism that fails to develop a new mode in the grounding of values.[66]

From today's vantage point, then, both London's and Nietzsche's naturalist ontologies openly disclose their historicity. If some of their assumptions appear dated, it is to be recalled that it was their fictional and philosophical models that furthered the knowledge of the relational character of the modern world. The aporia in London's and Nietzsche's discourses of nature thus is intricately linked to a seemingly unresolvable dilemma in anti-metaphysical, modernist modes of thinking. The transcendence of metaphysical claims ineluctably involves metaphysical foundations, if only on a heuristic level. The solution to this problem that looms large in the ongoing discussions about the project of modernity, lies, to paraphrase Nietzsche, beyond good and evil, beyond the answers that London's and Nietzsche's writings could provide. Yet as early signposts towards a genealogy of modernity, their naturalist and postmodernist contributions cannot be overlooked and certainly deserve close attention.

Notes

[1] References to Jack London's and Friedrich Nietzsche's works are as follows: *HS* - "How I Became a Socialist" (1903), *Jack London: American Rebel*, ed. Philip S. Foner (New York, 1947), pp. 362–65; *CW - The Call of the Wild by Jack London*, ed. Earl J. Wilcox (Chicago, 1980); *SW - The Sea-Wolf* (New York, 1904); *IH - The Iron Heel* (New York, 1908); *ME - Martin Eden* (New York, 1909); *GM - On the Genealogy of Morals*, trans. Walter Kaufmann and R. J. Hollingdale (New York, 1967); *GS - The Gay Science*, trans. Walter Kaufmann (New York, 1974); *BGE - Beyond Good and Evil*, trans. Walter Kaufmann (New York, 1966); *ZA - Thus Spoke Zarathustra*, trans. R. J. Hollingdale (Harmondsworth, 1961); *EH - Ecce Homo*, trans. R. J. Hollingdale (Harmondsworth, 1979); *HH - Human, All Too Human*, trans. R. J. Hollingdale (Cambridge, 1986).

[2] This study has profited greatly from the pioneer work done by LeRoy Culbertson Kauffmann, "The Influence of Friedrich Nietzsche on American Literature" (Diss. U. of Pennsylvania, 1963); Melvin Drimmer, "Nietzsche in American Thought, 1895–1925" (Diss. U. of Rochester, 1965); Patrick Bridgwater, *Nietzsche in Anglosaxony* (Leicester, 1972); Michael Dunford, "Further Notes on Jack London's Introduction to the Philosophy of Friedrich Nietzsche," *Jack London Newsletter*, 10 (1977), 39–42; Katherine M. Littell, "The 'Nietzschean' and the Individualist in Jack London's Socialist Writings," *Amerikastudien*, 22 (1977), 309–23; and John E. Martin; "Martin Eden, a London Superman Adventurer: A Case Study of the Americanization of European Ideology," *Die amerikanische Literatur in der Weltliteratur: Themen und Aspekte*, eds. C. Uhlig and V. Bischoff (Berlin, 1982), pp. 218–30.

[3] London quoted in Bridgwater, p. 169.

[4] For a discussion of the significance of the novel's multiple perspectives, see Wolfgang Karrer, "Jack London: *The Iron Heel* (1908)," *Die Utopie in der angloamerikanischen Literatur*, eds. Hartmut Heuermann and Bernd-Peter Lange (Düsseldorf, 1984), pp. 176–95.

[5] For the most recent discussion of Nietzsche's "naturalistic" view of nature, see Theodore R. Schatzki, "Ancient and Naturalistic Themes in Nietzsche's Ethics," *Nietzsche-Studien*, 23 (1994), 146–67.

[6] London's early familiarity with Nietzsche in 1898 was only established at a comparatively late date. Charles Walcutt's influential study on naturalism, for example, does not yet discuss *The Call of the Wild* or *The Sea-Wolf* as Nietzschean documents because the initial encounter was assumed to have occurred as late as 1905. Even Patrick Bridgwater's pioneer study *Nietzsche in Anglosaxony* still suggests 1903 as a conjectural date.

[7] The discussion about London's attitude towards Nietzsche followed a cliche that has generally obscured London's work. As J. Tavernier-Courbin has pointed out, London is seen devoid of sophistication and hence has often been taken literally, a prominent example being his treatment of philosophical matters: "Did he portray a Nietzschean hero, it was concluded that he concurred with Nietzsche's theories." Jacqueline Tavernier-Courbin, "Jack London: A Professional," *Critical Essays on Jack London* (Boston, 1983), p. 4.

[8] Dunford conjectures that London, in the first phase, was familiar with W. Haussmann's 1897 version of Nietzsche's *Genealogy* since his characterization of the blond beast has "a striking similarity" with the words used in the translation. See Dunford, p. 40; Drimmer, p. 369.

[9] Schatzki, p. 154.

[10] Schatzki, p. 147. For a discussion of the ongoing debate, cf. also Dieter Henke, "Nietzsches Darwinismuskritik aus der Sicht gegenwärtiger Evolutionsforschung," *Nietzsche-Studien*, 13 (1984), 189–210; Werner Stegmaier, "Darwin, Darwinismus, Nietzsche: Zum Problem der Evolution," *Nietzsche-*

Studien, 16 (1987), 264–87; and George J. Stack, "Kant, Lange, Nietzsche: Critique of Knowledge," *Nietzsche and Modern German Thought*, ed. Keith Ansell-Pearson (London/New York, 1991), pp. 30–58.

[11] Detlef Brennecke, "Die Blonde Bestie: Vom Mißverständnis eines Schlagworts," *Nietzsche-Studien*, 5 (1976), pp. 128ff.

[12] Among early critics, Lewis Mumford set the pattern with his harsh repudiation: "The career of the Superman in America is an instructive spectacle. He sprang, this overman, out of the pages of Emerson . . . caught up by Nietzsche, and colored by the dark natural theology Darwin had inherited from Malthus, the Superman became the highest possibility of natural selection: he served as a symbol of contrast with the . . . 'slave morality' of Christianity. The point to notice is that in both Emerson and Nietzsche the Superman is a higher type . . . London . . . seized the suggestion of the Superman and attempted to turn it into a reality. . . . In short, London's Superman was little more than the infantile dream of the messenger boy or the barroom tough or the nice, respectable clerk whose muscles will never quite stand up under strain. He was the social platitude of the Old West, translated into literary epigram." Lewis Mumford quoted in Bridgwater, p. 166.

[13] Bridgwater, p. 165.

[14] Maudemarie Clark, *Nietzsche on Truth and Philosophy* (New York, 1990), pp. 5f.

[15] Walter Kaufmann, *Nietzsche: Philosopher, Psychologist, Antichrist* (Princeton, 1968), p. 8.

[16] All references in this paragraph are to Littell, pp. 318f.

[17] Kaufmann's respectively Littell's assessment is used, for instance, by Martin, pp. 218–230, and Carolyn Johnston, *Jack London: An American Radical?* (Westport, Conn., 1984), p. 81.

[18] Clark, pp. 3, 103.

[19] Alan D. Schrift, *Nietzsche and the Question of Interpretation: Between Hermeneutics and Deconstruction* (London/New York, 1990), pp. 189, 197f.

[20] The term "blond beast" has developed a significance of its own apart from Nietzsche's initial intention and London's adaptation. For a discussion of this political controversy, see Brennecke, pp. 113–45.

[21] Brennecke, pp. 128f.; *Friedrich Nietzsche: Werke*, ed. K. Schlechta (München, 1956), III, p. 846.

[22] Arthur C. Danto, "Nietzsche," *A Critical History of Western Philosophy*, ed. D. J. O'Connor (London, 1964), p. 397; Schatzki, p. 150. Heidrun Hesse recently reasserted that the *Genealogy* does not develop a coherent system of conclusive arguments: "Von Lämmern und Raubvögeln: Randbemerkungen zu Nietzsches 'Genealogie der Moral,'" *Deutsche Zeitschrift für Philosophie*, 41 (1993), 895–904.

[23] Schatzki explains: "He demanded that people abandon evaluative perspectives that appeal to non-natural phenomena and himself employed the bio-physiological nature of human life as the ground for appraising values and practices" (p. 151).

[24] Schatzki describes and analyzes Nietzsche's naturalist positions, but does not criticize the bias in his gendered discourse. *Ibid.*, p. 152.

[25] *Ibid*, p. 152.

[26] Stegmaier, p. 281.

[27] Danto, p. 397.

[28] All the while, Nietzsche is unequivocal in suggesting the type of authenticity he demands: "Nietzsche's distinction between slave and noble morality was based on physiological considerations, as were his correlative divisions between strong and weak, ascending and descending, and healthy and unhealthy forms of life" (Schatzki, p. 148).

[29] The original reads: "Ich zeige auf etwas Neues hin: gewiß, für ein . . . demokratisches Wesen gibt es die Gefahr des Barbaren, aber man sucht sie nur in der Tiefe. Es gibt auch eine *andere Art Barbaren,* die kommen aus der Höhe: eine Art von erobernden und herrschenden Naturen, welche nach einem Stoff suchen, den sie gestalten können." Schlechta, III, p. 846.

[30] Brennecke, p. 128

[31] Kaufmann, p. 225.

[32] Schatzki, p. 148. In contradistinction to Darwin, Nietzsche claimed that affluence and not scarcity is the rule in nature and that the struggle for existence is "only an *exception,* a temporary restriction of the will to life. The great and small struggle always revolves around superiority, around growth and expansion, around power — in accordance with the will to power which is the will to life" (*GS,* 292).

[33] Stegmaier, p. 269.

[34] London quoted in Bridgwater, p. 165.

[35] London quoted in Johnston, p. 80.

[36] Jack London, "What Communities Lose by the Competitive System" (1900), *Jack London: American Rebel,* pp. 419–30.

[37] John Perry, *Jack London: An American Myth* (Chicago, 1981), p. 138.

[38] The aesthetic dislocation is then continued throughout the story that "departs from traditional depictions of dogs in fiction at almost every point." James Lundquist, *Jack London: Adventures, Ideas, and Fiction* (New York, 1987), p. 107.

[39] Perry, p. 132. London's fascination with Nietzsche's positive atavism of the "blond beast" also surfaces in his obsession with dogs and wolves. Thus he

"signed his intimate letters 'Wolf,' named his mansion 'Wolf House,' owned a husky called 'Brown Wolf,' and had a wolf's head as a bookplate" (Lundquist, p. 97).

[40] London follows Herbert Spencer and Benjamin Kidd in arguing that for survival, cooperation is essential (Lundquist, pp. 115–140). The various strands of evolutionary theory in London's narratives cannot always be neatly separated because agreement and disagreement on basic positions lack clear lines of division. Thus the antipodes Spencer and Nietzsche both rely on Lamarckian elements in their Darwinian models. Their mutual privileging of individualism is rejected by London who follows the collective orientation in Marxist philosophy. Johnston, pp. 81ff; Andrew Sinclair, *Jack: A Biography of Jack London* (New York, 1977), pp. 32ff.

[41] While Nietzsche's concept of individualism certainly is the central concern of the essay, it also contains an attack on "orthodox bourgeois ethics" (*HS*, 363).

[42] London quoted in Lundquist, p. 128.

[43] For an assessment of the influence of Nietzsche's *Zarathustra* on the novel, see Forrest Winston Parkay, "The Influence of Nietzsche's *Thus Spoke Zarathustra* on London's *The Sea-Wolf*," *Jack London Newsletter*, 4 (1971), 16–24.

[44] For the extensive parallels between the two narratives, see Abraham Rothberg, "Land Dogs and Sea Wolves: A Jack London Dilemma," *Massachusetts Review*, 21 (1980), 569–93.

[45] Michael Qualtiere, "Nietzschean Psychology in London's The Sea-Wolf," *Western American Literature*, 16 (1982), p. 263.

[46] Qualtiere, p. 278.

[47] Rothberg, p. 591.

[48] London quoted in Drimmer, p. 399.

[49] Martin, p. 223.

[50] Carolyn Merchant, *The Death of Nature: Women, Ecology, and the Scientific Revolution* (San Francisco, 1980), pp. 162f.

[51] Sherry B. Ortner, "Is Female to Male as Nature Is to Culture?" *Woman, Culture, and Society*, eds. M. Z. Rosaldo and L. Lamphere (Stanford, 1974), pp. 67–87.

[52] For a discussion of Nietzsche's contradictory statements about woman, see also Gayle L. Ormiston, "Traces of Derrida: Nietzsche's Image of Woman," *Philosophy Today*, 28 (1984), 178–88.

[53] Naomi Scheman, "Individualism and the Objects of Psychology," *Discovering Realities*, eds. Sandra Harding and Merrill B. Hintikka (Boston, 1983), p. 240.

[54] Jorgen Kjaer, *Die Zerstörung der Humanität durch 'Mutterliebe'* (Opladen, 1990), pp. 273f. Nietzsche's apparent elevation of women in equating them with truth also assigns them to the insubstantial: truth, too, is an illusion.

55 Rothberg, p. 585.

56 Susan Marie Nuernberg, "The Call of Kind: Race in Jack London's Fiction" (Diss. U. of Massachusetts, 1990), pp. 229ff.

57 Henry Louis Gates, Jr., "Writing 'Race' and the Difference It Makes," 'Race,' Writing, and Difference (Chicago/London, 1985), p. 4.

58 It should be pointed out, however, that for the vocal anti-chauvinist Nietzsche, the Teutonic race is not privileged as the master race: he argues that blond beasts also existed among the Roman, Arabian, and Japanese nobility (GM, 41).

59 Nietzsche's remarks about guided selection and about rooting out the unhealthy are largely in keeping with Social Darwinist eugenics. Cf. Schatzki, pp. 150, 156.

60 Lundquist, pp. 116, 118.

61 Lundquist, p. 100; Lothar Jordan, "Nietzsche: Dekonstruktionist oder Konstruktivist?", Nietzsche-Studien, 23 (1994), 226–40. For a criticism of androcentric biologism, see Ruth Hubbard, "Have Only Men Evolved?", Discovering Realities, pp. 45–69.

62 See Lutz Ellrich, "Rhetorik und Metaphysik: Nietzsches ,neue' Schreibweise," Nietzsche-Studien, 23 (1994), 241–72.

63 Alexander Nehamas, Nietzsche: Life as Literature (Cambridge/London: Harvard UP, 1985), p. 164.

64 Stack, pp. 39f.

65 Richard Rorty, Contingency, Irony, and Solidarity (Cambridge: Cambridge UP, 1989), p. 106.

66 Cf. Theodore R. Schatzki, "Nietzsche's Wesensethik," Nietzsche-Studien, 20 (1991), 85.

Joseph C. Schöpp

Cowperwood's Will to Power: Dreiser's *Trilogy of Desire* in the Light of Nietzsche

THE NOTION OF power seems to be deeply inscribed in the matrix of American culture. From the days of Emerson down to the critical agendas that currently dominate American university discourse, this preoccupation with power and the empowerment of the individual has been a constant cultural concern. In his essay "Power" (1860), Emerson expresses unconcealed admiration for individuals of power. Fascinated by the "rough and ready style" of American tradesmen and politicians, he not only extols such reputed representatives of political power as Jefferson and Jackson but also the less refined Hoosier, Sucker, Wolverine or Badger types of Midwestern "rough riders" and "legislators in shirt sleeves." Since life for Emerson was basically "a search after power," the *"plus* man" invested with a "surcharge of arterial blood" and an "excess of virility" became a true object of his admiration as long as he controlled his rough energy and vigor and employed it for the common good. All *"plus* is good," Emerson argued, "only put it in the right place."[1]

Four decades later an equally prominent American of entirely different temperamental disposition painted a much darker picture of power. Strolling in the fairgrounds of the 1900 Great Paris Exposition, "aching to absorb knowledge, and helpless to find it," Henry Adams is haunted by a mysterious power, a "Primal Force" that threatens to annihilate the Emersonian ideal of the self-empowered *"plus* man." The power of the Virgin of Chartres, once regarded as the life-shaping and life-enhancing force of Western culture, he now sees undermined by the abstract energy of the Dynamo that, in his eyes, governs contemporary life. Whether it is a "Gentle Friend" or a

"Despotic Master" Adams, despite his anxious absorption of knowledge, is no longer able to determine. Due to his pessimistic temper, however, he is inclined to regard human beings as mere "atoms whirled apace,/Shaped and controlled" by this abstract primal force.[2] The Emersonian self-empowered "*plus* man" is now reduced, as it were, to a mere minus function. Once victorious "over his necessities," he has now become their victim.[3]

Theodore Dreiser seems to be caught between these two notions of power, which is not surprising for a writer who was indebted to both transcendentalist idealism and the darker philosophical reflections of Post-Emersonian America.[4] Revisiting Buffalo some twenty years after a previous visit, he witnesses the dramatic and irreversible changes in the "spirit of America," acknowledging to himself "that never again could [he] feel as [he] felt then." Once the city's "factories and high buildings and chimneys" had aroused in him feelings of awe and elation reminiscent of the at times similar feelings of his fictional characters vis-à-vis the urban grandeur of Chicago and New York. America was then "just entering on the vast, splendid, most lawless and most savage period in which the great financiers, now nearly all dead, were plotting and conniving the enslavement of the people and belaboring each other for power." And he concludes his reminiscence:

> Power, power, power — everyone was seeking power in the land of the free and the home of the brave. There was almost an angry dissatisfaction with inefficiency, or slowness, or age, or anything which did not tend directly to the accumulation of riches. The American world of that day wanted you to eat, sleep, and dream money and power.

Old Buffalo, a place of unprecedented and, as it seemed, limitless expansion in a period which Mark Twain and Charles Dudley Warner had termed the Gilded Age, twenty years later appears to be a different place, still a great "but hard and cold city." The possibilities for the individual now seem to be greatly reduced. The working people, once entirely absent from the scene, now enter the stage; "tired of the exactions of the money barons," they become rebellious and restless, and the elated rhetoric of the above passage suddenly changes its tone and gives way to more melancholy reflections.[5] The years when there was still room at the top, when dreams of self-empowering ambitions could still be realized seem to be over. For

Dreiser, the Gilded Age seems to have lost its thin veneer; "stratification, stagnation and rigidity" characterize the cultural climate of the 1910s.[6] Unlike Henry Adams, however, Dreiser is not inclined to prematurely abandon the notion of the empowered individual. Although some of the tycoons and financial buccaneers may have abused their power and may, at least in part, be held responsible for the cultural malaise of the country, although "artistically, intellectually, philosophically" Americans may be regarded as "weaklings," they are "financially and in all ways commercial" still to be seen as "very powerful."[7] In order to successfully retain this notion of power, Dreiser had to redefine it; he had to bridge the chasm between the spheres of art-intellect-philosophy on the one hand and the realm of finance on the other. To an artist "whose boyhood in Indiana had been characterized by physical poverty, religious bigotry, and aesthetic malnutrition," as Walter Blackstock argues, the idea of the powerful individual that was able to reconcile and incorporate, as it were, the two separate spheres in one person must have had a special appeal.[8] What had been denied to him in real life, Dreiser could perhaps make up for in his fiction.

The writer who was to provide the necessary philosophical underpinnings in this attempt to reconcile the two spheres was Friedrich Nietzsche, who at the turn of the century began to invade many intellectual circles of America. Hailed by the critics of American culture as the great iconoclast who would smash the cultural icons of the *bourgeoisie* and maligned by the latter as that "German monster Nitzky,"[9] his idea of power, which is so central to his philosophy, must have been especially attractive for Dreiser. It was Nietzsche's concept of power, I will argue in the following, which helped him "transvalue" the traditional notion of power with its largely political and financial connotations. Nietzsche, a critical witness of his time, is of course not immune to and unaware of the attractions of politico-financial power, when he asks what drives "the upper class [to] indulge in permitted fraud and have the stock exchange and speculations on their conscience." "Not real want," he answers,

> for their existence is by no means precarious . . . . But they are urged on day and night by a fearful impatience at the slow way in which their money is accumulating and by an equally fearful pleasure in and love of accumulated money. In this impatience and this

love, however, we see reappear once more that fanaticism of the
lust for power which was in former times inflamed by the belief one
was in possession of the truth . . . what one formerly did 'for the
sake of God' one now does for the sake of money, that is to say, for
the sake of that which now gives the highest feeling of power and a
good conscience. (*DD*, 204)[10]

To reduce the "lust for power," as articulated here, to a mere materialistic desire, would be a gross oversimplification of Nietzsche's
central concept. Money for Nietzsche serves merely as a synecdoche
for a much wider notion of power which includes both philosophy
and art. Since philosophy for him is "the most spiritual Will to
Power" (*BGE*, 9) and since it "desires, what art does, to give the
greatest possible depth and meaning to life and actions" (*HATH*, 6),
both art and philosophy may be regarded as the sublimated expressions of man's "basic will, the will to power" (*WP*, 658).

Dreiser had his first acquaintance with Nietzsche's philosophy
between his first and second visit to Buffalo when on a December
day in 1909 H. L. Mencken's newly published book *The Philosophy of
Friedrich Nietzsche* (1908) reached his desk. "If the outline of Mr.
Nietzsche's philosophy in the introduction is correct," Dreiser re-
marked in his letter to Mencken on December 6, 1909, acknowledging the arrival of the book, "he and myself are hale fellows well met."
Only ten days later, however, his enthusiasm already seemed to have
waned when he commented in a second letter to Mencken: "I am
deep in Nietche [*sic*] but I can't say I greatly admire him. He seems
to Schopenhauer confused and warmed over."[11] Yet to infer from
such a remark that Dreiser was not only a Non- but a declared Anti-
Nietzschean, as some critics have done, seems to me premature and
wholly unfounded.[12] When Dreiser claimed to be "deep in
Nietzsche" ten days after the arrival of Mencken's book, he was, of
course, saying nothing but that he was deep in Mencken's interpretation of Nietzsche which had mistaken and misread the latter's Will
to Power for Schopenhauer's limited desire for mere self-
preservation.[13] Did Dreiser ever get beyond Mencken and deeper
into Nietzsche's own writings? Judging from the persistent misspell-
ing of Nietzsche's name, one is inclined to believe that his acquaintance remained purely superficial.[14] Did he ever heed Mencken's
advice to read *The Genealogy of Morals* and *The Antichrist?*[15] The
sparse references in his diaries, letters, and essays make the reader

believe that his knowledge went hardly beyond the common knowledge of Nietzsche's basic philosophical assumptions. It is the popular Nietzsche with his memorable aphorisms, not the subtle thinker, whom the reader encounters in Dreiser's more private writings, so that one tends to agree with Donald Pizer who maintains that Nietzsche's philosophy "served primarily to confirm views already held by Dreiser. He and Nietzsche were 'hale fellows well met' because both rejected moral values which arose from supernatural sanctions and because both believed that life was essentially struggle."[16]

Unless Nietzsche's influence on Dreiser can be traced beyond such very general parallels, we are indeed entitled to speak of a mere superficial relationship between the two "hale fellows well met." More promising and profitable than a mere search for Nietzsche references in Dreiser's diaries and letters, it seems, is a closer look at, and a more detailed discussion of, the literary works which originated in the years of Dreiser's alleged proximity to Nietzsche. The description of a fictional setting, the portrayal of a character, allows a subtler unfolding of philosophical nuances than notes hastily jotted down in more or less private documents. Dreiser's great literary project conceived yet not completed at the time when he was "deep in Nietzsche" is his *Trilogy of Desire* consisting of *The Financier* (1912), *The Titan* (1914) and the posthumously published *The Stoic* (1947), describing the career of Frank Algernon Cowperwood, a character marked by an insatiable "pleasure in and love of accumulated money," a true "American Financier" whose "pathology" Dreiser was to portray a few years later in an essay as follows:

> Often humorless, shark-like, avid, yet among the greatest constructive forces imaginable; absolutely opposed to democracy in practice, yet as useful an implement for its accomplishment as for autocracy; either ignorant or contemptuous of ethical niceties as related to thine and mine, yet a stickler for all that concerns mine; moral and immoral sexually . . . and seeking always to perpetuate their own fame. In other words, typical men and women of an avid pagan world . . . yet surrounded by religious and ethical abstrusities for which they care little and of which they understand less. Such might be called the pathology of the genus financier.[17]

Here Dreiser already reflects a profounder awareness of the ramifications inherent in Nietzsche's Will to Power. Cowperwood, the

American financier, is more than a vulgar and rapacious money-grabber whose "lust for power" exhausts itself in a simple materialistic acquisitiveness; he is portrayed as the American equivalent and embodiment of the Nietzschean Overman who, in the course of the trilogy, gradually reconciles crude financial power with the more sublimated and refined forms of intellectual and artistic empowerment. Maligned and detested by the moralists both within and without the novels because of his profound immoral behavior, Cowperwood more and more assumes the features of Nietzsche's Overman, an equally "immoral" individual with a distinct Will to Power.[18]

The Overman and the Will to Power are closely intertwined notions in Nietzsche's philosophic thinking. The "extension of power" is the essence and the force of life; it is "the basic will" (*WP*, 658) and "the true, fundamental instinct of life" (*GS*, 349) or, as Zarathustra puts it: "Wherever I found a living creature, there found I Will to Power" (*TSZ*, II, 12). The Will to Power is a Nietzschean synonym of the human desire for self-transcendence and self-transformation; "we are pressing towards man as towards something that stands high above us" (*UM*, III, 5). Since the Overman is a projection of man's desires into the future, he remains purely intentional, a mere trajectory, an infinite process of becoming: "Never yet has there been an Overman" (*TSZ*, II, 4). The Overman can therefore never be conceived as a product, as Michael J. Matthis correctly remarks: "becoming does not aim at a *final state*, does not flow into 'being.'"[19] Zarathustra as the prophet of the Overman is therefore one who must always surpass and overcome himself; he must, as Zarathustra says, "be struggle, and becoming, and purpose, and cross-purpose" (*TSZ*, II, 12). Since the direction of the Will to Power is conceived more or less in terms of an unchannelled desire and since becoming as self-overcoming is seen as an infinite process of self-creation (*purpose*) and self-decreation (*cross-purpose*), it is the notion of indeterminate process and change rather than that of a determinate self-improvement which is privileged in Nietzsche's thinking: "the whole morality of amelioration," in his opinion, "has been a misunderstanding" (*TI*, II, 11).

In his essay "Change," which resonates with distinct Nietzschean echoes, Dreiser celebrates sudden indeterminate changes as an "outstanding tendency, which we must accept whether we will or not." Since "nothing is fixed" and everything in flux, we must be "ready to abandon at a moment's notice" what we may still consider an eternal verity or a moral absolute. Only thus, Dreiser continues, will we "be able to step out free and willing to accept new and radically different conditions."[20] When Dreiser scholarship now begins to abandon the naturalistic notion of the determined and will-less "waif amid forces" and to direct its attention to a more indeterminate and protean self, it privileges Nietzsche's dynamic concept of life as an infinite process of becoming over the more finite notion of the deterministic self as maintained by naturalism.[21]

The process of Frank Cowperwood's becoming, his career from a self-centered plutocrat to an aristocrat and patron of the fine arts, is framed by two highly symbolic passages in the first and final chapters of *The Financier*. The first episode depicts young Frank with his nose pressed to the glass of a fish-market tank in which he witnesses the bitter struggle of a lobster and a squid which, after a prolonged fight, the fittest is ultimately going to win. Although fascinated by the fight, Frank remains deeply troubled, if not dissatisfied by the too facile Darwinian interpretation of the by-standers. Since he had been "forever pondering . . . how this thing he had come into — this life — was organized," the Darwinian answer could only "in a rough way [solve] that riddle which had been annoying him so much in the past" (*F*, 7f.).[22] A subtler answer, in his opinion, was required. Thus begins Cowperwood's life-long quest which will eventually lead him beyond the deterministic interpretation of life as the survival of the physically fittest. In the final chapter of *The Financier*, Dreiser again employs the image of a sea-animal, the Black Grouper, a solitary bottom fish of immense size, which here symbolizes the stage that Cowperwood in the meantime has reached in his process of becoming. In contrast to the lobster, "the greenish-copperish engine of destruction" (*F*, 8), the grouper for Dreiser represents the "constructive genius of nature." Changing its color continuously according to the requirements of its surrounding, the black grouper appears as "spectral and unnatural, so brilliant is its power to deceive" (*F*, 447). Power remains a keyword in this concluding passage, but unlike the first episode which rests on mere physical strength, it is a power characterized by "subtlety, chicanery, trickery" (*F*, 447). It is "the creative power" (*F*, 446) that the black grouper symbolizes. As "a living lie" invested with "an almost unbelievable power of simulation" (*F*, 447), it bears the distinct characteristics of art, which Nietzsche defines as a "healing balm of illusion [*Balsam des Scheins*]" (*BT*, 19) that man, as it were, applies because he does not want to "*perish of the truth*" (*WP*, 822). The grouper, with "its very remarkable ability to adapt itself to conditions" (*F*, 446), furthermore illustrates Nietzsche's "power of adaption [*Anpassungs-Vermögen*]" (*WP*, 645) which, far from being a mere mechanism of adjustment, has to be understood as a human "ability [*Vermögen*]," as an artful, subtle act of continuous self-transformation.

Dreiser enacts the process of Cowperwood's self-surpassing on three different levels: Wealth, Woman, and Art. How closely these levels are interrelated, may be illustrated by the following quotation:

> Wealth in the beginning, had seemed the only goal, to which had been added the beauty of women. And now art, for art's sake — the first faint radiance of a rosy dawn — had begun to shine in upon him, and to the beauty of womanhood he was beginning to see how necessary it was to add the beauty of life — the beauty of material background — how, in fact, the only background for great beauty was great art. (*F*, 144f.)

The hierarchy of the three levels deserves closer attention because it is here that Dreiser shows his greatest indebtedness to Nietzsche's philosophy.

When Dreiser at first grounds his trilogy largely on the idea of the pursuit of material wealth, he does so in full accordance with both the historical setting of the novels in Post-Civil-War America and Nietzsche's concept of money as a bestower of "the highest feeling of power" (*DD*, 204). America's Gilded Age was undoubtedly an epoch dominated by such "organizers seeking power" as the Goulds, the Fisks, the Carnegies or the Morgans. "To the aggressive organizing mind," Dreiser remarks in a diction reminiscent of Zarathustra's rhetoric, "life is and always has been a free and practically uncharted sea. It finds itself blazing with an impulse to get some one new thing done; it conceives some great scheme, is inspired with some great enthusiasm for something; and thereafter all else is as nothing."[23] The financier, a "real man," had such a fascination for Dreiser because he "was never a tool. He used tools. He created. He led" (*F*, 42). Persons of influence he shrewdly uses and makes subservient to his very own interests; common people are brusquely shoved aside so that the stage can be set for the master-figure, the selfish and self-sufficient man of power. "I satisfy myself" (*F*, 121) becomes Cowperwood's characteristic motto which resonates through the entire trilogy. Self-reliant and indebted only to himself, he increasingly becomes the autocrat who, defying due democratic process, stands out from the slavish masses as the Nietzschean Overman for whom the notion that all men are created equal is "the greatest of all lies" (*WP*, 464). Here again, Cowperwood acts in full accordance with the captains of commerce in the Gilded Age to whom, as Eric Foner maintains, "egalitarian ideas seemed an anachronism, a throwback to the unscientific sentimentalism of an earlier era."[24] Yet for Dreiser the financier-figure, however admirable as one of "the greatest constructive forces imaginable," shows clear signs of limitation. Too raw and unrefined, too "full of thievery and selfishness," he reminds the reader still too much of the primitive aggressiveness of the lobster rather than the subtlety and artfulness of the grouper. That Dreiser was not satisfied with the merely money-grabbing plutocrat in shirt sleeves, that he deliberately searched for a more refined power-figure is reflected in his choice of Charles T. Yerkes as Cowperwood's model. Yerkes, according to Matthiessen,

> had none of "the book-keeper's soul" that was attributed to Rockefeller. He loved not only wealth and power, but also women. But he was very different from Jim Fisk. He was not a roisterer, and he also loved art. His collection was not acquired whole-sale, as was the case with many, but was a reflection of his own taste.[25]

Thus the triad of Wealth, Woman, and Art reemerges once again as one of Dreiser's governing principles in which Cowperwood's Will to Power articulates itself.

Cowperwood's selfishly immoral attitude towards women has offended many a reader's and critic's moral sentiments. Stuart P. Sherman's aphoristic remark that *The Titan* was hardly more than "a sort of huge club-sandwich composed of slices of business alternating with erotic episodes,"[26] is a case in point. Although accurate as a formal description of the novel's structure, which does indeed alternate between sex and business as Cowperwood's primary levels of interest, Sherman entirely disregards the deeper relationship that Dreiser construes between these two levels. Cowperwood's rise as a businessman from rugged plutocrat to refined aristocrat is mirrored in his changing attitude towards women. Between his first superficial sexual contact in a "house of ill repute" (*F*, 37) at the beginning of his financial career and his deep and fulfilling relationship to Berenice Fleming, which begins to develop in the latter half of *The Titan* and finds its consummation in *The Stoic*, Cowperwood experiences the whole spectrum of lust from a base animal instinct to a more and more sublimated form of desire.

His first marriage to Lillian Semple, "a Presbyterian girl, religious, conventional" (*T*, 464), entirely follows Nietzsche's formula of "marriages for a period" which he had interpreted "as an antidote to prostitution (or as its ennoblement)" (*WP*, 733). Within the morally sanctioned institution of marriage, Cowperwood not only fulfills his matrimonial duties by procreating two children with a "pale and rather anemic" woman (*T*, 57), but at the same time he channels his sexual instincts and impunitively satisfies his carnal desires within the moral framework of wedlock. Cowperwood, however, is still in his initial stage of becoming. Unaware of Zarathustra's commandment that "not only onward shalt thou procreate thyself, but upward" (*TSZ*, I, 20), procreation is still understood by Cowperwood in merely physical terms, while the connotative meaning of the word as "a *pro*-cess of self-*creation*" remains undetected. Aileen Butler, his second wife — young, attractive, sensuous, and "bursting with sheer physical vitality" (*T*, 57) — is "in some respects more intelligent . . . at least less conventional, more generous" (*T*, 464). With her, Cowperwood discovers the erotic pleasures of love, with her he visits the great galleries of Europe and begins to enjoy the beauties of art. Aileen thus reflects a more refined stage of his own pro-creation. Although "more generous" than the strictly religious Lillian, Aileen represents only a transitory period in Cowperwood's process of self-becoming; his marriage to her is still a "marriage for a period." Unable to keep "pace with him" (*T*, 495), she is literally left behind. Afraid of losing her husband, she anxiously clings to him and shows a most ungenerous behavior when she learns about his amorous affairs. Unable to see that desires are transient and subject to change, she resembles the Nietzschean type of women whose "quiet, regular, happily attuned existences operate unconsciously against the heroic impulse of the free spirit" (*HATH*, 431). Since women have "their greatest power in morals" (*HATH*, 425), she obstructs her husband's immoral Will to Power. Cowperwood, we may conclude, by now has reached a position which is almost beyond good and evil. The "trouble with marriage is," as Dreiser maintains and as Cow-

perwood would undoubtedly agree, "that in its extreme interpretation it conflicts with the law of change."[27] When he meets Berenice
Fleming after a series of erotic interludes, he seems to have reached a
stage of awareness which allows him to review his former relationships to women in a proper perspective. His confession to Berenice
reflects this new awareness:

> . . . my own ideals in regard to women have all the time been
> slowly changing. I have come to see, through various experiments,
> that she [Aileen] is not the ideal woman for me at all. She does not
> understand me. I don't pretend to understand myself, but it has
> occurred to me that there might be a woman somewhere who
> would understand me better than I understand myself, who would
> see the things that I don't see about myself, and would like me,
> anyhow. I might as well tell you that I have been a lover of women
> always. There is just one ideal thing in this world to me, and that is
> the woman that I would like to have. (*T*, 464f.)

For Cowperwood, Berenice is this "ideal thing" of which he has always dreamed. "Immensely superior" to Aileen (*T*, 494), Dreiser
casts her almost as Cowperwood's *alter ego*. Like Cowperwood she
loves life; she is strange, shrewd, subtle, and intelligent like him (*T*,
352, 359). A "beauty which is above sex and above age and above
wealth," shines in her "blowing hair and night-blue eyes" (*T*, 381).
With her "love of art, her love of power" (*T*, 467) she embodies "so
much of all that he desired" (*S*, 107). Unlike his previous amorous
relations, his love for Berenice is free and no longer infused with
Christian morality; it worships, as Donald Pizer remarks, "a pagan
god of love in opposition to the false god of marriage."[28] With
Berenice Fleming, Dreiser reintroduces a pristine and pagan kind of
love as erotic desire vitiated by Christian morals. "Christianity gave
Eros poison to drink; he did not die of it, certainly, but degenerated
to Vice" (*BGE*, 168). Greatly surpassing the mere gratification of his
physical lust, Cowperwood's relationship to Berenice represents a
higher union of free spirits from which, as Dreiser says,

> It does not follow that there need ever be physical satiation to
> complete this union. Spiritual pollination can spring from the mer-
> est accidental contact for a moment with a mate. But the fact re-
> mains that the greatest, most complete spiritual and physical
> responsiveness to the universe . . . springs from this responsiveness,
> which springs from love, and as such our so-called love (desire,

passionate chemical response, physical and spiritual) becomes the most significant fact in the universe as we now understand it.[29]

Thus Frank Cowperwood, not unlike Carrie Meeber, undergoes a gradual metamorphosis from lower to ever higher forms of erotic desire which becomes increasingly one with artistic pleasure and aesthetic enjoyment. Lillian, Aileen, and Berenice are, as Pizer convincingly argues, "beautiful women who are in different ways art objects, but they are so in ascending order. Put crudely, Lillian's beauty is surface, Aileen vitalizes beauty with animal force, and Berenice spiritualizes it by a subtlety and depth of spirit and mind."[30]

Art as the third component in Dreiser's triad is thus brought into play and intimately related to the two other notions of Wealth and Woman. Wealth provides the material basis for Cowperwood to become the collector and patron of the arts, while his various amorous relationships reflect his ever deeper appreciation of the world of art. Berenice as the embodiment of "all that he desired" represents Cowperwood's highest stage in his process of self-refinement. Finance as the lowest form of art which dominates *The Financier* is increasingly transformed into the higher art-forms of Woman and Art proper in *The Titan* and *The Stoic*. The simple and modest Philadelphia home which he shares with Lillian Semple, an equally simple and modest spouse, gradually gives way to a more luxurious Chicago mansion reflecting his much more sensuous form of desire for his new wife Aileen; and the Renaissance palace on Manhattan's Fifth Avenue, an architectural tribute to Berenice, mirrors Cowperwood's highest level of love and artistic refinement. It is the Italian Renaissance, Nietzsche's "last *great* age" (*TI*, 37) of nobility and power, which for Cowperwood comes to represent the state of art in its highest perfection. Therefore, he begins to fashion himself more and more as a Renaissance man of power. As a financier and patron of the arts he increasingly resembles Cosimo I. of the Medici whom Dreiser, in "The American Financier," would a few years later describe as a typical *uomo universale* in control of "all the financial channels of Italy, France, Greece, a portion of Egypt, and the lowlands."[31] Sitting "in the court of orchids" in his New York palazzo and reading the diary of Benvenuto Cellini (*T*, 502), Cowperwood once again shows his affinity to a great Renaissance artist. An avid collector of art works, he increasingly loses interest in American art and becomes more and more fascinated by the paintings of Luini, Previtali, Perugino, and

Pinturrichio, among them a portrait of Cesare Borgia whom Nietzsche had already declared a "sort of Overman" (*TI*, 37). As a strong, passionate, and radiant figure of Renaissance proportions, Cowperwood becomes the target of his political and moral adversaries who cast him, "that scoundrel from Philadelphia" (*T*, 95), more and more in the role of a Machiavellian powerful prince (*T*, 189). This admiration for the Florentine Renaissance makes Dreiser again a true disciple of Nietzsche. For Nietzsche, "the last *great* age" had generated not only great works of art which are always perfect expressions of "freedom from moral narrowness and corner-perspectives [*Winkel-Optik*]" (*WP*, 823); it had brought forth, above all, great men of "virtue." Fascinated by the Renaissance concept of *virtù* as "moraline-free virtue" (*WP*, 327), Nietzsche considered the Renaissance a time in history in which he could ground his notion of the Overman, a transgressor of moral constraints who positioned himself beyond good and evil. Since philosophy, as understood by Nietzsche, desires what art aspires to, and since art, not unlike his philosophy, is "an attempt to assassinate all *pudeurs*" (*WP*, 817), the artist and the philosopher again may be seen as identical figures. Cowperwood, cast as a connoisseur of Renaissance art, thus also becomes a philosopher of sorts who considers philosophy as "this tyrannical drive itself, the most spiritual Will to Power" (*BGE*, 9).

Every reading of *The Trilogy of Desire* as a tasteless club-sandwich composed of slices of sex and business reduces the figure of Cowperwood to a raw and ruthless grabber of women and wealth. Every reading which sees in the trilogy only "a curiously blurred dream that combined Horatio Alger with Darwin and Nietzsche," as F.O. Matthiessen has suggested,[32] cannot do full justice to the novel. Such readings disregard not only the aesthetic significance of the two episodes which frame *The Financier* and clearly reflect Dreiser's attempt to free himself from a limiting, purely Darwinian interpretation of life; they also ignore Cowperwood's metamorphosis, "whose financial genius and lust for power were," as Dreiser puts it in *The Stoic*, "tempered . . . by his love of art and beauty" (*S*, 179). Far from being a merely blurred dream of Alger, Darwin, and Nietzsche, this transformation is consistently described in Nietzschean terms as a process of infinite self-becoming. Cowperwood's initial lust for material power is gradually transformed into higher, more refined forms of power which reflect the Nietzschean Will to Power as "the unexhausted, procreating life-will" (*TSZ*, II, 12), generating ever new and surprising creations of the self.

By casting Cowperwood as a Nietzschean artist figure, Dreiser ultimately casts himself as an artist. By investing his fictional protagonist with a distinct Will to Power, Dreiser empowers himself as an artist in a country which he, in an essay titled "Life, Art and America," would later describe as "comfortable, commercial and industrious," yet "artistically, intellectually, philosophically" weak. Its "profound moral idealism," he went on to argue, was prone to prevent "a free mental development, a subtle understanding, art or life in its poetic or tragic moulds."[33] As the author of *Sister Carrie*, who had suffered under the devastating moral judgments of readers and critics alike, he now, if only in the form of a fictional substitute, recasts and recreates himself in Cowperwood as the great Nietzschean immoralist whose goal it is to liberate American culture from its deep-seated and contemptible moral constraints. Nietzsche, "the devilfish," hauled ashore at the turn of the century and hailed by the literary Bohème as America's liberator,[34] is indeed Dreiser's "hale fellow well met." Like Nietzsche, a determined fighter against cultural philistinism, Dreiser likes to cast himself as a transvaluator of the values of his time. By subverting the rigid system of American morals and undercutting the hardly less rigid stability of the self, Dreiser made a truly significant contribution to modern literature, and his "hale fellow" effectively helped him design his strategies of subversion.

Notes

[1] *Essays and Lectures* (New York: The Library of America, 1983), 971–986.

[2] "Prayer to the Dynamo," in *Letters to a Niece and Prayer to the Virgin of Chartres* (Boston: Houghton Mifflin, 1920), pp. 128–30. See also chapter 25 ("The Dynamo and the Virgin") in *The Education of Henry Adams* (Boston: Houghton Mifflin, 1918), pp. 379–90. For a perceptive discussion of the role of power in Henry Adams's writings, see Harold Kaplan, *Power and Order: Henry Adams and the Naturalist Tradition in American Fiction* (Chicago: U of Chicago P, 1981).

[3] See Emerson, "Man the Reformer," *The Collected Works of Ralph Waldo Emerson: Nature, Addresses and Lectures*, ed. Robert E. Spiller (Cambridge, MA: Belknap, 1977), pp. 151ff.

[4] The advice given to Dreiser by Miss Fleming, his one-time teacher, to read both Herbert Spencer and Ralph Waldo Emerson may, at least in part, account

for this oscillation between the self-empowered individual and a powerless "waif amid forces"; see *Dawn: A History of Myself* (New York: Liveright, 1931), p. 370. The posthumously published *Notes on Life*, eds. Marguerite Tjader and John J. McAleer (Tuscaloosa: U of Alabama P, 1974) still reflect this unresolved tension between transcendentalist und naturalist notions.

[5] For the detailed description of "Buffalo Old and New," see *A Hoosier Holiday* (New York: John Lane, 1916), pp. 169–75.

[6] Dreiser, *Hey Rub-A-Dub-Dub: A Book of the Mystery and Wonder and Terror of Life* (New York: Boni and Liveright, 1920), p. 19.

[7] *Ibid.*, p. 266.

[8] Walter Blackstock, "Dreiser's Dramatizations of Art, the Artist, and the Beautiful in American Life," *Southern Quarterly*, 1 (1962), 63.

[9] Ludwig Marcuse, "Nietzsche in America," *South Atlantic Quarterly*, 50 (1951), 333.

[10] The titles of Nietzsche's works will be abbreviated as follows: *BGE: Beyond Good and Evil*; *DD: The Day of Dawn*; *GS: The Gay Science*; *HATH: Human All-Too-Human*; *TI: Twilight of the Idols*; *TSZ: Thus Spoke Zarathustra*; *UM: Untimely Meditations*, and *WP: The Will to Power*. The numbers after the abbreviations refer to the sections of the books. The translations are my own, though at times greatly indebted to R. J. Hollingdale, Walter Kaufmann, Anthony M. Ludovici, and Helen Zimmern.

[11] Thomas P. Riggio (ed.), *Dreiser-Mencken Letters*, vol. I (Philadelphia: U of Pennsylvania P, 1986), 41–42.

[12] The most adamant advocate of Dreiser as an Anti-Nietzschean is Arun Mukherjee, *The Gospel of Wealth in the American Novel: The Rhetoric of Dreiser and Some of His Contemporaries* (Totowa: Barnes & Noble, 1987). For Mukherjee it is a "fact that Dreiser denied that he was a Nietzschean" (73). On the basis of this questionable assumption, he suggests a reading of the trilogy in which he sees Dreiser at work shredding "to pieces the myth of the Nietzschean Superman" (127).

[13] See Nietzsche's critique of Schopenhauer's limited concept in *The Gay Science*, 349. For an extensive discussion of Mencken's misreading of Nietzsche, see Chenliang Sheng, "Nietzsche's Superman Americanized: On Dreiser's *The Financier*" (Diss. U of Maryland, 1989), pp. 46–51.

[14] "Nietche" (as in his letter to Mencken) and "Neitche" are his most common misspellings. See *Theodore Dreiser's American Diaries, 1902–1926*, ed. Thomas P. Riggio (Philadelphia: U of Pennsylvania P, 1982), pp. 333–34.

[15] Mencken in a letter to Dreiser on October 25, 1911. See *Dreiser-Mencken Letters*, p. 79.

[16] Donald Pizer, *The Novels of Theodore Dreiser: A Critical Study* (Minneapolis: U of Minnesota P, 1976), p. 158.

[17] "The American Financier," *Hey Rub-A-Dub-Dub*, p. 74.

[18] Unlike Chenliang Sheng, "Nietzsche's Superman Americanized," and despite Dreiser's occasional usage of the term "superman," I prefer the term "Overman." It allows for the Nietzschean resonances and ramifications which are entirely muted in the term "superman" with its misleading popular cultural connotations.

[19] "Nietzsche as an Anti-Naturalist," *Philosophy Today*, 37 (1993), 175.

[20] "Change," *Hey Rub-A-Dub-Dub*, pp. 19–23.

[21] See, for instance, Paul A. Orlov, "The Subversion of the Self: Anti-Naturalistic Crux in *An American Tragedy*," *Modern Fiction Studies*, 23 (1977), 457–72, who discusses Dreiser's subversion of a stable and fixed identity. See also Philip Fisher, *Hard Facts: Setting and Form in the American Novel* (New York: Oxford UP, 1985).

[22] All further references in the text will be to the following editions: *The Financier* (New York: Signet Classics, 1967), *The Titan* (New York: John Lane, 1914), *The Stoic* (New York: Doubleday, 1947). The titles will be abbreviated as *F (Financier)*, *T (Titan)*, and *S (Stoic)*.

[23] "The American Financier," *Hey Rub-A-Dub-Dub*, pp. 80–82.

[24] *A Short History of Reconstruction, 1863–1877* (New York: Harper & Row, 1990), p. 212.

[25] Matthiessen, *Theodore Dreiser* (New York: William Sloane, 1951) p. 131.

[26] Stuart P. Sherman, "The Barbaric Naturalism of Theodore Dreiser," *The Stature of Theodore Dreiser: A Critical Survey of the Man and his Work*, eds. Alfred Kazin and Charles Shapiro (Bloomington: Indiana UP, 1965), p. 78.

[27] "Marriage and Divorce," *Hey-Rub-A-Dub-Dub*, p. 217.

[28] *The Novels of Theodore Dreiser*, p. 173.

[29] "Marriage and Divorce," *Hey Rub-A-Dub-Dub*, p. 224.

[30] *The Novels of Theodore Dreiser*, pp. 173f.

[31] "The American Financier," *Hey Rub-A-Dub-Dub*, p. 76.

[32] *Theodore Dreiser*, p. 158.

[33] *Hey Rub-A-Dub-Dub*, pp. 263 *passim*.

[34] See H. L. Mencken in an article on James Gibbons Huneker, *H. L. Mencken's Smart Set Criticism*, ed. William H. Nolte (Ithaca: Cornell UP, 1968), p. 203.

Kathryne V. Lindberg

In the Name of Nietzsche: Ezra Pound Becomes Himself and Others

Open up and cast up to me your fish and glittering crabs! With my
best bait I shall today bait the queerest human fish . . . . biting at
my sharp hidden hooks, they must come up to *my* height — the
most colorful abysmal groundlings, to the most sarcastic of all who
fish for men. For *that* is what I am through and through: reeling,
reeling in, raising up, raising, a raiser, cultivator, and disciplinarian,
who once counseled himself, not for nothing. Become who you
are! *Zarathustra*, IV ("The Honey Sacrifice")

> Hang it all, there can be but one *Sordello*!
> . . . .
> Your *Sordello*, and that the modern world
> Needs such a rag-bag to stuff all its thought in;
> Say that I dump my catch, shiny and silvery
> As fresh sardines flapping and slipping on the
> marginal cobbles?
> *Draft Canto I*

FOR A MOMENT, let us accept the implicit invitation to interpretation and to the unmasking of the writer(s) — and perhaps of us
readers — that my superposed epigraphs seem to offer. First, Pound
reading Nietzsche, if you will. You can (be made to) hear, for instance, the orphic voice and imperious posture of the deceptive yet
confessional Zarathustra echoed in the virtually forgotten lines of the
first and later radically revised version of Pound's Canto I (first published in *Poetry*, 1917). Second, some Nietzschean red herrings, as
you appreciate his — whose? — hyperbolically disingenuous style of

self-reflection. Parodying the lowly position of the biblical "fisher of men," Zarathustra, taken or given as a mask of Nietzsche, addresses the human sea of forms that will appear before him as failed versions of the higher man he seeks and would become. Third, Pound's self-occluding yet self-assertively colloquial address is similarly double-edged: by means of an ambiguous pronoun, he calls upon Robert Browning and the present reader's versions of *Sordello* as he prolifer-ates Sordellos. Pound at once promises absolute novelty and perhaps tedious philological recovery of earlier textual (poetic and historical) fragments. Finally, if Nietzsche plays with religio-philosophical seri-ousness, Pound certainly courts chaos and obsolescence as he de-mands the interactive production of a future American rag-bag — or epic? — that only a Pound Industry would cobble together. Neither of the above passages can, in any case, be taken as a straightforward attempt to present or "become" one's self — or, in Whitman's equally vexing terms, "a simple separate Self."

Nevertheless, if, through layers of irony, Nietzsche issues a call to "Become who you are," Pound's "impersonal" posture as poet, if not as critic, is a strangely adequate response to the paradox of revi-sionary and active self-fashioning suggested by "becoming" who one is and, at the same time, pretending to be a legitimate heir to several artistic lines. Before leaving behind my two not-quite-randomly-selected passages from Nietzsche and Pound, let me suggest that they economically summarize the ironic imperative that Nietzsche seemed to issue to Pound's generation: be, create, overcome yourself and/or Man; change in order to become yourself.[1]

Thanks to his sister and the other directors of the Nietzsche Ar-chives (something of a prototype of literary critical clearinghouses like the Pound Industry and the Joyce Industry?) Nietzsche was, even before his death, less the author of specific texts and ideas than the inspiration for rebels who would renew artistic and philosophical traditions and create the New Man. Various French, Italian, German, and a few English avant-gardists as well as romantic nationalists of several regions, syndicalists, socialists, and proto-fascists saw great interpretative potential in Nietzsche's aphoristic style and icono-clasm. Whether in the guise of disciplinary authority or the love of intellectual danger, any number of writers, including Pound's *Blast* group, claimed positively to deploy Nietzsche's destructive force.

Pound might have been about as aware of Nietzschean intellectual currents (including Sorel, Bergson, Hulme and, later, Breton) as many of today's casual adherents of more recent neo-Nietzscheanisms (differentially indebted to such as Derrida and Foucault). Nietzsche and Nietzscheans and Nietzscheanism(s) are just that way! Just so, Pound's phrase "Neo-Nietzschean clatter," from "Hugh Selwyn Mauberley" seems a useful vagary, if not proof of his true brotherhood with a certain strained American de(con)structive reading machine. Such hints have proved useful for various American fishing expeditions in intellectual and political genealogies centered around Pound.[2] Still, it makes little sense to bother with simple influence based on Pound's reading or direct quotation of the German poet-philosopher. It matters little what stunning proximity they can be forced into; these secret sharers of an impossible Emersonian skepsis, these "neighbors" — whether in Heidegger's sense or in my more vulgar or violent juxtaposition — would not recognize each other.[3] Moreover, rumors and evocations of Nietzsche's writings and promiscuous identifications with his life had a more profound and wider impact than scant textual references to him suggest. This does not mean that one can fix or isolate a strain of Nietzscheanism that might be cultured or killed in order to yield a politically correct or fully Fascist Pound. Precisely the opposite. Pound does, however, present a peculiar problem for (American?) readers of poetry, who persist in believing that good and evil can be separated absolutely — even as they might be made to correspond with the beautiful and the ugly. Here, anyway, Nietzsche might help. But *whose* — or who is — Nietzsche?

Wyndham Lewis provides one of the most interesting — and interested — accounts of the Nietzsche phenomenon in England. In a chapter in *The Art of Being Ruled*, "Nietzsche as Vulgarizer," he sketches the contradictory self-assertions among followers who would be a vanguard. Keep in mind that, in the following, Lewis means to complain more about Nietzsche's openness than to correct his elitism or caution against resentment:

> For what he set out to vulgarize, the notion of aristocracy and power, was surely the most absurd, illogical, and meaningless thing that he could have chosen for that purpose.[4]

Lewis ends his rant with a dismissal of those who were "self-made" yet timidly in need of the license provided in part by Bergson, James,

Croce, and others inflated by Nietzsche's virtually necrophilic vitality.[5] Lewis rejected the Nietzsche propagated by his English contemporaries before World War I in favor of the purer and more violently
energetic vanguardism of Vorticism — informed, as he sometimes
fails to note, by Hulme and Sorel.[6] Later, however, Lewis consistently rejected these youthful enthusiasms, and he called for a
sterner, more traditional, and politically responsible reactionary art.

In a retrospective assessment after World War II of London in the
teens, Lewis claims that artistic vanguardism was vitiated by democratic politics and desires to educate the masses. As consistently reactionary as his position remained, Lewis continued to celebrate his
own individuality, originality, and artistic rebellion; at the same time,
he dressed up his forbidden politics as formalism, suggesting that the
English avant-garde merely mimicked political gestures:

> Both Mr. Pound and myself were establishing *groups* . . . immedi-
> ately before World War I. I refer to 'Imagists' and 'Vorticists': both
> craft-groups, with no political implications — except in so far as all
> revolution in literature or art involves a radical bias . . . . Eventually
> all avantgardism became deeply coloured with politics — in Eng-
> land rather an aesthetic phenomenon than a political, but inspired
> by political models.[7]

Lewis, perpetually the "Blaster" and the "Enemy," wants to recover, at once rejecting and claiming as his own, what Fredric
Jameson calls "his attitude towards *fascism* as a historical force" and
"the great political expression of *revolutionary* opposition to the
status quo."[8] Jameson faults the vitalism and voluntarism — even the
metonymic prose style — of Lewis's alleged perpetual aesthetic
revolution as the transformation of thought and Self to the exclusion
of material history and Others.[9] Indeed, Jameson identifies Fascism
with just the force of untamed revolutionary change and revisionism,
a kind of generalized macho textual violence that renews its attraction in various writers of another strain of Nietzscheanism (Blanchot,
Bataille, perhaps Foucault and Derrida). He erroneously, I think,
finds this particular danger/attraction in Lewis.[10] Another, perhaps
more useful, approach to certain nagging questions about identity
politics and Fascism might begin with the injunction to avoid over-
psychologizing the motives of writers we want to admire. That way
we could finally leave behind Pound, Nietzsche, and even the present
unauthorized or de-authorizing genealogy. Right now we should not

be detained by Jameson "working out," if you will, his own anxious attraction to Lewis and hence to the wrong Nietzsche.[11]

Suffice it to say that a Nietzscheanism characterized by intellectual adventure and progressive politics *versus* another Nietzscheanism that demanded obedience to an arbitrary master existed alongside each other in avant-garde movements. Sometimes over the career of a single artist or politician, as he transformed himself from rebel against the establishment to policeman of his own movement, both or several attitudes equally attributable to readings or misreadings of Nietzsche can be mapped. Richard Huelsenbeck claims such a trajectory for Tzara, who, he says, "completely reversed all the values" of experimental irrationalism.[12]

When Pound arrived in London, even before he became the only partially mis-named "Foreign Correspondent" for several American small magazines, most notably *Poetry*, there were already several Nietzsches on the scene. A brash yet defensively American autodidact, Pound would have seen in various manifestations of "Nietzsche" but one way to make himself the revisionary dictator of American modernism. In 1955, *American Literature* published a short piece Pound had written in 1909, which confesses an ambivalent patriotism. Throughout his career, Pound would refer back to Whitman, his one American epic forebear. "What I Feel About Walt Whitman" outlines his ambition to renew and revalue American culture. Interestingly, he cites the Tuscan renaissance (subject of his master's thesis, his first book, *Spirit of Romance*) as model for his perfect poets' society, which his Italian contemporaries were linking to their own Risorgimento:

> From this side of the Atlantic I am for the first time able to read Whitman, and from the advantage of my education and — if it may be permitted a man of my scant years — my world citizenship: I see him America's poet . . . . He *is* America . . . . Personally I might be very glad to conceal my relationship to my spiritual father and brag my more congenial ancestry — Dante, Shakespeare, Theocritus, Villon, but the descent is a bit difficult to establish. Whitman is to my fatherland (*Patriam qua odi et amo* for no uncertain reasons) what Dante is to Italy and I at my best can only be a strife for a renaissance in America of all the lost or temporarily mislaid beauty, truth, valor, glory of Greece, Italy, England, and the rest of it.[13]

Just as Pound chose Whitman as metonym for the incomplete project of American self-definition — for convenience and for his notion of author(ity)? — his critics have tended to center an era, style, canon, High Modernism, on what must needs be, according to Pound, an interested and revisionary genealogy.

Pound's schemes and "movements," directly or implicitly fashioned to achieve the (American or English or Italian) renaissance, tended to promote friends and contemporaries (Eliot, T. E. Hulme, Wyndham Lewis, Henri Gaudier-Brzeska) who coupled his ideals of Whitmanesque projective genius and careful training in craftsmanship. Pound, who at once damned and practiced the Americans' economy of selling "their own souls for a quotation,"[14] might have tagged Nietzsche, iconoclastic classicist, as model for the kind of artist he privileged and hoped to become. But rather than remaking himself a Nietzschean, Pound preferred to promote "donative artists" and men of "virtù" of his acquaintance.[15] In a sense, Pound was a double agent: an American following the well-trod path to aesthetic exile and English legitimacy, he also worked the London Scene on behalf of the national tradition to which he aspired. In addition to offering the bitterest decoction of Pound's attack on the United States publishing and journal trades, "Patria Mia," as it appeared in *The New Age* in 1912, summarizes his life-long ambivalence about American culture. Notwithstanding the bluster, Pound outlines a plan: "It is cheering to reflect that America accepted Whitman when he was properly introduced to them by William Michael Rossetti, and not before then" (*New Age*, XIII, 539). This self-promotion worked: the same section of "Patria Mia" carries the following footnote: "This article was written some weeks before I had any notion that I should be made foreign representative of this new periodical" — Harriet Monroe's *Poetry* (*New Age*, XIII, 540).

By 1910, when A. R. Orage and *The New Age* began publishing fragments of English translations, interpretations, and applications of such texts as *Zarathustra, Beyond Good and Evil*, and *Will to Power*, Pound and his literary-critical fellow travellers had begun thinking of themselves as intellectual aristocrats out to renovate art and politics. For a time, prior to World War I, which made such affiliations "German" in a dangerous way, "Nietzsche" underwrote the critical ambition and performance of the international intellectual avantgarde.[16] It is noteworthy that this very cosmopolitan and fluid group of intellectuals, particularly its Italian branch, also led the charge to national culture and ethno-nationalism.[17] If he took more Nietzsche "from the air" — Pound's favorite figure, from "I Gather the Limbs of Osiris" to *Guide to Kulchur*, for the transmission of potent ideas — than from any particular text, Pound's "I Gather the Limbs of Osiris" and "Patria Mia," both published in *The New Age* during the time that Nietzsche was therein excerpted and analyzed, bear the mark of a notoriously slippery Nietzscheanism that remains the enigmatic prototype and weapon against Fascism. Pound used this "Nietzsche" — or at least the ideas of some of his cohorts who read the poet-philosopher — for his "overcoming" of America. It is to the vexed London Nietzschean context and thematic that I would now like to turn.

From 1910–1913 on, after publishing *Spirit of Romance*, Pound supplemented the small and irregular salary he earned as part-time lecturer in Romance literature at the London Polytechnic by publishing his lectures and other critical writings in A. R. Orage's *The New Age*. His lectures and translations, "I Gather the Limbs of Osiris" and "Patria Mia," his reflections back on America, were the longest of over three hundred contributions.[18] The group of writers, artists, occasional teachers and commentators who filled the pages of Orage's little magazine was something of a reading group as well as a repertory staff of art, music, politics, economics, and general culture reviewers.[19] Pound was hardly the only writer to range over various fields in the effort to educate himself and an erstwhile (Anglo-American) public. Neither was this the only group to which Pound belonged nor his only organ for publicizing his own deliberately pungent prose. In a long letter to Harriet Monroe, written right before he became "Foreign Correspondent" for her Chicago literary magazine, *Poetry*, Pound adopted a characteristic posture that tells volumes about his anxious nationalism, his deliberately combative (Nietzsche's "indigestible"?) style, and his ideas of how literary magazines should work. Since only part of this letter, at the University of Chicago's *Poetry* Collection, is reprinted in the standard edition of Pound's letters, I will quote it at some length:

> I think the worst betrayal you could make of American poetry is to pretend for a moment that you are content with a parochial standard.

You're subsidized. You don't have to placate the public at once.
I can only ask you to form an imaginary jury. Whistler and Walt
Whitman, I abide by their judgment.

Print me with an asbestos border & deplore my opinions in a
foot-note or in an editorial.[20]

To take Pound seriously, therefore, means being suspicious of his
harshest words, as well as those he managed to provoke from critics.
This was built into the group dynamic or publicity strategy of these
writers who prized enemies as proof of their own controversial and
"dangerous" ideas. Among the usual contributors thus suspect was
T. E. Hulme, whose "Jacob Epstein and the Critics" as well as his
analyses and translated fragments of Georges Sorel's *Reflections on
Violence* and Henri Bergson's *Introduction to Metaphysics* were first
advertised and excerpted by Orage. There was also Anthony M. Ludovici, *The New Age* art critic and lecturer in philosophy and aesthetics at London University. As principal translator of Oscar Levy's
projected *First Complete Works of Friedrich Nietzsche*, he also excerpted translations and applications of Nietzsche that were later
published as collected lectures.[21] As we will see, Hulme and Ludovici
would sling wild accusations of inaccuracy and abuse of the "real"
Nietzsche in the pages of *The New Age*. If they did not philosophize
"with a hammer," they surely beat out Poundian themes — ranging
from Egyptian models for art to the political and cultural dangers
and therapeutics of the modernism they attempted to dictate.

A. R. Orage's longstanding enthusiasm over Nietzsche hardly
prevented his editorial signatures — S. Verdad (*es verdad?*) and R. C.
H., the latter reviews were collected as *Readers and Writers*— from
endorsing variously positioned philosophical, literary, artistic, and
economic speculations. In 1907, T. N. Foulis, the Scottish publisher
of the Nietzsche translations, issued Orage's *Nietzsche in Outline
and Aphorism*, some hundred pages of unannotated Nietzschean
moral apothems and guidelines for living the aesthetic life according
to a new morality at once patriarchal and destructive. *The Dionysian
Spirit of the Age*, a 1906 monograph also from Foulis, lays out recurrent themes of *The New Age*, including the myths-in-progress of
"new age," "new man," and "new education." Weighting the scale
on the side of Dionysus, Orage characterizes the most productive
role of the poet-philosopher as one of radical opposition, anarchy,
struggle, and an "immorality" leading to a "super-morality" beyond

the outworn habits of an exhausted Western culture. Like Pound and others (particularly in the Vorticist Manifesto of Lewis's *Blast*), Orage used Nietzsche to endorse suggestive parallels between ancient and modern art and, thus, to construct genealogies from which his own ideas could descend. In the spirit of his Nietzsche, for example, Orage directs the perpetually renewed drama of heroic battle of young intellectuals:

> For the tragic Greeks, life was the Dionysian will-to-renew, at war with the Apollan [sic] will-to-preserve; life was intelligible only as an aesthetic spectacle; there was no finality, no purpose, no end, no goal; only the gods played ceaselessly. And the business of man was to assist at the spectacle and in the play. As joyous spectator-actor, he should enter the strife consciously aiding the unfolding of the eternal drama, of which he himself was both Dionysus and Apollo.[22]

Nietzsche provided Orage with models and metaphors for the vitality and conviction he hoped to inculcate in the writers and readers of works addressing major issues. "Nietzsche," therefore, meant more a style of thought than a particular methodological rigor or definite position. Naming the German thinker a "European Event" with "his name" the "warcry of opposing factions" in Germany and France, Orage suggests Nietzsche's diffuse utility for English "intellectual and aristocratically-minded circles": "Already half a dozen well-known English writers might be named who owe, if not half their ideas, at least half the courage of their ideas to Nietzsche."[23] Orage abbreviated his own *New Age* project in the allegedly Nietzschean terms of producing the avant-garde or futuristic (if contra-Futurist) individuals who might project, predict, pilot, and construct the New (Super) Man, thus: "the concept of the Superman, as the goal of human progress, immediately lays the foundation of a scientific formulation of education."[24]

For the pedagogical *New Age* stable of extra-curricular poet-philosophers, this self-aggrandizing self-improvement program was license to excerpt, review, and imitate provocative work in the fluid fields of art, literature, and economics. Just so, its title, *The New Age: A Review of Politics, Economics and the Arts*, announces the range of conceptual exchange common in avant-garde journals of the time. While the dissemination of *New Age* ideas cannot be accurately gauged, Orage felt that he had a useful and saleable item. Or at least he advertised it as such: "Volume X . . . can be had, bound in linen with Index, and Illustrated and Literary Supplements. It forms a contemporary history of Labour, Socialist, Literary, Artistic and Dramatic Movements" (*The New Age*, XI, 528).

With authority derived aphoristically from outlines of Nietzsche's gnomic phrases, Orage promoted the man of letters, the critic-as-artist. A chosen few artists worked for him as art critics, as general cultural critic, and, more actively, as the best producers of cultural myths and values. Most important for our purposes is his (some would insist "Poundian" others "Sorelean") claim, "that artists of all men are the most necessary in the economy of life, for not only do they give things value that before had no value, but they alone can destroy old values and old creations."[25]

One could attribute several of Pound's key "theories" — including the concept/metaphor of the "interpreting detail" that would master yet remain anarchic — to Orage's Nietzscheanisms.[26] However, we might also factor in Orage's 1915 disclaimer of *The New Age*'s responsibility for "inventing Mr. Ezra Pound" who, was "wilful like an American child." Orage distanced himself from the schemes, if not the man, thus: "I would part from his theories as often as I found him clinging to one, for they will in the end be his ruin."[27] Orage was referring, not to Pound's economics or politics, but to his adoption of theories from the bad "company" he kept, "Imagists," "Verselebrists."[28] In 1921 he replied as editor to Pound's "Axiomata," published as Pound's "Last Will and Testament" when the poet departed for Paris: "The two most serious defects in Mr. Pound's work are his enmity to religion and his lack of psychological depth" which lead to "bizarre or rationalistic *mannerisms.*" Orage concludes his complaints about the Poundian mixture of theory and poetry with his own version of the neo-Nietzschean avant-garde aesthetic and nationalistic dismissal, common as well to Italian proto-fascists and German socialists: "Paris has nothing to teach and nothing to learn from EP."[29]

Before turning to the contested text of Nietzsche, let me introduce a note of caution about searching out representative sources, incriminating analogs, and the context of a particular author or authority. One might construct a quite different *New Age*, a socialist magazine that would, not only in retrospect, shade into Fascism; this is, after all, a well-worn trajectory of several continental schools and individuals (including Mussolini). Orage's "guild socialist" paper, though, was not this coherent; it has lent itself to further excerpting of the sort its contributors practiced. I was struck recently as I was mucking, if you will, the Upton Sinclair archives at Indiana University's Lilly Library, by the fact that searching for authorial coherence can easily distort the context or conversation surrounding his/her writings, not to mention other material factors. The collectors of the complete prose output of Upton Sinclair carefully clipped from *The New Age* only the then muckraking socialist's reviews and his call for the support of new oppositional writers. In 1910 (XI, 333), Upton Sinclair's Letter to the Editor appeared to compliment *The New Age* on its successful promotion of a democratic socialist agenda. Orage also published Sinclair's review of two books on Marx(ism) as well as his manifesto-like notice for the group and capitalist endowment of free-thinking young writers. Incidentally, Sinclair's document proposing that writers learning from writers be funded by the wealthy and established is not unlike Pound's own projects, "A College of the Arts" and "Bel Esprit." In fact, Sinclair, American and socialist and populist, was something of a departure from *The New Age*'s largely Continental and elitist focus. Among his favorite "Socialists," Orage published G. K. Chesterton, G. B. Shaw, H. G. Wells, and Edward Carpenter — all of them being among the "Dionysian Spirits" appended to *Nietzsche in Outline and Aphorism*.

As with many a small publishing venture, the words of a well-known writer found a place, despite ideological disagreements that place contributors in very different camps and canons. *The New Age* did not issue a homogeneous doctrine or unified theory, yet its (Nietzschean?) shape-shifting collection of followers of the usual (proto-Fascist) suspects traces an important intellectual current. Focussing on either the single author or, worse, from an uncritical *ex post facto* slant, on, say, the Fascist tendencies of Orage's group would be a mistake — however interested and interesting. In this regard, it is useful to look at the first two volumes of Mussolini's *Collected Works*, which also reprint the coverpages of several of the heterodox journals to which he contributed.[30] That said, "Nietzsche" clearly presided over a group-spirit of intellectual experimentalism and various revisionisms that sought the practical results of a modern aesthetics and artistic mission. For some his authority was more central and explicit than for others.

The books and *New Age* opinions of Anthony M. Ludovici, which led to an acrimonious personal attack by T. E. Hulme, crystalize the roughly Nietzschean and deeply contradictory, if intellectually shallow, thrust of Orage's magazine and group. Ludovici's University of London lectures on Nietzsche appeared in 1909 as *Who is to be Master of the World?*[31] Introduced by Oscar Levy's witty and typically misogynist jibes about the mostly female audience for philosophy and art lectures, Ludovici's book surveys Nietzsche's most enigmatic formulae ("Superman," mostly from *Zarathustra*; "transvaluation of all values" and "moralist *versus* immoralist," mostly from *Will to Power*) with an eye to injecting the German's therapeutic danger into the sclerotic English artistic and intellectual scenes, reversing the feminization and general decadence of the intelligentsia. His other major gripe is that English empiricism, liberal theology, and parliamentarism have been responsible for "plebicizing thought." Ludovici answers with a (de-)definition of a new secular religion in terms open to revisionary mastery by just the intellectual he wishes to become:

> freed from all taint of morality! — virtue or vice in the old sense. It [this new religion] becomes an adjustable instrument in the hand of the moralist wherewith he can rear a species — a world-conquering species, provided the code he writes can be calculated to make such a type thrive.[32]

Finding in Nietzsche the ground for what he calls his own Machiavellian theories, Ludovici emphasizes the basic sacrifice of special individuals to race progress. Artists — among whom critics are conspicuously counted — make the cut that excludes common men and common sense from the Future Man Ludovici wishes to propagate. This elitism and self-fashioning of a critical aristocracy is the common currency of *The New Age*. Not surprisingly, though with a certain "dramatic irony," the most frequent contributors jockeyed for position as proper ephebe and legitimate sire of the new breed of (Nietzschean?) thinker.

Ludovici's *Nietzsche and Art*, the 1911 collection of his 1910 University of London lectures, attempts to dictate guidelines of practical criticism and, as he says, a "canon" that also indicts "a choice of type in manhood," reflecting its author and predicting intellectual progeny.[33] Like better remembered and variously canonized documents (including the "Do's and Don'ts of Imagism" and Lewis/Pound/Brzeska's vorticist Manifestoes), Ludovici's book lists the interpretive requirements for sexually and intellectually potent art and criticism, even as it claims to tease these out of "Will to Power" (both *posthumously written* book and revisionary concept). Criticism must be held accountable to a practical interrogation:

> what guidance does it give? . . . why is it so vague? The words 'beautiful model' mean absolutely nothing nowadays. How, then, can the critic employ them without defining the particular sense in which he wishes them to be understood?[34]

Rather than endorse contemporary artists, of whom he finds no fitting English examples, Ludovici memorializes the great "aristocratic" and "organic" cultures of the past — most notably Egypt:

> In identifying Nietzsche's art canon with that admired and respected by Egypt at its best, I have done nothing at all surprising to those who know Nietzsche's philosophy . . . . His maturest work, *The Will to Power*, drove me inevitably not to Italy, not to Greece . . . but to the Valley of the Nile.[35]

Ludovici's implausible use of the German iconoclast as authority for a conservative canon hardly suggests the firestorm of posturing, the identity and legitimation crises, Nietzsche ignited in the young proto-High Modernists', so to speak, "aristocratic rebellion." Ludovici's negative review, in his capacity as art critic of *The New Age*, was the immediate cause of T. E. Hulme's ire, but from this exchange one can gather both what was at stake in appropriating Nietzsche (or, in Hulme's case, other favored demi-gods like Bergson and Sorel) and the amusing futility of claiming a straight genealogy with him as univocal influence or responsible father. Hulme's "Mr. Epstein and the Critics," which first appeared as an epistolary response in December 23, 1913's *The New Age* and later as an appendix to *The Sculptor Speaks*, attacks Ludovici as representative of the whole crowd of "ignorant popularizers" who fail to understand the true challenges of Nietzsche. Issuing what would later be named by Fredric Jameson and others the "classical High Modernist" call for "New Formulae" of accurate expression, Hulme praises the "more serious kind of art" that "sprang out of organic societies like the Indian, Egyptian, and Byzantine.[36] He diminishes Ludovici's similar observations about the positively despotic Egyptian models in terms most embarrassing to avant-gardists who, at the same time, would be the most classical: "All educated people take [that] for granted."[37] The

"GREAT HAMITE VORTEX OF EGYPT" was, of course, key source and coinage (contradiction/conundrum intended) of Gaudier-Brzeska's and Pound's own "Vorticist Manifesto" in Lewis's last issue of *Blast*, "Number II: The War Issue."[38]

Hulme lets go with a stream of insults that should have sobered all those "wannabe" critic-aristocrats who translated, published, quoted, and otherwise promoted a mixture of old and new models and metaphors under the signature of Nietzsche. Remember that these words — only slightly in excess of what Pound, warning Harriet Monroe, called his own FIRE — appeared in *The New Age*, and that Hulme continued to be a fellow traveller and but one of many difficult individuals who claimed at once to exceed and to represent the New (English) Man. For Hulme, perhaps gunning for the fellow's job, Ludovici was

> a little Cockney intellect . . . drawn by a curious kind of vanity into
> a region the realities of which must for ever remain incomprehen-
> sible to him. Mr. Ludovici, writing on Nietzsche might be com-
> pared to a child of four in a theatre watching a tragedy based on
> adultery . . . . He sees only what is akin to his mind's manner of
> working . . . as a Red Indian in a great town for the first time sees
> only the horses . . . ignorant of the aims of the actors in that sub-
> ject, and yet maintaining an appearance of adequate treatment with
> the help of a few tags.[39]

There and elsewhere, Hulme was simply engaging in a favorite activity of those who would appropriate or dismiss Nietzsche. And all that vituperation only endeared him to Pound.

Pound took the unusual step of adopting Hulme's theories along with his poems into his own poetic corpus. In 1913, as Appendix to *Canzoni and Ripostes,* he — or rather Elkin Mathews, owner of the bookshop that bears his name — published "The Complete Poetical Works of T. E. Hulme" with a shamelessly programmatic "Prefatory Note." In a move that might explain Orage's attempt to police the poet's incursions into "theory" — as well as the American's invasion of Orage's own turf, promotional editing — Pound appropriates Hulme's aphoristic critical style and sententious though rather elliptical poems as exemplary of "Imagism," "Vorticism," or "Dichten=Condensare":

In publishing his *Complete Poetical Works* at thirty, Mr. Hulme has set an enviable example to many of his contemporaries who have had less to say . . . .

As for the "School of Images . . . its principles were not so interesting as those of the "inherent dynamists" . . . yet they were probably sounder than a certain French school that tried to dispense with verbs altogether . . . . or of the Post-Impressionists who beseech their ladies to let down slate-blue hair over their raspberry-coloured flanks.[40]

Always the self-promoter, Pound took advantage of Hulme's greater selling power and British philosophical credentials as he drew tighter the circle of his "spermatic artists" and "seminal thinkers" — textual/sexual figures he used in "The Translator's Postscript" to Remy de Gourmont's *Natural Philosophy of Love*. Besides, he owed Hulme a favor, since that swash-buckling extra-curricular teacher probably set him up with both Orage and Mathews.[41] Pound idealized their collaborative friendship, even as he again advertised his own field of expertise, Provençal poetics as well as the casual political/aesthetic "life-style," if you will, of such as Dante, Machiavelli, and Castiglioni. Allusively contextual as ever, he explains that Hulme's poems

are reprinted for the good of fellowship, for good custom, a custom out of Tuscany and Provence; and . . . for convenience, seeing their smallness of bulk; and for good memory, seeing that they recall certain evenings and meetings of two years gone, dull enough at the time though pleasant to look back upon.[42]

Beyond his control, Pound might have been alluding to contemporary avant-garde Italian and French political and aesthetic developments. For, beyond Marinetti, several Italian artist-critic-intellectuals were (to turn the Benjaminian tag) politicizing art and otherwise, in various degrees of aesthetic high living, hanging out together as the American proposed. However, as fast as Pound was supplementing his American-ness and expanding his literary diet, he still did not know of an obscure Italian socialist school teacher and minor journalist, whose name would feature importantly in the poet's life only after the former became Il Duce. While he was soon to rise to the challenge of Marinetti's style of manifesto writing and to attempt, with Lewis and others, responses to Italian Futurism and performance, Pound did not know of Mussolini, himself merely a proto-fascist, of the movement he would later name and lead. By the time Pound was adopting Gaudier-Brzeska and Lewis, Mussolini had already fought a duel with Claudio Treves, the popularizer of Nietzsche and Sorel and editor of *Avanti!*, which was but one of the Socialist fine arts political journals to which Mussolini had contributed in his early years.[43] The once-friendly rivals fought over whether Italy should enter the war; Mussolini, abandoning Internationalist political (and aesthetic?) vanguardism, was an interventionist. What would Pound, later so enchanted by Mussolini's macho charm but equally appalled by the imperialism he failed to recognize in Fascism, have made of that? After all, as any "Poundian" will tell you, citing *Hugh Selwyn Mauberley*, Pound's *Blast* contributions, and *Gaudier-Brzeska*, the poet never got over the loss of his most promising cohorts to that first Great War.

In any case, the name of Nietzsche and doctrines of Will, political mythologization, and self-creation derived from Nietzsche and Georges Sorel, the founder of sydicalism, figured prominently in the early milieu and writings of Mussolini, even as they were endemic to several modernist movements that bridged art and politics. It is worth reviewing Mussolini's earliest published thoughts on Nietzsche, which are nearly concurrent with *The New Age* introduction of Nietzsche into England. Indeed, this is the high point of publicity, publication, and translations from the Nietzsche Archives, which was promoting the myth and revising the texts of Nietzsche with a media blitz that adumbrates both avant-garde movements and Mussolini's own Fascist state propaganda apparatus. Not only are Mussolini's comments on Nietzsche characteristic of the projective reading habits to which the philosopher seems particularly open, however lightly or indirectly rooted in readings of a particular book, his observations about the Nietzsche industry or phenomenon are accurate to the extent that he recognized, even as he constructed, the appeal and utility of Nietzsche as a "new man" and source of new ideas and ideas of renewal. It is, of course, more accurate to say that Nietzsche was a name that underwrote the still impressionable Mussolini's licenses to self-creation and an assault weapon against sclerotic political and artistic systems and conventions. In terms that he will later direct against Marxism and liberal democracy, Mussolini cites with special approval the largely posthumous and otherwise problematic *Wille zur Macht* — both text and concept — for the refusal of System and its author's "arbitrary" and highly interpretative styles of thought and writing. About a 1908 lecture on Nietzsche, Mussolini writes: "The 'system' is precisely the short-lived, the sterile, the negative element in all philosophies: while his is an ideal construction, often arbitrary and illogical, such that it must be interpreted as a confessing, a myth, a poem."[44]

Mussolini had discovered Nietzsche at the same time that several Italian avant-gardists, particularly Prezollini and Marinetti, were incorporating the not-quite-German philosopher, whom they might well have first encountered in France, as an activist for Italian culture. It bears recalling that for the last ten years of his life and well into the Third Reich, Friedrich Nietzsche was Elizabeth Nietzsche's, and later Max Öhler's, simulacrum. It was virtually acknowledged that he was not simply the author of texts but an icon or instigator of an increasingly nationalistic set of German ventriloquists who interpreted his slippery words and had no scruples about supplementing his notions of *Übermensch* with the mythical and future history of such a race. Moreover, the Nietzsche Archives actively promoted and aided the production and dissemination of this Nietzsche, whose very pan-Germanism and centered Individualism (as against another strain of Surrealist and skeptical interrogations of the Subject) proved remarkably translatable or adaptable to foreign and warring programs.

Early on in his own career of self-fashioning and self-promotion, Mussolini was certain that Nietzsche was part of a great Roman (anti-Christian and anti-masses) tradition that might be renewed. Just so, he recognizes Nietzsche as neither properly German nor, in the end, wholly rational. He was Mussolini's and others' enigmatic prototype of rebellious youth and, by extension, an adaptable version of the New Italy only the Overman can embody. With tone and emphasis that adumbrate Pound's attacks against the academic readers of literature ("the philologers" of "I Gather the Limbs of Osiris"), Mussolini, amplifying Treves, summarily condemns the general reception of Nietzsche by the establishment:

> there are salaried philosophers whose religion is the 27th of the month — the academicians, the awkward, clumsy representatives of official knowledge — who urge the young not to be seduced by free-thinkers, since Friedrich Nietzsche, the recognized head of these *nove homines*, spent the last years of his life in the shadow of

insanity. In short, Nietzsche is the most widely discussed man of our time — *man*, I have said, because in this case it is precisely the man who can explain to us the great enigma.[45]

The "great enigma"? Is it still Hamlet's "who goes there?" or Nietzsche/Zarathustra's more affirmative "Become who you are"? It is, in any case, a useful enigma.[46] And, who's to say what still can happen when a young guy/gal with political — even micro-political academic and journalistic — ambitions reads Nietzsche. Many current literary historians and Cultural Critics (Jameson, Adamson, Sternhell, for instance) would have, given the revisionary or anachronistic chance, censored Mussolini's reading and quotation program in the bud. Therefore, to bend my concocted moral tale to our present purposes, Poundians remain innocent of Nietzsche and, the better sort of Nietzscheans innocent of the likes of Pound.

That aside, in folding his Nietzsche commentary into Mussolini's exemplary life, Margherita Sarfatti modifies her subject's quotation/motto from *The Genealogy of Morals*. Noting that this woman was wont to use Mussolini's life and words and name in ways perhaps even more impressive than those employed by her male avant-garde contemporaries, I choose to quote her supplementary quotation — one which finds precedents for her Fascist hero in the (despotic) "Orient" as well as Nietzsche's "blond beasts of prey":

> Their egoism as men of power does not admit of restrictions. Far from suppressing their primordial instinct of cruelty they gave it free scope. Their motto is the *mot d'ordre* of the Oriental sect of assassins: 'Nothing exists: all is permitted.' And they add 'To see men suffer is good, to make them suffer is better.'[47]

If we seem to have traveled some distance from the topic at hand, Nietzsche and Pound, let the present essay end by picking up — or spinning — the thread of "influence" in Pound's cryptic mystification or mythologization of Il Duce. Canto LXXIV brings us back to Nietzsche, always good for penal reading, thus:

> Thus Ben and la Clara *a Milano*
> by the heels at Milano
>
> . . . .
>
> DIGONOS, Δίγονος, but the twice crucified
> where in history will you find it?[48]

Curiously, *The Companion to the Cantos of Ezra Pound*, that jewel of the Pound Industry and promissory note to a Variorum, if not an "authorized," *Cantos* fails to identify a possible source. Perhaps in the Detention Center Library in Pisa or "from the air" Pound read and modified the last line of *Ecce Homo*: "Have I been Understood? — *Dionysus versus the Crucified*" (EH, 335).[49]

Notes

[1] The theme of renewal, not simply the neo-effect, is everywhere in Nietzschean writings. Alexander Nehamas, *Nietzsche: Life as Literature* (Cambridge: Harvard UP, 1985), testifies to the currency of Nietzsche's peculiar utility for exacerbating and resolving identity crises and living authentically, improvisationally, or dramatically.

[2] In quite different veins, my own *Reading Pound Reading: Modernism After Nietzsche* (New York/London: Oxford UP, 1987) and Robert Casillo's *The Genealogy of Demons: Anti-Semitism, Fascism, and the Myths of Ezra Pound* (Evanston: Northwestern UP, 1988) explore Pound's intellectual sources. My book challenges a simple and singular patriarchal genealogy of Fascist villainy, whereas Casillo draws hard and fast conclusions about what happens when one reads certain dangerous Enlightenment Masters. Conversely, a recent study of Italian Fascism, Zeev Sternhell with Mario Sznajder and Maia Asheri, *The Birth of Fascist Ideology* (Princeton: Princeton UP, 1994), finds in irrationalism or the counter-Enlightenment the seminal force of Fascism.

[3] It is amusing to speculate that Pound, self-exiled from America and especially from New England, met and mis-recognized Emersonian individualism and skepticism in the intellectual currents he entered. We do know that Marinetti, Pound's intimidating rival, was translator and fan of Whitman. In a discarded draft of "Why I am so Clever," Nietzsche, singling out "Emerson's skepsis," virtually credits the American with the motive force of his (anti-)system (EH, 339). Orage lists Emerson as well as Thoreau and Whitman among those who wrote in "The Dionysian Spirit."

[4] Wyndham Lewis, *The Art of Being Ruled* (New York/London: Harper, 1926), p. 124.

[5] *Ibid.*, p. 127. Lewis, who unfairly but suggestively attacks almost everyone around him, anticipates the now commonplace historical conjunction of Nietzsche-Sorel-Bergson-William James as compound fathers of vitalism, individualism, voluntarism, anti-system and, ultimately, Fascism. See also Hulme's 1911 translation of Sorel's *Reflections on Violence*.

[6] Wyndhan Lewis, *Writers and the Absolute* (London: Methuen, 1963), pp. 54–59.

[7] Wyndham Lewis, *The Art of Being Ruled* (New York/London: Harper, 1926), p. 81.

[8] Fredric Jameson, *Fables of Aggression: Wyndham Lewis, the Modernist as Fascist* (Berkeley: U of California P, 1979), p. 183.

[9] *Ibid.*, p. 131.

[10] Unlike some of his friendly critics (especially Kenner and Bridson), I would not defend Lewis; quite the opposite. Notwithstanding Jameson's allusions to Hitler, Lewis's positive analysis of National Socialism is more pernicious than sexual and intellectual attraction to energetic and arbitrary leadership. In that book and elsewhere, Lewis ponders the utility of replacing "class" with "race," state paternalism and ethno-nationalism with argument and advertisement. See especially "Race and Class," "Blutsgefühl," and "The Exotic Sense," all chapters of *Hitler* that attempt to turn modern culture from the very revolutions *Blast* might be thought to represent. In key with Hulme's and his own early revolutionary pronouncements, Lewis mocks Ludovici for endorsing the alleged opinion of a sort of law and order Nietzsche, stating that "the patriarchal family has always been the foundation of peoples who have been distinguished for their joy and power over life" (*The New Age*, X, 113).

[11] Jameson, *Fables of Aggression*, p. 131.

[12] Richard Huelsenbeck, *Memoirs of a Dada Drummer: Documents of 20th-Century Art* (New York: Viking, 1969), pp. 88, 158. Georges Bataille, *Visions of Excess: Selected Writings, 1927–1939*, ed. and trans. Allan Stoekl (Minneapolis: U of Minnesota P, 1985) offers another insider's correction to the authoritarian abuses of Nietzsche. Because his elitist attacks upon "labyrinthine thought turned into directives" and the "servile attitude and *use value* of Elisabeth Judas-Förster" share the problems I am trying to expose, his story of the Fascist Nietzsche Industry is compelling. Particularly telling against Pound's pantheon is Bataille's question "How can one not see the abyss that separates a Cesare Borgia, a Malatesta, from a Mussolini. The former were insolent scorners of tradition and of all morality . . . the latter has been slowly enslaved by everything he was able to set in motion only by paralyzing, little by little his earlier impulses" (p. 186).

[13] Ezra Pound, *Selected Prose 1909–1965*, ed. William Cookson (New York: New Directions, 1973), pp. 145–46.

[14] *Ibid.*, p. 102.

[15] See Pound's *Gaudier-Brzeska: A Memoir* (London/New York: John Lane, 1916) as the poet's memorial to the young sculptor whom Pound had supplied with the marble for the "Hieratic Head of Ezra Pound." See also Eva Hesse's account of the "Men of 1914's" all-male conceptualization and birth of New Art, *Die Achse Avantgarde-Faschismus: Reflexionen über Filippo Tommaso Marinetti und Ezra Pound* (Zürich: Arche Verlag, 1990), p. 210.

[16] Despite Oscar Levy's ecstatic 1914 announcement of the Nietzsche Archive's role as "an intellectual center for securing that cultural unity of Europe which must precede its political and commercial union" (H. F. Peters, *Zarathustra's*

Sister: The Case of Elisabeth and Friedrich Nietzsche, New York: Crown, 1977, p. 202), many would recant or simply forget their Nietzschean connections. In *Readers and Writers, 1917–1921* (London: G. Allen and Unwin, 1922), a collection of his *New Age* columns, Orage erased Nietzsche's name and claimed that Blake and other English "Dionysian Spirits" had preempted anything valuable in Nietzsche.

[17] Walter L. Adamson, *Avant-Garde Florence: From Modernism to Fascism* (Cambridge: Harvard UP, 1993), pp. 79–93.

[18] "I Gather the Limbs of Osiris" was published in thirteen parts, December 1911-February 1912; subsequent publications have separated the translations from Pound's essay that offers his "New Method of Scholarship." Chapter 1 of my *Reading Pound Reading* gives extensive commentary on this series and "method." "Patria Mia" appeared in eleven installments September-November 1912; the version in *Selected Prose 1909–1965* was made for simultaneous American publication, but the editor at McClurg's misplaced it. With Pound's urgings, and perhaps further inked-in revisions, it was published in 1955, rather than 1913.

[19] While perhaps overly skeptical about any group cohesion — which might well have involved agreements violently and publicly to disagree — Carpenter notes that the "'New Age-ites'" met weekly for tea. Humphrey Carpenter, *A Serious Character: The Life of Ezra Pound* (Boston: Houghton & Mifflin, 1988), pp. 168–69.

[20] Pound to Monroe, October 22, 1912; in the University of Chicago Regenstein Library, *Poetry* Collection.

[21] In his "Editorial Note" and "Nietzsche in England," Oscar Levy cautions against reading Nietzsche at too early an age (p. ix); in keeping with Ludovici's and Orage's challenges, he jabs at England's "feminine receptivity" to all the bad stuff (democracy, pity, Christian virtues) to ask "Why is there no male audience in England willing to listen to a many daring philosophy?" (p. xiii). Levy didn't miss a certain serious Nietzschean play in, for example, his anti-anti-semitism: "It is easy for me to be carried away by that favourite sport of mine, of which I am the first inventor among the Jews — Christian baiting" (p. xxv). See Oscar Levy and Anthony M. Ludovici (eds.), *The Complete Works of Friedrich Nietzsche: The First Complete and Authorized English Translation* (New York: Macmillan Co., 1924).

[22] A. R. Orage, *Nietzsche in Outline and Aphorism* (Chicago: A. R. McClurg; Edinburgh: T. N. Foulis, 1911), p. 37.

[23] *Ibid.,* p. 11.

[24] *Ibid.,* p. 80.

[25] *Ibid.,* p. 124.

[26] Pound, *Selected Prose 1909–1965,* p. 23.

[27] See Wallace Martin, *A. R. Orage as Critic* (London: Routledge & Kegan Paul, 1974), p. 142.

[28] *Ibid.*, p. 143.

[29] *Ibid.*, p. 146.

[30] Benito Mussolini, "La Filosofia della Forza: Postille alla Conferenza dell'on Treves," in *Opera Omni di Benito Mussolini* (36 volumes), ed. Edoardo & Duilio Susmel (Firenzi: Fenice, 1951–63), II, 174–84.

[31] Anthony M. Ludovici, *Who is to be Master of the World? An Introduction to the Philosophy of Friedrich Nietzsche* (Edinburgh: T. N. Foulis, 1909).

[32] *Ibid.*, pp. 40–41.

[33] Anthony M. Ludovici, *Nietzsche and Art* (London: Constable, 1911), p. 8.

[34] *Ibid.*, pp. 30–31.

[35] *Ibid.*, p. 234.

[36] T. E. Hulme, "Epstein and the Critics," in *The Sculptor Speaks: Jacob Epstein to Arnold L. Haskell* (London: William Heinemann, 1931), pp. 157, 162.

[37] Ezra Pound, *Gaudier-Brzeska: A Memoir* (London/New York: John Lane, 1916), p. 163.

[38] *Ibid.*, p. 9.

[39] Hulme, *The Sculptor Speaks*, pp. 160–64.

[40] Ezra Pound, *Canzoni and Ripostes of Ezra Pound* (London: Elkin Mathews, 1913), p. 59.

[41] Humphrey Carpenter, *A Serious Character: The Life of Ezra Pound* (Boston: Houghton & Mifflin, 1988), p. 17.

[42] Pound, *Canzoni and Ripostes*, p. 59.

[43] Margherita Sarfatti, *The Life of Benito Mussolini*, trans. Frederic Whyte (New York: Frederich A. Stokes, 1925), p. 211.

[44] Mussolini, *Opera Omni di Benito Mussolini*, II, 175; my thanks for the ms translation given me by Lawrence Rainey.

[45] *Ibid.*

[46] If Mussolini soon became too engaged in political activities and/or tangled in other lines of influence to write about Nietzsche, he exchanged many letters with the philosopher's sister. Like Hitler, he visited the Archive, and Frau Förster enabled the Weimar performance, in 1932, of Il Duce's play *Campo di Maggio*, a fictionalized life of Napoleon. Cf. also H. F. Peters, *Zarathustra's Sister*, pp. 218–19.

[47] Sarfatti, *The Life of Benito Mussolini*, p. 143. In order to spread the guilt and glory around Mussolini's circle, one should consider Sarfatti's influence, which even Benito Mussolini — not to mention Rachelle, other family members and

the Mussolini Industry at large — revised out of history and biographies; cf. Philip V. Cannistraro and Brian R. Sullivan, *Il Duce's Other Woman: The Untold Story of Margherita Sarfatti, Benito Mussolini's Jewish Mistress, and How She Helped Him Come to Power* (New York: William Morrow, 1993).

[48] *The Cantos of Ezra Pound* (New York: New Directions, 1970), p. 425.

[49] Carroll F. Terrell, *A Companion to the "Cantos" of Ezra Pound*, 2 vols. (Berkeley: U of California P in conjunction with the National Poetry Foundation, Orono, 1984), p. 48, simply notes that there is no record of "twice crucified." Of "Digones," *twice-born* let me note the Dionysian Spirit of Pound's ms footnote to "The Translator's Postscript" to Remy de Gourmont's *Natural Philosophy of Love*, Pound's clearest Nietzschean formula: "*an* idea once born does lead an independent life, very much like a member of the vegetable kingdom, blowing seed ideas from the paradisal garden at the summit of Dante's *Purgatoria*, capable of lodging and sprouting where they fall. Or in Gourmont's phrase 'fecundating a generation of bodies as Genius fecundates a generation of minds' not in relation to the paternal brain that begat it" (Lilly, mss [192]).

Elmar Schenkel

Dionysus and the Word: The Nietzschean Context of American Modernist Poetry (Cummings, Eliot, Stevens)

WHEN T. S. ELIOT, in his *Notes Towards the Definition of Culture* (1948), claimed that "only a Christian culture could have produced a Voltaire or a Nietzsche," he may not have suspected the pivotal role Nietzsche was to play in Western philosophy from the nineteen-seventies onwards. Eliot went on to say that he did not believe "that the culture of Europe could survive the complete disappearance of the Christian Faith," and he was more Nietzschean than anything else when he described himself as a "student of social biology."[1] In any event, Eliot saw Nietzsche as being indissolubly bound up with the project of European culture. For Eliot, the very absence or disappearance of Christianity heralded by Nietzsche seems to have had a specifically European flavor.

With the return of Nietzsche's work to academic studies — via Heidegger, Derrida, Bloom, and Neo-Nietzschean philosophers in the United States — this view sounds outdated only at first sight. Nietzsche's discomfort with European or rather Christian civilization was a reaction to a form of philosophical discourse that had become a deeply ingrained and largely unconscious habit among Westerners. In this sense, Nietzsche has been seen as one of the great archeologists of modernism — one who, like Freud, pointed out the great fallacies and illusions produced by a society in which instinct and rationality had inexorably diverged. And yet, Nietzsche's attempt to pierce the veil of untruths and even his praise of lying and illusions are unthinkable without a deeper sense of what truth and falsehood are. Hence his thinking depends on values that he continually undermines.

As Robert Ackermann has pointed out, however, current American thought on Nietzsche — represented by such influential works as Nehamas's *Nietzsche: Life as Literature* — has focussed predominantly on aestheticism and textuality. In other words, Nietzsche's incongruities have been simplified in order to call them perspectivist and pluralist. Such labeling ignores the bass notes in his philosophy:

> Nietzsche has been transformed from an incomprehensible foreigner into a safe and predictable contemporary. But when Nietzsche is presented in such terms, he is trivialized into a King-Kong-in-chains, appearing under heavy sedation to English-speaking academic audiences.[2]

In this pluralistic view, *Übermenschen* "could meet like Rotarians, each with a colorful and unmistakable personality, ready to engage in a provocative Monday luncheon conversation" (*ibid.*).

This cosy model seems to domesticate and ultimately to marginalize Nietzsche and is thus a far cry from Eliot's view of Nietzsche as a major protagonist in Western culture. Because the "poets lie too much," as Nietzsche wrote and as Robinson Jeffers was to reiterate, they come closer to carrying out Nietzsche's thought than to understanding it. What philosophers by their very vocation tend to neglect — the illogical and irrational, the unclassifiable and irreconcilable — may turn out to be the essence of poetry, or, as Adorno put it, the non-identical, that which cannot be identified within a theoretical or ideological system or a set of beliefs.

Ackermann's main criticism is that recent American philosophers have neglected or even ignored the most important non-textual dimension of Nietzsche's thought — the Dionysian element. In this paper I try to argue that modernist poets have tried to embody this Dionysian dimension in their texts, or have reacted to Nietzsche's diagnosis of the absence of Dionysus in modern culture.

Dionysus assumes different guises and can be discovered in a human figure, a principle, a physical movement, sensory ecstasy, or an emotional obsession — but at any rate, this god is ultimately of a somatic nature. All his attributes stem from bodily experience. Nietzsche's philosophy of the body derives from his fascination with Dionysus and the Dionysian powers inhabiting the body. In light of Dionysus as a somatic force, the modern condition could be expressed thus: "When you have lost your body, you need an ism."[3] Paradoxically, Nietzsche, who unearthed this relationship between ideology and asceticism produced a work that fuelled the very isms that he fought — socialism, anti-semitism, nationalism, etc.

Any discussion of Nietzsche and literature will be confronted with the problem of intertextuality. The poet who has been most frequently linked with Nietzsche, Wallace Stevens, has also been the center of a debate concerning 'influence' and the 'intertextual'. The most sophisticated attempt to create an intertextual understanding of Stevens to date has come from Bobby J. Leggett in his *Early Stevens: The Nietzschean Intertext*. The gist of his methodological discussion is the following:

> not to say anything about the origins of Stevens' poems or to identify sources but to produce readings. The value of intertextuality is to allow us to read aspects of a text that are otherwise unreadable, to propose new perspectives, and these results obtain even when the question of influence is deferred.[4]

I endorse this understanding of intertextuality and wish to apply it to some modernist poets — in particular, Cummings, Eliot, and Stevens — who seem to have reacted in similar ways as Nietzsche to the same cultural phenomena. The most important of these phenomena is the Christian element that Eliot alludes to in his *Notes*.

II

Nietzsche has been hailed as "our pivotal Modernist," and his key text is *The Birth of Tragedy*. As Frederick Karl puts it: "Nietzsche was seeking a new form of thought that went beneath and beyond texts, one that, moving outside normal restraints, defined itself as having come from a different source."[5] Karl emphasizes the "bifocal experience" — of the mind versus the senses — that Nietzsche's thought shares with Stevenson's and H. G. Wells's fantasies as anticipations of Freudian psychology. For the first time, the struggle between the conscious and the unconscious received a nomenclature. It is no coincidence that Nietzsche as well as Freud resorted to Greek myths in order to elaborate their respective concepts.

If we understand the opposition of Dionysian and Apollonian as a dichotomy that is fundamental to the modern experience, we will discover that this opposition is seminal to themes and techniques of modernist poetics, too. Nietzsche asserts that "Dionysian man resembles Hamlet, in that both have peered into essences, have gained knowledge."[6] This knowledge, when directed to everyday reality, creates a nausea that prevents action. According to Nietzsche, it is not an excess of reflexion that paralyzes Hamlet but an insight into the nauseating abyss of truth. Only in art can there be redemption for this type of knowledge, art being "the saving sorceress, expert at healing" (*BT*, 60). As Karl points out, Nietzsche here "prefigures that small army of Hamlets who will emerge in the latter part of the century and culminate in Eliot's Prufrock, Pound's Mauberley, Rilke's narrator in Duino" [sic, Karl probably means Malte Laurids Brigge]. By aligning Hamlet with Dionysus and by redefining Greek serenity ("griechische Heiterkeit") as the inversion and, hence, mirror of the tragic view, Nietzsche rejects the silly optimism of his age. So did those American modernist poets who subverted the American Dream or tried to escape from it into cosmopolitanism or regionalism. Eliot and Pound expressed their dissatisfaction with American values both by pursuing European and non-European concepts and by choosing Greek myths as landmarks of cultural orientation.

It is important to note that the Apollonian and the Dionysian are not simply opposites. It is the Dionysian that is fundamental for Nietzsche, while the "Apollonian is a mode of representation that allows human beings to have a grasp of the Dionysian in a bearable form."[7] Modernism can then be seen as an attempt to reassert the Dionysian foundations of all cultural experience rather than the result of the struggle between two principles. This assertion occurs on the level of self and other, or rather through the recognition of the other within the self. It is to the tune of Rimbaud's "Je est un autre" that later poets will compose their songs of self. This otherness may reside in the claims of the unconscious and the body that make themselves felt in a shift of signs or in a symbolic subversion, a return to metaphor and self-referential language. The Dionysian body also reasserts its presence in music, which is "the key Dionysian art."[8] While Apollonian art forms emerge from dreams, the Dionysian is found in dance, rhythm and music. Wherever music takes over in poetry — from Mallarmé to Yeats — the somatic element is manifested in language: alliteration, repetition, assonances, consonances, and metrical devices stress poetry's affinity with bodily movement and testify to the psychophysical origin of the poetic.

Myth is a further attribute of the Dionysian spirit. Dionysian music actually creates myths (*BT*, 17), and any culture that cuts itself off from its mythical roots is bound to lose its creativity (*BT*, 23). But Dionysian processes are also related to play. Nietzsche developed this idea later in *The Gay Science* and in *Zarathustra*: "A child is concealed in the true man: it wants to play" ("Im ächten Mann ist ein Kind versteckt: das will spielen").[9] This slogan became a beacon for a whole generation of German proto-Dadaists and in particular for the poet Christian Morgenstern. But even in *The Birth of Tragedy* Nietzsche emphasized the playful nature of the Dionysian Urlust, the "primordial delight," with its "playful construction and destruction of the individual world" and likened this view to Heraclitus's idea of history as a child playing with stones and sands (*BT*, 142).

Again, the Dionysian manifests a corporeal dimension. Myths often concern the incarnation of spiritual principles and imagination embodied in play. This return of the body through Dionysus can even be seen in Nietzsche's concept of truth. His perspectivism, far from superseding the Dionysian impulse, derives from his insight that truth can never be an object. Hence it can never be objectively perceived and involves a subject-object relationship. Truth, in this sense, depends on the perspective and, above all, the vested interests of the viewer, which, for Nietzsche, are inextricably bound up with the somatic aspects of a person. Or, as an English author, who lived in the United States, wrote under the Nietzschean spell: " . . . truth is not knowledge. Truth is not the recognition of an external fact. Truth is a creative gesture. It is a ritual, a rhythmic poise, a balance deliberately sustained between eternal contradictions."[10]

III

One of the poets who has not yet been seen in relation to Nietzsche's philosophy is E. E. Cummings. While Yeats, Hart Crane, Stevens, Jeffers, and Ezra Pound all show signs of having come under the influence of the philosopher, lower-case Cummings seems to be harder to pinpoint. Yet the affinity with Nietzsche, in spite of all differences, is striking. As an inhabitant of Greenwich Village he was bound to have been exposed to Nietzsche's work, just as he was to Freud's work, whom he apparently read more carefully than most of his intellectual contemporaries. In fact, Cumming's reading of Freud can be seen as analogous to his reading of Nietzsche. Both authors may have made him conscious of the triple form of repression that his background weighed him down with, namely an inheritance "from Puritanism, from the stifling propriety of bourgeois Cambridge, and more immediately, from the prudery of his upbringing under the aegis of Reverend Edward Cummings."[11]

Milton A. Cohen traces certain techniques — like juxtaposition and oxymorons — in Cummings's paintings and poetry back to Freud's *Interpretation of Dreams* and *Wit and Its Relation to the Unconscious*. This sense of duality and talent for juxtapositions, however, is also part of a Nietzschean outlook that helped Cummings to overcome his repressive past. Cummings owned a copy of *Thus Spoke Zarathustra*, which he had marked heavily.[12] In *Zarathustra*, Nietzsche deconstructs the Western self in a similar way as Cummings does in his poetry and prose. Cummings's concept of self, however, is ambivalent, as Martin Heusser has demonstrated: "Thus we find on the one hand a traditional or metaphysical understanding of the self and on the other an attitude that is best described as Nietzschean."[13] Heusser shows that the Nietzschean view of self — as outlined in Nietzsche's posthumous fragments after 1885 and to some extent in *Zarathustra* — keeps appearing in Cummings's poetry as a disruptive force that produces heterogeneity and fundamental instability: "i am a birdcage without any bird."[14] This line recalls Kafka's haunted phrase "a birdcage went in search of a bird"[15] in a curious fashion. It describes an absence in search of a presence, emptiness in search of a subject that will fill it. If absence is characteristic of Cummings's work on one level, presence of self is also articulated in his work and reflects Cummings's debt to the values of American Transcendentalism. Here the self is vindicated by going beyond the physical world into the realm of metaphysics, which Nietzsche had already abrogated.

In much of his poetry, Cummings tries to find terms to reconcile these two concepts of the self. Heterogeneity and multiplicity are bound up with the condition of Keatsian negative capability and are essential to the recreation of wholeness, or even holiness; but Henri Bergson's intuitions about the "very inwardness of life" are also central to Cummings's view.[16] In light of Nietzsche's opposition of Apollonian and Dionysian forces, one can interpret Cummings's concept of the self as the fundamentally Dionysian process of "playful construction and destruction" stemming from an "overflow of primordial delight" (*BT*, 142). In this, Cummings's quest for the child in himself coincides with the "essential act of 'primitivism'" that is "elimination":

> ... the inexcusable and spontaneous scribblings which children make on sidewalks, walls, anywhere ... cannot be grasped until we have accomplished the thorough destruction of the world. By this destruction alone we cease to be spectators of a ludicrous and ineffectual striving and involving ourselves in a new and fundamental kinesis, become protagonists of the child's vision.[17]

Like Nietzsche in *Untimely Meditations*, Cummings rejects the dead knowledge accumulated by history and the stifling power of historicism, which is the arch-enemy of feeling. The ultimate value in Cummings's poetry is nowness and it is only here that feeling, intuition and even morality are localized. As he wrote to his sister in 1922: "THE MORE WE KNOW THE LESS WE FEEL !!!!!!!! ... Destroy, first of all!!! ... TO DESTROY IS ALWAYS THE FIRST STEP IN ANY CREATION."[18] Death comes from mechanistic, routine-like thinking, and from science and its measuring: "who cares if some oneeyed son of a bitch / invents an instrument to measure Spring with?[19] Spring is one of the recurrent images in Cummings's poetry denoting rejuvenation and a new life-giving freshness, in which the assertion of Dionysian forces and the body is felt. As in "La Guerre II":

> to the incomparable
> couch of death thy
> rhythmic
> lover
>
> thou answerest
>
> them only with
>
> spring[20]

In a similar fashion, Cummings writes in "i thank You God for most this Amazing": "i who have died am alive again today, / and this is the sun's birthday ..."[21] Mind and matter can only be reconciled with the help of the Dionysian element. Characteristically, Cummings expresses the two types of self — the paradoxical and the monolithic — in a contrast of the two cities that shaped him:

> [In Paris] I participated in an actual marriage of material and im-
> material things; I celebrated an immediate reconciling of spirit and
> flesh, forever and now, heaven and earth. Paris was for me precisely
> and complexly this homogeneous duality: this accepting transcen-
> dence; this living and dying more than death or life. Whereas — by
> the very act of becoming its improbably gigantic self— New York
> had reduced mankind to a tribe of pygmies, Paris (in each shape
> and gesture and avenue and cranny of her being) was continuously
> expressing the humanness of humanity.[22]

Paris allows him to become himself through the marriage of mind
and matter, body and spirit: "Now, finally and first, I was myself: a
temporal citizen of eternity . . . ."[23] Cummings not only expresses his
affirmation of life in such images, but also enacts his great 'Yes' in
the ecstasies of his language which transcends grammar and the linearity of writing. The written word is only a temporary appearance
"from spirally ecstatically this," or a flash of "perhapsless mystery of
paradise."[24] In the same vein, anti-metaphysical Zarathustra resorts to
similar means of representing his ecstasies. As in Cummings's and
Wordsworth's work, it is the child who represents Dionysian freshness for Zarathustra: "The child is innocence and forgetfulness, a
new beginning, a sport, a self-propelling wheel, a first motion, a sacred Yes. Yes, a sacred Yes is needed, my brothers, for the sport of
creation . . . ."[25]

IV

Forgetfulness (as recommended by Nietzsche in *Human, All Too
Human, I*, 92), is the necessary precondition for the Dionysian to re-
enter life through vital processes in nature and history. One of the
most important forms the Dionysian can assume in order to stimu-
late earth and humanity is, according to Nietzsche, music and
rhythm. T. S. Eliot's use of music is related to his early familiarity
with the French symbolists, and music appears to be closely connected to myth in *The Waste Land*. This affinity was first explored by
Nietzsche in *The Birth of Tragedy* and in his discussions of Wagner in
Untimely Meditations. Eliot, as a student of philosophy, had some
knowledge of Nietzsche as is shown by his review of Wolf's *The Philosophy of Nietzsche*, which ends with his regretting "the omission of
any account of Nietzsche's view on art" and a reference to *Human*,

All Too Human.[26] It is a well-balanced review that does not support the notion of Nietzsche's militarism — a remarkable feat when one considers that just three years later, Hart Crane felt it necessary to defend Nietzsche against the simplifiers by stating that "Nietzsche, Zeppelins, and poisoned-gas go ill together."[27]

As Michael Beehler put it, "it is Nietzsche's voice that resonates in *The Waste Land*, although it is a voice suppressed by Eliot's explanatory notes."[28] Thus Eliot's quotation from Wagner's *Tristan and Isolde*, "Oed und leer das Meer," in *The Waste Land* re-echoes *The Birth of Tragedy*, in which Nietzsche describes the resurgence of Apollonian forces and their play in *Tristan*:

> . . . suddenly we imagine we see only Tristan, motionless, asking himself dully: "The old tune, why does it wake me?" And what once seemed to us like a hollow sigh from the core of being now merely wants to tell us how "desolate and empty the sea." (*BT*, 127)

Yet only the explanations suppress the Nietzschean intertext in Eliot. The modernist poet builds up a new field of relationships and tensions which partly reproduces Nietzschean images and cultural criticism ("Culturlüge"), but also partly anticipates the non-Nietzschean solutions Eliot was to produce in his later works.

In all events, Eliot's analysis of culture is here very close to Nietzsche's views. There is a great affinity with Nietzsche's attack on historicism in *Of the Use and Disadvantage of History for Life* and, in consequence, with his cult of youthfulness as an attack on gerontocratic society. This is reflected in *The Waste Land* in images of age, ruins, dryness, or decrepit bodies and a general physical and psychic seediness. The very fact that Eliot provides explanatory notes shows his ambivalence about historicist culture. The vitality that is championed in the text is counteracted by the attendant paralysis caused by the weight of knowledge in the subtext.

While in his later works Eliot searches for "a sign of meaningful presence, as the eternal still point and center of the turning world of time,"[29] *The Waste Land* is sprinkled with signs of absence and dissonance, which, for Nietzsche, express the Dionysian: "The joy aroused by the tragic myth has the same origin as the joyous sensation of dissonance in music" (*BT*, 142). But Eliot's is an absence yearning for presence. One of Madame Sosostris's cards is blank, "is something he carries on his back / which I am forbidden to see. I do not find / The Hanged Man."[30] Eliot was to fill in this blank and find the Hanged Man, as we know from hindsight. Both Eliot and Nietzsche evince an increasing sense of the separation of body and spirit. In *The Waste Land* any allusion to the body politic turns into a corpse politic. The unreal city is inhabited by husks and spiritless shells, while bodiless spirits flow over London Bridge. Characteristically, the speaker alludes to the classical world when he tries to address Stetson, "You who were with me in the ships at Mylae!"[31] a quotation that is embedded within a number of references to Greek and Mediterranean fertility rites and myths. As depicted by *The Waste Land*, myths contain memories of other mental and bodily states, of participation and oneness. Hence they are fit to become vehicles for atonement. Cultural malaise goes beyond the text, and this may be a comment on the knowledge stored in the footnotes: "'You! hypocrite lecteur! — mon semblable, — mon frère!'"

This state of infertility, drowsiness and paralysis can only be redeemed by undergoing a form of initiation that is deeply related to the Dionysian. In "Death by Water" disorder is emphasized. Here we find the "whirlpool" which promises rejuvenation. As in "Gerontion," protagonists wait for the "juvescence of the year" and "Christ the tiger." In the latter poem, history is a maze that leads people astray and continues to cause the general fragmentation:

> After such knowledge, what forgiveness? Think now
> History has many cunning passages, contrived corridors
> And issues, deceives with whispering ambitions,
> Guides us by vanities . . . . [32]

The speaker feels separated from his body: "I have lost my sight, smell, hearing, taste, and touch."[33]

In Jessie L. Weston's and Frazer's interpretation of the fertility myths underlying the Arthurian cycle, Eliot finds hope for the reconstruction of the individual as well as the social body. Water provides a living link between the dissociated worlds; it is this element which will help overcome the spiritual drought. This process is depicted in "What the Thunder Said." However, the signs of hope which Eliot sees in the larger context of Indo-European myths ultimately depend on a Schopenhauerian and Wagnerian belief in transcendence: "Shantih shantih shantih" or, as the note explains, "The Peace which passeth understanding." Here Eliot departs from

Nietzsche's bolder attempt to negate any metaphysical or ascetic construction — a turn that characterizes his attitude towards Wagner in *Untimely Meditations* ("The Case of Wagner"). While Eliot reconstructs the shattered body in transcendence and tries to go beyond the lurking nemo[34] in the modern psyche, Nietzsche perceives the illusionary nature of this type of asceticism which only increases the modern sense of futility, and thus produces more illusions and ideologies and eventually precipitates the catastrophes of the twentieth century. Cummings seems to come closer to Nietzsche's intentions by staying firmly within the material world, since the immaterial can be located only here. The senses cannot contradict the divine. On the contrary:

> how should tasting touching hearing seeing
> breathing any — lifted from the no
> of all nothing — human merely being
> doubt unimaginable You?

> (now the ears of my ears awake and
> now the eyes of my eyes are opened)[35]

V

Eliot's technique of collage and montage, as practised in his earlier work, employs a multiplicity of perspectives, which were replaced in his later work by an older, religious model of perception. In *The Waste Land*, however, 'truth' appears in flashes, in the gaps produced by dissonance. In much of his work, Wallace Stevens concentrated on just these flashes, in which the bodily and the spiritual converge. He is the modern American poet who has most consistently been discussed in connection with Nietzsche. Bloom, Bates, Leonard/Wharton, Leggett and others have scrutinized most of Stevens's explicit and implicit responses to Nietzsche.[36] As Milton Bates has summarized: "Nowhere else in Stevens does one have an intellectual influence whose sources and extent can be specified with as much certainty."[37] As documentary evidence (in particular Stevens's correspondence with Henry Church) suggests, Stevens was "actively interested in Nietzsche during two widely separated periods — the years before and during World War I, and the last years of World

War II."[38] The latter period is especially interesting in view of 1940 newspaper headlines such as "HITLER WAR URGE BLAMED ON INSANE PHILOSOPHER; NIETZSCHE NAZI CHIEF'S FAVORITE AUTHOR."[39] Critics have designated a canon of works by Stevens that possibly reflect a Nietzschean influence, poems such as "Montrachet-le-Jardin," "Lettres d'un soldat," "The Surprises of the Superhuman," "Description without Place," "Esthétique du Mal," "Notes Towards a Supreme Fiction," and his essays "A Collect of Philosophy" and "Two or Three Ideas." Affinities in themes and style of thought have been analyzed: the attitude towards the hero and the Overman;[40] 'truth' as the making of fiction;[41] the view of symbolism in Stevens, Zarathustra, and Cassirer's philosophy.[42] The most sophisticated approach has been undertaken by Leggett, who studies the transvaluation of values, pluralism, and the arts of untruth in his Nietzschean reading of early Stevens.

Here I should like to concentrate on those traces of the Dionysian that are characteristic of Stevens's "Notes Towards a Supreme Fiction." Nietzsche's essential uncertainty about the future — vacillating as it did between euphoria (as in *The Birth of Tragedy*) and deepest scepticism (as in significant parts of *Zarathustra*) — entails difficulties in nomenclature. As Humpty Dumpty would confirm: When the master leaves his house, words lose their precise meanings. Tensions develop between the instinctual biological forces that condition history and the new free spirits as envisaged in the idea of the *Übermensch*.[43] Hence Nietzsche's emphasis on the unnameable qualities of emergent phenomena: "Being new, nameless, hard to understand, we premature births of an as yet unproven future . . . ."[44]

In "Notes" Stevens stresses a similar duality: "the uncertain light of single, certain truth."[45] The death of God is also the death of Adam's project — the death of naming as a process that not only defines but also creates:

> Phoebus is dead, ephebe. But Phoebus was
> A name for something that never could be named.
> There was a project for the sun and is.
>
> (100)

Creating reality by naming, however, always bears the seeds of destruction within itself; naming is a result of "desiring," and desire is permanently reproduced by an absence or the inward nemo: "And not to have is the beginning of desire" (100). Nietzsche closes his thoughts on the unnameable by returning to the only norm that seems to be left for experience — the body. But the present body cannot fill this void: " . . . how could we still be satisfied with present-day man?"[46] The future dimension of the body is implied in Nietzsche's metaphor of "the great health,"[47] which he judges as necessary for the expedition into the unknown. "Expedition" ("discoverer and conqueror of the ideal") can be read as a metaphor that is deeply related to another image, that of exile. In Stevens's poetry, desire and exile are inextricable: "To have what is not is its ancient cycle . . . . It knows that what it has is what is not" (100f.). Although the sun itself cannot be named, it has a project. There is an eternal difference between what is and what is not, which appears "in the difficulty of what it is to be" (100). As Beehler writes, in Stevens, there "is never identity without the trace of difference . . . . Signs, then, do not begin in a paradise of meaning or intentionality; they begin differentially in the original displacement of exile . . . ."[48]

Just as Nietzsche tries to visualize health as a supreme state of being, which has discarded the burden of history, Stevens's symbols and signs in "Notes" keep referring, at least negatively, to paradisal meanings that stress an existence beyond history. Here the Dionysian impulse can be perceived in the interplay between difference (negation, exile, abstraction) and identity (sensual experience, affirmation, creation, metaphor, phenomenon). In "Notes," Stevens keeps alluding to the "first idea," the origins, to Adam and Eve. However, the "first idea was not our own" (102). Even in paradise, there is a primordial split between body and mind. Paradise nourishes the seeds of the modern age, self-reflexion and alienation: "Adam / In Eden was the father of Descartes / And Eve made air the mirror of herself" (*ibid.*). In this world where truth is ravished again and again — "ravishments . . . so fatal to / The truth itself" (100) — the original (and ever present) namelessness is pivotal for humans trying to create ideas of order by using the imagination. Because there "was a myth before the myth began" (102), the nameless world is in a perpetual process of becoming. All secondary myths reflect the non-human mythmaking that informs creation. Any image referring to such primary unity is bound to be exiled: "the first idea becomes / The hermit in a poet's metaphors" (100). Or, as Owen Barfield put it:

Reality, once self-evident, and therefore not conceptually experienced, but which can now only be reached by an effort of the individual mind — this is what is contained in a true poetic metaphor; and every metaphor is 'true' only in so far as it contains such a reality, or hints at it. The world, like Dionysus, is torn to pieces by pure intellect; but the poet is Zeus; he has swallowed the heart of the world; and he can reproduce it as a living body.[49]

This reconstruction in metaphor is the starting point for Stevens's reflections on poetry. In the interplay between absence and presence that the rhetoric of metaphor creates, the Dionysian body can be found in the somatic unity of idea and image, of allusion and illusion:

> The poem refreshes life so that we share,
> For a moment, the first idea . . . It satisfies
> Belief in an immaculate beginning.
>
> (101)

"Notes" represents an effort to reflect on the difficulty of maintaining such a belief in an immaculate beginning:

> The fragrance of the magnolias comes close,
> False flick, false form, but falseness close to kin.
>
> It must be visible or invisible,
> Invisible or visible or both:
> A seeing and unseeing in the eye.
>
> (104)

Origins and bodily experience can only be celebrated because there is a continual effort to invent the world, to embody that which lies beyond the physical and is as yet nameless. It is a world in parenthesis, suspended between matter and that which matters. Stevens's poetic universe, like Nietzsche's, is "a universe of inconstancy" (109), a play between absence and presence, exile and return. His view of spring can be contrasted to Eliot's and Cummings's: "Is spring a sleep?" (110). The Apollonian and Dionysian polarities of winter and spring, day and night, real and imaginary (112) render the sense of touch invaluable, since the visual no longer suffices:

The partaker partakes of that which changes him.
The child that touches takes character from the thing,
The body, it touches.

(112)

In the "fluctuations of certainty" (115), the sparrow's "Bethou me"
(114) announces what anthropologists would call original participation,[50] a world in which primeval unity can be experienced, far surpassing the Cartesian dreams Adam dreamt in paradise. It is
reconstructed in the "fiction of an absolute — Angel" (125).

There are few dashes in modern poetry upon which rests so much
pressure; this dash expresses a breathtaking moment of hesitation.
The cause for such hesitation may well lie in the knowledge that this
kind of fiction is always abroad, in exile. In this respect, Stevens's
Dionysian unity, as represented by the fiction of the absolute, can be
likened to Paul Klee's angels, who, with their unfinished nature, lin-
ger in some limbo between past and present or present and future, as
indicated by the titles of his pictures: "Forgetful Angel," "Angel in
the kindergarten," "Angel still groping," "Angel full of hope,"
"Angel in the process of becoming." Both Klee's and Stevens's creations share Nietzsche's sense of the unrealized and unfinished nature
of human evolution; both reside in worlds that are no longer or are
yet to come into being.

The Dionysian reality Nietzsche pursued cannot be realized in
modern poetry. Yet in modern poetry and poetics, we may experience the unending search for this reality, in the interstices between
somatic, mental and spiritual processes, or in the manifold attempts
to rethink and reinvent beginnings and transitions, in which

. . . the freshness of transformation is
The transformation of a world. It is our own,
It is ourselves, the freshness of ourselves.

(118)

Nietzsche's walk along the Silvaplaner lake prefigures this freshness,
this transformation: "Perhaps / The truth depends on a walk around
a lake" (105).

Notes

[1] T. S. Eliot, *Notes Towards the Definition of Culture* (London: Faber, 1962),
p. 122.

[2] Robert Ackermann, "Current American Thought on Nietzsche," in Sigrid Bauschinger, Susan L. Cocalis, and Sara Lennox, eds., *Nietzsche heute: Die Rezeption seines Werkes nach 1968* (Bern: Francke 1988), pp. 129–36 (here 129).

[3] Morris Berman, *Coming to Our Senses: Body and Spirit in the Hidden History of the West* (New York: Bantam, 1990), p. 343.

[4] Bobby J. Leggett, *Early Stevens: The Nietzschean Intertext* (Duke UP, 1992), p. viii.

[5] Frederick R. Karl, *Modern and Modernism: The Sovereignty of the Artist 1885–1925* (New York: Atheneum, 1988), p. 81.

[6] *The Birth of Tragedy*, trans. W. Kaufmann (New York: Vintage, 1967), pp. 59f. Hereafter, this edition will be quoted as *BT* with page references in parentheses.

[7] Robert Ackermann, *Nietzsche: A Frenzied Look* (Amherst: U of Massachusetts P, 1990), p. 15.

[8] *Ibid.*, 16.

[9] *Thus Spoke Zarathustra*, trans. R. J. Hollingdale (Harmondsworth: Penguin, 1961), p. 92.

[10] John Cowper Powys, *The Complex Vision* (New York: Dodd, Mead & Co., 1920), p. 69. Powys occupied an apartment on Washington Square, in the same house with E. E. Cummings. He made many American friends during the two decades he lived and lectured in the United States, some of whom were interested in Nietzsche such as Theodore Dreiser and Henry Miller. Powys gave lectures on Nietzsche and visited Nietzsche's sister in Weimar in 1909. See Patrick Bridgwater, *Nietzsche in Anglo-Saxony* (Leicester: UP, 1972), pp. 104–13, and Elmar Schenkel, "Taking Tea With Nietzsche's Sister — J.C. Powys in Weimar," *The Powys Society Newsletter*, 22 (1994), 2–11.

[11] Milton A. Cohen, "Cummings and Freud," *American Literature*, 55 (1983), 591–610 (here 593).

[12] He owned Thomas Common's translation (New York, 1917). Cf. Martin Heusser in his forthcoming book on E. E. Cummings, Chap. 1.

[13] Martin Heusser, "Unity Through Duality: Paradox in the Relation between Self and Other in the Poetry of E. E. Cummings," in Paul Geyer and Roland Hagenbüchle (eds.), *Das Paradox: Eine Herausforderung des abendländischen Denkens* (Tübingen: Stauffenburg, 1992), pp. 577–95 (here 579).

[14] E. E. Cummings, *Complete Poems 1913–1962* (New York: Harcourt, 1972), p. 360.

[15] Franz Kafka, *Hochzeitsvorbereitungen auf dem Lande und andere Prosa aus dem Nachlaß* (Frankfurt: Fischer, 1953), p. 41.

[16] Milton A. Cohen, *Poet and Painter: The Aesthetics of E. E. Cummings's Early Work* (Detroit: Wayne State UP, 1987), pp. 78f.

[17] Cf. Cummings, p. 68.

[18] *Ibid.*, p. 76.

[19] Cummings, *Complete Poems*, p. 264.

[20] *Ibid.*, p. 46.

[21] *Ibid.*, p. 663.

[22] Cummings, *i – six nonlectures* (New York: Atheneum, 1962), p. 53.

[23] *Ibid.*

[24] Cummings, *Complete Poems*, p. 714.

[25] *Zarathustra*, p. 55.

[26] Eliot, "Review of Wolf's *The Philosophy of Nietzsche*," *International Journal of Ethics*, 26 (1915/16), 426–27.

[27] Hart Crane, *The Complete Poems and Selected Letters and Prose* (New York: Anchor, 1966), p. 198.

[28] Michael Beehler, "Eliot, Burglary, and Musical Order," *Bucknell Review*, 30,2 (1987), 117–29 (here 118).

[29] *Ibid.*, p. 126.

[30] Eliot, *The Waste Land and Other Poems* (London: Faber, 1971), p. 28.

[31] *Ibid.*, p. 29.

[32] *Ibid.*, p. 19.

[33] *Ibid.*

[34] Cf. John Fowles's concept of the nemo in *The Aristo* (London: Triad/Granada, 1981), p. 47: "The nemo is a man's sense of his own futility and ephemerality . . . ." See also Berman, *Coming to Our Senses*, pp. 20ff.

[35] Cummings, *Complete Poems*, p. 663.

[36] Cf. Harold Bloom, *Wallace Stevens: The Poems of Our Climate* (Ithaca NY: Cornell UP, 1977); Milton J. Bates, *Wallace Stevens: A Mythology of Self* (Berkeley: U of California P, 1985); J.S. Leonard and S. E. Wharton, *The Fluent Mundo: Wallace Stevens and the Structure of Reality* (Athens, GA: U of Georgia P, 1988); Bobby J. Leggett, *Early Stevens: The Nietzschean Intertext* (Duke UP, 1992).

[37] Bates, *Wallace Stevens*, p. 248.

[38] Milton J. Bates, "Major Man and Overman: Wallace Stevens's Use of Nietzsche," *Southern Review*, 15 (1979), 811–39 (here 812).

[39] Quoted *ibid.*, p. 815.

[40] Cf. Joseph G. Kronick, "Large White Man Reading: Stevens's Genealogy of the Giant," *The Wallace Stevens Journal*, 7 (1983), 89–98; David Bromwich, "Stevens and the Idea of the Hero," *Raritan*, 7,1 (1987), 1–27.

[41] Cf. Patrick Bridgwater, *Nietzsche in Anglo-Saxony* (Leicester: UP, 1972), pp. 191–201.

[42] Cf. Leonard and Wharton, *The Fluent Mundo*, pp. 103–39.

[43] Nobody recognized this conflict in Nietzsche's thought earlier or more clearly than Rudolf Steiner in his 1895 study *Friedrich Nietzsche: Fighter for Freedom* (trans. 1960). It is one of the enigmas of modern scholarship that this work is rarely mentioned, though it is one of the best introductions to Nietzsche's thought.

[44] *The Gay Science*, trans. W. Kaufmann (New York: Vintage, 1974), p. 346.

[45] Wallace Stevens, *Selected Poems* (London: Faber, 1965). Numbers in parentheses refer to this edition.

[46] *The Gay Science*, p. 347.

[47] *Ibid.*, p. 346.

[48] Michael Beehler, *T. S. Eliot, Wallace Stevens, and the Discourses of Difference* (Baton Rouge: Louisiana State UP, 1987), pp. 44, 47.

[49] Owen Barfield, *Poetic Diction: A Study in Meaning* (Middletown: Wesleyan UP, 1973), p. 88.

[50] As, for instance, defined by Owen Barfield in *Saving the Appearances* (London: Faber, 1957).

Gerhard Hoffmann

Eugene O'Neill: America's Nietzschean Playwright

NIETZSCHE'S INFLUENCE ON Eugene O'Neill was probably
greater than it was on any other English-speaking playwright.[1]
Beyond the simple provision of ideas and motifs, it furnished the
dramatist with the thematic framework for his plays, with general
patterns of contrast and polarity among his characters, with the recurrent plot of suffering and redemption, and even with specific formal elements like the use of masks and laughter as expressive
dramatic means. When asked, in 1928, whether he had a literary
idol, O'Neill's response could not have been clearer: "Nietzsche."[2]
Years later, in his acceptance speech for the Nobel Prize, he claimed
that Nietzsche, like Strindberg as dramatist, "remains, in his sphere,
the master, . . . still our leader."[3] Most explicit of all, however, is a
letter dated June 22, 1927, to his friend and fellow Nietzsche en-
thusiast Benjamin De Casseres:

> What you say of "Lazarus Laughed" deeply pleases me — particu-
> larly that you found something of "Zarathustra" in it.
> "Zarathustra" . . . has influenced me more than any book I've ever
> read. I ran into it, through the bookshop of Benjamin Tucker, the
> old philosophical anarchist, when I was eighteen and I've always
> possessed a copy since then and every year or so I reread it and am
> never disappointed, which is more than I can say of almost any
> other book (That is, never disappointed in it as a work of art. Spots
> of its teaching I no longer concede).[4]

And yet, it was not only *Zarathustra* that affected him to such an
unusual degree, but also *The Birth of Tragedy*,[5] the work O'Neill
once referred to as the "most stimulating book on drama ever writ-

ten!"[6] External proof of this book's influence on the playwright can be gleaned from Barrett H. Clark's statement that when he met O'Neill in 1926 he was carrying "a worn copy of Nietzsche's *Birth of Tragedy*."[7] Furthermore, O'Neill himself saw to it that two longer quotations from the book were placed on the playbill of *The Great God Brown*. O'Neill also thought Nietzsche's *The Gay Science* "wonderful stuff,"[8] and he probably read *Ecce Homo*,[9] but clearly the two most important works for him were *The Birth of Tragedy* and *Zarathustra*, which provided the key to the religious ideas and to an understanding of the overall conceptual basis of O'Neill's works.

Although Nietzsche's influence on O'Neill was all-pervasive and accompanied the dramatist throughout his career, it cannot be easily defined in specific terms. It is noteworthy that O'Neill, in spite of his whole-hearted enthusiasm for Nietzsche, also had some reservations: "spots of teaching I no longer concede." Nowhere did he explain which "spots of teaching" he would not concede, nor did he specify the point in time when such differences with the philosopher arose. There is reason to assume with Agnes Boulton that *Zarathustra* and other books by Nietzsche "moved his emotion rather than his mind,"[10] so that individual points of difference did not matter so much. The basis for O'Neill's life-long proximity to Nietzsche is obviously a spiritual affinity between the two writers that goes beyond the details of influence, and encompasses mentality, poetics, and rhetorics of style. In Boulton's words: "He had read the magnificent prose of this great and exciting man over and over again, so that at times it seemed an expression of himself."[11] What the playwright ultimately derived from Nietzsche's complex and partly ambivalent ideas was a set of parameters, a system of differentiation (Luhmann), which included within it such oppositions as Reason/Life, Apollonian/Dionysian, and suffering/yes-saying.

This is not to say, however, that O'Neill took his literary inspiration from a single source. On the contrary, he was a conscious eclecticist whose syncretism included a highly selective choice and combination of ideas taken from Nietzsche, but also from Schopenhauer and from Buddhist and Taoist philosophy,[12] from Freud, Jung, Ibsen, Strindberg, and others. "I've tried to make myself a melting pot for all these methods,"[13] O'Neill once wrote. In this atmosphere of the literary fusion of different forms of belief and practice, and in consonance with Nietzsche's accent on experimentation, O'Neill himself often referred to his plays as "experiments."[14]

II

O'Neill frequently followed Nietzsche in his most fundamental concepts. He took over Nietzsche's basic idea that "God is dead," a notion which robs this world of ultimate significance and leaves, as an antidote to nihilism, only the affirmation of *Life* as an alternative religious attitude. Nietzsche never exactly defined what he meant by life but characterized its meaning through its constitutive phenomena: the Dionysian, the will to power, eternal becoming, perspectivism, and (perspective) appearance. Against the fictive dichotomy of being and truth, he set the "real" dichotomy of becoming and appearance.[15] The playwright accepted the religious aspects of life and the ground for its affirmation, the Nietzschean belief in eternal becoming and eternal recurrence, which sets the human spirit free from the bonds of time and is the "highest formula of affirmation which is at all attainable."[16] This Nietzschean belief, which links the earlier *Birth of Tragedy* with the later *Zarathustra*, teaches "that all things recur eternally, and we ourselves too; and that we have already existed an eternal number of times, and all things with us" (*Z*, III, 13).[17] It also provides the basis for an encompassing aesthetic principle. For Nietzsche, we derive "metaphysical comfort" from every tragedy because "life is at the bottom of things, despite all the changes of appearances, indestructably powerful and pleasurable" (*BT*, 7). And when O'Neill writes that "The only way we can get religion back is . . . through an exultant acceptance of life,"[18] who can fail to detect the source?

The notion of eternal recurrence serves as a bridge between individuation and oneness, the oppositional basis of Nietzsche's and O'Neill's concepts of tragedy. For Nietzsche, tragedy is "the expression of two interwoven artistic impulses, *the Apollonian and the Dionysian*" (*BT*, 12), and the struggle between them. The Apollonian principle stands for individualism, for "boundaries . . . as the most sacred laws of the world." It actively calls for "self-knowledge and measure" (*BT*, 9), while the "Dionysian state . . . represents the shattering of the individual and his fusion with primal being" (*BT*, 8). Out of this dialectic grows, for both Nietzsche and O'Neill, the burden of individuation, and "the primordial contradiction that is concealed in things" (*BT*, 9), which causes the terrible tension that, in Nietzsche's phrase, "tears us up."

The opposition between individuation and oneness unfolds in *Zarathustra* in the concepts of will to power, self-overcoming, and superman, the Dionysian yea-sayer. Although O'Neill neither used these exact terms nor systematically connected them, their underlying conceptual interrelation influenced his plays in one way or another. The will to power in *Zarathustra*, contrary to its partly negative evaluation in Nietzsche's earlier works, is generally regarded as the fundamental impulse that dominates all life, and more specifically as a manifestation of both its negative and positive sides. As a "negative" force it craves possession and determines, for instance, the antagonism between man and woman, adding fuel, as it were, to the mutual power drive responsible for "the eternal war between the sexes" (*EH*, "Why I Write Such Good Books," 5), which itself, in turn, energizes the dramatic conflicts in O'Neill's plays, for example in *Before Breakfast, Ile, Beyond the Horizon, Gold, Welded, All God's Chillun Got Wings, Desire Under the Elms, The Great God Brown,* and *Strange Interlude*. As a positive force, the will to power means self-overcoming. For Nietzsche's superman, the power drive is essentially the eternal defiance and self-creative force of the free spirit, for whom the maxim "I am that which must always overcome itself" (*Z*, II, 12) is the guiding axiom of self-fulfillment and self-realization. This includes unrelenting severity in respect to oneself in the conquest of the passions and, if necessary, severity against others. The will to power of "higher men" annihilates conventional values, the old ideals of happiness in this world and in other-worldly hopes. By breaking existing rules, it destroys habit and custom, and sets up its own standards of a life "beyond good and evil." Its highest desire strives for self-transcendence (cf. *Z*, I, 15), i.e., the desire for perfection, which results not only from the endurance but also from the love of necessity, and from the ultimate, free, and creative fusion of passion and reason — though there always remains, in tragedy as much as in life, in society as well as in the individual personality, the lasting conflict between the irrational and the rational, chaos and order, pain and joy. O'Neill dramatically combined the ideas of will to power, self-overcoming, and the superman as Dionysian affirmer of life only in one play, *Lazarus Laughed*, which is based directly on

Zarathustra. For both the playwright and Nietzsche, however, the overcoming of the animal nature of man, and the reaching-out for a spiritual good (or the failure to do so) generally distinguish people either as creative spiritual types or weak mediocre ones.

The death of God, implicitly the substitution of the myth of eternal recurrence for dogmatic Christianity, as well as the opposition between individuation and oneness, civilization and life, order and chaos, combine to make life (and death) an insoluble mystery — which is another basic idea O'Neill found appealing in Nietzsche. For the playwright, life in its eternal repetition and with its lack of a reasonable goal beyond itself embodies a "mystic pattern," an idea again prefigured in *The Birth of Tragedy* by what is called "the *mystery doctrine of tragedy*: the fundamental knowledge of the oneness of everything existent, the conception of individuation as the primal cause of evil, and of art as the joyous hope that the spell of individuation may be broken in augury of a restored oneness" (*BT*, 10). Interesting in this context is O'Neill's perception of himself as "a most confirmed mystic."[19] In 1926, he explained with regard to *The Great God Brown* that the "mystic pattern" manifests itself only "dimly behind and beyond the words and actions of the characters."[20] The "mystery" O'Neill wanted to expose in this play is "the mystery any one man or woman can feel but not understand as the meaning of any event — or accident — in any life on earth."[21] For the playwright, the most important symbol of the unfathomable mystery of life, as well as of the doctrine of eternal recurrence, is the sea: " . . . the sea — fate — the symbol of life."[22] In O'Neill, people come to fear or to affirm the sea, or both to fear and affirm it at the same time, as do the characters at the end of *Anna Christie*. The fog frequently overflowing the sea becomes the veil which prevents humans from seeing their ways clearly and finding a "true" meaning in life. The mysterious intransparency of both sea and fog prefigure and reflect the ambivalent human situation as such; but the yea-sayers in O'Neill's plays accept and affirm it as a symbol of the mystery of life, as, for instance, Anna does at the end of *Anna Christie*.

Yet Nietzsche's philosophy does not exhaust itself in the praise of mystery and affirmation; it also includes a reflection of the ever-present aspects of pain, suffering, and destruction. O'Neill would have heartily agreed with Nietzsche's famous description of the paradoxical human predicament:

Man is a rope, tied between beast and overman as a rope over an
abyss. A dangerous across, a dangerous on-the-way, and a dangerous looking-back, a dangerous shuddering and stopping. What is
great in man is that he is a bridge and not an end. (*Z,* Prologue, 4)

In *The Hairy Ape,* O'Neill has Yank walk on such "a rope over an
abyss," when he becomes, in the playwright's own words, "the symbol of a man, who has lost his old harmony with nature, the harmony which he used to have as an animal and has not yet acquired in
a spiritual way."[23] The play is the psychological unfolding of this idea;
it is close to Nietzsche not only in its underlying concepts, but also
in the unabating polarity of thought and feeling, the never-resolved
antagonism of attitudes, and the fascinating mysteries of life. The
effort of some critics to ontologize Nietzsche's ideas neglects the fact
that the philosopher did not wish to codify an ontology and that he
rather let himself be guided by "intuitions" and "experiments." Such
attempts in fact ignore Nietzsche's philosophy of "perspectivism,"
according to which there is no such thing as Being in itself, but only
appearances and perspective views, so that appearance and truth actually merge. Even Zarathustra cannot define the "truth" in order to
rest in it; he praises life simply because he loves it. Interpretations of
Nietzsche generally shift between an ontological and a psychological
reading, and O'Neill's view of Nietzsche is no different. Yet the notion of perspectivism that accepts no "objective" truth but sees in
truth a subjective category of experienced life — "truth" being what
intensifies life — is a dominant idea in Nietzsche that O'Neill responded to.

III

Everything O'Neill found attractive in Nietzsche came together
in the playwright's concept of tragedy. Like Nietzsche, O'Neill believed in the importance of aesthetic values as meaningful for life because they create, in Nietzsche's words, "the beauty of . . . tragic art"
out of the horrible "witches brew of sensuality and cruelty" (*BT,* 2).
Both writers believed the task of the artist to lie in the propagation of
a vision of life, in which the blind human strife against the forces of
nature became meaningful. In this respect, both felt Greek tragedy
to be the epitome of the fusion of art and religion. "The tragic
alone," O'Neill noted in 1921, has "that significant beauty which is

truth. It is the meaning of life — and the hope. The noblest is eternally the most tragic."[24] In 1929 he added: "What has influenced my plays the most, is my knowledge of the drama of all time — particularly Greek tragedy."[25] Rather than a theory, the playwright had a vision of tragedy that adopted at least four aspects of the Nietzschean model.

(1) The mystery of life results from the opposition between two worlds of separating forces and rationalities: one to which the "spiritual middle classers" (O'Neill) remain bound, and the other indicative of the forces of oneness, which remain hidden as the "Force behind." The basic theme in many of O'Neill's plays deals with the tensions between these two worlds. He claimed that even in one of his earliest plays, *The Moon of the Caribbees* (and the same can surely be said of *The Web*), he was "always acutely conscious of the Force behind." His predominant aim was "to interpret Life in terms of lives, never just lives in terms of character."[26] In this way his tragic heroes appear, in Nietzsche's terms, as "masks of the original hero, Dionysus" (*BT*, 10).

(2) The "morality" of Life demands the abandonment (or relativization) of the dichotomy of good and evil. With Nietzsche the "primordial contradiction in things" that ends in the "shattering of the individual and his fusion with primal being" makes the moral opposition of good and evil ultimately irrelevant, for "All that exists is just and unjust and equally justified in both" (*BT*, 9). O'Neill followed Nietzsche on this point.[27] He once told an interviewer: "To me there are no good people or bad people, just people. The same with deeds. 'Good' and 'evil' are stupidities, as misleading and outworn fetishes as Brutus Jones's silver bullet . . . ."[28]

(3) For Nietzsche, the only worthwhile struggle (and "metaphysical comfort") is the struggle of the tragic hero, who "prepares himself" for a "higher pleasure . . . by means of his destruction, not by means of his triumphs" (*BT*, 21) in order to attain a Dionysian sense of oneness with life. For O'Neill, the one eternal tragedy of man was "his glorious, self-destructive struggle to make the Force express him instead of being, as an animal is, an infinitesimal incident in its expression."[29] In another interview of 1922, O'Neill held: " . . . a man wills his own defeat when he pursues the unattainable. But his *struggle* is his success . . . when the individual

fights all the hostile forces within and without himself to achieve a future of nobler values."[30]

(4) Out of Nietzsche's concept of tragedy grows the antagonism between life and civilization, creativity and reason (or, rather, rationality). As Nietzsche saw it, tragedy began to draw individualized portraits with Euripides; it was then that it lost its religious spirit and its mythopoetic sense of wholeness, and substituted for the self-destructive experience of primordial oneness logical reasoning in the form of "life-consuming . . . Socratic optimism" (*BT,* 24). Socrates, in Nietzsche's view, introduced "a life guided by concepts" (*BT,* 24) and optimistic rationalism, and hence a new era of Western civilization, which replaced the depth of spirit and desire with the dominance of logical reason, science, and the worship of power and worldly success. Nietzsche's opposing concepts of life/mystery and civilization/decadence induced O'Neill to deal conceptually with the American experience from a similar angle. For O'Neill, this meant setting the American Dream of renewal and reunion with nature against the reality of American materialism, acquisitiveness, competitiveness, and the mania for owning things on the one hand, and the values of Christian life-denial and the doctrines of the church on the other. In a famous letter to George Jean Nathan, O'Neill specified what he considered the "sickness" of American civilization in Nietzschean terms:

> The playwright today must dig at the roots of the sickness of today as he feels it — the death of the Old God and the failure of science and materialism to give any satisfying new One for the surviving primitive religious instinct to find a meaning for life in, and to comfort its fears of death with.[31]

True influence, however, is seldom one-dimensional. And so it was with Nietzsche and O'Neill. As some other comments by O'Neill show, there are also important differences between the philosopher's and the playwright's concept of tragedy, differences which point, at least in part, to those "spots of teaching" in Nietzsche he could no longer concede.

(1) O'Neill did not share Nietzsche's contempt of the masses. For the playwright, "the transfiguring nobility of tragedy" showed not only in the "noble" man, the "superman" but also in "the most ignoble, debased lives."[32] The "metaphysical comfort" to be derived from tragedy was as important for O'Neill as it was for Nietzsche,

but for the former the resulting affirmation of life was frequently further specified, often even negated. The playwright tended towards emphasizing the universal human predicament: isolation, suffering and struggle. His heroes are everything but self-confident; they are — perhaps with the exception of Lazarus in *Lazarus Laughed* and the "philosopher ruler" Kublai Khan in *Marco Millions* (*MM*, I, vi, 411–12)[33] — not supermen at all.

(2) The names O'Neill gave to life's "Force behind" vary greatly, combining pagan, Christian, and scientific or technological concepts. In O'Neill, the "Force behind" is not only called Life but also "Fate, God, our biological past creating our present, whatever one calls it — Mystery certainly."[34] It may also appear as the force of electricity or the Dynamo, figuring as the "Mother of life" and as "God the Mother" (*D*, II, iii, 872). O'Neill indeed could not be inclusive enough in his religious concepts, if he wanted "to develop a tragic expression in terms of transfigured modern values and symbols," especially of American extraction. One is here reminded of Agnes Boulton's remark that O'Neill, as a Catholic renegade, remained "haunted by the God whom he had discarded."[35]

(3) O'Neill frequently "de-ideologized" the concept of "mystery." To be sure, mystery keeps its exultant Nietzschean note, but it can also imply the frustrating aspect of not-knowing since it both defines and does not define life. Nietzsche's call for existential experience, for the full immersion in life, may not be enough in view of the impossibility of fully *understanding* life, much less of rationally analyzing it or establishing a value system for judging it in terms of good and bad. O'Neill's reservations regarding those "spots of teaching I no longer concede" might have originated in the fact that beyond the acceptance of Nietzsche's basic antitheses and an orientation towards the mysticism of the life force, which he shared whole-heartedly with Nietzsche, he allowed himself a wider intellectual margin of interpretation that included components of Schopenhauer's darker, more resigned vision of tragedy, as well as the possibility of a moral point of view and a revitalization of communal values (e.g., in *Servitude*, *The Hairy Ape*, *All God's Chillun Got Wings*, *The Great God Brown*). Or, to argue the point in Nietzschean terms, the O'Neill of the later plays, from *Strange Interlude* on, emphasized the psychological aspects of perspectivism to the detriment of the ontological view of Nietzsche's philosophy. Consequently, the

experience of oneness gains the status of a (pipe) dream (e.g., in *Mourning Becomes Electra*, *Long Day's Journey Into Night*).

(4) Freud's analysis of the unconscious, together with the Jungian idea of the collective unconscious, both served to reinforce and focus the influence of Nietzsche's psychological ideas on O'Neill. Lending credence to the extensive parallels between Nietzsche and Freud is Freud's own admission that he had long avoided reading the philosopher because "his premonitions and insights so often agree in the most amazing manner with the laborious results of psychoanalysis."[36] The contribution of psychoanalysis to O'Neill's stock of ideas lies, among others, in a stronger conceptualization of the dualism between conscience and its moral restrictions on the one hand, and instinct/sensual drive on the other. In O'Neill's plays, this dualism provides the basis for the characters' tragic struggle between two equally valid and necessary but also eternally antagonistic forces, as can be seen, for instance, in *Mourning Becomes Electra*. An impressive early example for the complex Nietzsche-Freud-O'Neill parallels is *The Emperor Jones*, a play that leans heavily on the destructive influence of the unconscious and the guilt complex. Here the self-styled black emperor of an island in the West Indies, the counterpart to the civilized and decadent white American materialist, flees from the rebellious natives he has exploited and confronts the regressive visions of his personal and collective unconscious, rediscovering, to describe it in Nietzsche's words, "in outbursts of passion, and in the fantasizing of dreams and insanity, . . . his own and mankind's prehistory: animality and its savage grimaces" (*D*, 312). Jones's power drive succumbs in these hallucinations to the hidden forces of nature and its superior will to power. The same parallelism is evident in *Diff'rent* with its traces of the Freudian theory of sexual repression and what Nietzsche calls "malicious idealism," a phenomenon of which he held that "every expression of contempt for the sexual life, every befouling of it through the concept 'impure', is *the* crime against life" (*EH*, IV, 5).

IV

O'Neill's adaptation (and modification) of such fundamental Nietzschean ideas as eternal recurrence, self-overcoming, affirmation of life, and inevitable perspectivism influenced the dramatic structure of his plays in decisive ways, though they never combined into a single complex in any specific case. Like Nietzsche, O'Neill was driven from style to style, from one form to another in his ceaseless striving for an adequate expression of his ideas in both philosophical and literary terms. By using the highly rhetorical and emotionalized language of "a poet who has labored with the spoken word to evolve original rhythm of beauty where beauty apparently isn't,"[37] O'Neill followed Nietzsche's example and the philosopher's concept of tragedy as the intricate synthesis of Dionysian and Apollonian forces, as the artistic conquest of the horrors of existence. Though many parallels in details, especially between Nietzsche's *Zarathustra* and O'Neill's plays conceived in the twenties, cannot be discussed here, three points should be noted.

First, for Nietzsche and O'Neill alike the overcoming of the limitations of the world in order to become a "noble man," a "creator," and a "yea-sayer" requires a number of stations or metamorphoses on the way. *The Emperor Jones, The Hairy Ape, The Fountain, Marco Millions,* and *Lazarus Laughed* all present examples of spiritual and physical journeys, as do Strindberg's so-called "Wander Plays" (*Lucky Per's Journey, The Keys to Heaven, To Damascus, A Dreamplay* and *The Highway*). These latter plays also clearly influenced O'Neill, and actually strengthened the Nietzschean connection, since Strindberg himself was one of Nietzsche's ardent followers. In the manner of Nietzsche, many of O'Neill's plays (*The First Man, The Fountain, Welded, All God's Chillun Got Wings, Marco Millions, The Great God Brown,* and *Lazarus Laughed*) transcribe a rising line of development and often end in a mystical union with elemental being. *The Great God Brown,* for instance, structurally reflects the doctrine of eternal recurrence by interlacing beginning and end, and it finally establishes the idea of mystery (as in many other of O'Neill's plays) as the conceptual basis for the author's "super-naturalism" or "unreal realism."[38] Such plays give expression to the *ontological* aspects of Nietzsche's thought in dramatic form. The definition of the spiritual quest in terms of doubt and pain, as well as self-overcoming and the resulting perspectivism of thought and feeling, however, keep open the option of dramatizing *and* internalizing the action by foregrounding its *psychological* aspects.

Second, Nietzsche provided the concept and the components of the mystic moment of primordial union in O'Neill. Such moments are for Nietzsche distinguished by Dionysian ecstasy, a feeling "as if the veil of the *máyá* . . . were now merely fluttering in tatters before the mysterious primordial unity" (*BT*, 1) — the veil of the *máyá* being Schopenhauer's image, borrowed from oriental philosophy, for the illusionary world of appearances. In such moments of "ecstasy," and "enchantment," "in these paroxysms of intoxication the artistic power of all nature reveals itself to the highest gratification of the primordial unity" (*BT*, 1). In modern literature, these exemplary "moments of being," "vision," "revelation," or "recognition" abound (Virginia Woolf, Henry James, Conrad, Joyce, D. H. Lawrence, Thomas Wolfe), and they become the model of an ecstatic "mythic" knowledge. O'Neill, deeply influenced by Nietzsche, made extensive dramatic use of this state of Dionysian intoxication, which is to say of moments he characterized as an "intensified feeling of the significant worth of man's being and becoming," and an ecstatic happiness resulting from being "in harmony with any deep rhythm in life."[39] This complex also includes Nietzsche's association of laughter and music with the experience of the "mysterious primordial unity." Yet while in Nietzsche's theory of tragedy exultation and pain are the two sides of *one* feeling, O'Neill frequently separates pain and joy, thus isolating the mystic moment of primordial unity,[40] and, in some cases, depriving the end of his plays of tragic tension (e.g., *Welded*, *Desire Under the Elms*). After *Lazarus Laughed*, O'Neill added his own kind of ambivalence to these moments of exultation by opposing them, in a quite un-Nietzschean way, to "reality."

Finally, Nietzsche anticipated in his own way the Freudian tension between the conscious and the unconscious, and understood internal human conflicts as struggles between an outer mask and an inner being. This comes close to O'Neill's specific use of the mask (though masks were, of course, a stock property of the Art Theatre and their usefulness had been celebrated by, among others, Gordon Craig, William Butler Yeats, and Kenneth Macgowan, a close associate of O'Neill). For the American playwright, quite generally, "One's outer life passes in a solitude haunted by the masks of others; one's inner life passes in a solitude hounded by the masks of oneself."[41] Consequently, what O'Neill aimed at in his copious and diversified use of masks up to *Mourning Becomes Electra* (where he also planned to use masks but finally left the characters with mask-like faces), was "a drama of souls, and the adventures of 'Free Wills,' with the masks that govern them and constitute their fates."[42]

V

The Great God Brown is O'Neill's most complex and intricate experiment with Nietzschean ideas and attitudes and may thus serve, together with *Lazarus Laughed*, to illustrate the extent to which Nietzsche influenced O'Neill's conception of dramatic theme and design. The drama stages the conflict between Christianity and Dionysian religion, and expresses it psychologically "in the pattern of conflicting tides in the soul of Man."[43] In O'Neill's own words, the play is "a Mystery,"[44] and the mystical perspective here serves as an all-encompassing frame of reference for theme and dramatic technique, by absorbing the enigma of personal identity in ecstatic moments of vision; by solving the problem of an over-all evaluation of life in favor of the irrational and a mysticism both of the universe and the human soul; by mystifying the personality in the stark contrast of face and mask; by using the mask to transfer the personality of one man (Dion) to another (Brown); and finally, by transforming the prostitute Cybel into a pagan Earth Mother.

O'Neill's equivalent to Nietzsche's contrast of nobleman/creator/overman with small/Alexandrine/theoretical man can be seen in the character constellation of Dion Anthony versus his foil William Brown. Similarly, the Nietzschean dichotomy of mask and face finds its counterpart, in Dion Anthony's case, in the opposition of "Pan" (Dionysus) versus "Anthony." Elsewhere, O'Neill has explicitly commented on the nature of this agonistic struggle, referring to it as "the creative pagan acceptance of life, fighting eternal war with the masochistic, life-denying spirit of Christianity as represented by St. Anthony — the whole struggle resulting in this modern day in mutual exhaustion."[45] Dion, on the one hand, approaches St. Anthony's God and receives no answer; on the other hand, he tries to live according to the demands of the Pan mask and fails. His ecstatically phrased belief that marital closeness and love deliver one from painful disguise is soon shattered by the Nietzschean realization that love in marriage is mostly a striving after possession and is subject to illusion, misunderstanding, and injustice. When Dion finally sees no chance of bridging the gulf between man and woman in love and marriage and to overcome "the duality of human character,"[46] he falls into an attitude of cynicism that makes his Pan mask change its features into those of Mephistopheles. He finally gives in to the enemy, the Great God Brown: "Now I'll have to foreswear my quest for Him and go in for the Omnipresent Successful Serious One, The Great God Mr. Brown, instead" (*GGB*, I, iii, 496).

Dion Anthony remains bound, as it were, in "perspectivism," and dies as a defeated character. His fate covers conflict and fight, isolation and suffering, and ultimately prefigures the fate of O'Neill's later protagonists (from *Strange Interlude* on), who often end their struggle over affirmation or denial of life "in mutual exhaustion" and resignation. For the final achievement of oneness, the playwright paradoxically reserves the worldly Brown who, after Dion's death, out of a feeling of emptiness takes on Dion's mask of Mephistopheles that the latter had mockingly bequeathed to him as his "last will and testament" (*GGB*, II, iii, 510). Hoping to gain "the power to live creatively,"[47] Brown paradoxically inherits Dion's problems of identity. With Dion's mask, Brown — now Dion/Brown — usurps the place of Margaret's husband without her recognizing his true identity. Having himself pronounced Brown dead and having been shot by policemen who ironically see in him Brown's murderer, he dies in the arms of Cybel, who is both a prostitute and a kind of Earth Mother (and who as friend and educator had already tried "to inspire Dion Anthony with her certainty in life for its own sake" [*GGB*, 492–94]).

Here, at the end of the metamorphoses, the Dionysian spirit and its affirmation of life transform doubt and suffering into ecstatic "yes-saying," and the play ends on an unmistakably Nietzschean note. Before he dies like a child in Cybel's arms, Brown asks her as Dion had asked him: "What's the prayer you taught me — Our Father — ?" and Cybel answers: "(*with calm exultance*) Our Father Who Art!" In his death, then, Brown experiences the ecstasy of unity, and formulates a philosophy of "stations" in his psychic preparation for the ultimate experience of primordial unity:

> (*taking her tone — exultantly*) Who art! Who art! (*Suddenly — with ecstacy*) I know! I have found Him! I hear Him speak! 'Blessed are they that weep, for they shall laugh!' Only he that has wept can laugh!'

Immediately after Brown's death, Cybel, now clearly in her role as Earth Mother (whom Dion Brown in his last words had connected with God the Father in the generation of eternal recurrence), formulates the final message of the play as an ecstatic Dionysian affirmation of primordial being, now replete with — quite in Zarathustra's sense — "profound pain":

> (gets up and fixes his body on the couch. She bends down and kisses him gently — she straightens up and looks into space — with a profound pain) Always spring comes again bearing life! Always again! Always, always forever again! — Spring again! — life again! — summer and fall and death and peace again! — (with agonized sorrow) — but always, always, love and conception and birth and pain again — spring bearing the intolerable chalice of life again! — (then with agonized exultance) — bearing the glorious, blazing crown of life again! (She stands like an idol of Earth, her eyes staring out over the world.) (IV, ii, 532)

Lazarus Laughed, not only in theme, motifs, and design, but also in many other details of phrasing and tone, is a play based on Nietzsche's *Zarathustra*. The author here pursues the ultimate attempt to celebrate not primarily the human struggle to overcome the self, as he does in *The Great God Brown*, but the final stage of ecstatic harmony, of "yea-saying," and unconditional affirmation of life, reflecting Nietzsche's *amor fati* in "A Play for an Imaginative Theatre," which, in O'Neill's view, is "a legitimate descendant of the first theatre that sprang . . . out of [man's] worship of Dionysus."[48] The play has "no plot of any sort as one knows plot,"[49] and it works with an enormous number of characters and an intricate scheme for masking them. Following Nietzsche's high regard for Christ's actual life (not the Christian doctrines), O'Neill attempts to fuse the image of Christ with that of Dionysus, or rather, he attempts to "complete" Christ who, measured against the Dionysian religious spirit, remains, as it were, in the stage of suffering without ever attaining the joyful Dionysian affirmation of Life. The resurrected Lazarus, freed from the fear of death and without mask, takes over and carries further Christ's role as savior. He fights against religious dogmatism, worldly hopes of superficial success and pleasure, and the cult of materialism, as well as against "the coldest of all cold monsters" (Z, I, 11), the State, represented by Tiberius's and Caligula's negative authority vested in their power of the "Thou shalt." Lazarus preaches the "love of life" (*LL*, I, i, 547), the "sacred 'yes,'" the all-overcoming mystical laughter, as his divine message.[50] Travelling like Zarathustra by land and sea, exhorting the people to destroy their false gods and values, Lazarus wanders with a retinue of enthusiastic followers all over the old world from Palestine to Greece, Rome, and Tiberius's palace on Capri, preaching the Nietzschean messages of eternal recurrence and joyful affirmation of life: "Laugh! Laugh!/Fear is no more!/There is no death!/There is only life!/There is only laughter!" (*LL*, I, ii, 559). In the end, Lazarus, the Dionysian yea-sayer, is burned at the stake by Tiberius's order, but he meets his fate with divine laughter. As earlier in *Marco Millions*, O'Neill's *Lazarus Laughed* restricts the struggle of life to the conflict between two powerful forces, the one worldly, functional, and death-oriented, the other religious, joyous, and life-affirmative. In this most Nietzschean of O'Neill's plays, the mystery of the sacred "yes" overcomes psychological struggle and historical antagonism, in fact, it "epicizes" the drama and ontologizes its message and, in so doing, reaches the peak of the dramatist's "super-naturalism."

VI

Lazarus Laughed exhausts the form of the mystery play prefigured in O'Neill by *The Fountain*, *Marco Millions*, and *The Great God Brown*. For a variety of reasons that cannot be discussed in detail, there is no numinous reality, no absolute truth evoked in O'Neill's later work. The flux of creation and the idea of eternal recurrence no longer contain a meaningful synthesis of life that offers joyful rest. The ecstatic moment of transcendent meaning has lost perhaps not its charm but its absolute truth, and is now relativized by reality. As with Nietzsche, individuation remains a curse, but it no longer makes sense to abandon it joyfully. The result of this development is an emphasis on *aspects* of life, and on attitudes towards life, which are united by pain and together reflect the mystery of life as a concept that unites O'Neill's earlier with his later plays. For the characters of O'Neill's later plays the yearning for oneness is still there, but skepticism has overgrown it. The desire for oneness turns into a form of resignation reminiscent of Schopenhauer's view of tragedy, and into an all-pervasive perspectivism with its attendant inability to provide any ultimate truth or faith. This can be illustrated in reference to *Strange Interlude* and *Mourning Becomes Electra*.

In *Strange Interlude*, the familiar Nietzschean themes of women's "vampirism" and the war of the sexes, or, in more general terms, the drive of all human beings to possess each other, are combined with the struggle in all men and women between two opposite dimensions of human existence, passion and reason, the instinctual and the rational, and the failure to achieve a harmonious balance between the two poles. The drama sacrifices the idea of the wholeness of individuality and turns into a play of aspects, roles, perspectives, and oppositions. Only the central female protagonist, Nina Leeds, revealing a growing vampirism by using all men in her attempt to fulfill herself, experiences a form of oneness in her will to power as woman, not as individual character, but this oneness is fleeting. The experience of unity comes when Nina, who like Cybel in *The Great God Brown* bears both the traits of seductress and mother, has gathered all her men around her and, while "looking from one to the other with triumphant possession," celebrates her ecstatic feeling of power and perfect completeness as a woman:

> My three men! . . . I feel their desires converge in me! . . . to form one complete beautiful male desire which I absorb . . . and am whole . . . they dissolve in me, their life is my life . . . I am pregnant with the three! . . . husband! . . . lover! . . . father! . . . and the fourth man! . . . little man! . . . little Gordon! . . . he is mine too! . . . that makes it perfect! (*SI*, VI, 756)

While the men are reduced to aspects and facets of one male personality that completes the woman, Nina takes on the role of "Everywoman," or simply "Woman" (with a capital W), and thus becomes the daughter of the "Life Force" and the "Earth Mother" ("I am a mother . . . God is a Mother . . ." [*SI*, V, 715]). Her substitution of God the Mother for the possessive Christian God the Father, who has caused the misery of the world, is a typically Nietzschean feature. And like Nietzsche, Nina has no illusions about who has won the eternal power game: it is the church of God the Father. Yet she also goes beyond Nietzsche, when Life appears to her as a "joke" of the Gods, and individual lives seem to her "merely strange dark interludes in the electrical display of God the Father" (*SI*, IX, 817). Nietzsche's and Schopenhauer's concepts mix in a dramatic combination of ideas. Doris M. Alexander is unquestionably right when she argues that *Strange Interlude* has a "clear-cut intellectual design,"[51] and that this design shows Schopenhauer's influence, for instance, in the treatment of love and exhaustion. *Strange Interlude* indeed verifies Schopenhauer's concept that "No attained object of desire can give lasting satisfaction, but merely a fleeting gratification."[52] Yet in characters like Nina and her lover Darrell, who gives up a promising career as a scientist for love, there is still the Nietzschean opposition of life and science, as well as the striving for oneness in love, even if it leads to no final achievement but rather fails.

In *Strange Interlude*, then, the various dimensions of life can no longer be reconciled. As a result of this insight, O'Neill writes *Mourning Becomes Electra*, a drama of life and death impulses which drive the characters to their horrible fate, thus exemplifying Nietzsche's belief that the renunciation of life always results in broken personalities and a state of death-in-life. All members of the Mannon family are torn apart by the Nietzschean-Freudian conflict between sensuality/love and the life-denying (Puritan) moral code which they fail to integrate into an idea of oneness. O'Neill once again emphasizes the variety of perspectives and individual choices by having the four Mannons respond in completely different ways to their family curse. Ezra, the exponent of Puritan negation and self-denial, is poisoned by his wife, Christine, the representative of the life principle, and dies in terror. After the murder of her lover, Adam Brant, by her own son, Christine commits suicide with a grotesque laugh of despair and rebellion. Her son, Orin, also takes his life, but with an apparant ecstatic feeling of expiating his guilt in the mystic reunion with his mother. After the failure of Lavinia's and Orin's attempt at escape, their visit to the Blessed Isles — the symbol of life for both Nietzsche and O'Neill — Lavinia finally faces the tragic consequences of individuation, guilt, and a split self by renouncing the world forever and by shutting herself up in the house of the Mannons as a veritable temple of death.

In O'Neill's late plays, Nietzsche's evaluation of the contrast between life/oneness and civilization/individuation is reversed in terms of what is actually real. In *Long Day's Journey Into Night, A Moon for the Misbegotten*, and *A Touch of the Poet*, delight in the affirmation of life and an envisioned feeling of oneness have become dreams, yet not in Zarathustra's sense, but rather as "pipe dreams" or "lies." Both, the playwright's obvious closeness to Nietzsche and the differences between them are revealed in the dramatic treatment of two prominent themes, namely the function of pipe dreams and the role of pity, and their integration into the struggle between life and death after God is pronounced dead. In this context, O'Neill dramatizes the role of pipe dreams in terms of Nietzschean perspectivism. For Nietzsche, self-deception and illusion were never compatible with self-perfection and ultimate happiness, and consequently had to be overcome; committing oneself to lying meant "wishing *not* to see something that one does see . . . . The most common lie is that with which one lies to oneself."[53] Only the weak "have at all times had need of entrancing *visions* to endure life" (*WP*, 852). The drunken and chanting crowd in Harry Hope's establishment, the "End of the Line Cafe," otherwise known as "the No Chance Saloon" (I, 577), in *The Iceman Cometh* are the herd animals, the weak ones, who invariably must live by illusion or die. But then another idea is introduced in O'Neill that, to a certain extent, invalidates any clear-cut antithesis, and again Nietzsche could be the source: "That lies are necessary in order to live is itself part of the terrifying and questionable character of existence" (*WP*, 853). In the opening scene of the play, Larry Slade, who has "taken a seat in the grandstand of philosophical detachment" (*IC*, I, 570), notes: "The lie of a pipe dream is what gives life to the whole misbegotten mad lot of us, drunk or sober" (*IC*, I, 569f). People are not only herd animals and weaklings in O'Neill's later plays, and they are not to blame if they need pipe dreams in order to be able to exist. The *Iceman Cometh* demonstrates, again in Nietzsche's terms, that "illusions are certainly expensive amusements: but the destruction of illusions is even more expensive . . . ." (*HAH*, II, 2, 312). This is illustrated in the play by the fate of the three "outsiders," Hickey, Parritt, and Larry, who lose their pipe dreams and face death, or rather death in life, in one way or other. For O'Neill, Nietzsche's visionary moment of union with life now becomes one of the meaning-giving perspectives and, as such, part of the opposition between "pipe dream" and reality, as *A Long Day's Journey Into Night* shows, where Edmund Tyrone, O'Neill's alter ego in this strongly autobiographical play, conjures up the now lost but never forgotten experience of mystical oneness in a mixture of nostalgia and utopian longing, however, without ever being able to transform it into a force shaping reality.

Yet, from O'Neill's redemptive perspective, consolations are not altogether absent. They mainly lie in the possibility of human understanding and the humanizing potential of pity. However, under the reign of moral perspectivism nothing is ever unequivocal, not even pity. Its various aspects in O'Neill again parallel Nietzschean views, though they also transcend them. First, any acceptable kind of pity, according to Zarathustra, should not evade but precisely confront the truth, which, in Jamie's words from *Long Day's Journey*, comprises "the infinite sorrow of life" (*LDJN*, IV, 816). Moreover, pity can also confirm and reinforce the *avoidance* of the fundamental truth in the name of a more human truth that admits and accepts the inability of facing the truth, because the destruction of the lie would invariably lead, as in Larry Slade's case, to death-in-life. But then again, since pity hurts the pride of the sufferer and creates shame, it may cause revolt, even contempt, because, as Zarathustra puts it, "indebtedness does not make men grateful but vengeful; it turns into a growing worm" (*Z*, II, 3). When the "ugly one" speaks to Zarathustra about the death of God, he holds that God had to die because man could not bear his pity. And Hickey, the salesman, who comes back, in *The Iceman Cometh*, for the yearly celebration of his birthday admits to having killed his wife, but not because he wanted to spare her pain and free her from her pipe dream but rather, as he comes to realize (destroying in the process his own pipe dream), because he felt he was the victim of his wife's "sweetness and love and pity and forgiveness" (*IC*, IV, 698), which he could not bear. Finally, in *Long Day's Journey*, Edmund exclaims: "Then Nietzsche must be right . . . 'God is dead: of His pity for man hath God died'" (*LDJN*, II, ii, 759). By quoting Nietzsche's *Zarathustra*, Edmund ironically but unconsciously provides a link between the death of God, or rather, of God's pity, and the (un-Nietzschean) urge of creating an exclusively human bond of pity with one's fellow beings, as we frequently find it in O'Neill. In this sense, pity can be something one cannot avoid, as in the case of Larry Slade, who in the first scene says, "To hell with pity! It does no good, I'm through with it" (*IC*, I, 572), but cannot sustain the role of aloof observer and continues to pity the others against his own will; the same is true of Hickey's wife, who cannot but pity her husband for his inability to reform.

As is well known, O'Neill dedicated *Long Day's Journey Into Night* to his wife, Carlotta, with the inscription: "I give you the original script of this play of old sorrow, written in tears and blood . . . faith in love . . . enabled me to face my dead at last and write this play — write it with deep pity and understanding and forgiveness for *all* the four haunted Tyrones."[54] O'Neill's Lazarus, like Nietzsche's Zarathustra, refuses to be seduced by the "sin" of pity (*Z*, IV, 2), because "god's pity or man's . . . offends the sense of shame" and is the "virtue . . . among all the little people" (*Z*, IV, 7). Instead, Lazarus responds with gentle laughter to the death of his followers, indicating that, for him, there is no death or fear of death in the irrevocable affirmation of life and eternal recurrence. In O'Neills later plays, however, pity, understanding, and forgiveness once more enter the scene — affirming and transcending Nietzsche's perspectivism — in an effort to bridge the gulf between Schopenhauer's resignation and Nietzsche's hope. Life is mystery, but also energy, and energy creates hope, if it is true that energy in all forms of life has "an insatiable desire to manifest power" (*WP*, 619). The power of hope creates the power of human sympathy; the necessary acceptance of deception and pity, however, reduces this power, in O'Neill's famous paradoxical phrase, to the power of "hopeless hope" (*The Straw*, III, 793).

Notes

[1]Cf. Patrick Bridgwater, *Nietzsche in Anglosaxony: A Study of Nietzsche's Impact on English and American Literature* (Leicester: Leicester UP, 1972), pp. 184–90; and Egil Törnqvist, "Nietzsche and O'Neill: A Study in Affinity," *Orbis Litterarum*, 23 (1968), 97–126 (here 99f). For the relationship between O'Neill and Nietzsche, see also Esther Olson, *An Analysis of the Nietzschean Elements in the Plays of Eugene O'Neill* (Diss. U. of Minnesota, 1956); Herwig Friedl, "Power/Play: Nietzsche and O'Neill," in *Eugene O'Neill 1988*, ed. Ulrich Halfmann (Tübingen: Narr, 1990), pp. 203–21; Reinhold Grimm, "The Hidden Heritage: Repercussions of Nietzsche in Modern Theatre and its Theory," *Nietzsche-Studien*, 12 (1983), 355–71.

[2]See Louis Sheaffer, *O'Neill: Son and Playwright* (Boston: Little, Brown, 1968), p. 122.

[3]Arthur and Barbara Gelb, *O'Neill* (New York: Harper & Row, 1962), p. 814.

[4]See Törnqvist, "Nietzsche and O'Neill," pp. 97f. In 1912 O'Neill gave Maibelle Dodge a copy of *Thus Spake Zarathustra* inscribed with two quotations from the text (Gelb, *O'Neill*, p. 209). In 1914 he seems to have read "the whole

of *Also sprach Zarathustra*" in German with the help of "a German grammar and a dictionary" (Barrett H. Clark, *Eugene O'Neill: The Man and His Plays* [New York: Dover, 1947], p. 25); and, aside from "copiously" marking his copies of Nietzsche (which Agnes Boulton reports in her *Part of a Long Story* [Garden City, NY: Doubleday, 1958], p. 61), he copied passages from *Zarathustra*, from 50 chapters out of about eighty, in all nine pages long. Some of these excerpts are now in the O'Neill Collection in the Yale University Library. See Törnqvist, "Nietzsche and O'Neill," p. 100.

[5]When O'Neill read the book is not clear. For a discussion of several possibilities (before the First World War or after, even after he wrote *The Great God Brown*), see Michael Hinden, "*The Birth of Tragedy* and *The Great God Brown*," *Modern Drama*, 16 (1973), 129–40 (here 129f).

[6]Quoted after Louis Sheaffer, *O'Neill: Son and Artist* (Boston: Little, Brown, 1973), p. 174.

[7]Clark, *Eugene O'Neill*, p. 5.

[8]Sheaffer, *O'Neill: Son and Artist*, p. 174.

[9]Nietzsche's influence, of course, came not only from the philosopher's books but also, as Agnes Boulton in the above-quoted passage notes, from conversations with friends. See Törnqvist, "Nietzsche and O'Neill," pp. 98f. Furthermore, O'Neill read texts by other authors that showed Nietzsche's influence (See Linda Ben-Zvi, "*Exiles, The Great God Brown*, and the Spectre of Nietzsche," *Modern Drama*, 24, 1 [1981], 251–63), and of course the plays of his favorite dramatist, Strindberg, another ardent disciple of Nietzsche. For Nietzsche's influence on Strindberg, see in particular Robert Brustein, *The Theatre of Revolt: An Approach to Modern Drama* (London: Methuen, 1964), p. 102.

[10] Boulton, *Part of a Long Story*, p. 61.

[11] *Ibid*.

[12] See, for example, James A. Robinson, *Eugene O'Neill and Oriental Thought* (Carbondale: Southern Illinois UP, 1982); Doris M. Alexander, "*Lazarus Laughed* and Buddha," *Modern Language Quarterly*, 17, 4 (1956), 357–65; Sheng-chuan Lai, "Mysticism and Noh in O'Neill," *Theatre Journal*, 35, 1 (March, 1983), 74–87; An Min Hsia, "Cycle of Return: O'Neill and the Tao," *Eugene O'Neill's Critics: Voices from Abroad*, eds. Horst Frenz and Susan Tuck (Carbondale: Southern Illinois UP, 1984), pp. 169–73.

[13] Arthur Hobson Quinn, *A History of the American Drama* (New York: Appleton-Century-Crofts, 1936), II, p. 199. See similar remarks quoted by Gelb, *O'Neill*, p. 770.

[14] See Clark, *Eugene O'Neill*, pp. 69,72; "Eugene O'Neill, Playwright and Critic," in *O'Neill and His Plays*, eds. Oscar Cargill *et al.* (New York: New York UP, 1961), p. 102.

[15] See Theo Meyer, *Nietzsche: Kunstauffassung und Lebensbegriff* (Tübingen: Francke, 1991), pp. 114ff.

[16] *Thus Spoke Zarathustra (Z)*, trans. Walter Kaufmann (New York: Viking Penguin, 1978), p. xxii. Further quotations from Nietzsche's works will indicate section numbers in parentheses, preceeded by the following abbreviations: *(HAH) Human, All Too Human*, trans. R. J. Hollingdale (Cambridge: Cambridge UP, 1986); *(D) Daybreak*, trans. R. J. Hollingdale (Cambridge: Cambridge UP, 1982); *(GM) On the Genealogy of Morals* and *Ecce Homo (EH)*, trans. Walter Kaufmann and R. J. Hollingdale (New York: Vintage, 1967); *(BGE) Beyond Good and Evil*, trans. R. J. Hollingdale (New York/London: Viking Penguin, 1990); *(BT) The Birth of Tragedy and the Case of Wagner*, trans. Walter Kaufmann (New York: Vintage, 1967); *(WP) The Will to Power*, trans. Walter Kaufmann and R. J. Hollingdale (New York: Vintage, 1968).

[17] Cyrus Day points out certain differences in Nietzsche's and O'Neill's concepts of eternal recurrence; he holds that Nietzsche stresses "the unconditional and endlessly repeated circular course of all things," while O'Neill refers to "the cyclical regeneration of the biological abstraction Man." See Cyrus Day, "*Amor Fati*: O'Neill's Lazarus as Superman and Saviour," *Modern Drama*, 3 (1960), 297–305 (here 301).

[18] Gelb, *O'Neill*, p. 520.

[19] Quinn, *A History of the American Drama*, II, p. 199.

[20] Letter to the *New York Evening Post*, Feb. 13, 1926; rpt. in Clark, *Eugene O'Neill*, pp. 104–6.

[21] See Clark, *Eugene O'Neill*, p. 106.

[22] O'Neill, "Prefatory Notes" to the *Wilderness-Edition* of *The Plays of Eugene O'Neill* (New York: Scribner's, 1934–35), vol. XII.

[23] Quoted in Clark, *Eugene O'Neill*, p. 127.

[24] "Damn the Optimists!" *New York Tribune*, Feb. 13, 1921; rpt. in *O'Neill and His Plays*, p. 104.

[25] Quoted in Arthur Nethercot, "The Psychoanalyzing of Eugene O'Neill," *Modern Drama*, 3 (1960), 248.

[26] See Quinn, *A History of the American Drama*, II, p. 199.

[27] The two quotations O'Neill used for the inscription of the copy of *Zarathustra* he presented to Maibelle Dodge in 1912 are indicative of this relativism: "Almost in the cradle we are given heavy words and values. 'Good' and 'Evil' such cradle-gift is called . . . . But he hath discovered himself who saith: 'This is *my* good and evil.' Thereby he maketh mute the dwarf who saith: 'Good for all, evil for all.'" (Gelb, *O'Neill*, p. 209).

[28] Gelb, *O'Neill*, p. 487.

[29] Quinn, *A History of the American Drama*, II, p. 199.

[30] Mary B. Mullet, "The Extraordinary Story of Eugene O'Neill," *American Magazine*, 94 (1922), pp. 118, 120.

[31] Letter rpt. in *O'Neill and his Plays*, p. 115. See also Doris M. Alexander, "Eugene O'Neill as a Social Critic," *American Quarterly*, 6 (1954), 349–63; Michael Hinden, "*The Emperor Jones:* O'Neill, Nietzsche, and the American Past," *Eugene O'Neill Newsletter*, 3 (1980), 2–4.

[32] Quinn, *A History of the American Drama*, II, p. 199.

[33] All references to O'Neill's plays are to *Complete Plays 1913–43* (New York: The Library of America, 1988), 3 vols. The following abbreviations will be used: Vol. II, 1920–31: *Dynamo* - *D*; *The Great God Brown* - *GGB*; *Marco Millions* - *MM*; *Lazarus Laughed* - *LL*; *Strange Interlude* - *SI*. Vol. III, 1932–43: *The Iceman Cometh* - *IC*; *Long Day's Journey Into Night* - *LDJN*. References in parentheses are to acts, scenes, and page numbers.

[34] Quinn, *A History of the American Drama*, II, p. 199.

[35] Boulton, *Part of a Long Story*, p. 280; cf. also Richard Dana Skinner, *Eugene O'Neill: A Poet's Quest* (New York: Russell & Russell, 1963), p. 115.

[36] *The Basic Writings of Sigmund Freud* (New York: Modern Library Edition, 1938), p. 939; see also p. 103.

[37] Letter to Arthur Hobson Quinn, "Eugene O'Neill, Poet and Mystic," *Scribner's Magazine*, 80 (October, 1926), 368.

[38] O'Neill used the term "super-naturalism" with regard to Strindberg (H. Deutsch and S. Hanau, *The Provincetown: A Story of the Theatre* [New York, 1931], pp. 191ff). The phrase "unreal realism" appears in "Working Notes and Extracts from a Fragmentary Work Diary," in *European Theories of the Drama*, ed. B.H. Clark (New York, 1959), p. 535.

[39] Quoted in Clark, *Eugene O'Neill*, pp. 146–47.

[40] See also Reinhold Grimm, "A Note on O'Neill, Nietzsche, and Naturalism: *Long Day's Journey Into Night* in European Perspective," *Modern Drama*, 26 (1983), 331–34.

[41] O'Neill, "Memoranda on Masks," *The American Spectator*, Nov. 1932; rpt. in *O'Neill and His Plays*, p. 117.

[42] *Ibid.*, p. 116.

[43] *Ibid.*

[44] See *Playwrights on Playwriting*, ed. Toby Cole (New York: Hill and Wang, 1961), p. 239.

[45] O'Neill as quoted in Clark, *Eugene O'Neill*, p. 104.

[46] O'Neill in "A Note for this Edition" (*Wilderness Edition*, vol. X, p. XI).

[47] See Clark, *Eugene O'Neill*, p. 161.

[48] See "A Dramatist's Notebook," *The American Spectator*, Jan. 1933; rpt. in *O'Neill and His Plays*, p. 121.

[49] O'Neill in a letter to Macgowan, May 14, 1926; quoted in Gelb, *O'Neill*, p. 601.

[50] Cf. Nietzsche's *Zarathustra*: "How much is still possible! So *learn* to laugh away over yourselves! Lift up your hearts, you good dancers, high, higher! And do not forget good laughter . . . . Laughter I have pronounced holy; you higher men, *learn* to laugh!" (*Z*, 295f).

[51] Doris M. Alexander, "*Strange Interlude* and Schopenhauer," *American Literature*, 25 (1953), 211–28 (here 211). See also William R. Brashear, "O'Neill's Schopenhauer Interlude," *Criticism*, 6 (1964), 256–65.

[52] Schopenhauer as quoted in Alexander, "*Strange Interlude* and Schopenhauer," p. 217.

[53] *The Antichrist* (sec. 55), in *The Portable Nietzsche*, ed. and trans. Walter Kaufmann (New York/London: Viking Penguin, 1982), p. 640.

[54] See Gelb, *O'Neill*, p. 841.

Christoph Kuhn

Hemingway and Nietzsche: The Context of Ideas

CONSIDERING THE VAST number of articles and books on Hemingway published in the last five decades, contributions that claim or suggest a direct relationship between Hemingway's and Nietzsche's work certainly play a marginal role. Nevertheless, references to Nietzsche have, since the 1950s, persistently turned up in Hemingway criticism. Until the early seventies such critics as Michael F. Moloney, John Killinger, Josette Smetana, and Philip Young have either claimed that Nietzsche was a source for Hemingway's writing, dispensing with any explanation of how and when Hemingway came into contact with Nietzsche's philosophy; or they have simply mentioned Nietzsche's name in this or that context, a strategy which, if anything, seems to serve as a convenient method for papering over cracks in the critical arguments.[1] The publication of Hemingway's library cards of the legendary Paris bookshop Shakespeare and Company in 1975 released two more studies which follow another hypothetical track of Nietzsche's influence on Hemingway. Both critics, Gregory Green and Nicholas Gerogiannis, support their claims of an alleged influence with the fact that on May 5th, 1926, Hemingway borrowed a Thomas Common edition of *Thus Spoke Zarathustra* and did not return it until September 13th. However, the conclusions of both critics are as weak as the basis for their assumptions. Green, in particular, puts his readers' patience to a severe test with his suggestion that Hemingway waited twenty-five years to replace Nietzsche's images of the camel and the desert with Santiago and the sea, and to promote Manolin to some kind of superman. Gerogiannis, on the other hand, comes up with interesting details about Hemingway and the "Nietzsche disciple" d'Annunzio; however, his random collection of "points where Nietzsche and Hemingway meet" fails on closer examination, since it is dressed up in a vague rhetoric of possibility, which culminates in the conjecture that "Hemingway's fictions are the dramatizations of Zarathustra's teaching."[2]

Simple answers rarely do justice to complex questions. Literary influence is usually not a matter of monocausal effect (as Green and Gerogiannis seem to believe) but an intricate process of creative reception. Besides, any critical evaluation of Nietzsche's influence would certainly have to begin with a most careful study of Hemingway's reading. His library at Finca Vigia might help to prove the point: Among some six thousand books and magazines there is a copy of *Thus Spoke Zarathustra*, translated by Thomas Common, and a 1927 issue of Alfred Flechtheim's periodical *Der Querschnitt*, which contains an essay, "Nietzsche als Popularphilosoph," translated from Wyndham Lewis's book *The Art of Being Ruled*; finally, there is Guy de Pourtalès's biographical work *Nietzsche en Italie*.[3] However, as long as those items have not been searched for potential comments and marginals put down by Hemingway, we should take care not to overrate their value.

As yet, we do not know if Hemingway actually ever took special notice of Nietzsche's philosophy. This situation leaves us with an alternative approach to the subject, which is to some extent indebted to Charles Taylor's attempt to read *The Old Man and the Sea* as a Nietzschean tragedy. Taylor's article makes us aware that Santiago's adventure has more in common with Nietzsche's notion of tragic affirmation of life than with the Christian themes of sin, punishment, and salvation. On the other hand, Taylor does not fulfill his promise to present a new interpretation of Hemingway's parable, since he ignores, among other things, some twenty-five years of Hemingway criticism.[4]

The aim of the following investigation is to set crucial aspects of Hemingway's early fiction in relation to Nietzsche's *The Birth of Tragedy*, a book whose insights anticipated if not shaped the modern mind. As I hope to show, both authors' concepts of reality are founded on (to some extent surprisingly) similar modes of thought. "Reality," however individually characteristic its expression may be on the textual surface of Nietzsche's philosophical essays and of Hemingway's literary narratives, is here taken as a pattern structured by certain distinctive features, which can be identified in the texts of both authors. With this pattern as a frame of reference, our approach not only helps to find coherence in what looks like random details in Hemingway but also qualifies the context of both Nietzsche's and Hemingway's views of life.

Hemingway's first work to be published in book form in America, *In Our Time* (1925), provides — by way of its suggestive title — an entry point for our discussion. This book presents an inventory of contemporary experience that places man in a fragmented, meaningless world which seems to offer little consolation but, instead, imposes the prospect of physical and psychic destruction. The key to the emergent theme of the book lies in one of its most striking features, i.e. the heterogeneous body of the text. The italicized vignettes, or interchapters, of *In Our Time* are set apart from the short stories not only in terms of typography; most of them also display extremely drastic scenes of maximum cruelty and suffering compared to their rather subdued reverberations in short stories such as "Indian Camp" or "The Battler." The discrepancy between the interchapters and the stories is emphasized by the principle of contrast, one of the major structural patterns making for the book's unity. This has brought critics to the conclusion that the concept of reality in *In Our Time* is essentially dualistic: beneath a smooth surface of everyday life lingers an abyss of suffering and violence, threatening to distort and destroy human life at any moment.[5]

Such observations lead us to the attitude towards life described in Nietzsche's *The Birth of Tragedy*. A brief review of this work directs our attention to the essence of human existence as sketched in the interchapters of *In Our Time*, which Hemingway himself called "the picture of the whole." An essay on the "continuous development of art"[6] was what Nietzsche originally had in mind when he set out to write his first book; however, *The Birth of Tragedy* turned out to be (and by the subsequent generation of critics and writers was acknowledged as) the outline of a philosophy of life and a critical picture of the cultural situation of modern man. The basic idea presented in *The Birth of Tragedy* is the never-ending struggle of the Apollonian and the Dionysian — encompassing philosophical categories that explain the development of history and civilization. Everyday reality is illusory, for beneath its surface lies the essence of life, the "primordial unity," with Dionysus figuring as its supreme symbol. This "eternally suffering and contradictory" force "needs the rapturous vision, the pleasurable illusion, for its continuous redemption" (45) — a process accomplished by the Apollonian force of individuation. The Dionysian force is, paradoxically, both creative and destructive,[7] giving birth to the manifestations of the Apollonian, the world of appearance, which man, entangled in it, takes for his reality (45). Simultaneously the Dionysian force destroys the original Oneness and, decomposing the fragile world of individuation, reconstitutes the unity of all existence. Suddenness is the temporal condition of Dionysus' revelation (36): In a moment of vision man encounters the transitoriness and insignificance of the Apollonian, and any form of order, knowledge, morals, intelligible organization, or interpretation of life is swept away. The sudden impact of the chaotic force of the Dionysian cannot be grasped by the intellect, and so it resists expression through language (55). It is not only Nietzsche's rhetoric of seeing and feeling which implies that the experience of Dionysus is perceptible only at the sensory level; the paradoxical reaction of man is also responsible, as he is thrilled with "terror" and "blissful ecstasy" (36).

Man's experience of his individual existence, based on contradiction, chaos, and suffering, makes him susceptible to the negation of life (60). On the other hand, this most profound insight into the core of existence also offers man the utmost participation in life. "Tragic wisdom," as Nietzsche names this perceptiveness in his late autobiographical book *Ecce Homo*,[8] keeps in mind the universal truth about Dionysus, and tragic culture is committed to the Janus-faced "comprehensive view of the world" (112).

Nietzsche, however, condemns contemporary culture as decadent because it thoroughly misses, even rejects, the tragic vision: The Apollonian has asserted itself to the full exclusion of its antagonist; appearance has become absolute, and any manifestation of Being has been frozen into "little circles" and confined to "Egyptian rigidity" (72). At the final stage of Apollo's sole triumph, man turns upon life itself and eventually finds himself in the Waste Land of Alexandrian culture: "everywhere there is dust and sand; everything has become rigid and languishes" (123). Decadent culture, which clings to conventional morals as a touchstone for evaluating life, is radically opposed to Nietzsche's postulate that justifies the existence of the world only as an "aesthetical phenomenon" (22, 52, 141):

For, confronted with morality (especially Christian, or unconditional, morality) life *must* continually and inevitably be in the
wrong, because life *is* something essentially amoral. (23)

Nietzsche will later repeat this idea in *Ecce Homo*: "Nothing in existence may be substracted, nothing is dispensable" (728).

Nietzsche's formula for the ambiguity of life will be taken here as
the starting point for an exploration of *In Our Time*, in which the
opening sequence of the interchapters — scenes of World War I and
the Greco-Turkish conflict — is of primary interest. The first interchapter pictures a battery of drunken soldiers making their way
through the night, with a lieutenant heedless of military discipline,
riding into the fields and talking to his horse: an epitome of utter
disintegration. The impact of this scene is heightened by the adjutant
who keeps worrying about the fire in the field kitchen, although the
front line is fifty kilometers away. The traditional image of the fire,
which implies warmth and shelter, is inverted, now revealing itself to
the adjutant as a potential source of danger, whereas the surrounding
darkness, the unknown, appears to provide protection.[9] This interchapter presents a glimpse of a world which is chaotic, contradictory,
and unpredictable, and, consequently, the narrator's only comment
remains characteristically vague, failing to find the suitable words for
what he has witnessed on his way to the front: "It was funny going
along that road."

The road motif is picked up in the second interchapter, but now
it is daytime, and the sketch deals with a movement away from the
war zone. Compared to the other interchapters of *In Our Time*, this
one perhaps carries the most complex meaning, and, dealing with
refugees, it links military to civilian life. Once more, chaos and contradiction dominate a scene perceived through the eyes of a nameless
narrator:

> There was no end and no beginning. Just carts loaded with every-
> thing they owned . . . . Carts were jammed solid on the bridge with
> camels bobbing along through them . . . . The women and children
> were in the carts, crouched with mattresses, mirrors, sewing ma-
> chines, bundles. There was a woman having a baby with a young
> girl holding a blanket over her and crying. Scared sick looking at it.
> It rained all through the evacuation.

The atmosphere of unspeakable suffering indicated by the image of
the girl's emotional state pervades the whole of this interchapter. Just

as the rain, which serves, along with "mud" and "water," as a major objective correlative, relentlessly pours down on the refugees, the most intimate situation of two individuals is singled out by the narrator in order to evoke the existential plight of mankind as a basic *conditio humana*. Turning to the context of the vignette, the contrast of old and young, as well as the birth scene, echo the dramatic climax of "Indian Camp," the short story immediately preceding the interchapter. The simultaneousness of birth and violent death that Nick Adams witnesses, or, on a more general level, the coexistence of creation and destruction, of life and annihilation, is a central theme in Hemingway's works.[10]

The "picture of the whole," another expression for the undisguised presentation of the essential ingredients of life, bears close resemblance to Nietzsche's Dionysian ground of existence. There is certainly no question of a literal similarity but rather of a structural one between Nietzsche's concepts and the fictional world view of Hemingway's *In Our Time*, both of which conspicuously share the features of paradox, chaos, and suffering. These elements can also be located elsewhere in Hemingway's stories: The execution scene in the fifth interchapter, picking up the rain motif of the second, juxtaposes the beginning of day to the sudden end of six cabinet ministers; at the same time, this section points forward to the hanging of Sam Cardinella at dawn in the fifteenth interchapter. The thematic link between both vignettes is enforced by the identical syntax of the opening sentences, by the precise identification of setting and time, as well as by the similar postures of the sick minister and Cardinella at the moment of death. Moreover, times of war in Europe and times of peace in the United States become interchangeable; anarchy and chaos prevail in both cases, as for instance in the eighth interchapter where Hungarian shop-lifters are taken for "wops" and are consequently shot dead by the police, or in the thirteenth interchapter, which is a vivid description of the *riau-riau*-dancers' drunken revelry.

In *The Birth of Tragedy*, the sudden experience of Dionysus goes along with the immediate destruction of the Apollonian, and this is precisely what happens to Nick Adams in the sixth interchapter of *In Our Time*, which has been regarded as the "symbolic center of the whole book."[11] After his serious injury Nick finds himself sitting against the wall of a church, looking "straight ahead brilliantly," "smiling sweatily" — a paradoxical reaction considering his situation — declaring to his comrade Rinaldi: "You and me we've made a separate peace . . . . We're not patriots." Ideologies suddenly collapse, and the church, a place of spiritual consolation, is reduced to a mere physical shelter. Conventional values lose their meaning to those who have been exposed to the absurdities of existence in a moment of mortal danger. In his later novel *A Farewell to Arms* (1929), Hemingway has his protagonist Frederic Henry dwell on exactly this point: "I was always embarrassed by the words sacred, glorious, and sacrifice and the expression in vain . . . . Abstract words such as glory, honor, courage or hallow were obscene."[12]

The violence of war and peace, particularly imminent death at close range, is the catalytic agent which sets those apart from society, from social norms and habits, who have had a glimpse of the contradictory condition of existence. Regarding the question of how to live with this experience, a separate peace seems to be the only viable option left, whereas the attempt to return to the roots of one's childhood and adolescence ("Soldier's Home") is doomed to lead to a dead end, to mental corruption brought about by an ignorant Midwestern society.

In Hemingway, a first step towards a separate peace, at least for the time being, seems to be the solitary retreat into nature, performed by the nominal protagonist of *In Our Time*, Nick Adams, in the final two-part story of the book. After a series of psychic and physical injuries inflicted upon him through the exposure to a violent and chaotic reality, he returns to the fishing grounds of his youth. Among Hemingway critics there seems to be general agreement that Nick's activities in "Big Two-Hearted River," which provide for "the re-establishment of an harmonious and therapeutic intimacy with nature; the flight from bad memories and unpleasant thoughts,"[13] represent a complete psychological convalescence; but, in fact, the rhythm of success and failure, of expectation and disappointment in the story suggests that Nick has not fully regained his emotional balance.[14] Despite his deliberate movements and ritualized actions, Nick lets the coffee boil over, a mosquito gets inside his tent despite the cloth he fixes across its opening, and next morning a big trout breaks the leader of his fishing rod and escapes. Finally, Nick postpones his plan to fish in the swamp. "Nick did not want to go in there now . . . . In the swamp fishing was a tragic adventure."[15]

Towards the end of the story, the swamp is mentioned eight times within three paragraphs (210f.), and the final word of the text is also "swamp." As one of the key images in "Big Two-Hearted River," the swamp has been variously interpreted as an "area of the sinister," as "the lower depths of Nick's unconscious mind," or as "the earthly terrain of nada, the opposite of . . . the sun-drenched world offering its sharp and well-lit particulars."[16] In terms of Nietzsche's concept of the Dionysian essence of life, however, these symbolic meanings attributed to the swamp are inadequate. In my view, the swamp, as depicted in "Big Two-Hearted River," is a metaphor for Hemingway's picture of the whole, for the comprehensive essence of life. The swamp carries the connotations of chaos, paradox, and suffering. In its very substance it has no palpable texture; it is treacherous, both solid and unsolid. It feeds the trout: "they were rising to insects come from the swamp" (184), a natural image unifying the duality of life and death. The appearance of the swamp is also paradoxical, in that it is covered with white mist in the dark, while producing a twilight during daytime.

The swamp is a complex image not to be confused with what the leftovers of Seney stand for — the burned town which is the point of departure at the beginning of "Big Two-Hearted River"; nor is the swamp to be juxtaposed to the meadow and the river. Instead, its ambiguity comprises both the figures of equivalence evoked by the burnt-over country — darkness equals barrenness and destruction — and the metaphoric implications of the sunny stretch of the scenery. The white mist and the sunny patches provide a link to the brightness of meadow and river, i.e. the prospect of an area of pure happiness and unspoilt sensation.

The topographical ground opposed to the swamp is, in fact, the place where Nick has pitched his tent; if the pattern of metonymical references associates the swamp with the Dionysian, the camp site is related to the Apollonian: It is located within range of sight but furthest away from the swamp, slightly elevated, "wooded and sandy, to overlook the meadow, the stretch of river and the swamp" (185). The tent is Nick's temporary home, evoking safety and order for the time being: "Nothing could touch him . . . . He was in his home where he had made it" (186f). Nick's impression of something "mysterious and homelike" touches the borderline of illusion: "It was quite dark outside. It was lighter in the tent" (187). The camp stands in opposition to the swamp, the river, and the meadow — a microcosm created by man, and set apart from the surroundings of nature. Also, it is the only dry place, which adds to its illusory, unreal character; even the adjacent meadow is wet with dew in the evening, and on the next morning, when Nick climbs out of the river, "water [was] running down his trousers and out of his shoes" (204, cf. also 212). In its temporariness, the tent serves as a provisional shelter keeping the disturbing presence of the swamp at bay, at least for a night: a presence which the mosquito reminds us of before Nick burns this presumptive emissary of the swamp with a match.

In the course of "Big Two-Hearted River II," action gradually shifts away from the camp as Nick approaches the swamp, the image of inevitable, tragic reality. Figuratively speaking, fishing in the swamp means unreserved re-immersion into the paradoxical world: Nick finds himself on the threshold to what Nietzsche calls the tragic affirmation of life. In trying to face reality, Nick's attitude toward life widely differs from the viewpoint attributed to an opposite cast of characters in *In Our Time*. Its most prominent members are Nick's mother in "The Doctor and The Doctor's Wife," who pronounces moral judgments on the world from a room with the blinds drawn, and the society of "Soldier's Home," in whose morally rigid Midwestern view of life Nietzsche's notion of Alexandrian culture seems to have materialized. Their preconceived attitude is based on anticipations which do not match reality, just as the picture of Krebs on the Rhine does not match their ideas of radiant heroes, beautiful German girls, and the romantic Rhine valley.[17] Illusions replace fact, Apollo has set himself absolute. To Harold Krebs life in his hometown has come to a complete standstill: "Nothing was changed," even his father's car is "still the same" (92). Stagnation and uniformity — all the girls are dressed alike — as much as empty conventions are ubiquitous. Life in Krebs's family, *pars pro toto* for the surrounding community, is propelled by the belief that "God has some work for everyone to do . . . . There can be no idle hands in His kingdom" (98), as Mrs Krebs insists in the final dialogue with her son.

The contrast between the Wastelanders of Krebs's hometown and Nick Adams of "Big Two-Hearted River" is obvious. On his way to confronting life not as an act of reason or moralizing, Nick experiences the world as an aesthetic phenomenon in the literal sense of the word. He relies on the evidence of his senses as the only verifiable truth, and he tries "not to rush his sensations" (204), taking care to pay attention to each single sense impression — "smells, feels, above all sights."[18] In this respect, he figures as the prototype for a long series of subsequent Hemingway protagonists, who, sensuously grasping the complex reality of the world, strive for the precious moments of feeling at one with the earth, a guidance towards the highest possible participation in life.

The notion of tragic affirmation also yields the key to the world of the bullfight, whose great importance to the author's works has been well documented by the *aficionado* Hemingway himself in his semi-fictional book *Death in the Afternoon* (1932), and has also been discussed at length in Hemingway criticism. The tragic implications of the bullfight come very close to Nietzsche's idea of tragedy as the dramatization of tragic myth. According to *The Birth of Tragedy*, tragic myth originates in the Dionysian vision and "expresses Dionysian knowledge in symbols" (103). It "wants to be experienced vividly as a unique example of a universality and truth that gaze into the infinite" (107). Cast into the mold of Attic tragedy, tragic myth, the concentrated image of the world, is revealed to the audience identifying itself with the chorus on stage, and thereby living to experience the sudden overwhelming sensation of transcendence, the "bustle of the changing figures":

> We are to recognize that all that comes into being must be ready for a sorrowful end . . . . We are really for a brief moment primordial being itself . . . ; the struggle, the pain, the destruction of phenomena now appear necessary to us . . . , we have become, as it were, one with the infinite primordial joy in existence, and . . . we anticipate, in Dionysian ecstasy, the indestructibility and eternity of this joy. (104f)

Tragedy serves as a therapy to those who have seen into the abyss of the Dionysian; it sublimates existential experience. The Apollonian "objectification of a Dionysian state" makes the sudden "shattering of the individual and his fusion with primal being" aesthetically perceptible (65) and, thereby, brings about the consolation that "life is at the bottom of things, despite all the changes of appearances, indestructibly powerful and pleasurable" (59). As myth is the "necessary prerequisite of every religion" (111), tragedy assumes the function of a religious ritual, resulting in the revelation of the mystery of Dionysus.

To the reader of *Death in the Afternoon*, Nietzsche's idea of tragic myth may well appear as an anticipation of what bullfighting essentially means.[19] On the very first page of the book, the narrator insists on seeing the bullfight as a work of art which gives aesthetic pleasure: judging it by standards of Christian morality means completely missing its message. Like the chorus in Attic tragedy, the matador acts as the agent on behalf of the audience which collectively identifies with him. The *faena*, the climactic last act of the bullfight, centers on the revelation of an otherwise hidden universal truth and causes the same effects as tragedy does in Nietzsche: The primordial truth of a paradoxical reality is the substance of the tragic myth which is put on stage in the bull ring, or, in Hemingway's own words, the "feeling of life and death and mortality and immortality."[20] Leading to the final sword thrust, the *faena* "takes a man out of himself and makes him feel immortal"; it "gives him an ecstasy, that is, while momentary, as profound as any religious ecstasy, moving all the people in the ring together and increasing in emotional intensity" (206f):

> Now the essence of the greatest emotional appeal of bullfighting is the feeling that the bullfighter feels in the middle of a great faena and that he gives to the spectators. He is performing a work of art and he is playing with death, bringing it closer, closer, closer, to himself.... He gives the feeling of his immortality, and, as you watch it, it becomes yours. Then when it belongs to both of you, he proves it with the sword. (213)

The moment of truth unites man and beast, the boundary lines of individual existence fade, and the original oneness of nature is reestablished:

> The beauty of the moment of killing is that flash when man and bull form one figure as the sword goes all the way in, the man leaning after it, death uniting the two figures in the emotional, aesthetic and artistic climax of the fight. (247)

In the twelfth interchapter of *In Our Time*, the decisive ingredients of the bullfight are laid bare: a *spectacle* which gives *emotion* to the audience, culminating in an *instant of time* when the matador and the bull form *one figure*:

> If it happened right down close in front of you, you could *see* Villalta snarl at the bull and curse him .... Then he ... swung back

from the charge, his feet firm, the muleta curving and at each swing the crowd *roaring*.

When he started to kill it was all in the same rush . . . . He drew out the sword from the folds of the muleta and sighted with the same movement and called to the bull, Toro! Toro! and the bull charged and Villalta charged and just *for a moment they became one*. Villalta became *one with the bull* and then it was over [emphasis added].

Finally, the bullfight, like Attic tragedy, comprises a spiritual dimension which produces a therapeutic effect. If, in *The Birth of Tragedy*, the dramatization of the tragic reconciles man with the absurdities of his existence, so does the bullfight, helping the spectator to the cherished moments of maximum participation in life. As a quasi-religious ritual it provides the chance to live through the most fundamental truth again and again, a synthesis of all possible experience: "The only place where you could see life and death, i.e. violent death now that the wars were over, was in the bull ring," says Hemingway in the second paragraph of *Death in the Afternoon*, and those of his characters who have been in the war and have felt the impact of the Dionysian seem to have the urge to repeat this experience. Jake Barnes, the narrator of *The Sun Also Rises* (1926), for example, is an *aficionado* and war veteran who does not simply tell the story of a vacation trip to Spain. As his detailed itinerary suggests, he is well aware of the fact that his journey follows the ancient pilgrimage route from the "Rue Saint Jacques"[21] in Paris to Santiago de Compostela. He covers more than half of the distance of the historical highway, of which Roncevalles and Pamplona were two important stations in former times. Jake Barnes is a modern pilgrim, however not seeking consolation in Christian belief, but in the pagan ritual of the bullfight. Paganism and Christianity, dominant antagonistic features of the *Chanson du Roland*, are implicitly referred to when Jake mentions "the old chapel of the monastery" (128) in Roncevalles which is said to be built over the remains of Roland.[22]

In Jake's description, the beginning of the fiesta reads like a frontline report, as if his memories of war mingled with the present of his narrative:

At noon of Sunday, the 6th of July, the fiesta exploded . . . . The café was like a battleship stripped for action . . . . Before the waiter brought the sherry the rocket that announced the fiesta went up in the square. It burst and there was a grey ball of smoke high up above the Theatre Gayarre, across on the other side of the plaza. The ball of smoke hung in the sky like a shrapnel burst and as I watched, another rocket came up to it, trickling smoke in the bright sunlight. I saw the bright flash as it burst and another little cloud of smoke appeared. (152f)

The overall impression of the fiesta is that of a chaotic, Dionysian bacchanal. Conventions such as the value of money lose their meaning (152); individuation fades, as the crowd absorbs even tourists who are as strange to the events as their clothes are to the black smocks of the Spanish peasants (205). Fundamental contradictions such as the pagan and Christian sources of the fiesta are fused in the procession: It is framed by *riau-riau* dancers and presents not only the statue of San Fermin but also "great giants, cigarstore Indians, thirty feet hight, Moors, a King and Queen" (155). The fiesta turns into an image of the Dionysian carrying everything and everyone with it, preparing the participants for the sudden and intense feeling of the "tragic sensations" (214) that Romero is to give them in the bull ring: visionary moments when man and beast merge into "one sharply etched mass" (217). To the *aficionado*, the fiesta, far from offering mere amusement, answers an existential need for essential experience. Its boiling-point, the bullfight and, in particular, the moment of truth, grants a deep penetration into reality. In *The Birth of Tragedy*, Nietzsche similarly welcomes such precious moments when nature celebrates "her reconciliation with her lost son, man" (37).

Although Hemingway was far from well-acquainted with the German cultural tradition, there are clear parallels between his literary presentation of reality and Nietzsche's view of life, as well as between the two writers' concepts of the tragic. Even if an assessment of direct influence seems, as yet, to be a difficult enterprise, our contextual approach is of some cognitive value: It offers, for instance, an alternative to many readings and misreadings of topography in "Big Two-Hearted River" and of the story's ending. It also elucidates the significance of the bullfight in Hemingway. Moreover, the coordinates which make up the patterns of correspondence between Nietzsche and Hemingway, namely their points of intersection and their structural and semantic contiguities, lead to a re-evaluation of Hemingway's position in literary modernism. The Janus face of reality and the sense of chaos beneath an ordered surface of life, which play such a prominent role in Hemingway's works, also deeply concerned other modern writers, such as Joseph Conrad, Thomas Mann, and Robert Musil. What is more, the meaning of tragic myth, both in the bull ring and in Nietzsche's Attic tragedy, echoes what T.S. Eliot, in his famous essay "Ulysses, Order, and Myth" (1923), has called a way "of giving a shape and a significance to the immense panorama of futility and anarchy which is contemporary history."[23] Finally, the sudden appearance of the moment of truth in Hemingway, as much as the revelation of the Dionysian in Nietzsche, i.e. the sudden visualization of an otherwise hidden universal coherence, are prominent features in the works of Virginia Woolf, Joyce, and, again, Conrad: The moment of vision becomes the manifestation of the discontinuous and incommensurable.

If the commanding presence of Nietzsche's legacy in the collective consciousness of the modern mind has left its traces almost everywhere, it is no wonder that the philosopher's ideas appear to us as a model for comprehending and re-assessing typical modernist aspects in Hemingway. In *The Autobiography of Alice B. Toklas,* Gertrude Stein claimed that her ex-disciple looked like a modern and smelled like a museum.[24] This may be so, but a recognition of the pervasive Nietzschean attitudes and ideas in Hemingway can help us to shift the balance back from the scent to the looks of this central figure in American and modernist literature.

Notes

[1] Michael F. Moloney, "Ernest Hemingway: The Missing Third Dimension," *Hemingway and His Critics: An International Anthology,* ed. Carlos Baker (New York: Hill and Wang, 1961), pp. 187–188; John Killinger, *Hemingway and the Dead Gods: A Study in Existentialism* (Lexington: U. of Kentucky Press, 1960), p. 101; Josette Smetana, *La philosophie de l'action chez Hemingway et Saint-Exupéry* (Paris: J.A.M.-Edartec., 1965), pp. 42–47; Philip Young, *Ernest Hemingway: A Reconsideration* (University Park and London: The Pennsylvania State UP, 1966), pp. 199–200. The fact that Young erroneously ascribes the motto of his book to Nietzsche's *Zarathustra* — it is a passage out of *The Gay Science* — perhaps indicates an all-too-careless way of dealing with the critical term "influence."

[2] Richard Layman, "Hemingway's Library Cards at Shakespeare and Company," *Fitzgerald/Hemingway Annual* (1975), 191–207; Noel Fitch, "Ernest Hemingway — c/o Shakespeare and Company," *Fitzgerald/Hemingway Annual*

(1977), 157–181; Gregory Green, "The Old Superman and the Sea: Nietzsche, the Lions, and 'The Will to Power'," *Hemingway Notes*, 5 (1979), 14–19; Nicholas Gerogiannis, "Hemingway's Poetry: Angry Notes of an Ambivalent Overman," *Ernest Hemingway: The Papers of a Writer*, ed. Bernard Oldsey (New York and London: Garland, 1981), pp. 73–87 (here: pp. 74, 78).

[3] Michael S. Reynolds, *Hemingway's Reading 1910–1940: An Inventory* (New Jersey: Princeton UP, 1981); "A Supplement to 'Hemingway's Reading 1910–1940,'" *Studies in American Fiction*, 14, 1 (1986), 99–108. See also James D. Brasch and Joseph Sigman, *Hemingway's Library: A Composite Record* (New York: Garland, 1981).

[4] Charles Taylor, "'The Old Man and the Sea': A Nietzschean Tragic Vision," *Dalhousie Review*, 61 (1981–82), 631–643; there is next to nothing in Taylor which has not been said before by Leo Gurko in his thorough study *Ernest Hemingway and the Pursuit of Heroism* (New York: Crowell, 1968), pp. 159–174.

[5] Gerhard Hoffmann, "Kontrast und Parallelität in den Kurzgeschichten Hemingways," *Anglia*, 83, 2 (1965), 201–203; Ernest M. Halliday, "Hemingway's Ambiguity: Symbolism and Irony," in Carlos Baker, pp. 174–182. Cf. also Robert M. Slabey, "The Structure of *In Our Time*," pp. 76–78; Clinton S. Burhans, Jr., "The Complex Unity of *In Our Time*," pp. 88–102, in *Critical Essays on Hemingway's In Our Time*, ed. Michael S. Reynolds (Boston: Hall, 1983).

[6] *Basic Writings of Nietzsche*, ed. and trans. Walter Kaufmann (New York: Random House, 1966), p. 33; in all following quotations page numbers in the text refer to this edition.

[7] Peter Heller, *Dialectics and Nihilism* (Amherst: U of Massachusetts P, 1960), p. 82.

[8] *Basic Writings of Nietzsche*, p. 729.

[9] Charles G. Hoffmann and A. C. Hoffmann, "'The Truest Sentence': Words as Equivalents of Time and Space in *In Our Time*," *Hemingway: A Reconsideration*, ed. Donald R. Noble (New York: Whitston, 1983), p. 102.

[10] Carlos Baker, *Hemingway: The Writer as Artist* (Princeton: Princeton UP, 1972), pp. 152f.; Robert O. Stephens, *Hemingway's Non-Fiction: The Public Voice* (Chapel Hill: U of North Carolina P, 1968), p. 91.

[11] Cf. Reynolds, *Critical Essays*, p. 77. Most of Philip Young's critical work on Hemingway is centered on the theme of the wounded hero.

[12] *A Farewell to Arms* (New York: Scribner's, 1929), p. 191.

[13] Tony Tanner, "Ernest Hemingway's Unhurried Sensations," *The Reign of Wonder: Naivety and Reality in American Literature* (London: Cambridge UP, 1965), p. 254. Cf. for similar positions, Joseph DeFalco, *The Hero in Hemingway's Short Fiction* (Pittsburgh: U of Pittsburgh P, 1963), p. 147; Hoffmann and

Hoffmann, p. 105; Joseph M. Flora, *Ernest Hemingway: A Study of the Short Fiction* (Boston: G. K. Hall, 1989), p. 59.

[14] S. P. Jain, *Hemingway: A Study of His Short Stories* (New Delhi: Arnold-Heinemann, 1985), p. 106; Arthur Waldhorn, *A Reader's Guide to Ernest Hemingway* (New York: Farrar, Straus, and Giroux, 1972), p. 66.

[15] *In Our Time* (New York: Scribner's, 1967), p. 211; page numbers in parenthesis refer to this edition.

[16] In the order of citation: Baker, p. 127; William Adair, "Landscapes of the Mind: 'Big Two-Hearted River',", in Reynolds, p. 260; Tanner, p. 254.

[17] DeFalco, pp. 139–140; cf. Hoffmann, p. 207.

[18] See Tanner, p. 229.

[19] In his study "Hemingway and the Bullfight: Archetypes of Tragedy," *Arizona Quarterly*, 29 (1973), 37–56, Stephen R. Philipps associates the bullfight with ancient Dionysian rites but does not mention Nietzsche.

[20] *Death in the Afternoon* (New York: Scribner's, 1955); page numbers in parenthesis refer to this edition.

[21] *The Sun Also Rises* (New York: Scribner's, 1955); page numbers in parenthesis refer to this edition.

[22] Cf. H. R. Stoneback, "Hemingway and Faulkner on the Road to Roncevaux," in Noble, pp. 136–144 *pass.*; Mary Ann C. Curtis, "*The Sun Also Rises*: Its Relation to the Song of Roland," *American Literature*, 60, 2 (1988), 274–280.

[23] *Selected Prose of T. S. Eliot*, ed. Frank Kermode (London: Faber & Faber, 1975), p. 177.

[24] *The Autobiography of Alice B. Toklas* (London: Arrow Books, 1960), p. 219.

Hays Steilberg

From Dolson to Kaufmann: Philosophical Nietzsche Reception in America, 1901–1950

URING THE FIRST half of our century, Nietzsche did not enjoy the diplomatic immunity of a 'philosopher's philosopher' in America. Often enough, he was either grilled on the scholastic witness stand for crimes not committed, or completely ignored in the proceedings of the academic court. It is not without good reason that later interpreters such as Kaufmann and Danto conspicuously include the word *philosopher* in the titles of their studies on Nietzsche, for with their generation lay the burden of proof in the case of academia versus Nietzsche. To help illustrate why these scholars and others who succeeded them considered the establishment, once and for all, of Nietzsche's true status as philosopher and the refutation of the circumstantial evidence mounted against him a paramount task of philosophic justice, as well as in order to indicate what achievements were made by Nietzsche's early philosophic advocates in America, I wish to present a brief overview of American monographs on Nietzsche from 1901 — the appearance of Grace Neal Dolson's 1899 dissertation in book form — to 1950 — the publication date of Walter Kaufmann's Nietzsche-book. I employ Kaufmann's study as a temporal line of demarcation because it dramatically altered the course of American Nietzsche reception and because it has the character of a crossover work. Kaufmann belongs in some senses to the tradition that went before him, while in other ways preparing all that comes after him.

From the beginning, the academic mainstream was loath to take Nietzsche seriously as a philosopher, in part because of the anti-systematic nature of his presentation; but even more than this, the obsession with the moral and political ramifications of Nietzsche's thought determined the philosophical reception of his work in America. In this regard, the philosophical reception mirrors the popular handling of Nietzsche in America. What we will see in examining these studies is that the question of morals or values in the light of Nietzsche's philosophy of power has dominated almost every extensive American interpretation of his thought within this time frame. In the cases of Grace Neal Dolson, Paul Elmer More, Paul Carus, William Salter, and George Burman Foster, the moral approach tended to obscure or even compromise the quality of interpretation, whereas in the instances of H. L. Mencken, George Morgan, and Walter Kaufmann the question of values and, specifically, the inquiry into whether Nietzsche conceived of his "highest types" as egoistic, animalistic tyrants or meritorious new intellectuals, led to the most fruitful American interpretations of Nietzsche in the first fifty years of reception.

At the turn of the century, the center stage of American philosophy was without a doubt in Harvard. Although the philosophy department at Columbia under Dewey later got on the main circuit, Cambridge boasted the true cast of stars, counting William James, Josiah Royce, and George Santayana among its ranks. Although all three of these thinkers were aware of Nietzsche and even granted him some mention, none ever came to produce any serious work on his thought. James mentions Nietzsche only once, in *The Varieties of Religious Experience* (cf. "The Value of Saintliness"). There James elucidates, among other things, the social value of the religious impulse, while dubbing Nietzsche "The most inimical critic of the saintly impulses whom I know."[1] So much for the question of Nietzsche's usefulness for the "melioristic universe" of the Harvard sage. Curiously, James's personal friend and professional foe, the idealist Josiah Royce, found more use for Nietzsche in his own philosophy than the "radical empiricist" James. But Royce's adaptation of Nietzsche's overman for the purposes of his own "philosophy of loyalty" has all to do with Royce and little to do with Nietzsche.[2] Lastly, George Santayana stands out as the one among these three American philosophers who outright denounced Nietzsche. Santayana considered him an ideological forerunner of the imperialistic stance taken by the Wilhelminian Empire that eventually led to the outbreak of World War I. In his wartime study *Egotism in German Philosophy*, Santayana attempted to trace the development of totalitarian thought in Germany within the history of German philosophy from the Reformation onwards and saw Nietzsche as part of this sinister tradition.[3]

Thus, one must first of all note that none of the major names in American philosophy dealt extensively with Nietzsche's philosophy. Second, and more important, in all three of these cases, involving omission (James), misapplication (Royce) and rejection (Santayana), the respective interpretations on which these reactions were based all view Nietzsche as a philosopher of morals who wishes to institute a new program of ethics.

This moral(istic) interpretation also affects all monographic works on Nietzsche — be they favorable or inimical — written before the 1950s. The first of these works was presented as a doctoral dissertation at Cornell University in 1899 by Grace Neal Dolson. The importance of this study, subsequently published by Macmillan as *The Philosophy of Friedrich Nietzsche* in 1901, rests perhaps foremost on its having been written at all. As late as 1881, Santayana was not allowed by his advisor, Royce, to write his dissertation on Schopenhauer, the *grandseigneur* of pessimism being for Royce too much of a philosophical lightweight for a doctoral thesis.

The structure of Dolson's study relies on a thesis established in the earliest German literature on Nietzsche which divides his work into three distinct chronological and thematic periods. Period one is said to range roughly from *The Birth of Tragedy* to *Human, All to Human*, period two from *Dawn* to *The Gay Science*, and period three from *Thus Spake Zarathustra* to the posthumous notes. This provides Dolson with the scaffolding for an interpretation of Nietzsche's intellectual development as an organic process. She explains Nietzsche's thought as the progressive quest for a *summum bonum*, which Nietzsche ostensibly identifies varyingly in period one as beauty, in period two as truth and in period three as power. While she dismisses the first two periods as epigonus variations on traditional philosophical themes, she asserts that Nietzsche finally came into his own in the third period. Significantly, Dolson also declares this phase to be the era in Nietzsche's philosophy in which he formulated the principles of a new moral system. She shows mostly disregard for Nietzsche's expeditions into the fields of truth-theory and metaphysics, concluding that

> Nietzsche tells us everything that truth is not, but makes no attempt at any positive definition, although he constantly implies that there is an objective standard somewhere.[4]

Indeed, Dolson's identification of this apparent aporia, which leads right into the core of Nietzsche's epistemological and ontological thought, is exemplary, but she does not get beyond singling out the problem. In order to circumnavigate this barrier, she concentrates on the new, "Nietzschean" moral system, which appears in her interpretation as a vitalistic rehabilitation of the *physis* (ignoring higher cerebration) as the standard of all morals. All of this seems to come together in isolated aphorisms in which Nietzsche risks descriptions of his new vision. "The falseness of a judgment," he writes in *Beyond Good and Evil*,

> is to us not necessarily an objection to a judgment: it is here that our new language perhaps sounds strangest. The question is to what extent it is life-advancing, life-preserving, species-preserving, perhaps even species-breeding . . . .[5]

At first hearing, this sounds clearly like the proclamation of a new vitalistic ethic. But such a reading makes a drastic reduction of Nietzsche's 'experimentalism' (what might "falseness" mean to Nietzsche? — he warns us, after all, about the "strangeness" of this "new language"), for he simultaneously proposes that we measure the "strength" of an individual on the basis of how much "truth" he can stand (*BGE*, 39).

Dolson's combination of the three-period division and the concentration on a vitalist ethic was, nonetheless, quickly accepted as a standard assumption in the interpretation of Nietzsche. Both elements show up, for instance, in the next American monographic study of Nietzsche to follow Dolson's: H. L. Mencken's *The Philosophy of Friedrich Nietzsche*. The influence alone of Mencken's book, which was the first to have a broad sway, necessitates discussing it in any summary of the major works in American Nietzsche reception. Between 1908, the publication date, and 1913, Mencken's 300-page monograph saw three printings and one special British edition. The reviewers of the daily papers and the smaller journals quickly elected his study the "most complete exposition of the Nietzschean philosophy."[6] Mencken wanted to prove first that Nietzsche was understandable and logical, and second that Nietzsche had a definite importance for current events in America (a traditional thesis of American Nietzsche-supporters). He did admittedly adopt much of the already extant exegetic strategies for his own study. Mencken adheres, for example, to the three-period division of Nietzsche's thought, sees his philosophy as a search for the highest good, and incorporates vitalistic tenets into his examination of Nietzsche's critique of morals. But he was also led by an original interpretative instinct that drove him to look for an answer to the question of what Nietzsche's "highest types" really are. Mixed with this 'instinct' is Mencken's own identification with Nietzsche, since he considered himself, as rationalistic (and rabid) culture critic, one of the higher specimens of the species, and thought that he had found in Nietzsche a comrade in arms.

The *Untimely Meditations* (particularly the third one) form a consistent undercurrent in Mencken's exposition and what he discovered in these essays was the idea that Nietzsche rejected the 'mass' of mankind because of their 'mediocre intelligence' and unwillingness to think independently or to break away from cultural and moral convention. In *Schopenhauer as Educator*, Nietzsche puts forth his (Schopenhauerian) theory of why most people avoid thinking for themselves, accusing them of timidity and conventionality. Nietzsche encourages his readers to "become themselves," just as he later speaks of how "one becomes what one is." This nurtured in Mencken the conviction that Nietzsche's highest types were not physically superior dumb brutes, but intellectuals with the courage to be nonconformist and to reject the metaphysical "prejudices" of conventional mores. According to Mencken, Nietzsche's ideal vision of the higher individuals or "free spirits" involves, then, the practice of a critical philosophy which, in the best manner of the Enlightenment, strives ultimately toward the "overthrow of superstition and unreasoning faith."[7] In Mencken's portrayal, the Nietzschean hero no longer runs with the blond beasts of the master morality, but is rather to be found among "the men who go most violently counter to the view of the herd, and who battle most strenuously to prevail against it . . . sham-smashers and truth-tellers and mob-fighters after the type of Huxley, Lincoln, Bismarck, Darwin . . . ."[8] Thus,

Mencken rejects the social Darwinian cum vitalist interpretation of Nietzsche's ideal. His interpretation suffers, however, from one severe and complex flaw (discounting other less important problems) that at the same time contains one of its best perceptions. Mencken recognized that Nietzsche attacks conventional morals because, as a thoroughgoing empiricist, he identified all moral systems as historical, functionalistic products of the human imagination. (The more torpid and craven the imagination that makes values, the baser and more poltroonish the morals.) In all these systems, excepting the so-called "master morality," Nietzsche discovered a fundamental appeal to a supernatural or transcendent entity which justified all principles contained in the specific ethical codex. The master morality interests Nietzsche as the hypothetical construct of a completely *immanent* moral code. No concepts of justice resting on the invocation of an otherworldly, empirically nondemonstrable idea or entity cloud the immanent clarity of a master morality.

Mencken grasped that Nietzsche posited only one observable principle present in all being to which any immanent value system would have to recur: the will to power. He was unable, however, to reconcile will to power with the ideal of critical reason. Nietzsche does apparently reject worldly power or mere brute domination of one's environment as the highest form of power, but can this be taken as a standard for claiming that critical reason is the highest epiphenomenal outgrowth of will to power? This is the point at which Mencken's interpretation falters and he himself falls back upon vitalist banality. "How is man to define and determine his own welfare and that of the race after him?" he asks. "The answer, of course, lies in the obvious fact that, in every healthy man, instinct supplies a very reliable guide."[9]

Reason is no instinct, though. On the contrary, reason in its highest critical functions can, in Nietzsche's opinion, be most threatening to man's existence. The vitalist's will to illogical but "healthy" illusion is subordinate to biological ends. The higher activities of the intellect or the "intellectual conscience" are actually at cross-purposes with the *physis* in man and yet are at the same time called "sublime" by Nietzsche. This is a logical conflict which Mencken apparently was not qualified to take on. The problem itself, however, is the key to the best American interpretations of Nietzsche's philosophy, and its definition is first present in Mencken's book.

Two extremely hostile and rather tendentious short monographs followed on Mencken's heels and may to a certain extent be seen as a reaction to the popularity or even acceptability Mencken was helping Nietzsche achieve. Paul Elmer More, classicist, New Jersey hermit and second in command of the so-called "new humanist" movement begun by Irving Babbitt and himself at Harvard, lashed out at the enemy in 1912 with his study, *Nietzsche*. Babbitt displayed some amity toward Nietzsche because he sensed in the philosophy of the highest types an air of aristocratic "decorum," which was a programmatic term in the new humanist canon. Babbitt leaned toward classical tastes with a shot of social Darwinism on top and shared the exclusivity of Nietzsche's interest in the natural *aristoi* (he also shared Nietzsche's vehement hatred of Rousseau, whom Babbitt made responsible for the general misery of the modern age). In compliance with new humanist doctrine, More did at least concur that Nietzsche had good arguments against humanitarianism (the very name "humanist" was intended by Babbitt and More as a counterterm to "humanitarian," which they identified with exaggerated and undifferentiated philanthropic sympathy):

> That much of Nietzsche's protest against the excesses of humanitarians was sound and well directed, I for one am quite ready to admit. He saw, as few other men of our day have seen, the danger that threatens true progress in any system of education and government which makes the advantage of the average rather than the distinguished man its first object.[10]

This, too, is a strictly moral/political interpretation of Nietzsche's thought and contains nothing new or innovative. In addition, anti-humanitarianism makes up the only aspect in Nietzsche's work deemed worthy of praise by More. In all other points, he resorts to the conventional prejudices and clichés brought against Nietzsche at the time in order to argue his philosophical insignificance. More drudges through Nietzsche's biography looking for incriminating evidence, stresses the discrepancy between Nietzsche's own 'paltry' existence and the 'virile' physique he gave to the body of this thought, declares him incapable of serious philosophical work and indebted to the irrationalist school. Nietzsche's final dementia dominates More's interpretation as the most characteristic biographical expression of Nietzsche's philosophical ailment:

> We begin to see that the roots of disease were more deeply im-
> planted in his nature than those would have us believe who think to
> find in his words a return to sanity and strength.[11]

Nietzsche's so-called philosophy, More solemnly instructs us, contains nothing more than "the sort of spasmodic commonplace that
enraptures the half-cultured."[12]

Paul Carus, German-American philosopher and editor of *The
Monist* and *The Open Court*, began polemicizing against Nietzsche
early on in journalistic publications and summarized his displeasure
in *Nietzsche and Other Exponents of Individualism*, which appeared
in 1914. Carus's objections to Nietzsche rest on slightly more philosophical foundations than More's. In his own philosophical writings,
Carus practices a rather labored and eclectic mixture of Platonism,
monism, and positivism which today seems like something from the
old curiosity shop of ideas. Although Carus was an atheist in the
sense that he denied the existence of a superpersonal god, he was at
the same time quirky enough to propose that science should be con-
secrated as the new deity.[13] Recognizing the arch-skeptic Nietzsche
as an anti-systematic and anti-mechanistic philosopher, Carus had,
from his own standpoint, no other choice than to dismiss him as
solipsistic and unscientific:

> In modern times Friedrich Nietzsche expressed the most sovereign
> contempt for science. Among all the philosophies of modern times
> there is perhaps none which in its inmost principle is more thor-
> oughly opposed to our own than Nietzsche's.[14]

Carus also maligned Nietzsche for his ethical 'depravity' and made
no bones about employing the same arguments as More, accusing
Nietzsche of megalomania, theomania, and just plain insanity. For
the most part, though, Carus simply possessed no philosophical organ for even hearing what Nietzsche was talking about. His idola-
trous positivism caused him to miss completely the newest
philosophical developments in the United States — pragmatism
struck Carus as being hardly any better than Nietzscheanism.

Carus's study was the last to appear before the outbreak of World
War I. During the war era, much was made of the possibility that
Nietzsche's philosophy might have contributed to the bellicose,
chauvinistic nationalism of the Wilhelminian Empire that came to a
head in the years from 1914 to 1918. And yet, although a sizable

propaganda program directed against him diminished Nietzsche's public image in the United States and Great Britain, the study of Nietzsche continued more or less unhampered. In the penultimate year of the war, the ethical theorist William Salter published the longest American monograph on Nietzsche to date. Salter's 500-page excursion into Nietzsche's philosophical 'system' was a very congenial and thus timely contribution to the American literature on Nietzsche (Salter had also published articles in which he defended Nietzsche against the associations drawn between his philosophy and the German *Reich*). Philosophically speaking, however, Salter's *Nietzsche the Thinker* offers little in the way of new insight into Nietzsche's thought, and the goodwill plus the sheer mass of the book cannot compensate for its dearth of ingenuity. Salter's method is, similarly to Carus's, in large determined by his own philosophical standpoint, to which he tries to make Nietzsche conform. He had begun his university studies in theology at Knox College, moving on to Yale and Harvard, but eventually became an apostate from church orthodoxy. Salter continued to concern himself with ethical questions, but sought his answers outside the kingdom of faith, turning mainly to the domains of classical philosophy. Under the influence of the German-American ethical philosopher Felix Adler, Salter struck out on his own search for a new *summum bonum* to fill the moral void of the atheistic modern age. James Cadello observes quite correctly that Salter's Nietzsche-interpretation represents his attempt to find the missing link in the deductive chains of his own philosophy via Nietzsche's critique of morals and the "transvaluation."[15]

Salter recognized, as had Mencken before him, that if, as Nietzsche says, "*This world is the will to power — and nothing besides!*"[16] then any immanent scale of goods would have to reflect levels of will to power. But also like Mencken before him, Salter fails at the attempt to reconcile will to power with reason or intellect. To add insult to injury, the remainder of his interpretation is devoted to convincing the reader of an essentially innocuous Nietzsche who purportedly equated the highest power with the highest rationality and the highest rationality, in turn, with a utilitarian social ethics. This, in Salter's words, was Nietzsche's point in redefining the terms "good" and "evil": the good is merely intelligence, which enables society to cooperate better, the evil is merely ignorance, which creates social discord. Thus, Nietzsche's scale of values reveals that

"some actions are . . . more intelligent than others, and this fact gives
rise to diverse judgements . . . . Acts called evil are really stupid."[17]
Intelligence may mirror the levels of strength or "power" in the
world and in man, but Salter sets an *apriori* synonym of power to
harmonious spirituality.

This outline of a Nietzscheanism with a heart becomes simply
more and more absurd as Salter tries harder and harder to prove the
truly benevolent interest Nietzsche supposedly took in the welfare of
mankind. Salter's Nietzsche even dons the garb of partisan of the
working classes in this revisionist pastoral. He assures the reader that
if Nietzsche

> had lived to complete the work on which he was bent in his later
> years, he would have supplemented his doctrine of the higher
> man . . . with some adequate exposition of the place and functions
> of the average worker in society.[18]

At this point, Salter has completely left the orbits of all possible
worlds of interpretation. The working classes interested Nietzsche
only in their relation to the higher individuals. As already mentioned,
these higher individuals are undoubtedly "free spirts," grand intel-
lects as opposed to ruthless thugs, but Salter could not explain why
this is the case. One must take into account that Salter may have exaggerated his image of an essentially harmless and more or less philanthropic Nietzsche in order to rout the many erroneous
defamations directed against this "German" philosopher during the
war, but on one level at least, his interpretation is equally as corrupt
as that of the oppositionists and propagandists.

A similarly conciliatory Nietzsche takes the stage in the study
Friedrich Nietzsche by George Burman Foster, professor of the philosophy of religion at the University of Chicago. Foster wrote the
work during the war years, but it did not appear until 1931, posthumously. In his own philosophical and theological outlook, Foster had
run up against an impasse precisely like Salter's. Foster criticized
what he referred to as the "supernatural" element in religion (as if
this were not what religion is about), but also considered empiricism
alone incapable of fulfilling man's spiritual needs, whether as individual or as a group. Foster characterized the aim of his own philosophy
as "spiritualistic evolutionism" — as the attempt "to defend against
supernaturalism the ideal of understanding and . . . against naturalism the ideal of meaning."[19]

As indicated by the title of an early study, *The Function of Religion in Man's Struggle for Existence* (1909), Foster had grown to view religion functionalistically. His reading of Nietzsche at least partially inspired him to this revision, for Nietzsche, as a nominalistic proto-semiotician, also teaches that religions and all other codes of belief (among others, rationalism as well) merely record mankind's sundry trials to assign systems of meaning to the world with the intention of making experience more understandable, controllable and, thus, more bearable. Foster deems man "incurably religious,"[20] meaning that he cannot face life without some formalized faith in the significance of his being. Foster rightly understands Nietzsche to say that the will to power in man, as the fundamental ingredient of being, simply manipulates the epiphenomenal intellect in order to further its own purposes, but Foster is also wont to portray the striving of the will as a functioning toward biological ends only. Also, Foster himself adhered to a form of Vaihinger-like "as if" theory to justify the necessity of religious belief. That is, even if factual belief is not possible in an empiristic age, for Foster a *contrafactual* belief may indeed be thinkable and even desirable if it avails the biological purposes of life:

> The question of the "truth of religion," as a former generation used the phrase, has died out of the consciousness of modern man. The man of today must think of religion as a necessary creation of human nature and evaluate it from that point of view.[21]

Nietzsche considers this idea, but never accepts it as a strategy for the higher individuals or "free spirits" of whom he requires that they recognize the "truth." Nietzsche is speaking of just these higher types when he writes that "No one is likely to consider a doctrine true merely because it makes him happy or virtuous . . ." (*BGE*, 39). For Nietzsche, the truth unveils before us a world containing no virtue or justice or even particular meaning, and this is precisely the nihilistic tenet that endangers the normally unreflective *physis*. Such truth is indeed dangerous, but again, for Nietzsche the "strength of a spirit could be measured by how much 'truth' it could take . . ." (*BGE*, 39). Foster, however, extrapolates from his own position to his interpretation of Nietzsche and comes to the conclusion that the latter acknowledged the "necessity" of religion (which traditionally brings forth varying theodicies to cover up this 'dangerous' truth) even if he could not believe in its premises: "He [Nietzsche] confirms a law which operates everywhere; namely, that religion, under one form or another, is a sociological necessity . . . ."[22]

Nietzsche does admit the function of religion, yet one must recognize that in his view, which always judges such phenomena perspectively, the loss of religion and God at once weakens the community while at the same time opening up new horizons for the "free spirits." As he writes in the *Gay Science*:

> Indeed, we philosophers and "free spirits" feel, when we hear the news that "the old god" is dead, as if a new dawn shown on us; our heart overflows with gratitude, amazement, premonitions, expectation. At long last the horizon appears free to us again . . . . [23]

Foster does not attempt to turn Nietzsche into a philanthropist after Salter's manner, but his endeavor to replace religion as a social necessity in Nietzsche's thought falls equally wide of the mark. Like Salter — and generally all the authors whom we have viewed up to now — Foster also employs a decidedly ethical approach in his interpretation and basically ignores the epistemological and metaphysical subtleties of Nietzsche's philosophy.

During the 20s and 30s, not a single monographic study on Nietzsche by an American author appeared. It was not until the 1940s, curiously enough the next great war era, that academic interest in Nietzsche again began to blossom. This is in part a function of German immigration to the United States at this time. Countless German intellectuals fled persecution under Hitler and found a scholarly refuge in America's universities. The conspicuous presence of German scholars (among them Karl Löwith and Paul Tillich) at the symposium held (under the ægis of the Conference on Methods in Philosophy and the Sciences) in New York on December 3, 1944, in celebration of the centennial of Nietzsche's birth,[24] reflects this influence, and certainly Walter Kaufmann is the best known German emigré to play a role in American Nietzsche circles. During the Second World War, hostile propaganda once again tarnished Nietzsche's image in America, particularly as the Nazis actively tried to create a tailor-made Nietzsche for the justification of their own ideology. This association, even supported in works by known names in German Nietzsche scholarship like Alfred Bäumler, was not without effect: the Harvard historian Crane Brinton, for instance, swallowed the Nazi version of Nietzsche hook, line and sinker and presented an excoriating derision of his supposedly proto-fascistic philosophy in the study *Nietzsche*, which came out in 1941. Brinton faithfully relays almost every flagrant misconception of Nietzsche's philosophy on the market, from Pan-Germanism to race-hygiene to anti-semitism. I therefore devote no more space here to Brinton's interpretation (which, embarrassingly enough, saw two printings), but close this aside with Brinton's own self-incriminating words: "Nietzsche called for the Supermen. Mussolini and Hitler answered the call."[25] In general, though, as in the case of the First World War, this propagandistic libel by no means brought Nietzsche scholarship in America to a halt, as the New York conference demonstrates. And, again, German scholars contributed greatly to keeping interest in Nietzsche alive.

The first monograph (excluding Brinton) written after two decades of relative inactivity came, however, from an American scholar, George Allen Morgan of Duke University. Morgan's study *What Nietzsche Means* (1941), something of a landmark in American philosophical Nietzsche reception, unfortunately escaped the broad interest of the world of letters. Morgan essentially picks up where Mencken and Salter had left off — with the paradox of reason and power in Nietzsche's thought. This is, however, certainly not the only idea which informs Morgan's interpretation. Like those before him, he also attempts to rehabilitate Nietzsche's image and convince his readers that Nietzsche was above all else a serious philosopher. This judicious restoration is not cheapened by philanthropic makeover, though. Morgan's is also the first American study to place Nietzsche's critique of morals in proper perspective by pointing out that Nietzsche actually opposes the dogmatic metaphysical dualism implicit in both the philosophy and morals of the occidental tradition and does not simply attack Christianity out of iconoclasm for iconoclasm's sake. What appears modestly clad in Morgan's matter-of-fact presentation is in truth an extremely significant insight:

> Essentially *what* morality does Nietzsche propose to criticize? As just stated, it is one claiming absolute status: its imperatives are categorical, its values supreme . . . its content consists in absolute antitheses: certain qualities are utterly good, others utterly evil.[26]

This explains precisely what Nietzsche means by a philosophical position "beyond good and evil" — recognizing that a world without transcendence provides no basis for the Manichaean separation of being into opposites that characterizes Western thought. Morgan condenses all this in the remark that "Moral distinctions are 'perspectival', all actions are the same at bottom . . . ."[27] As Nietzsche says, now "grades of apparentness" supplant the absolutism of opposites (*BGE*, 34). This clarification of Nietzsche's attitude toward moralism or dualistic dogmatism in ethics and philosophy leads Morgan to the above mentioned conflict. If the world is non-transcendent and free of dualistic valuations, then being can be grounded only in itself, which seems to mean that being is not grounded at all: "So, for Nietzsche, reality is literally bottomless."[28] This limitless regression is, however, like Hegel's "night in which . . . all cows are black,"[29] untenable, because being would thus become thoroughly unrecognizable — unless some immanent monadic stuff might be discovered that infuses, even *is* all being. In Nietzsche's view, this monadic stuff is, of course, will to power.

Once again, if all being is will to power, then any and all valuations of being would have to correspond to various qualities of will to power. Nietzsche "must grade the *kinds* of life," and "power . . . is the standard of value which Nietzsche affirms . . . ."[30] If also, as Morgan correctly assumes, Nietzsche maintains "not only that the most spiritual or intellectual man — other things being equal — is most valuable, but also that he is strongest,"[31] then some connection must obtain between the intellect and a higher quality of *will to power* (or simply *power*, as Morgan interprets Nietzsche's meaning). The first scholar to devote his attention to Nietzsche's concept of sublimation as the redirection of primal energies toward higher intellectual pursuits (cf. aphorism 290 of *The Gay Science*), Morgan utilizes this concept to explain sublimation or "self-overcoming" as the substantiate trait of the most powerful. If will to power always seeks obstacles which it wants to overcome and the greatest obstacles are within the self — the primal drives — then overcoming these drives means turning all energies toward the purposes of the intellect and at the same time attaining the highest power (as mastery over the self). Yet, this understanding of the highest types betrays a basic fault later identified by Kaufmann. How can and why should intellect overcome will if everything, including these two phenomena, is will to power? What is the individual overcoming when he appears to be overcoming *himself*? As Nietzsche says, the free spirits all possess their sublime inclination to truth "thanks to a superfluity of 'free will'" (*BGE*, 44), by which he means will to power. Intellect remains merely the tool of the fundamental will. Morgan comes closer than anyone before him to a solution of the problem, but his interpretation remains, in the end, incomplete.

We must now consider one final attempt to solve this conflict of will to power and intellect in the interpretation by Walter Kaufmann. It would be grand foolishness to essay to an exhaustive treatment of Walter Kaufmann's *Nietzsche: Philosopher, Psychologist, Antichrist* (1950) in but a few pages. Hence, I restrict myself here to Kaufmann's interpretation of Nietzsche as it deals with the central idea of will to power. As Kaufmann himself writes in his Preface, after all, "will to power *is* the core of Nietzsche's thought."[32] One must also at least intimate, however, what a tremendous influence Kaufmann had on the course of American Nietzsche reception. Through this study and his translations of Nietzsche's works that followed it, Kaufmann did more than any other American scholar to dispel preconceived notions about Nietzsche's philosophy while at the same time popularizing it. The initial reviews of Kaufmann's book already bespeak the epochal role of this work.[33] One must grant that the author achieved his expressed intent: "to buck the current prejudice against Nietzsche" (xi). He would have earned his laurels if for this service alone, but Kaufmann was foremost a professor of philosophy, and we should concentrate first on the philosophical content of his argument and only second on the influence thereof.

Kaufmann pays tribute to Morgan's achievement in stressing the importance of sublimation for Nietzsche's philosophy. Not only had the concept been far too long neglected, but it also demonstrates that Nietzsche did not, as both his critics and some of his vitalistic followers have presumed, put forth the unbridled release of all primal passions as an ideal form of higher existence. Kaufmann also concurs with Morgan that Nietzsche's thought strives in the main toward the resolution of a "value problem" (the discovery of an immanent, non-transcendent good, that is) by posing one central question: "How can he [Nietzsche] determine what specimens are the most valuable?" (174). Yet, at the same time Kaufmann identifies the contradiction in Morgan's solution to the riddle of the 'highest power' as complete self-overcoming. If Nietzsche presumes the intellect to be the epiphenomenon of the will, then an intolerable dualism arises when one makes self-overcoming the main drive of the will and an absolute measure of power, for why should intellect as *dominatio*, or in other words the will in an instrumentalized form, overcome the will as *dynamis*, and if everything is will to power, how can there be various wills?

> The simile of overcoming . . . implies the presence of two forces, one of which overcomes the other. "Self-overcoming" is conceivable and meaningful when the self is analyzed into two forces, such as reason and the inclinations. Apart from such a duality, apart from the picture of one force as overcoming and controlling another, self-overcoming seems impossible. (215)

And yet, Nietzsche certainly believes that higher intellect can be achieved only at the cost of sublimating the primal urges. Kaufmann views Nietzsche's philosophy as an organic development (echoes of Dolson) and sees this very contradiction as present not only in such a dualistic interpretation as Morgan's, but even in the early Nietzsche himself: "The philosophy of his [Nietzsche's] youth was marked by a cleft which all but broke it in two" (178). Nietzsche saw, according to Kaufmann, that this cleft rent his thought, because his philosophical method, which Kaufmann calls dialectical (meant mostly in a Socratic, but also Hegelian sense), enabled him to see the internal contradictions in all traditional philosophical terms. Thus, Nietzsche came to spot the transcendent metaphysical residue that blurred the empiricist vision of Western philosophy. Kaufmann encapsulates all this in his neologistic term for Nietzsche's philosophy, to which he refers as "dialectical monism" (235). Monism describes the reduction of all being to one principle, will to power, with which Nietzsche resolves the conflict of will and intellect. Here once more, the thesis of gradation or degrees now replaces the older theories of dualistic opposition:

> Instead of assuming two qualitatively different principles, such as strength and reason, he would reduce both to a single, more fundamental force: the will to power. And the distinction of brawn and brains he would explain in terms of a qualitative difference between degrees of power. (202)

Now, this still does not explain *why* the element of "brains" in this equation represents a higher degree of power. Kaufmann makes no secret of this logical lapse and tries to take up the slack by proving the identical nature of intellect and highest power in Nietzsche's thought. He begins *ex negativo* by asking what makes the followers of "slave moralities" weak in Nietzsche's opinion. The weak are weak, says Kaufmann, because they must define themselves in relation to others (this idea was prefigured by Mencken). Their entire life is *reaction* or, in Kaufmann's reading, dependency (250). This dependency or weakness also expresses itself in the need for categorically accepted truths. If dependency characterizes the essence of weak individuals, then the opposition of weak and strong may be viewed as one of heteronomy over against autarky. The strongest individuals would be those capable of the greatest independence, and absolute independence, or absolute freedom, would hypostatize the highest attainable level of power. If the will wants power, then the highest will, as Kaufmann would have it, strives toward the highest freedom which is reachable only through the highest intellect. This would then be the conversion formula for Nietzsche's new scale of values. In this light, Kaufmann sees an even stronger parallel between Nietzsche and Hegel, having first indicated such a similarity in the function of dialectics in the philosophy of both:

> Power is enjoyed only as *more* power. One enjoys not its possession but its increase: the overcoming of impotence. Since impotence is the equivalent of dependence, one might say that the achievement of independence is the source of pleasure . . . . Even closer is [now] the relation of the will to power to Hegel's notion of spirit, which was conceived as essentially a striving for freedom . . . . (186)

Nietzsche would indeed appear to substantiate this interpretation. When speaking of independence in *Beyond Good and Evil*, he remarks that "Few are made for independence — it is a privilege of the strong" (*BGE*, 29). This independence also complies with the danger Nietzsche envisions as bound up with this "sublime" inclination of the intellect, because the highest freedom implies the rejection of all the categorical truths of the weak, the repudiation of all certainty. Nietzsche considers a "pleasure and power of self-determination, . . . a *freedom* of the will" possible in which "the spirit would take leave of all faith and every wish for certainty . . . . Such a spirit would be *the free spirit* par excellence" (*GS*, 347). Only the strongest intellect could, then, attain the highest freedom, because this spiritual autarky demands that one cast overboard all the comforts of certain truth — this would be the recognition of absolute relativity. The highest types are the freest. If one accepts this, then Mencken was actually not that far off in his interpretation of Nietzsche.

One may, of course, prefer challenging this interpretation to accepting it, and it is time that such a critique be ventured. I do not have space here to expound upon a detailed test of this theory, but I would like at least to indicate that the assumption of freedom as the goal of the will's striving is not quite as clear-cut in Nietzsche as it may appear. For one thing, freedom is identified here with power, and both Morgan and Kaufmann seem to take power to be the substance of being in Nietzsche's philosophy, which results in a new dualism: here will, there power (whatever it might be). Nietzsche never says, however, that the world "is power and nothing besides" — he calls the world "*will* to power and nothing besides." The will is the substance of being and the will desires above all . . . to will (cf. *On the Genealogy of Morals,* III, 28) — which keeps it in the monadic context. Nietzsche also never says that freedom is the highest form of existence. He calls it a "drive" or "privilege" of the highest types, but indicates that these individuals are first superior and then free. They become free "thanks to a superfluity of 'free will'" which has *already* made them strong and superior. Again, the will is primary, the intellect secondary as epiphenomenon. Nietzsche *does*, on the other hand, explicitly name the "highest state a philosopher can attain" and calls it *amor fati* (*WP*, 1041). I should like to suggest that *amor fati*, not freedom, might be the goal of the highest will — which wishes to will *everything*. He who can will all (even nihilism, the necessity of which for Nietzsche Kaufmann neglects to include in his system) reaches the ultimate power of being because his will is suppressed by nothing: he sees that the entire cosmos is structured to his complete advantage, he could not wish for anything to be changed. Dissatisfaction with the world would be unthinkable for him. But why nihilism if this love of fate is the ultimate goal of the highest will?

Nietzsche's thought is nihilism, but not in the mere sense of a pessimism taken to extremes. Elsewhere I have emphasized the status of Nietzsche's ontology as a wholly immanent metaphysics, which means that his is a thoroughly closed system. Nietzsche does not choose this approach out of fancy or desire for the shock of the new, but as the description of the fundamental nature of being and the logical prerequisite of *amor fati*. Let us, taking a cue from Kaufmann, describe this point *ex negativo* as well. What characterizes the opposite of *amor fati*, the attitude contrary to the devaluation of this

world that Nietzsche associates with all "slave-morality"? To criticize
the state of being as the pessimist does presumes an appeal to a transcendent standard — only some superior measure outside this world
(be it God or *eidos* or what have you) can indicate to us that something is wrong with this world. But Nietzsche rejects this appeal to
the transcendent as the great moralistic or dualistic flaw of Western
metaphysics. We might regard his thought, then, as an affirmative
monistic nihilism. He calls it an "experimental philosophy" that anticipates "even the possibilities of the most fundamental nihilism,"

> but this does not mean that it must halt at a negation, a No, a will
> to negation. It wants rather to cross over to the opposite of this —
> to a Dionysian affirmation of the world as it is, without subtraction,
> exception, or selection . . . . (*WP*, 1041)

If, then, like Nietzsche we look to our experience alone, or "the
world as it is," instead of to a "beyond" for a standard of value for
fixing our attitude toward the world and exclude the very possibility
of any transcendent essence (as a "higher individual" would do),
then the world must by definition look immaculate to us, for we can
measure it by its own standards alone. *Amor fati* is thus possible only
in a completely self-referential (or *immanent*) and non-teleological
system. As Nietzsche says, "If the motion of the world aimed at a final state, that state would have been reached. The sole fundamental
fact, however, is that it does not aim at a final state . . ." (*WP*, 708).
This encloses also, in part, the idea of eternal return, which is
Nietzsche's model of an evolving world that at the same time never
changes, that has no *telos*.[34]

The *significance* of Kaufmann's solution cannot be contested, for
his interpretation is the first to remain within the immanent premises
of Nietzsche's own philosophy. It also provides a solution which,
however, has a somewhat humanistic temper not really germane to
Nietzsche, but is nevertheless useful for the popularization of his
thought. Hardly any reader, especially in the American public, would
object to the desire for freedom as the highest good in a philosophical system, and Kaufmann even goes so far as to compare Nietzsche's
philosophy to the Declaration of Independence (270). This borders
on the abstruse, but the most important aspect of this explanation is
Kaufmann's resistance to the supposition of a transcendent entity in
attempting to solve the Nietzschean conundrum of will and intellect.
Kaufmann's "new" method, which seeks to understand Nietzsche on

his own terms, cleared the way for the next generation of scholars to enter the Nietzschean labyrinth and discover many secret passageways that had heretofore remained unseen. And yet, Kaufmann also retains traditional elements in his view of Nietzsche. His theory of "dialectical monism" treats Nietzsche's thought as a program for solving a value problem, which in other words is an aspect of moral philosophy. Kaufmann has effectively freed Nietzsche of moralistic readings and has laid to rest the belief that Nietzsche supposedly wanted to enthrone a new set of mercenary master mores in our culture, but he also concentrated strongly on the question of what forms of human existence are to be admired, to be "valued." Admittedly, this is one of the principal ideas in Nietzsche's thought, but Kaufmann's examination of Nietzschean perspectivism, in contrast, pales next to his treatment of power philosophy and *Entlarvungspsychologie*. Nevertheless, the overall development of new Nietzschean readings (such as those of the deconstructionists) perhaps necessitated first the thorough exhaustion of the issue of morality and valuation.

Walter Kaufmann is remembered mainly as the great enlightener, who dispelled the myths of the eugenicist, militant, anti-semitic, vitalist, hedonistic Nietzsche, and (especially in America) as the discoverer of the proto-Freudian psychological insights in Nietzsche's work.[35] In his zeal, Kaufmann occasionally tends toward a whitewashing of Nietzsche's image, which cannot be treated here in any detail. Suffice it to say, however, that he has been heavily criticized for his decidedly one-sided handling of Nietzsche's ambivalent views on Socrates[36] and has also been called the creator of an "antiseptic" Nietzsche.[37] Kaufmann is guilty on both counts, but his service to American and international Nietzsche scholarship should not be belittled, for he is the originator of a serious interpretation that does not simply dismiss the possibility of comprehension because of "contradictions" in Nietzsche's thought, but takes up the often thankless task of lucid explication.

In every instance we have seen, the fascination with the effects of Nietzsche's thought on values has played a prominent role in the philosophical interpretations of his work in America. Today, questions of perspectivism and the artificiality of language and logic loom large in the discussion of Nietzsche, but this re-direction of interest presupposes the earlier concentration on Nietzsche and morals. The turmoil of change that overshadows the beginning of the twentieth century brought forth an almost panic-stricken insecurity about the validity of all accepted values (which was paradoxically accompanied by a manic hopefulness regarding the possibility of achieving new values). We need not be surprised that this affected the readings of a philosopher who envisioned the modern era as one of a decisive "transvaluation." The one surprise that really comes unexpectedly, perhaps, is that among the monographs predating Morgan and Kaufmann, H. L. Mencken's interpretation comes closest to an innovative discussion of the topics that concerned Nietzsche. Despite its blemishes, Mencken's *The Philosophy of Friedrich Nietzsche* lays bare the conflict that is actually at the bottom of Kaufmann's argument: if we accept Nietzsche's nihilistic rejection of transcendent values, with what right can we consider the great intellect the highest goal of mankind? And Mencken's criterion of non-conformity and intellectual independence parallels Kaufmann's stress on the will's striving for absolute freedom.

The dominant strains in the 'first wave' of philosophical Nietzsche reception in America were, undoubtedly, political and moral: phrased as the questions of power and new values. This befits the era. The age of modernism responded to the fin de siècle's paralytic obsession with the double burden of hypertrophic historical consciousness and exhausted culture by producing a cult of the new man who must needs find completely new values in order to redefine the human as the superhuman. It is only logical that early twentieth-century readers should see the question of values popping up on every page of Nietzsche's work. Nietzsche himself was at first cocooned in the cobwebs of this musty age-old *Zeitgeist* that he tried to exorcize. Wherever Nietzsche looked, he saw the snares and traps of moralism — especially in philosophy. Nietzsche did escape, though. The half-philippic, half-confessional tract *The Case of Wagner* records this liberation. The new territory he discovered and mapped is full of cartographic signs, however, that must first be reconstructed — painstakingly, like deciphering an unknown tongue without the aid of a Rosetta stone. Not many took it upon themselves to retrace Nietzsche's steps with the Argus-eyes of the philosophic scout. Nine books in fifty years may seem like quite a lot, or very little if one considers the magnitude of the task.

The tables have, of course, now been turned and the lecture halls of American universities resound with Nietzsche's name. Nietzsche's proponents of earlier days had no easy way of it getting him there, though. Some of the works here discussed show us what obstacles the serious philosophical reception of Nietzsche's thought was up against in America (most obviously in the cases of Carus, More, and Brinton); but other works — like Mencken's, Morgan's, and Kaufmann's — demonstrate how much of the Nietzschean palimpsest was faithfully, if fragmentarily, decoded for the next generation of explorers to descend into the labyrinthine depths of the Nietzschean mind. Of course, hindsight always does a superb job of recognizing mistakes, but one should also give a nod to achievements. American Nietzsche scholarship is now among the most productive internationally; let us not forget that it has its heritage — both of delinquents who deserve censure, but also of pioneers who deserve a place of honor in the family tree.

Notes

[1] William James, "The Varieties of Religious Experience," *Writings, 1902–1910*, ed. Bruce Kuklick (New York: Viking, 1987), p. 336.

[2] See Josiah Royce, *The Philosophy of Loyalty* (1908; New York: Haffner, 1971), pp. 381–82.

[3] George Santayana, *Egotism in German Philosophy* (1916; London: J. M. Dent, 1939).

[4] Grace Neal Dolson, *The Philosophy of Friedrich Nietzsche* (Diss. Cornell, 1899; New York: Macmillan, 1901), p. 42. I quote here from the dissertation manuscript.

[5] *Beyond Good and Evil*, trans. R. J. Hollingdale (1973; Middlesex: Penguin, 1981), 17. Cited hereafter in the text as *BGE* with number of aphorism.

[6] Edwin Slosson, "The Philosopher With the Hammer," *The Independent*, 65 (1908), 697.

[7] H. L. Mencken, *The Philosophy of Friedrich Nietzsche* (Boston: Luce, 1908), p. 98.

[8] *Ibid.*, p. 198.

[9] *Ibid.*, p. 103.

[10] Paul Elmer More, *Nietzsche* (New York: Houghton Mifflin, 1912), p. 75.

[11] *Ibid.*, p. 4.

[12] *Ibid.*, 19.

[13] Paul Carus, *Nietzsche and Other Exponents of Individualism* (Chicago: Open Court, 1914), p. 144.

[14] *Ibid.*, p. 5.

[15] James Peter Cadello, *Nietzsche in America: The Spectrum of Perspectives, 1895–1925* (Diss. Purdue, 1990); see chapter six, "William Mackintire Salter: Ethical Idealist." Cadello also includes a detailed examination of George Burman Foster with much additional information on Foster's own philosophy.

[16] *The Will to Power*, trans. Walter Kaufmann and R.J. Hollingdale (New York: Random House, 1968), 1067. Cited hereafter in text as *WP* with number of aphorism.

[17] William Salter, *Nietzsche the Thinker* (New York: Henry Holt, 1917; London, 1917), p. 118.

[18] *Ibid.*, p. 435.

[19] George Burman Foster, *The Finality of the Christian Religion* (Chicago: U of Chicago P, 1906), p. 217.

[20] George Burman Foster, *The Function of Religion in Man's Struggle for Existence* (Chicago: U of Chicago P, 1909), p. 153.

[21] *Ibid.*, p. 88.

[22] George Burman Foster, *Friedrich Nietzsche* (New York: Macmillan, 1931), p. 199.

[23] *The Gay Science*, trans. Walter Kaufmann (New York: Random House, 1974), 343. Cited hereafter in text as *GS* with number of aphorism.

[24] The papers delivered and discussions held at this conference can be found in *The Journal of the History of Ideas*, 6 (1945), 259–324.

[25] Crane Brinton, *Nietzsche* (Cambridge: Harvard UP, 1941), p. 171.

[26] George Allen Morgan, *What Nietzsche Means* (1941; Connecticut: Greenwood Press, 1975), pp. 162–63.

[27] *Ibid.*, p. 174.

[28] *Ibid.*, pp. 50–51.

[29] G. W. F. Hegel, *Phänomenologie des Geistes* (1807; Hamburg: Meiner, 1988), p. 13 (my translation).

[30] Morgan, *What Nietzsche Means*, pp. 117–18.

[31] *Ibid.*, p. 128.

[32] Walter Kaufmann, *Nietzsche: Philosopher, Psychologist, Antichrist* (1950; Princeton: Princeton UP, 1974), p. xiv. Cited hereafter in text with page number in parentheses.

[33] Walter Cerf of Brooklyn College, for example, was prompted by Kaufmann's monograph to a confession that many other American scholars dealing with

Nietzsche probably should have made as well: "I have shared the generally accepted ideas about Nietzsche without bothering to winnow the chaff from the wheat, thus helping to spread gossip about his work. I am now convinced, or almost so, that the Nietzsche whom Mr. Kaufmann discovered comes closer to the true Nietzsche than the various images and idols which, accepted by layman and professional alike, have blocked a fuller comprehension of Nietzsche's thought." See Walter Cerf, "Review of Walter Kaufmann's *Nietzsche: Philosopher, Psychologist, Antichrist,*" *Philosophy and Phenomenological Research*, XII (1951/52), 287.

[34] Eckhard Heftrich's *Nietzsches Philosophie: Identität von Welt und Nichts* (Frankfurt: Klostermann, 1962) is most enlightening on this point. Heftrich's study deals in the main with the theme of being and nothingness in Nietzsche's thought, but I specifically refer to his interpretation of eternal return here. Cf. especially the compact summary of his conclusions, p. 264.

[35] Indeed, Ludwig Klages may be seen as a significant forerunner of Kaufmann in this regard. See Klages, *Die psychologischen Errungenschaften Nietzsches* (Leipzig: Barth, 1926).

[36] Thomas Jovanovski, "Critique of Walter Kaufmann's 'Nietzsche's Attitude Toward Socrates,'" *Nietzsche-Studien*, 20 (1991), 329–58.

[37] Walter Sokel, "Political Uses and Abuses of Nietzsche in Walter Kaufmann's Image of Nietzsche," *Nietzsche-Studien*, 6 (1977), 442.

Stanley Corngold

The Subject of Nietzsche: Danto, Nehamas, Staten

Arthur Danto's *Nietzsche as Philosopher*, published in 1965 and again in paper in 1980, continues to be read for its logical acuity, coherence, and even-handedness.[1] Certainly, its strengths are evident. Danto tackles thorny issues directly — for example, the question of Nietzsche's personal stake in his rhetoric (that stake is a variable one, and Danto proceeds to distinguish Nietzsche's argument from his style). The systematic character of the book, without being Procrustean, aids in the grasp and reproduction of Nietzsche's leading ideas (Apollonian and "Dionysiac," Nihilism, Master/Herd moralities, Will to Power, Eternal Recurrence), and its flashes of critique reveal Danto to be more than Nietzsche's expositor. He is his commentator, and his sense of loyalty to his author leads him to query tenaciously the truth value of his claims (a perfect love casteth out anxiety). This means: Danto has come neither to praise Nietzsche nor to bury him. His reward would be, presumably, his felt success at having gotten Nietzsche into a system founded on the attention Nietzsche demonstrably paid to a few famous and traditional questions (e.g. What can we know? What is the self? What can we will?), which, for Danto, is the hallmark of qualification as a "philosopher." Speaking pragmatically, this meant in 1965 qualification as a professor of philosophy doing work consistent with ordinary language philosophy and mathematically-informed logical analysis.

There are a number of passages that explain, with different emphases, the book's title *Nietzsche as Philosopher* which, in 1965, Danto thought the most interesting general feature of his argument. But this assumption — that Nietzsche requires academic credentials — now seems to be the least productive, the most dated, and in the last resort the least perspicuous dimension of the book. It leaves unsettled the question: What, for Danto, was most at stake in writing it?

The answer is tangled in the circumstances of its composition. According to the Preface of the Morningside edition (1980), the book arose as a youthful snookcocking at an "esteemed senior colleague" who had assured Danto that "Nietzsche isn't really a philosopher." His title, Danto confesses, *was* therefore intended to be "(mildly) offensive."[2] In the years immediately before 1965, Nietzsche seemed to have been scheduled into graduate programs of philosophy only for lack of a more fitting place and was looked at skeptically there. This prompted Danto to write a book aiming "to show that whatever else Nietzsche was or was not, he was certainly a philosopher . . ." — and here the reader's dismay sets in — "[a philosopher] in just the way that everyone who is one is one: that he thought systematically and deeply about each of the closed set of questions which define what philosophy is . . . ." (D, 9). Then came Rorty, to ask how useful it might be to water with the lifeblood of Nietzsche's rhetoric the garden-preserve of warrior-priests immured in the famous "closed set of questions"; and furthermore how bold Danto's "offensive" might be, when it consists, finally, of propitiating this clergy with one more sacrifice of style. I shall offend against my peers, the program runs, but so mildly, indeed, that they will henceforth admit my protégé as perfectly qualified for analysis. Well and good, but the question gets overlooked whether his new-won qualification might not be "(mildly) offensive" to Nietzsche, not only as the author of *The Birth of Tragedy* but as one generally no longer able to prosper for being denied the ability "to generate a set of paradoxes" (Alexander Nehamas)[3]: namely, for being set down among those "who know a good deal more philosophy today" and can read "Nietzsche's analyses in terms of logical features which he was unable to make explicit but toward which he was unmistakably groping." Indeed, adds Danto, actually turning a corner, Nietzsche's "language would have been less colorful had he known what he was trying to say, but then he would not have been the original thinker he was, working through a set of problems which had hardly ever been charted before" (D, 13–14). These lines from the Preface of 1965 in fact inflect matters differently — and more generously —

than the lines from the Preface to the Morningside edition just quoted above. For if, now, the "closed set of problems" that defines philosophy appears to be original with Nietzsche, then it is clear that what we, who know a good deal more philosophy today, know is, precisely — Nietzsche.

Now it may be that Danto's touch in 1980 is simply off, and hence he is not a reliable guide to his intentions before 1965, especially when his second Preface evokes a conversation between Nietzsche and Croom Robertson, then editor of *Mind*, which has Nietzsche "declaiming" over the Eternal Return (Danto in 1980 has evidently forgotten to read page 203 of his own book, which records Nietzsche's awe before this idea — "so terrifying, in fact, that . . . Overbeck tells us Nietzsche spoke of it in whispers"), let alone "over the potato soup and sauerbraten" (D, 8), at a time when Nietzsche could imagine nothing tastier than a "risotto" of rice boiled in water. The more free-wheeling Danto, certain in 1980 that he had been ready as early as 1965 to give offense to his peers, forgot that he had also written, "I should not be dismayed . . . were someone to say that any [philosophical] construction is misguided, that Nietzsche was a topical writer, an aphorist, unformed or undominated by the systematic specter of philosophy" (D, 230).

I read this latter concession as part of a developing thrust in Danto's book from which Nietzsche's thought acquires an ever more powerful and commanding face of its own, a moment acknowledged by Danto's distinction between "real philosophers" and mere "philosophical critics" who, "as long as they remain only that, are instruments in the service of a philosophical Will-to-Power, but they are not philosophers as yet" (D, 228). "*Genuine philosophers*," wrote Nietzsche, "*are commanders and legislators.*"[4] *Nietzsche as Philosopher* began, and continued, with Danto himself as an "instrument in the service of a philosophical Will-to-Power," appropriating his hitherto recalcitrant source to professional uses. By the end of the book, however, the reversal appears to be complete, and Nietzsche, by Danto's own admission, has made him see what is truly at stake: namely, doing the work of "real philosophers."

They say, "*thus* it *shall* be!" They first determine the Whither and For What of man, and in so doing have at their disposal the preliminary labor of all philosophical laborers, all who have overcome the past. With a creative hand they reach for the future, and all that is and has been becomes a means for them, an instrument, a hammer. Their "knowing" is *creating*, is a legislation, their will to truth is — *will to power.*[5]

Which inspires Danto to conclude his book powerfully: "How we shall live, and what we shall mean, is up to us to say" (D, 228). This ending is no longer a matter of cocking one's snook at senior colleagues by buying into a professionalism as solid as theirs, in a move that Thomas Mann would call "noble parody."

One could justify the anecdotal and not-so-edifying misremembering of the second Preface as a local illustration of Danto's insight into Nietzsche's difficulty. Nietzsche produces confusion by offering as a principle what is in fact its illustration, a procedure especially troubling when principle and illustration go by the same name. Notice that the "offense" which Danto thought he meant to give to his senior colleagues for withholding from Nietzsche (and from the author?) a sort of philosophical civility, could pass for the "offensiveness" of the ever active will to power and therefore feel right with respect to that will, the great vehicle of Danto's argument. This mixing of levels of argument is a mistake, a telling one, which as Danto shows, runs through many different aspects of Nietzsche's argument. Here are some other examples.

Nietzsche's analysis of the religious character as asceticism does not allow for the distinction between the man who is religious in the wide sense of worshiping God yet "antireligious in the narrow sense when he calls religion into question in the name of something else, such as reason, or science, or historical criticism, or truth . . . . [For] both are *personae* of the religious impulses which only incidentally are expressed in actual religious forms" (D, 190). Or, again, "If the *Übermensch* has been taken to be a bully, whose joy is in the brute exercise of strength, Nietzsche has only himself to blame. His illustrations have obscured his principles" (D, 200). This sort of mistake, the confusing of the illustration with the principle, is one which only a philosopher, Danto appears to be saying, is able to sort out. As such, this claim acts like a date stamp. For since this mistake involves not only confusion between the particular instance of a thesis and its general form but rests on a verbal confusion or *paronomasia*, the same mistake might be grasped as a feature of Nietzsche's rhetoric and hence a subject better suited to a philological, indeed a deconstructionist critique *avant la lettre*. Interestingly, Danto's 1980 Preface does indeed re-imagine his thesis as one essentially about Nietzsche's claims for language (viz. "we have learnt to see conformably with our language" [D, 91–92]). In truth it is so only intermittently. In the last resort, *Nietzsche as Philosopher* reveals its character as preceding the full linguistic turn marked by deconstruction precisely by its subordination of Nietzsche's language to a factor of (authorial) intention and moral purpose, viz. Danto's comminatory phrase "the irresponsibility of Nietzsche's style," which makes of style the vehicle of the "lurid, expressionist illustration" marring the "more philosophical and abstract text" (D, 229). Imagine, instead, Derrida's understanding of "the irresponsibility of style."

Danto's more or less determined snookcocking in 1965 (its stake overdramatized in 1980) does resurface with a different target in a lengthy footnote holding "Professor" Walter Kaufmann responsible for the abuse of suspended dots, by means of which Kaufmann intends to show that Nietzsche, a "pious man" (D, 190), strove after and loved the truth. In 1980, Danto, fearless, has ceased to refer to Kaufmann as "Professor," who has been transmogrified, if I understand him, into the "photographer [*sic*] from Princeton," from under whose all-too-humane camera eye the younger Danto meant to remove his fiercer subject. But the attack in the footnote is justified, and upon it depends the pillar of Danto's reading of Nietzsche, namely, "the antimetaphysical bias which drove him to attack the Correspondence Theory of Truth." Danto continues:

> I fear we must take seriously Nietzsche's claim that everything is false . . . . The motto of Book Five of *Die Fröhliche Wissenschaft* is: '*Carcasse, tu trembles: tu tremblerais bien davantage, si tu savais où je te mène.*' It is hard to suppose that he then had in mind something so comforting as truth exists and God is truth. The *destruction* of this idea was what was frightening and intoxicating. (D, 192)

There is a great deal of this pungent exposition and critique in Danto that has proved seminal, quite apart from one's assent to his unclear program of preparing Nietzsche as the topic for a seminar in analytical philosophy of language ca. 1965. It has also put him outside and beyond it.

At the end of his book, Danto restates the problem of perspectivism in Nietzsche: "Was his philosophy, too, a matter of mere convention, fiction, and Will-to-Power? To put it sophomorically but no less vexingly, was it his intention, in saying that nothing is true, to say something true?" (D, 230).

This question is taken up directly in Alexander Nehamas's *Nietzsche: Life as Literature* (1985), a lustrous, finely-textured work whose argument flows from a position on Nietzsche's perspectivism that proves the seriousness and maturity of the question. Nehamas argues that "perspectivism is not equivalent to relativism" (N, 49) and can therefore support truth claims based on arguments for utility. In this and in other ways, his responsiveness to Danto is plain. It is once more as if Nehamas had just laid down his Danto, when he defines his own procedure as arising from the certainty that "Nietzsche's thinking is inseparable from his writing and that coming to terms with his style is essential to understanding him at all" (N, 13). In this case Danto's claim is explicitly the opposite one: coming to terms with Nietzsche's thought is in many cases a necessary knowing better than to follow Nietzsche's style, which at the end of his writing life turned into clownish polemic. But it still needs to be asked (in the question raised by Henry Staten at the outset of his book) whether Nehamas ever actually reads Nietzsche's style beyond affirming it as "essential."[6]

Nehamas's approach is like Danto's in proposing to organize all of Nietzsche's texts; the difference is in the organizing principle. For Danto it is a logical coherence, a set of relations between ideas, structured by principles of identity and opposition: the unity is in the coherence of the system. Nehamas argues that this is so but precisely in being so it is empty of positive meaning. The unity of Nietzsche's work can be intuited only as a virtual subjective unity, assigned to Nietzsche's writing by Nietzsche's "self" bent on becoming what it is. The conatus indwelling of Nietzsche's work is not the will to system, which might then be reproduced by the commentator's will to systematic exposition, but the will to construct a "character" for oneself— indeed "a literary character," which might then prompt the reader to try the same thing: to construct himself on the model of Nietzsche's own self-construction. The first task of the commentator, however, is to evoke Nietzsche's character as a certain effect of Nietzsche's will to power: again, as a phenomenon of style. But this task is not actually performed by Nehamas, partly because it is impossible. (It is one of the virtues of this crystalline work that it brings this aporia to the fore.)

Nehamas's thesis throughout makes Nietzsche's exercise of style the goal of Nietzsche's life and work. Insisting tenaciously on understanding Nietzsche through clear paraphrase or not at all, Nehamas concludes that the main lines of Nietzsche's thought (cf. Danto's "system") do not add up to doctrine: "there is no type of life that is in itself to be commended or damned" (N, 229). But this very meagerness has rich implications for Nehamas's thesis on self-representation:[7] "Nietzsche's effort [is] to create an artwork out of himself" (N, 8); "Nietzsche's texts . . . do not describe but, in exquisitely elaborate detail, *exemplify* the perfect instance of his ideal character. And this character is none other than the character these very texts constitute: Nietzsche himself" (N, 232–33).

This ruling notion, however, has a built-in proclivity to slip into a register of elusive generality, viz. "The self-creation Nietzsche has in mind involves accepting everything that we have done and, in the ideal case, blending it into a perfectly coherent whole" (N, 188). I have tried to imagine the totality of Nietzsche's experience of life — the totality of his actions, utterances, feelings, wishes, and dreams, all the sentences that ever rose up in his head, the sights and sounds of his experience . . . "blended" into a "perfectly coherent whole." But I do not have much uptake from this, Nietzsche's allegedly best idea. I make this cavil about Nehamas's rigorous, determined study only out of concern that his thesis on Nietzsche's self and work *not* be remembered this way. What is wrong in the view that Nietzsche's entire work strove toward and to some degree achieved the perfect "blend" of everything he'd done is the glib substantialist connotation. The difficulty is more than an infelicitous phrase. The metaphor rises out of the disturbance of the thesis by the substantialist trouble at the root of Nietzsche's own thinking on the self. Is the self deep down its own granite-like fate, as Nietzsche once said: "At the bottom of us, really 'deep down,' there is . . . some granite of spiritual *fatum*"?[8] Or is it, rather, the ineffable striving in Nietzsche's most telling description: "No subject 'atoms' . . . . "No 'substance,' rather something that in itself strives after greater strength, and that wants to preserve itself only indirectly (it wants to *surpass* itself —)"?[9] "No 'substance'"; hence, no attributes — and hence no features. Certainly Nehamas intends to put as much distance as possible between the substantialist view and his own. But he does also write, "Each 'thing' [the subject-'thing' included] is nothing more, and nothing less, than the sum of all its effects *and features*" (N, 179) (emphasis added). The italicized phrase introduces a factor different from effects — one that makes sense only on the model that constitutes identity as a substance and its attributes (or features). Indeed, earlier, Nehamas insisted that "a subject is nothing more than its properties and that these properties are nothing more than a thing's effects on other things . . ." (N, 164). I do not find perspicuous the term "properties" considered as the equivalent of a subject's effects; but here, at any rate, there is no mention of "features" apart from effects, and rightly so. Effects might have features: the Nietzschean subject does not.

In addition to the difficulty of deriving the features of a self from its effects, there are special problems in deriving them from effects termed "literary." What, finally, is the benefit of calling the self a work of literature? Can a self conceived this way indeed amount to a unity? It is, for one, shredded by a history of reader-receptions, not blent into a coherent whole. Nor do I think the matter is illuminated when the self is compared to a literary character. There is more difference than sameness to the comparison. One difference stands out: a literary character, if it is to be one, needs a literary context — the fictional world. What, in Nehamas's comparison of the self with a literary character, embeds the self the way the literary work of art embeds the literary character? It is a fact that for Nietzsche the world is in a certain sense a text. But even the textual world, for Nietzsche, is not a literary work of art.

In fact, Nehamas's argument employs two different senses of character, and they are incompatible. One is anthropomorphic: it identifies Nietzsche with the embodied character, for example, in *Ecce Homo* who, despite "the torments that go with an uninterrupted three-day migraine, accompanied by laborious vomiting of phlegm, . . . possessed a dialectician's clarity *par excellence*, and thought through with very cold blood matters for which under healthier circumstances" he was "not subtle, not *cold* enough."[10] But, vivid as it may be, this Nietzsche-figure finally belongs to only one biographical-sounding aphorism from one of the works and doesn't essentially shape the literary character who, in Nehamas's other sense, is equal to the totality of the work. In principle, "Nietzsche" could be found just as strikingly in any other passage, which could then be construed as a privileged synecdoche: Nietzsche's description of Sterne's *Tristram Shandy*, for example, could be an equally decisive (if nonetheless an esoteric and coded) representation of himself. The enterprise of identifying a determinate stratum of literary representation depends on point of view, a reading perspective; and one such point of view, of course, is already in play in every reading of Nietzsche. This is the perspective provided by the narrator, a dimension not often mentioned in Nehamas's account. A literary entity is twilighted by the narrative perspective, which might make that entity "unreliable," ironical, oneiric, hallucinatory, contradictory, etc. Characters in literature appear across different distances, in different tonalities — a distance in presentation which isn't encompassed by the idea of character itself. It is impossible in such a critical construction to do without the idea of narrator. But if the narrator is included under the head of the self-in-the-work, it is also true that that narrator (as the fiction of a person intending all the effects of narration in the story) cannot coincide with the character. The problem of unity is not so much generated by the many various characters whom Nietzsche constructs (N, 196) as by Nehamas's implicitly posited unity of narrator and narrated selves.

Grasped as a research program to articulate the self that Nietzsche constitutes through the totality of his work, Nehamas's work has a strong pertinence. But in its present form the thesis needs further mediation. It diminishes too much the relevance of the empirical self — allegedly, "the miserable little man who wrote [the works]" (N, 234) — and hence it evades too readily the imperative described by Walter Benjamin as "the great acquiescence of authentic biographism in serving as the archive of the documents, in themselves undecodable, of this existence."[11] The point is that the empirical self continues to keep a privilege as the factor of identity through which the constructed literary self arises in and through a range of substitutive relations — relations of sacrifice, renunciation, transcendence, surrogation, imitation, and more. The great question of whether Nietzsche writes his self in his work is answered only tautologically when the self is defined as something always already only constituted in writing. For then nothing (of the self) could be lost in the act of writing, and nothing is finally at stake in this conversion.

Henry Staten's *Nietzsche's Voice* profiles, on the other hand, a Dionysian dimension of wastage, squandering, discharge, absent from Nehamas's more nearly Apollonian view of Nietzsche's self as the blent unity of captured possibilities. Nietzsche's philosophy cannot be a philosophy of immediate self-actualization because the individual self is a scene of conflict: the "restricted" economy, which aims at appropriating and holding fast, constructing and enduring as a particular being, fights against the "grand economy," which urges that it spend itself and die. The contest of forces in Nietzsche's thought is not only or even principally a contest of themes and concepts, one of which might be proved more truthful and valuable than its opposite, with the result that the other is annihilated. Instead, it is a play of rhetorics and styles — of cross-conceptual attractions and repulsions, advances and withdrawals, driven by the Dionysian "pathos" of the will to power. Words like "contest" and "play" are more fitting here than "structure." Nietzsche proposes not so much arguments as contests within arguments fought at a micrological level: at every moment key terms strive toward and away from one another. It can never be a matter of eliminating an apparently weaker term when Christ the Jew inheres in Dionysus.

Staten's book, therefore, doesn't so much aim to recover an explicit doctrine — or, indeed, to discover the lack of one — as trace the velleities of Nietzsche's expression, "map the economy of Nietzsche's texts . . . , listen to Nietzsche's voice, listen for the way various tonalities resound in the neighborhood of specific themes . . . ." (S, 32). Hermeneutical restraint is the *mot d'ordre*; the reader must attend the most minute oppositions flowing through Nietzsche's arguments at the expense of positive doctrine. The reward for his vigilance, however, is another sort of conceptual uptake. Staten motivates these opposing tonalities as symptoms of a heterogenous libidinal economy, whose chief terms are attraction and repulsion, fusion and shattering, complexes of the erotic and death drives found in Freud's meta-psychological writings. *Nietzsche's Voice* takes literally Nietzsche's dictum that philosophizing is a form of instinctual expression. Hence Staten's "psychodialectical" method, which reads Nietzsche's texts along channels connecting them with Nietzsche's deep personality.

Nietzsche was himself "a problematic and fractured unity" (S, 6), and in this sense Staten's readings of Nietzsche's texts map the unity of Nietzsche's unconscious. How much unity, however, informs such a fund of motivations, how much disparity? In dealing with pulsions of whatever sort, are we also dealing with the features of an "individual"? Nietzsche wrote early and negatively in *The Birth of Tragedy* of the (artistic) subject insofar as it is individually specifiable: it "can be conceived of only as the antagonist, not as the origin of art. Insofar as the subject is the artist, however, he has already been released from his individual will . . . ."[12] This is exactly the sort of double movement and paradox that Staten identifies as Nietzsche's DNA, threading through the entire corpus, from the earliest to the latest writings on will to power: "The individual . . . matters only as an expression of forces that transcend his individuality." But there is a dialectical turn to this paradox, which Staten repeatedly discovers and names with admirable intensity: "The individual who *is* an expression of such forces *does* matter as individual, because he is more than individual . . . , constantly overflowing his own boundaries; and because this individual is precious, because he justifies the rest of the species, the boundary of his self-overflowing self-identity must be kept intact . . . ." (S, 120–21).

This tension between individuality and self-unbinding may not be resolved in a single picture of personality, but some such formulation correctly describes Nietzsche's view of the self: "Nietzsche has a very strong tendency to preserve within the outline of the expansion the identity of the being that expands" (S, 123). This point upsets the deconstructionist dogma on the question of the subject in Nietzsche so dominant in the 70s and 80s, which asserts a hegemony of the terms "irony" and "language" at the expense of "the self," even as Staten's paradoxical "correction" evokes some of the difficulty in representing this term.

Staten's responsiveness to Nietzsche's play of affects uncovers one surprising mutation of sense after another: he takes to an unwonted point of complication, for example, the sameness/distinction of master and herd moralities, exceeding analytic "solutions" ("they will 'solve' ['dissolve'] you all right, they are already hungry for your 'solution'"), short of affirming their merely vertiginous and undecidable character.[13] Under his attack the will to eternal recurrence turns out unexpectedly to fit into the second position, into the "restricted" economy of self-saving over self-spending, and hence it does not belong to Nietzsche's grand style at all. Staten is indefatigably alert to Nietzsche's psychic excitement, pursuing his text as it "oscillates or vacillates in its evaluations according to the way in which his subject matter attracts one or another type of charge from him as he writes" (S, 50–51). The outcome are endlessly chiastic readings of the key thematic complexes: man/woman; self-love/pity; pain/pleasure; master/ascetic priest; will to power as conservative/spendthrift. You have to conclude from the sustained intricacy of these readings that if Nietzsche ends on a position, it can only be one of psychic exhaustion, of the evacuation of affect, and not because his argument is conclusive. Arguments ending otherwise than as an acknowledgment of spent power are only a ruse of reason. Staten suggests that it is Nietzsche's subliminal awareness of the ebb and reflux of his own affective life that moves him to assert the semblance-like character of all constructed unities: they exist by masking the destruction at their origin, and by staying blind to their impending dissolution.

"Suggests" is the important word here. Today one is quick to value the effort to identify an extralinguistic component in Nietzsche's writing — still quicker, a component in excess of empirical reference, through hints like "mood," "tone," "voice," "affect," "force." But what, finally, is the aptness of describing Nietzsche's rhetorical excess as the product of a *psycho*dialectics? There is no ascertainable connection between Nietzsche's linguistic complications and events allegedly occurring in Nietzsche's psyche. Why is this something other-than-dialectics rightly got at by a Freudian analytical diction which, as Staten knows, is itself as knotted as any text of Nietzsche's? There isn't, pace Danto and to some extent pace Nehamas, a single privileged explanatory language for Nietzsche's work; but how good, one asks, is the Freudian meta-psychology?

In a forthcoming book significantly titled not *Nietzsche's Voice* but *Nietzsche's Corps(e)*, Geoffrey Waite suggests another motive governing Nietzsche's conceptual velleities that is certainly as good: it is Nietzsche's concern for the *practical* applicability in the particular case.[14] What forces Nietzsche to shrink from or draw near, let us say, the ascetic priest is the imagination of this figure as an institution. Is it a step in the right direction to move from a Nietzschean political dialectics to a Freudian meta-psychological erotics?

In fact, Staten's readings are only intermittently indebted to psychodialectics, which for long stretches disappears entirely. In other places, it is modulated into a general discourse on the affects, viz. "I am trying to identify the trace left on Nietzsche's discourse on will to power by the movements of that fear and desire the lineaments of which we discovered in the writings on tragedy" (S, 129). Here, Staten's language is revealing. The authority for his psychodialectical reading of will to power appears to be secured by the intertextual association. But his tracing of the affective charge on Nietzsche's writing at the time of *Birth of Tragedy* is itself dogmatically guided by Freudian (cum Laplanchian) categories, so this foundation is only an extension of authority based on an initial decision. Furthermore, though "fear" and "desire" are motives appropriately *elicited* by a discourse on tragedy, it does not follow that they are also the motives *inspiring* a discourse on tragedy. Yet this assumed homology between the charging affect and the named affect is central to Staten's argument, viz. "Whether language is performative or constative, or whether it oscillates undecidedly between the two, it is always a network of cathetic pathways, no matter how repressed or sublimated or cunningly disguised." What is the evidence? "In Nietzsche the repressions and disguises are very thin because his explicit themes are the abstract structures of libidinal economy: storing-up, blockage, and discharge of 'animal energy'; self-preservation, self-dispersal, self-enjoyment" (S, 129). This is not (necessarily) true. These themes are certainly present in Nietzsche's work, but this fact does not guarantee that they also name the motives that led him to set them down. "Power" is not (necessarily) charged with power; "altitude," as Derrida likes to say, is not high. Freud's metapsychology is not (necessarily) sexed; Nietzsche is not (necessarily) answerably Nietzschean.

The highlighting of this division makes vivid the connection between the different strivings for coherence in the above three key American receptions of Nietzsche. Danto's work, for plain reasons much determined by his *zeitgeist*, produces a decisive articulation of features of Nietzsche's conceptual "system." Staten, focusing on these very constellations (Dionysian/Apollonian, master/slave moralities, will to power), shows that they are in fact oscillations. Terms ostensibly opposed incessantly cross over the bar of their division and take on the charge (of eros or death) attached to their opposite number. On the other hand, Staten asserts an immediate kind of coherence between theme and motivation, text and affect. Earlier, I noted the cogent but unpicturable quality of Staten's view that Nietzsche means to keep intact the boundary of even the self-overflowing individual (S, 120–21). Does it not now seem that such relations of boundary-setting and also overflowing can only be conceived with the appropriate richness on the model of the literary work? This point returns us to the aptness of Nehamas's project of grasping Nietzsche's life as a text — as long as it actively solicits a factor of *différance*, of negative dialectics. What I am here setting down is less a conclusion than a program to draw the connections between Nietzsche's various *autobiographies*.

Notes

[1] Arthur C. Danto, *Nietzsche as Philosopher*, Morningside edition (New York: Columbia UP, 1980).

[2] *Ibid.*, p. 9. Further quotations from this book are identified in the text by page numbers in parenthesis, preceded by D.

[3] Alexander Nehamas, *Nietzsche: Life as Literature* (Cambridge: Harvard UP, 1985), p. 1. Further quotations from this book are identified in the text by page numbers in parenthesis, preceded by N.

[4] *Beyond Good and Evil*, trans. Walter Kaufmann (New York: Vintage, 1966), VI, 211.

[5] *Ibid.*

[6] Henry Staten, *Nietzsche's Voice* (Ithaca: Cornell UP, 1990), p. 26. Further quotations from this book are identified in the text by page numbers in parenthesis, preceded by S.

[7] He achieves this proof by explaining Nietzsche in ways more patient, detailed, and circumspect than Nietzsche's own ways. This is partly why the stroke and sting of Nietzsche's style does not come over, but conveying the shock by imitation of the "intonation, modulation, the tempo of talk, 'the way of speaking'" is by now the least of what Nehamas needs to do (Cf. Martin Heidegger, *Being and Time*, trans. John Macquarrie and Edward Robinson [New York and Evanston: Harper & Row, 1962], p. 205). He comes *after Danto*. Nietzsche has already seduced readers in high places in philosophy departments and certainly more than enough in departments of comparative literature. The task now is to understand him — in detail and as a whole. In this latter respect Nehamas is the hedgehog to Danto's fox. The interest of the argument consists in the slow unfolding of one great idea.

[8] *Beyond Good and Evil*, VII, 231.

[9] *The Will to Power*, trans. Walter Kaufmann and R.J. Hollingdale (New York: Vintage, 1967), 488.

[10] *Ecce Homo*, in *Basic Writings of Nietzsche*, trans. Walter Kaufmann (New York: Modern Library, 1966), "Why I am So Wise," 1.

[11] Walter Benjamin, "Goethe's *Elective Affinities*," translation of "Goethes *Wahlverwandtschaften*," in *Works of Walter Benjamin*, eds. Michael Jennings and Marcus Bullock (Cambridge: Harvard UP, forthcoming).

[12] *The Birth of Tragedy* and *The Case of Wagner*, trans. Walter Kaufmann (New York: Vintage, 1967), 5.

[13] Nietzsche, "Zwischen Raubvögeln," *Dionysos-Dithyramben*, in *Werke in drei Bänden*, ed. Karl Schlechta (Munich: Hanser, 1954–56), II, p. 1252. Translation in my *The Fate of the Self: German Writers and French Theory*, 2nd ed. (Durham, NC: Duke UP, 1994), p. 248.

[14] Geoffrey Waite, *Nietzsche's Corps(e)* (Durham, NC: Duke UP, forthcoming).

Olaf Hansen

Stanley Cavell Reading Nietzsche Reading Emerson

Le oui, le non immédiats, c'est salubre
en dépit des corrections qui vont suivre.
René Char

THROUGHOUT HIS WRITINGS Stanley Cavell tells a complicated
story of knowing and forgetting that is also a history, or at least
part of a history, in which Emerson and Nietzsche play an important
role.[1] The shape of Cavell's narrative is genealogical, which means
that his arguments tend to be specific rather than general in a sys-
tematical, theoretical sense, even though the critical impact of the
specific may eventually have a theoretical meaning. Hence, I think, it
is not important to discuss such questions as how Cavell's skepticism
came about or how one can defend it against its critics; our interest
should rather focus on the ways in which skepticism has been regularly and differently used in philosophy, and how it has been useful
for Cavell in certain contexts. This is, of course, another way of saying that it does not make much sense to look for a beginning in the
story which Cavell has to tell, unless we agree, as we certainly do,
that the sentence "Call me Ishmael" is the beginning of a story
called *Moby-Dick*, an agreement which seems fairly conventional at
first, but not in the long run. In the case of Stanley Cavell, "in the
long run" means that he has associated the fate of his thinking with
the question that Heidegger has tried to rephrase again and again
since the publication of *Being and Time*, namely the question of
what the task of thinking can be if philosophy, as we know and have

accepted it, has come to its legitimate end or, as Heidegger puts it,
to its fulfillment in its rightful place.[2]

The answer to this question, according to Heidegger, is clear: the
fate of philosophy, as its history indicates, is that from the very beginning of philosophy as platonic metaphysics there has been a task
for thinking which philosophy itself has missed. In fact, the history of
philosophy is essentially nothing but the history of the continuous
suppression of what Heidegger calls thinking. Heidegger's use of his
basic quarrel with Parmenides and his translation of the term *aletheia*
as openness, the unhidden [das Unverborgene], has the purpose of
pointing out the only place where thinking and being coincide without the intrusion of philosophy. Heidegger's transformation of
aletheia's place as one of Light is highly metaphorical; it goes back to
the lines of Parmenides' fragment: "And you must ascertain everything — both the unmoving heart of well-rounded truth, and the
opinions of mortals in which there is no true trust (pistis). But nevertheless you will learn those too."[3]

The "unmoving heart of the well-rounded truth" is the kind of
religious, pre-philosophical experience for which the equivalent
metaphor is found in Emerson's first chapter of *Nature*: "I become a
transparent eyeball; I am nothing; I see all; the currents of the Universal Being circulate through me; I am part or particle of God"
(10).[4] The task of thinking, if we follow these lines, is therefore not
the establishment of truth as certitude or *adaequatio*, it is rather to
allow thinking to happen in the dimension of its yet unknown form
and fate. The right form of thinking has yet to be invented and remains to be found. If this influence of Heidegger on Cavell makes
sense, the way to Nietzsche and Emerson is wide open, but in a
highly particular form, namely in the shape of negation.

In both philosophers, Emerson as well as Nietzsche, Cavell observes an intellectual energy that derives its momentum from a radical quarrel with the ways of the world; Emerson's polemics against
conformity and his anger about the shape, which society more and
more clearly has assumed, is reflected in Nietzsche's fury about the
way mankind has become what it is. Zarathustra comes down from
the mountain after ten years of solitude with the message that, if
people stop giving birth to a dancing star, the time of the ultimate
despicable man has come. Cavell looks at Emerson and is fascinated
that, without an academic history of philosophy at his disposal, Em-

erson's stars are dancing to an orphic melody unheard of before (or after) Emerson and Thoreau. How could Emerson, how could Thoreau, this is the crucial question Cavell asks, occupy the intellectual space which they inhabit and emphasize life against society in such a variety of intellectual styles, and how did they not become part of their own culture (*IQO*, 13–15)? In a way, Cavell has been busy, ever since he asked his famous question about the inability of America to express itself philosophically, to find an adequate answer leading him beyond his first tentative suspicion that America does express itself only in the metaphysical riots of its greatest literature (*SW*, 123–24). I am not sure whether in 1978, when Cavell first raised his perspicacious question, American literature included philosophy. But reading Nietzsche and Emerson must certainly have resulted for him in a heightened awareness of to what extent writing can indeed be thinking. Writing and reading are ways of negating negativity, acts of creation, not necessarily part of philosophy as we know it as part of our tradition, but definitely in tune with Zarathustra's decision to come down from his mountain in order to speak to the crowds. Zarathustra's mountain has its equivalent in Emerson's walking in the Berkshires, coming to the decision to do everything by himself from now on, or in Thoreau's epiphany on Mount Ktaadn. But what does it mean, in the end, to come down and to speak, what kind of thinking is appropriate, and which form of language is the adequate one as philosophical language? To what extent may thinking be a kind of performance? To answer these questions, we have to return briefly to Heidegger reading Parmenides.

Heidegger's dispute with Parmenides is about the meaning, even the thinkability of what in an adverbial and nominal sense Heidegger calls "nothingness." This is not the place to enter into the fray over Heidegger's radical philology, but the consequences of Heidegger's own path into the history of philosophy are substantial for Cavell's approach to Nietzsche, to Emerson and Thoreau, and finally to America itself. Ever since his early and ongoing quarrel with Parmenides, Heidegger tried to go back in time beyond Parmenides to ask over and over again the fundamental philosophical question, why do things exist rather than not, a question which became central for the religious interpretation of God as the creator, while the tensions embodied in this question came from the Aristotelian and Neoplatonic understanding of the phrase "nihil ex nihilo fit." The legacy of

this verdict shaped large parts of the nineteenth-century dispute between theology and philosophy: one only has to remember
Schelling's philosophy of revelation and what reverberated around it.
But before we go too far into this direction, we should also remember Emerson's statement that he did not want to be taught out of
Leibniz and Schelling, but rather wanted to learn everything on his
own.

However, a long history of thinking lies behind us, and if we want
to accept Cavell's maxim that he prefers "sets of texts" to systems of
philosophy, we will have to address sooner or later the relationship of
the fragment to the system, and also Cavell's intuition that any given
system is constructed around voids. Cavell's skepticism, like
Nietzsche's, does not simply negate logic or reason; both thinkers
merely distrust deductions within given systems, deductions which
have little or no evidence at all in the context of an individual's life.
By concentrating on the heterogeneous rather than on the systematic, Cavell, of course, sharpens our senses for the empty spaces
within the contexts in which we like to think, and when all we have
to say is said, I presume the religious dimensions of the emptiness
around and in our way of thinking will be more important than the
epistemological ones.

If we read Cavell reading Emerson and Nietzsche against this
background, we shall have little difficulty in understanding the energy which his philosophizing draws from skepticism. The skeptic's
voice, not his epistemology, wonders forever about its own truth or
success. Will the spoken word arrive, is the skeptic's fundamental
question, will it become truthful? The Greek phrase for both, speaking truthfully and successfully, is *aletheuein,* and if we accept the
meaning of *aletheia* as well-rounded truth, we can better understand
the skeptic's fundamental ambition, namely to speak truthfully, not
so much in an epistemological sense, but rather from a pre-
epistemological position of, perhaps, unmediated experience. But in
order to be truthful, the skeptic's voice has to reach its audience,
which means that the audience must be willing to accept the utterances of epistemologically unmediated experience. The work of the
skeptic, therefore, is to make his statements evident.

It seems sensible, I hope, to emphasize the phenomenon of the
voice this early in our argument, because it helps us to understand
Cavell's own way of thinking and reading. When Cavell thinks, he

speaks, and when he reads, he listens. Language as voice is a recurrent theme in Cavell, as much as in Nietzsche and Emerson. Zarathustra does not write but he speaks, and Emerson's essays have to be heard as sermons and/or lyceum lectures. Socrates, as Nietzsche pointed out, was the man who did not write, and Nietzsche himself wanted to put some of his writings into music. Proleptically speaking, using a brief passage from Heidegger on Nietzsche's *Zarathustra*: "Who is Zarathustra? . . . Zarathustra speaks. He is a speaker. . . . The speaker Zarathustra is an "advocate" — a *Fürsprecher* . . . . An advocate is ultimately the man who interprets and explains that of and for which he speaks."[5] In Cavell's terms, anticipating a topic we will have to deal with later, the problem is indeed: "how to do things with words!"

As Heidegger points out, referring to the image of Zarathustra as a convalescent, the sickness of Zarathustra is the kind of longing which the soul, in Plato's description, develops in conversation with itself: the self-gathering that the soul undergoes on its way to itself in the context of whatever it perceives. Why does all of this sound so familiar when we think of Stanley Cavell and of Emerson? Both speak frequently about a process of healing, of "leading words home" — a phrase which Cavell appropriated from Wittgenstein — and of language finding its proper place in infancy, as Emerson says, then calling it poetry.

If we look at Cavell's essay "Austin at Criticism" (*MMS*, 97–114) and his introduction to *The Claim of Reason*, we are confronted by descriptions of crisis and recovery. But the crisis is not limited to Cavell's self-confessed fall after having been exposed to the teaching and the writings of Austin. Worse: for Cavell, the meaning of the implications of doing things with words is at first an experience of doing damage. As Cavell understands it, the damage is done not because we do not choose the right words, but because the right words are seemingly without essence; they have been harmed during the time of their usage, they have been around for too long. If we want to talk about philosophy, we have to use the words of philosophy, unless we are willing to risk a collapse of the self or the sickness unto death, as in Nietzsche, Kierkegaard, and Emerson. Unmasking the workings of myth, as Cavell points out, can mean many things, for instance in the case of Nietzsche:

> It can mean what Nietzsche was doing in trying to break the soul,
> especially those parts about its origin (from nothing, by creation)
> and its existence (as opposed to the body) and its end (in a world
> beyond) — to break it by replacing it, or by removing the place for
> it, which meant breaking all our interpretations of experience,
> breaking belief, breaking the self. (*CR*, 366)

Cavell's reading of Emerson's essay "Experience" brings out the
same radical breakings and commitments in Emerson. The word
"whim" on the lintelstone (in Emersons's famous phrase) corre-
sponds to a large number of other places where Emerson, like
Nietzsche, points out that one should not accept what is said at face
value, a warning which Emerson re-emphasizes when he refers to
himself as an experimenter and as someone who does not care to
explain or justify himself. In this context, two aspects of Cavell's
thinking become rather obvious: on the one hand, his long-term
project is to establish the exact task for what we call thinking, and,
on the other hand, Cavell's use of the skeptic mode allows for a genealogical approach to the problem, for which we will later use Sextus Empiricus as a model.

At this point of the discussion it is advisable to turn to the connection between Emerson and Nietzsche as an influence story that has
been discussed for quite some time. Philologists with a penchant for
philosophy have been busy on both sides of the Atlantic, and the
philological work has recently come to a point of culmination in
George J. Stack's book *Nietzsche and Emerson: An Elective Affinity*
(1992). It is perhaps not quite correct to call Stack's book a work of
philology, because it also addresses so many other questions, as the
author's programmatic statements indicate:

> In the case of the profound and long-lasting influence of Ralph
> Waldo Emerson on Nietzsche the thinker and Nietzsche the man,
> we are dealing with a deep one-way relationship between a polished
> essayist, an original poet, an admired teacher in the art of wisdom
> and literary style and an unknown philologist-turned-philosopher
> who became the former's ardent and unsuspected admirer. We are
> dealing with an intellectual and spiritual relationship that is so

profound and pervasive that the word *influence* doesn't do justice to it.[6]

However, one does not have to dig very deep in order to realize that what Stack has done in his study is quite different from what Cavell means when he emphasizes that

> The depth of the connection between them [Emerson and Nietzsche] is unknown. Everyone has to discover that for themselves. No matter how many people tell you the connection exists, you forget it, and you can't believe, and not until you have both voices in your ears do you recognize what a transfiguration of an Emerson sentence sounds like when Nietzsche rewrites it.[7]

To follow the story, then, which Cavell has to tell in relation to Emerson and Nietzsche is perhaps risky, but philosophically more promising and closer to the heart of the matter: it is the story of philosophy in Emerson and Nietzsche.

In this context, it is helpful to take a closer look at Cavell's concept of philosophical time or how time works in the unfolding of philosophy. Cavell explicitly does not share Heidegger's view of philosophy having an obvious beginning and an end, and perhaps this is so because he does not like the Heidegger who was also a critic of modernism and who displayed such indefensible attitudes during the period of the Third Reich. However, the way in which Cavell himself sees Emerson, Thoreau, Nietzsche, Heidegger, and Wittgenstein "underlying" each other has much to do with Heidegger's emphasis on simultaneity in philosophy or the problem of a congruence between future and past. As we know from *Being and Time*, for Heidegger the past is not merely what exists no more, nor is the future that which does not yet have existence. Philosophy, in other words, creates its own idea of time and development — which brings us back to the story Cavell tries to tell and to the implications of such concepts as narrative time and space. Certainly, anybody who tells a story is not alone, not entirely autonomous, not without an audience, and he will always try to be authentic. Authenticity, in this sense, is fundamentally connected to the idea of selfhood, and this idea has much to do with what we care to remember and what we would like to forget or not. (To what extent, for example, is it important for Cavell's thinking that he almost became a musician and then decided not to?)

In regard to such questions, it is interesting to read interviews with Stanley Cavell, but his explanation of how his career as a phi- losopher came about through times of crises is not exactly what I mean when I call remembering and forgetting, and consequently authenticity, the major topic of his thought. To make a convenient shortcut: in a precise pragmatic way, about which William James knew so much that he spent the better part of his life explaining what he thought it was, authenticity, for Cavell, is an effect of making sense. This explains also why Richard Rorty misses the point of Cavell's *The Claim of Reason*, when he looks for, and insists on, clear results — a strange demand when one reads Cavell.[8] *The Claim of Reason*, for the most part, brings together what seems so far apart in philosophy and in Cavell's career, namely the tradition of Heidegger and the tradition of analytic philosophy. The book bears witness of its author's distress when he finds himself at crossroads, but more important, it documents a consistency in Cavell's thinking that he himself is reluctant to point out explicitly. But then again, how much does an author know about his own story? Probably more than his audience, but maybe in some cases also less. Perhaps a brief reminder will help us to understand the continuity in Cavell's thinking better, a continuity which exists, not despite, but because he so frequently dramatizes the rift between continental and analytic philosophy in British and American universities, two directions of philosophy which now seem so different, but originally were closer to each other than one would suppose.

At about the same time when Heidegger began to pursue his idea of what metaphysics could possibly be in a post-metaphysical age, the Vienna School of analytic philosophy began its destruction of Hei- degger's efforts to reestablish philosophy against its own ontological premises. Heidegger's insight that the metaphysical momentum in philosophy had reached its point of absolute exhaustion with Hegel led him to a rethinking of the possibilities of philosophy, a rethinking centered on linguistic interpretations of such terms as *being* and *nothingness* which, in turn, did not make sense in the eyes of the founders of analytic philosophy. However, Heidegger as well as the members of the Vienna circle (Rudolf Carnap, for example) shared the idea that the time of metaphysics had come to an end, as much as the feeling that this particular end was bound to have existential consequences. Hence, contemporary readers of Heidegger saw him as an existentialist, as the founder of an existential ontology, and as a philosopher close to Kierkegaard and Nietzsche. The Vienna circle (to which Wittgenstein did not really belong) regarded Heidegger's interpretations of "nothingness" as nonsense and tried to develop its own logical construction of the world without the help of ontology or metaphysics. Cavell, who seriously tried to think his way through these two opposing schools of philosophy, obviously wanted to find a terrain at once within and without these two modes of looking at the world. It is here that we must take up our earlier reference to Sextus Empiricus and the tradition of Pyrrhonic skepticism. Even though Cavell consistently underlines his debt to Thompson Clarke when the issue of the tenability or untenability of skepticism comes up, the essay by Clarke cannot be his only source and inspiration.[9] I simply do not believe that Cavell's skepticism is an extension — and only an extension — of epistemological skepticism in the tradition of Hume, Moore and, finally, Nozick.

Epistemological criticism has been afraid, since David Hume's *Treatise of Human Nature*, of Pyrrhonic skepticism, although Hume was ultimately convinced that the strength of nature would protect us against it. By strength of nature, I take it, Hume meant our natural inclination of finally avoiding any "senseless" form of radical doubt, i.e. the kind of doubt for which Hume reproached Berkeley because it only produces confusion and irresolution. But how unconvincing was this invalidation of skepticism in the context of the profound, sometimes panic-stricken doubts which Emerson harbored. Emerson frequently had severe problems with concepts such as "habit" or "custom," and for him a theory of human nature would necessarily have to include a theory of "dream and beast." The tradition of epistemological skepticism, leading to the overlabored problem of "the external world," seemed to need an image of Pyrrhonism that threatened to lead to absolute doubt and consequently to absolute disaster. However, Hume's understanding of Pyrrhonism was not accurate, and a brief look at Sextus Empiricus will help us understand the nature of Cavell's skepticism, if not better then at least in a different way. It will also allow us to understand Cavell's debt to Austin in its full dimensions. Austin, even though he must have shared the early critical impulses of logical positivism, never developed a theory for his own way of philosophizing. The most internally coherent parts of his published work are the last five

lectures in *How to Do Things with Words*. If we accept that Austin's
style of teaching concentrated on picking sets of problems, adding
one particular cluster of them to another, we are closer to Pyrrhonic
skepticism than one might expect. Pyrrhonic skepticism, as we know
it by way of Sextus Empiricus, took epistemological doubt as a point
of departure, not because its followers doubted the human ability to
know the truth, but rather because they did not trust the dogmatic
eagerness of wanting to know the truth. They did not want to deny
the possibility of criteria, instead they criticized the insistence upon
such a possibility. The impetus of Pyrrhonism, then, was a form of
cognitive self-reference that would result in a state of *ataraxia*, a
state of benevolent indifference, we might say, very close to the description Cavell puts forth of the particular frame of mind resulting
from a specific use of ordinary language philosophy: " . . . one is not
finally interested at all in how "other" people talk, but in determin-
ing where and why one wishes, or hesitates, to use a particular expression oneself" (*MMS*, 99).

The question of knowing, of knowledge in the tradition of Greek
philosophy, was not an end in itself for Pyrrhonic skepticism; it
rather had a thorough dimension of interpreting the self for the purpose of its own well-being. The epistemological question consequently turned into a question of ethics. Somewhere between these
two points of equidistance, of truth and wisdom, we will have to account for moods of anger or frustration and, sometimes, for a feeling
of exhaustion. Emerson courted these moods in many ways, often in
an extremely radical form: "There is no virtue which is final; all are
initial" (411). Such statements imply the necessity of constant work
to achieve a quiet state of mind. Emerson, in his *Conduct of Life*, describes this kind of work as a form of transformation: for him, the
question about the "Spirit of the Times," discussed in Boston, New
York, and London, "resolved itself into a practical question of the
conduct of life. How shall I live?" (943). He points out that we cannot really hope to bring into harmony the world of divergent ideas,
but he also insists that against all odds there is something which he
calls a "private solution." Private, but not without method, sounds
like a familiar method indeed.

> If one would study his own time, it must be by this method of
> taking up in turn each of the leading topics which belong to our
> scheme of life, and, by firmly stating all that is agreeable to experi-

ence on one, and doing the same justice to the opposing facts in
the others, the true limitations will appear. Any excess of emphasis
on one part, would be corrected, and a just balance would be
made . . . . But let us honestly state the facts. Our America has a
bad name for superficialness . . . . (944)

Picking up the leading topics that belong to one's own scheme follows a kind of existential blueprint; it has something to do with Heidegger's notion of grasping something, of turning "toward what
desires to be thought."[10]

In a similar vein, Nietzsche's break with traditional philosophy —
his Zarathustra speaking of knowledge and selfhood — elevated and
in the end celebrated the process of personal becoming, or establishing a scheme for an exemplary counterlife radically conceived as an
aesthetic one. The image of the wanderer, in the third part of
Zarathustra, is an image in which finally, in an almost Hegelian
fashion, the summit and the abyss "are now united in one!"[11] The
ultimate danger, as Zarathustra reminds himself, has become the ultimate refuge, and this is a sign of greatness in exactly the sense Emerson liked to think of it. Yet this way to greatness, merely another
formula for selfhood in Emerson's art of troping, is a way that leads
to knowledge by sorting out what one would like to remember. Pro-
gressing toward the self implies the necessity of leaving something
behind. Emerson's essays "Experience," "History," and "Self-
Reliance" dramatize this process in an abrupt rhetoric of messianic
exultation. In *The Conduct of Life,* Emerson seems to be commenting on himself in a fashion which Nietzsche also employs when he
reflects on himself in his epigrammatic manner. Fragments and epi-
grams address their audience by way of allegoric self-reference. So
the Emerson of *The Conduct of Life* is on his way to become a
thinker, not a teacher, if we apply Nietzsche's distinction. The
thinker has arrived at possessing a certain wisdom, he knows about
tranquility, a knowledge that becomes part of him, but a part only.
Emerson's knowledge of the "lubricity" of whatever you want to
grasp includes the kind of joyful despair that Nietzsche liked to cultivate as an "adequate" attitude for his own time.

In the third part of his *Untimely Meditations,* Nietzsche discusses
the merits of self-perfection, and if we want to understand how
Cavell reads texts "underlying" each other, we can here establish our
point of departure. Self-perfection was not a fixed ideal for

Nietzsche, but it rather meant fundamental "self-preservation" as a guarding against the despair which all knowledge of truth effects in such a devastating way. Schopenhauer the educator is Nietzsche's example of how the knowledge of truth opens vistas upon greatness and marginality. In the end, the central figure is not the philosopher but the thinker, i.e. a person who suffers. Suffering, in this sense, is the result of allowing thinking to happen against all philosophy and philosophizing. Emerson's warnings about what would happen if a great thinker were let loose on this planet make up the final paragraph of Nietzsche's third untimely meditation, and surely Nietzsche here appropriates the voice of Emerson's "Circles" in order to break with academic philosophy, as much as he adopted it and made it his profession to use it, in future works, as a style of thinking, of which he had already decided that it was the adequate one for himself and for his time. It is indeed Emerson's voice with Nietzschean overtones that Cavell hears in "Circles," and only if we allow the two voices to blend into each other will we understand what Cavell means by saying that, even if we know about these voices overlapping, we still have to be constantly reminded of this phenomenon and its uncanniness. We have to be reminded of it, because it is so easy and so comfortable to point out such affinities instead of realizing the tremendous echo that Heidegger traced back to Parmenides and the two ways of knowledge the goddess promises to the young poet whom she addresses.[12] Apart from the philosophically central part of the poem Heidegger refers to in this context, we should remember that when the goddess speaks of "mortal opinions," she points out the way of falsehood and untruth. However, that is the way of mortals, the secular way, the way which Emerson tried to avoid, as did Nietzsche, with their styles of avoidance converging in the epigrammatic and aphoristic forms they used for the expression of their insights. Heidegger, in his interpretation of Parmenides, calls the place where the true path of thinking leads to a clearing, and without too much mystification it is obvious that this clearing is a holy place, a location, as he puts it, "that first grants Being and thinking their presence to and for each other."[13] The experience of unconcealment, the advent of a thinker whom God let loose on this planet, is like a catastrophe in Emerson's view: "then all things are at risk" (407). Nevertheless, with Emerson, with Nietzsche, and with Cavell reading both within the context of philosophical skepticism, this is also a moment of self-recovery. In the traditional sense, self-recovery as *cara sui* is an ongoing work of recovering and, with so much history behind us, what could be more useful for the damaged self within a damaged world. Cavell's readings of Nietzsche reading Emerson, as well as his readings of Kierkegaard and Wittgenstein, take shape as works of recovery that are also works of conservation. If the influence of Austin on Cavell had an ethical dimension, it is plausible that his subsequent readings of Nietzsche and Emerson had one major purpose: to reestablish and to reconnect central aspects of philosophy that had gone under, so to speak, and consequently had to be recovered. This orientation may confuse readers of Cavell whose seeming eclecticism makes them nervous, but exactly these readers would also be confused by Nietzsche, by Emerson, by Kierkegaard, and by all forms of literary romanticism.

As a coda to my reflections on the close interrelation between Emerson, Nietzsche, and Cavell, I would like to address the subject of negative theology which, once more, binds the three thinkers inextricably together. Since Nicholas of Cusa's treatise *De docta igno-rantia*, we are familiar with the term negative theology, signifying the holy ignorance that has taught us to conceive of God as something for which we have no adequate name or concept. According to Hilarius of Poitiers, whom Cusa quotes, 'God' is the infinite in the eternal, the idea in the image, the useful in the gift. Emerson's and Nietzsche's metaphors for God, Kierkegaard's despair, and Cavell's elaborate procedures of bringing something into focus that has been lost for a long time, are all negative theologies in their own right. Yet in which ways does Cavell's voice blend in with those of Emerson, Nietzsche, and Kierkegaard? What exactly, if we look at each philosopher's wealth and poverty, is Cavell underwriting as a thinker whose readings demand returns which then become new beginnings? If, as Parmenides tells us through Nietzsche and Heidegger, the beginning of ontology and ontotheology is tragic from the time of its earliest conception, the adequate topos of Cavell's philosophy must be that of negative theology. How could a Greek philosopher, thus Nietzsche's irritated question, arrive at forms of abstract logic in the first place, and then react against himself in an orphic impulse that collapses thinking and the well-rounded truth into identity? Is this identity not in total opposition to what our senses register? Nietzsche's answer to the question implies, of course, that this identity is not derived from the realm of our senses at all. It was by way of terrible abstractions Parmenides arrived at the conviction that unconcealed truth exists.

Zarathustra tells us that willing is an act of creation and hence a source of joy. Cavell's use of Nietzsche in this context is connected to the question of what the meaning of Emerson could possibly be for America, if we take him seriously as a philosopher. And furthermore: what is the meaning of America in the works of philosophers such as Emerson and Thoreau? In Cavell's view, Nietzsche leads the way towards a whole set of answers to both questions. The first step is to realize that Nietzsche's negativity, his resentment, is the result of an effort to escape from something concrete and contemporary, rather than reacting against reality as such. Nietzsche's resentment indicates the full extent to which he replicates the mood of resentment in Emerson. Emerson's theory of friendship, approval, and our feeble ways of dealing with superiority poses a view of resentment as an active force of memory. If "every man believes that he has a greater possibility," as Emerson tells us in "Circles" (406), there must be something of which he is not aware, apart from its existence as a kind of anticipatory memory. Aversive thinking, as Cavell calls it, is a way of conditioning resentment into the shape of compensation. We concentrate on our failures to exercise resentment until we know how to benefit from this tragic mood instead of developing the "unhappy consciousness" Hegel evokes and overcomes by way of dialectical reasoning. The tragic disposition in Emerson, Nietzsche, and Kierkegaard as read by Cavell is a result of having overcome the limitations of resentment, in Emerson, for example, by putting the problem of the self into the center of his essay "Circles." Thinking *after* Nietzsche is not possible without transposing the self into the very position where all philosophy starts from, and such a beginning knows about the unavoidable pain which the act of naming the self involves. Thoreau's distressed comments upon the fact that we are never able to articulate the best part of what we want to say are turned into another version of the same regret at the beginning of his journals where he states: "That which properly constitutes the life of every man is a profound secret. Yet this is what every one would give most to know, but is himself most backward to impart."[14] And so he proceeds with what another passage describes thus: "I am only introduced once again to myself."[15]

Thoreau's *Journal* is the most gigantic effort imaginable at introducing the "I" to the "Me" in the course of the nineteenth century in America, and if we hypothetically put it on Cavell's tablet of heroic readings, one would probably be inclined to see in it a gigantic Nietzschean effort of self-creation. We must become what we are, Nietzsche held, and his anti-moralism was probably one of the central forces in the process of making the self what it is. Nietzsche's key text on how this can be achieved is *Thus Spoke Zarathustra*, in particular the passages where Zarathustra addresses the pride of the people and then undermines this pride by speaking to them of the most contemptible man he knows, the Ultimate Man. For Zarathustra, "The earth has become small, and upon it hops the Ultimate Man, who makes everything small. His race is as inexterminable as the flea; the Ultimate Man lives longest."[16] In contrast to what follows, we learn a different lesson from *Ecce Homo*. Zarathustra speaks, but in *Ecce Homo* the author withdraws, only to return when everybody has rejected him. To a certain extent, the style of Nietzsche's later works is artistic, as opposed to a style of conceptual reification, but in a formidable way this epigrammatic style is also an attempt to transcend the limitations of chronological time. It is not *chronos* but the Greek notion of *aion* Nietzsche is interested in, not our limited life-time but the convergence of life and time in an exercise of joyful power. Nietzsche's will to power is nothing else than this, and Stanley Cavell acknowledges, in his own fashion, exactly this idea, when he puts America back into the works of Emerson and Thoreau. America has rarely offered itself to timeless contemplation, it has hardly ever been considered as existing beyond chronological time. Cavell's efforts to recapture moments and reactions in Emerson, Thoreau, Poe, even Melville against the transitory and violent passing of time as America's destiny, are efforts to locate and relocate the promise *behind* the promise of American life. The idea of America's timelessness in Cavell's re-reading Emerson and Thoreau back into American culture with the help of Nietzsche is negative theology in its purest form. Perhaps F. Scott Fitzgerald found the perfect image, at the end of *The Great Gatsby*, for what happens in this process: "So we beat on, boats against the current, borne back ceaselessly into the past."[17] Cavell's life-long endeavours to lead words home, or simply to bring ideas back to their original contexts, are acts of thinking that attempt to evoke the first path which the goddess explained to Parmenides' poet, namely the path of well-rounded truth, of unconcealment. America, in the eyes of Stanley Cavell, is both, a place of irrefutable realities, perhaps philosophically impoverished, but at the same time also the clearing where Being and thinking belong together.

Notes

[1] References to Cavell's works will be given in parentheses in the text. I have used the following abbreviations: *(CR) The Claim of Reason* (Oxford/New York: Oxford UP, 1979); *(SW) The Senses of Walden* (San Francisco: North Point Press, 1981); *(IQO) In Quest of the Ordinary* (Chicago/London: U of Chicago P, 1988); *(MMS) Must We Mean What We Say* (Cambridge: Cambridge UP, 1976); *(NYUA) This New Yet Unapproachable America* (Albuquerque, 1989).

[2] Martin Heidegger, "The End Of Philosophy and the Task of Thinking," in David F. Krell (ed.), *Martin Heidegger: Basic Writings* (London/New York: Routledge, 1993), pp. 431–36.

[3] Heidegger's comment on the Parmenides fragment in question is the following: "*Aletheia*, unconcealment, is named here. It is called well-rounded because it is turned in the pure sphere of the circle in which beginning and end are everywhere the same. In this turning there is no possibility of twisting, distortion, and closure. The meditative man is to experience the untrembling heart of unconcealment. What does the phrase about the untrembling heart of unconcealment mean? It means unconcealment itself in what is most its own, means the place of stillness that gathers in itself what first grants unconcealment. That is the clearing of what is open. We ask: openness for what? We have already reflected upon the fact that the path of thinking, speculative and intuitive, needs the traversable clearing. But in that clearing rests possible radiance, that is, the possible presencing of presence itself" ("The End of Philosophy and the Task of Thinking," pp. 444–45).

[4] Emerson's works are here quoted from the "Library of America" edition of his writings: *Ralph Waldo Emerson* (New York: Library of America, 1983). References in parentheses are to page numbers of this edition.

[5] Martin Heidegger, "Who is Nietzsche's Zarathustra?", in David B. Allison (ed.), *The New Nietzsche: Contemporary Styles of Interpretation* (New York: Dell, 1977), p. 64.

[6] George J. Stack, *Nietzsche and Emerson* (Athens: Ohio UP, 1992), pp. 2–3.

[7] Quoted from an interview with Stanley Cavell: "An Apology for Skepticism," in Giovanna Borradori (ed.), *The American Philosopher* (Chicago: U of Chicago P, 1994), pp. 131–32.

[8] See Richard Rorty, *Consequences of Pragmatism* (Minneapolis: U of Minnesota P, 1982), pp. 176–90.

[9] Thompson Clarke, "The Legacy of Skepticism," *The Journal of Philosophy*, 69 (1972), 754–69. In this context, it is also significant that Cavell never followed the example of Austin by participating in the further development of speech-act theory. Cavell must have been immediately fascinated by the ethical dimension of Austin's work.

[10] See Heidegger, "What Calls for Thinking," *Basic Writings*, p. 372.

[11] *Thus Spoke Zarathustra*, trans. R. J. Hollingdale (London/New York: Penguin, 1969), p. 173.

[12] The goddess points out that the way of truth is the way of poetry. She thereby brings back to memory a time when poetry and prose were not yet separated. It makes sense, therefore, to assume that the way of truth refers to a time of all-encompassing religious experience, a time of myth and mythology. Cf. Vigdis Songe-Möller, *Zwiefältige Wahrheit und zeitliches Sein* (Würzburg: Königshausen & Neumann, 1980), and Simon Tugwell, "The Way of Truth," *The Classical Quarterly*, N. S. 14 (1964), 36–41.

[13] "The End of Philosophy and the Task of Thinking," p. 445.

[14] *The Journal of Henry D. Thoreau*, 2 vols. (New York: Dover Publications, 1962), I, p. 35.

[15] *Ibid.*, I, p. 107.

[16] *Zarathustra*, p. 46.

[17] F. Scott Fitzgerald, *The Great Gatsby* (New York: Charles Scribner's, 1952), p. 182.

Lutz Ellrich

Richard Rorty's Pragmatic Appropriation of Nietzsche

W ITH HIS CONCEPT of different world-describing vocabularies and his provocative theses about the contingency of language, Richard Rorty occupies positions that have already been adumbrated in Nietzsche's work.[1] Consequently, Rorty's explicit references to Nietzsche as the precursor of his own pragmatist outlook do not come as a surprise.[2] In the following, however, I do not intend to demonstrate how similar or different Nietzsche's and Rorty's theories are.[3] I rather want to show that Rorty's readings of Nietzsche on the one hand undercut the standards of his own pragmatist theory of interpretation and, on the other hand, do not make full use of the philosophical possibilities Nietzsche's analyses have to offer.

Rorty regards Nietzsche as an astute critic of metaphysical thought, but he does not interpret Nietzsche's reflections as prefiguring deconstructive analyses such as those performed by Derrida and de Man in recent years. While deconstructive readings act within the traditional patterns of thought in order to subvert and undermine them from within, Nietzsche attempts to find a new vocabulary to describe his "self" as being formed in the process of linguistic articulation and being created by it. According to Rorty, deconstruction directs its critical endeavours "against the use of a familiar and time-honored vocabulary" by demonstrating

> that central elements in that vocabulary are 'inconsistent in their own terms' or that they 'deconstruct themselves.' But that can *never* be shown. Any argument to the effect that our familiar use of a familiar term is incoherent, or empty, or confused, or vague, or 'merely metaphorical' is bound to be inconclusive and question-

begging. For such use is, after all, the paradigm of coherent, meaningful, literal, speech. (*CI*, 8–9)

Where deconstructive analyses misinterpret the process of replacing a received vocabulary, Nietzsche realizes that effective criticism initiates a contest "between an entrenched vocabulary which has become a nuisance and a half-formed new vocabulary which vaguely promises great things" (*CI*, 9). Rorty considers Nietzsche's experimental philosophy an attempt to establish a vocabulary for the self-interpretation of someone "who faces up to the contingency of his or her own most central beliefs and desires" (*CI*, XV) and is able to live with the thought that there is no convergence between language and reality in itself (*OR*, 32). Nietzsche's creative achievement consists in replacing "inherited with self-made contingencies" and to describe himself "as doing exactly that" (*CI*, 98). Consequently, Nietzsche assumes the stance of the "ironist," for whom "there is nothing more powerful or important than self-redescription." A "thoroughgoing ironist" does not foster the illusion of being able to construct better and better descriptions of the world and his own self, since he does not believe in the possibility of a 'right' description. Instead, he takes his actions as a way of rearranging "little mortal things" by redescribing them (*CI*, 99). The ironist pursues but one single aim, Rorty holds, and that is to be responsible himself for any new descriptions and vocabularies of his own invention: "The perfect life will be one which closes in the assurance that the last of his final vocabularies, at least, really was wholly his" (*CI*, 97).

Rorty understands Nietzsche's project of viewing and describing himself from ever-changing new perspectives as an aesthetic gesture of play, which in turn implies a specific concept of beauty. This concept allows us to appreciate the contingency of the new perspectives as stimulants for the affirmation of a finite life: "Beauty, depending as it does on giving shape to a multiplicity, is notoriously transitory, because it is likely to be destroyed when new elements are added to that multiplicity. Beauty requires a frame, and death will provide that frame" (*CI*, 105). With this laconic remark Rorty merges the aspects of contingency, beauty, and tragedy into a suggestive idea of the very project Nietzsche is said to have first developed and then betrayed. According to Rorty, Nietzsche abandons his own project when he is no longer content with the beauty of a newly created vocabulary but instead begins to pursue sublimity. For sublimity "is neither transitory, relational, reactive, nor finite" (*CI*, 105), but instead figures as a metaphysical remnant.

For Rorty, Nietzsche is not at all successful in transcending metaphysics by leaving it to itself.[4] Although he loves "to show . . . that every description of anything is relative to the needs of some historically conditioned situation" (*CI*, 174), he finally succumbs to the temptations of reaching out for a "historical sublime, a future which has broken all relations with the past, and therefore can be linked to the philosopher's redescriptions of the past only by negation" (*CI*, 105). When Nietzsche conjures up "pure self-creation" and "pure spontaneity" (*CI*, 106) with his new vocabulary envisioning the advent of the Overman, he claims a meta-perspective "from which to look back on the perspectives he inherited" (*CI*, 106). Thus, his rhetorical self-creation culminates in the hypostatization of a force no longer subject to relativization. In his attempt "to affiliate himself with 'Becoming' and 'Power'"(*CI*, 107), Nietzsche follows one of the cardinal patterns of traditional metaphysical thought.

In his sketch of Nietzsche's philosophy, Rorty attempts to show why Nietzsche — in spite of his creditable approach — was not successful in solving his alleged central problem: "namely, how we can write a historical narrative about metaphysics . . . without ourselves becoming metaphysicians" (*CI*, 108).[5] In Rorty's view, Nietzsche himself inadequately assessed his own redescription of inherited vocabularies. He believed the difference between his new interpretations and the old terms, arguments, and figures of thought to be totally different, and thereby unwittingly established his own new vocabulary as something absolute.

Now Rorty himself has claimed — against deconstruction — that the invalidation of existent and familiar vocabularies is an act of distancing, which allows one to take an external, para-argumentative stance that does not exhaust itself in efforts of internal decomposition. Rorty conceives of this act as a *rhetorical* process, as a kind of battle between deviating vocabularies. But in doing so, he gives a wrong meaning to Nietzsche's mode of distancing. Rorty regards it as a series of constative speech-acts rather than performative ones, and he interprets the terms (sublimity, will to power, Overman, etc.), which are rhetorically used by Nietzsche, in a literal sense and therefore as a form of representation of a higher authority. Rorty simply does not see in Nietzsche the figurative distancing of a new vocabulary, on whose function he himself so vigorously insists. Consequently, he mostly ignores the rhetorical orientation of Nietzschean redescription, a point he himself has used against the outdated model of immanent de(con)struction. Rorty does not understand the performative act in which the new vocabulary introduces itself *as* new in terms of an aesthetic enactment of the inaugurated conflict between two vocabularies, but rather takes it to be a form of traditional representation.

There are decidedly good reasons to read Nietzsche's later (as much as his earlier) vocabulary metaphysically. Nietzsche has criticized himself unsparingly in this respect when he re-read his own early publications. But Rorty's reading of Nietzsche undermines the premises of the *pragmatist* redescription of what new vocabularies accomplish when they attempt to replace existent patterns of thought. For instance, Rorty interprets Nietzsche's references to the "Übermensch" or to the "will to power" bluntly as concepts with a literal or proper meaning, only to fill them with metaphysical content.[6] Thus he overlooks precisely the practical frame in which a new subversive theory must assert itself against inherited ideas. Nietzsche has shown that any rhetoric that suggests the surmounting of all perspectivity and all forms of conditionality is itself merely the expression of a perspective, namely the perspective that guides creative acts. In this context, a new description can only assert itself successfully if, at the moment of its formation, it blinds itself to its own conditionality.

Perhaps Rorty's tendency to interpret certain statements by Nietzsche not rhetorically but rather in terms of a conventional content analysis conceals a basic problem that the pragmatist approach invites whenever it confronts the phenomenon of power.[7] Nietzsche's theory of the will that is directed towards itself is not the initial context in which he tackles the issue of power. On the contrary, the holistic concept of interpretation that Rorty pays tribute to is from the outset inextricably tied to the concept of power. "All occurrences" are to Nietzsche "interpretive in character."[8] Interpretation "has itself existence,"[9] it is nothing but an ongoing process of arranging and overpowering. Any new interpretation may thus be understood as a means "to master something,"[10] a violent act "through which any previous 'meaning' and 'purpose' are necessarily obscured or even obliterated."[11] Hence power is not something to which interpretation refers as if it were a transcendental signified, but rather the process interpretation itself transcribes. That Rorty pays almost no attention to this point is all the more surprising, if one considers how enthusiastically he applauds Harold Bloom's openly Nietzschean theory of the struggle for survival between poetic texts.[12] Taken by so much enthusiasm for Bloom's concept of intentional misreading, which sweeps aside all hermeneutic probings for a correct interpretation, Rorty seems to have lost all sense for the rhetoric of power and the *agon* that makes itself heard in Bloom's distinction between "weak" and "strong misreading."[13] But this view is misleading, since Bloom, like Rorty himself, delimits the otherwise unrestrained contest between innovative language games — where the rule of self-assertion is the only law — to a specific area. In the case of Bloom, this area is the poetic license of aesthetic practice; in the case of Rorty, it is a poetic culture that comes into its own in the private sphere and may help to form, but must not dominate, the public realm.

However, is this the appropriate way to avoid the difficulties that the concept of a totalized interpretative performance must lead to? Neither Nietzsche nor the pragmatists James, Dewey, and Rorty conceive of this performance as only a mental manipulation of symbols; they rather regard it as closely bound to a physical process of action. Action and interpretation form an inseparable unity that penetrates all areas of life with its agonistic impulses and that invalidates the difference between facts (whether aesthetic or moral) and values.[14] Given these assumptions, then, how is it still possible to differentiate between types of interpretation? How can we identify criteria to define their function and range? And what will eventually tell us when and under what circumstances a particular interpretive practice will prove to be either useful or detrimental?

Rorty tries to answer such questions by linking the recognition of the contingency of language, selfhood, and community with the acute awareness of the non-contingency of each historical perspective and point-of-view.[15] At the heart of Rorty's version of pragmatism, which explains the complicated synergy of freedom and obligation, lies the distinction between the private and the public sphere. This controversial distinction has two roots: on an abstract level, it is based on Rorty's theory of truth, which combines a fundamental idea of Nietzsche's with insights of James and Davidson; on another level, it is prefigured by traditional liberal theories of society which have frequently influenced Rorty. In attempting to radicalize and surpass liberalism in important respects, Rorty constructs a dualistic model that presents interesting parallels and differences to Nietzsche's varying definition of the relation between Dionysian art and Socratic culture.

Rorty agrees with Nietzsche's "definition of truth as a 'mobile army of metaphors'" (CI, 17)[16] and explains it in reference to Davidson's theory of metaphor, in which the distinction between literal and metaphorical sense is "not a distinction between two sorts of interpretation," but a "distinction between familiar and unfamiliar uses of noises and marks" (CI, 17). Truth has no special form and expression: it is a "way of producing effects on our interlocutor or our reader, but not conveying a message" (CI, 18). Thus truth is rendered trivial and becomes a non-definable or non-analyzable element (OR, 50); it is a kind of label that we stick on statements which we consider authoritative. Truth "is simply an automatic and empty compliment which we pay to those beliefs which are successful in helping us do what we want to do" (PMN, 10). Following Davidson, Rorty "breaks with the notion that language is a medium — a medium either of representation or of expression" (CI, 10). For him, "not the world . . . not experience, not surface irritations" (OR, 50) make our sentences true, but rather the way in which we take our actual interpretations to be relevant for our practical life.

With this concept of truth, Rorty no longer believes in two classical projects of analytical philosophy which, in his opinion, amount to the same thing: on the one hand, the attempt to construe an ideal language, and on the other hand, the fixation on ordinary language as the ultimate meta-language, in the light of which the problems of metaphysics decompose into mere linguistic entanglements. Rorty refutes the recurrent accusations of relativism raised against pragmatism (and, of course, against Nietzsche) with the following argument: since it is not the world that makes sentences true, talking about *different worlds,* which are unintelligible to each other yet equally valid, no longer makes sense. Thus the standard argument against relativism becomes trite. This argument usually holds that the relativist position entangles itself in performative contradictions because, in order to be consistent, relativists must assume that alternative worlds exist which are mutually exclusive yet comparable in one undisclosed respect. Otherwise, no similarity or connection that allows an identification of fundamentally incongruent worlds as equally possible or equally good, could be determined. In other words, in order to affirm his point of view the relativist would have to claim a knowledge which he has already declared impossible.

Viewing Rorty's theory in the light of this simple argument, we are faced with the following question: if Rorty's "ethnocentrism" amounts to the claim "that our own *present* beliefs are the ones we use to decide how to apply the term true, even though 'true' cannot be defined in terms of those beliefs" (*OR*, 50),[17] what allows us then to believe that historically changing concepts of what is held to be true deserve the uniform predicate 'true'? Why is it that precisely the pragmatist point of view permits such a recognition, although it rejects an overall and external standard for the fixation of truth? The answer to such questions, which Rorty does not give explicitly, though it is implied in his theory, might run as follows: the generalization that the pragmatist here promotes is unproblematical, because the term 'true' in the given context merely serves as a marker for what particular people at a particular place and time consider valid. Such a marker, which only refers to a functional property of the term in question, can be ascribed to highly varying concepts without assuming an objective standard of judgement for the various concrete claims involved. To operate with the term 'true' indicates, then, that humans apparently cannot do without the notion of validity, although there is no unrefutable basis available for their reliance on the idea of universal validity. What is valid is valid because of an ultimately contingent yet inevitable decision. Humans connect language and action in a specific way by tautologically designating that as 'true' what they have chosen as valid in their own actions.

This pragmatist view of the role that the concept of truth plays in different cultures and in different historical periods is equivocal: opposed to the generalizing view that sees all attributions as groundless but indifferently equal, it acknowledges singular acts of ethnocentric validation, which are made by individuals or groups sharing a given "we-consciousness" (*CI*, 190). In the former case, the term 'true' is defined functionally, but in the latter it is used according to pragmatic rules which — as Davidson has shown — do not allow a definition. The equivocality in Rorty's concept of truth increases and becomes more specific as soon as the historical and social contexts, to which all innovative interpretations (especially of the concept of truth) are bound, are taken into account, just as it is demanded by the principal maxim of pragmatism.

The traditional concept of truth that Rorty abandons implies the assumption that there is only one *single* correct interpretation of given things and events possible and that this interpretation can be reliably stated with the help of language. From the perspective of pragmatism, the formation, assertion, and persistence of this traditional concept can only be explained by its considerable practical efficiency. The belief in the existence of a single correct description or "adequate interpretation"[18] of the world was simply a conviction useful for the project of individual and collective modes of action. With reference to Nietzsche, Rorty assumes that this belief lost its persuasive power and dominant social function in the course of the nineteenth century. The rise of liberal concepts of society and their gradual political institutionalization created the conditions for ways of life that could do without this belief. Rorty does not hesitate to refer to the founding and the historical development of the United States as evidence for his thesis. However, the new liberal ideologies Rorty refers to did not draw their power primarily from a new belief in the infinity of interpretation,[19] but from the belief in moral, economic, and political principles to which a similar absolute validity was ascribed as in the case of the traditional concept of truth. Yet because of these principles, liberal societies open up certain areas, in which all kinds of interpretations can be put to a test and all kinds of standpoints assumed. This applies, for instance, to works of art, religious beliefs, erotic passions, and with certain qualifications to scientific hypotheses. In the theories liberal societies use in order to describe themselves, a distinction has taken root that designates core areas where either the free play of contingency or the preservation of established principles predominates. This is the distinction between 'private' and 'public' sphere to which Rorty has called attention. The area that is chiefly relieved of an orientation towards the absolute and the objective is called the private sphere, and the public sphere that stands in contrast to it is seen as still governed by fixed principles. Despite this separation, classical liberalism assumes that the two spheres complement one another harmoniously according to a quasi-transcendental law. The publicly approved principles are considered preconditions for the contingencies of self-creation in the private sphere, and the individual scope of free play in turn appears as an indispensable and irrevocable source for the general progress in the social sphere.

In reference to this situation, Rorty advocates that contemporary liberal societies renounce two premises which were once "very useful in creating modern democratic societies" (*CI*, 194): first, the assumption that their values and forms of organization are rooted in reason or human nature, and second, the belief in an ultimately harmonious interaction between the private and the public sphere.[20] Liberal societies would then be in a position to understand that their basic values are contingent starting points and, furthermore, they would be able "to treat the demands of (private) self-creation and of (public) human solidarity as equally valid, yet *forever* incommensurable" (*CI*, XV).

However, Rorty's program contains two highly questionable implications if seen from Nietzsche's perspective: first, the astonishing courage to postulate a rather metaphysically sounding universal difference (private versus public), and second, the equally astonishing confidence in the stability of democratic forms of life and the tradition of historically grown "shared habits" (*OR*, 26). Of course, Rorty as model pragmatist immediately concedes that this tradition is neither a safe stronghold against potential anti-democratic movements, nor is it able to offer *objective* reasons for condemning a future generation that would, perhaps, accept fascism, and find its truth in the vocabulary of this ideology (*CP*, XLII). It is here that Rorty senses a potential danger, which even a socially established universalist canon of values cannot eliminate.

Rorty's argument is based on the assumption that Western democratic societies have changed so much in the course of their historical development that they are now ready to part company with metaphysical presuppositions which have fulfilled their historical purpose and can be relegated to the museum of the history of ideas. As is well known, Nietzsche considered bourgeois democracy an entirely metaphysical project and a part of the Socratic culture of enlightenment that would inevitably break down as soon as it would revoke its belief in basic principles. Rorty, however, considers it possible to redescribe liberal democracy without appealing to metaphysical elements and still maintain its cultural achievements. Yet Rorty's belief in this possibility is somewhat ambiguous. At first sight, it is not clear whether Rorty envisions a society whose members (like Nietzsche's "Übermenschen") no longer feel any need for certainty and therefore see all their rules and institutions as contingent affirmations, or whether he merely assumes that liberal societies, due to their historical development, have created new certainties and habits which render the old ones (grounded in religious beliefs or principles of Reason) superfluous and are able to replace them completely. Rorty attempts to settle this ambiguity by defending both positions at the same time and proposing them as new redescriptions for the ideal interrelation of the public and the private sphere. Liberal society is thus able to face overall contingency, but to handle it in two different ways: in the private sphere through a narcissistic quest for free self-realization, in the public sphere with an appeal to an encompassing "ethic of mutual accommodation" (*CI,* 34). The boundary between the private and the public sphere would then not be marked according to different degrees of contingency, but only by different practices of dealing with the awareness of contingency: on the one side we would find the experimental play of self-creation, and on the other the cultivation of communal solidarity.

There are, then, two mutually exclusive vocabularies of describing contingency possible for Rorty: "A liberal culture whose public rhetoric is *nominalist* and *historicist* is both possible and desirable," but a liberal culture "whose public rhetoric is ironist" (*CI,* 87) is not desirable.[21] As a result, Rorty's Nietzschean "recommendation that culture should be poeticized" (*CI,* 67), because "only poets . . . can truly appreciate contingency" (*CI,* 28), is subject to certain restrictions. The ironic attitude of the private realm should not penetrate and dominate the rhetoric of the public sphere. Rorty "cannot imagine a culture which socialized its youth in such a way as to make them continually dubious about their own process of socialization" (*CI,* 87). Seen against the background of these assumptions, it does not come as a surprise that Nietzsche's propaganda for the "free spirits" is only useful in the private sphere, but detrimental in the public sphere. Consequently, Rorty sees Nietzsche as "invaluable in our attempt to form a private self-image, but pretty much useless when it comes to politics" (*CI,* 83).

The assumption that societies cannot do without the support of stable structures in the process of socialization, however, is to Rorty's mind not an argument against his theory of "the contingency of a liberal community" (*CI*, 44). For he claims that liberal society produces people who can face contingency without losing their ability to maintain unequivocal moral positions as members of this society. According to Schumpeter, civilized people are able "to realize the relative validity of one's convictions and yet stand for them unflinchingly" (*CI*, 46). Yet this stance which combines an awareness of contingency with unflinching determination is possible only if we maintain an ethnocentristic position,[22] i.e. if we "privilege our own group" (*OR*, 29) and feel "responsible only to (our) own traditions" (*OR*, 199).[23] Only this identification with our own group seems to counterbalance the irritation that seizes us as soon as we accept the general contingency of language, self, and social institutions. Rorty has no doubts that the identification with the community provides an even greater moral and political force than any identification with universal values ever could (*CI*, 190–192). That we should at all harbor feelings of solidarity with our fellow beings (whether mainly directed towards the members of our own group or towards all mankind), is something that Rorty can only explain on pragmatic grounds. In this context, he again turns to the argument that an awareness of contingency allows only the choice of certain specific attachments. If the world of things no longer unequivocally determines the interpretations we form, then the only determinants affecting us in a strict sense are the interpretations that our fellow-inquirers have presented. We simply turn necessity into a virtue. The acceptance of contingency always establishes a curious solidarity with our precursors, and this form of bond can easily be transferred to the members of our specific community. This is also the reason why Rorty expects a new and intensified sense of community to arise when we abandon the belief in timeless and universally applicable values.[24]

The crucial point of Rorty's presentation rests on the assumption that the two spheres of liberal society, the private realm of individual self-creation and the public realm of mutual accommodation, are "forever incommensurable" (*CI*, XV) yet nonetheless "compatible" in practical life (*CI*, 87). Rorty believes that it is possible both to identify ethnocentristically with the society we happen to be born into and to keep private that area which grants us a poetically inspired redescription of the self. As long as we participate in social life, we must try hard to believe in something that we can deny as private persons. But how are we to establish the *necessity* of the distinction between these two contrary ways of dealing with the awareness of contingency? Will the difference between two practices of coping with contingency not inevitably, sooner or later, itself appear to be contingent, and will the members of liberal society then not develop concomitantly into public actors of a cultural identity and private fools of an inconsequential critique of communal life?

Nietzsche has proposed a different solution to this problem, which, against the background of Rorty's theory, gains an unexpected profile. Nietzsche's intricate analyses lead to the recognition that we cannot first totalize the awareness of contingency and then de-activate it with the help of a historically established difference (e. g. the private/public scheme). The gist of his reflections points to an inevitable opposition and compromise between two cultural projects which developed during Modernism in close relation to each other, but which could not be reconciled: Dionysian art and Socratic culture.[25] Nietzsche's view of the relation between these two concepts has undergone a telling modification. Initially, Nietzsche had represented the metaphysical foundationalism and the essentialism of enlightenment in his suggestive model of Socratic culture, and then summoned up Dionysian art against it. The Dionysian art of tragedy, in this context, recalls the mythical awareness of primal pain caused by individuation which individualistic rationalism (i.e. Socratic dialectics and irony) had repressed, and it overcomes Socratic culture in a collective aesthetic ecstasy. But since the Dionysian remedy can only be administered in the medium of art, it is chained to Apollonian appearance. Only in this insoluble amalgamation, and that means only partly, can the Dionysian emerge. The effects on the collective consciousness that Nietzsche hoped to achieve with an aesthetic revitalization of the Dionysian are tied to formal laws of art that necessarily endanger these very effects. The only cure for the pain of individuation, Nietzsche concludes from the disenchanting insights of *The Birth of Tragedy*, is an intensified individualism. This raging individualism is the program of the "free spirits," who create themselves in full awareness of their own contingency.[26] In pursuit of this program, the free spirits transform the tragic sense of collective ecstasy into a figure of purely artistic distance that separates them from the social processes of life. But even the attitude of the free spirits, as Nietzsche eventually has to concede, cannot conquer all bastions of traditional thought and action, which forever attempt to secure their foundations of irrevocable and timeless existence. The free spirits survive only as elements in a game which not only effectively undermines the fundamentalist and universalist edifice, but also strengthens and reconfirms it as a necessary "Gegengewicht."[27] Hence Nietzsche develops the panorama of a culture that presents itself in two mutually dependent practices: the radical experiments of the free spirits, who create their autonomy out of contingent elements, and the foundational discourses of the champions of universally binding norms and values, who do not want to abandon their belief in universal ideals as implicit preconditions or explicit ends of their actions.

Nietzsche's early attempts to dismiss rational justifications in favor of a self-regulation of social life arrives in a philosophical detour at the dialectical image of divided power. The cult of principles Socratic culture engages in thus proves to be viable, because it acts as an indispensable antagonist to the subversive practices of the free spirits, and not because of the indestructibility or undeniable evidence of its leading values. Nietzsche presents his model of a total and never-ending interpretation, which is so attractive to pragmatism, in terms of a concept of power that engages in self-referential acts of play. If power, however, in the last analysis is only interested in the staging of its own performance, it must in each act of domination supply the dominated part with enough force to allow it to become an eternal antagonist. In Nietzsche's view, a pragmatist philosophy of contingency that establishes a holistic interpretation of all interpretation would only misinterpret itself; it would turn into a bad metaphysics of infinite regression. The only scenario for a game of power that would be truly holistic is that in which each discovery of contingency entails the creation of necessity, and in which each detection of necessity entails an assertion of contingency.

Rorty misses the strict consequence of the infinite gesture of interpretation as *agon* in Nietzsche, a consequence that could have made him aware of the limitations of pragmatism. He initially totalizes the experience of contingency and then addresses himself to various forms of responding to this experience (e. g. individual self-creation and communal solidarity). Moreover, he classifies these practices of coping with contingency according to their adequacy and usefulness in different social contexts. Consequently, he must claim a knowledge about the practical value of actions and attitudes which at the same time admits and conceals its own contingency. For the acknowledgment of contingency loses its destructive or liberating force, if it is merely taken as the starting point for a form of life excelling in the capacity of perseverance. The forms of communal life that Rorty describes have a tendency of starting as contingent, then gaining a structural resistance which transcends the appearance of complete arbitrariness. As apparently reliable traditions, they provide precisely those standards that help to assess the utility or harmfulness of attitudes and actions. It is these historically developed perspectives themselves that judge their own range and force, and thus open up a limited area within which they can be played out, that is to say, thrown back onto their own contingent point of departure.

However, if Rorty had made full use of Nietzsche's analytical tools, this devious theoretical approach would have been unnecessary. Rorty advocates a self-reflexive theory that binds itself to what it describes. It conceives itself as an inventory and utopian continuation of an existent tradition, but applies its own perspectivism only partly to the basic concepts that it uses. Following Nietzsche, Rorty should admit that even the experience of contingency is dependent on a certain perspective, and he should suspect that this experience might lead to actions (whether of self-creation or solidarity) which were already intended and decided before a subsequent motivation was invented in order to legitimize them. Nietzsche's famous figure of the reversal between cause and effect here almost imposes itself as a leading aspect of interpretation. For without a previous *positing* of language and world as contingent, the act of construction cannot be grasped as an act of autonomy and self-creation. If we follow Nietzsche's path of reflection, we discover a diagnosis of the problem of contingency which Rorty — although coming close — finally misses. We simply cannot know whether the discovery of contingency does not deny determination in order to grant us an illusion of freedom, or whether, in granting necessity, we do not abandon an idea of freedom that we cannot bear. All we can see is that there exists a mutual relationship between the two perspectives, which instigates a persistent dispute between two parties that cannot live with, but also cannot do without one another.

Notes

[1] In quoting Rorty's books I use the following abbreviations: *(PMN) Philosophy and the Mirror of Nature* (Princeton: Princeton UP, 1979); *(CP) Consequences of Pragmatism* (Minneapolis: U. of Minnesota P., 1982); *(CI) Contingency, Irony, and Solidarity* (Cambridge: Cambridge UP, 1989); *(OR) Objectivity, Relativism, and Truth* (Cambridge: Cambridge UP, 1991); *(EH) Essays on Heidegger and Others* (Cambridge: Cambridge UP, 1991).

[2] Rorty claims that Nietzsche and the father of pragmatism, William James, share the same opinions concerning knowledge and truth while diverging in political matters: " . . . the Emersonian combination of self-reliance and patriotism found in James and Dewey" was alien to Nietzsche (*EH*, 2).

[3] This is the point in the articles by D. Shaw, "Rorty and Nietzsche: Some Elective Affinities," and W. R. Schroeder, "Nietzsche's Synoptic and Utopian Vision," *International Studies in Philosophy*, 21 (1989), 3–15 and 15–20.

[4] This is what Heidegger proposes in a famous sentence of his essay "Zeit und Sein" (1962), which Rorty quotes and underlines (*CI*, 97).

[5] I have dealt with this problem more closely in my essay "Rhetorik und Metaphysik," *Nietzsche-Studien, 23* (1993), 242–47.

[6] Among others, Sarah Kofman has attempted to show that Nietzsche's rhetoric of the will to power displays a decidedly anti-metaphysical tendency. See Kofman, *Nietzsche et la métaphore* (Paris, 1972).

[7] Rorty assumes that the supposition of a "connection between redescription and power" promises a metaphysical certainty that the true ironist disdains (*CI*, 90). In this assumption, he misunderstands from the very beginning Nietzsche's rhetoric of power, which does not strive to reach a safe position, but rather illustrates the never-ending process of reflexive self-overpowering.

[8] Nietzsche, *Kritische Gesamtausgabe (KGW)*, ed. G. Colli and M. Montinari (Berlin/New York, 1967ff.), VIII, 1, 1 [115] (my translation).

[9] *KGW*, VIII, 1, 2 [151] (my translation).

[10] *KGW*, VIII, 1, 2 [148] (my translation).

[11] *On the Genealogy of Morals*, trans. Walter Kaufmann (New York: Random House, 1967), II, 12.

[12] See *CI*, 39–42.

[13] See Harold Bloom, *The Anxiety of Influence* (New York/Oxford: Oxford UP, 1973); *Agon* (New York/Oxford: Oxford UP, 1982). Cf. also Rorty's statement: "Nietzsche's history of culture . . . sees language . . . as a form of life constantly *killing off* old forms — not to accomplish a higher purpose, but *blindly*" (*CI*, 19).

[14] With due consistency, pragmatism explicitly eliminates "the distinction between theoretical inquiry and practical deliberation" (*EH*, 33).

[15] See, for example, *OR*, 29. Some critics fail to notice this point in their critique of Rorty's allegedly indeterministic conception of autonomy. See, for instance, D. W. Conway, "Disembodied Perspectives," *Nietzsche-Studien*, 21 (1991), 281–89, and Keith Ansell-Pearson, "Toward the *Übermensch*: Reflections on the Year of Nietzsche's Daybreak," *Nietzsche-Studien*, 23 (1993), 142–45.

[16] See also for further references to this quotation in Rorty: *CI*, 27; *OR*, 32; *EH*, 13. However, Rorty also emphasizes that "Nietzsche has caused a lot of confusion by inferring from 'truth is not a matter of correspondence to reality' to 'what we call 'truth' are just useful lies'"(*CI*, 8).

[17] Cf. also *OR*, 26, 29–32, 197–210.

[18] *KGW*, VIII, 1, 1 [120] (my translation).

[19] Cf. *The Gay Science*, trans. W. Kaufmann (New York: Random House, 1974), V, 374.

[20] Rorty even wants "to show that the vocabulary of Enlightenment rationalism, although it was essential to the beginnings of liberal democracy, has become an *impediment* to the preservation and progress of democratic societies" (*CI*, 44).

[21] "Irony is, if not intrinsically resentful, at least reactive. Ironists have to have something to have doubts about, something from which to be alienated" *(CI, 88)*.

[22] I have elaborated on this issue in my essay "Zulassung und Ausschluß: Der Umgang mit Verschiedenheit," *Deutsche Zeitschrift für Philosophie*, 41, 6 (1993), 1059–71.

[23] Rorty further holds that, therefore, "we . . . think of enemies of liberal democracy like Nietzsche or Loyola . . . as 'mad' . . . . They are crazy because the limits of sanity are set by what *we* can take seriously. This, in turn, is determined by our upbringing, our historical situation" (*OR*, 188). This remark and the general admission that there are "no lives which are not largely parasitical on an unredescribed past" (*CI*, 42) once more argue against the interpretation of Rorty by Conway and Ansell-Pearson. While for Nietzsche the perspectives governing interpretation are rooted in affections, Rorty sees interpretations — despite the strong poets — as linked to existing forms of social life.

[24] See the critical comments on this assumption in C. B. Guignon and D. R. Hiley, "Biting the Bullet: Rorty on Private and Public Morality," *Reading Rorty*, ed. Alan Malachowski (Oxford: Basil Blackwell, 1990), 339–64.

[25] See Ch. Menke, "Distanz und Experiment: Zu zwei Aspekten ästhetischer Freiheit bei Nietzsche," *Deutsche Zeitschrift für Philosophie*, 41, 1 (1993), 61–77.

[26] *The Gay Science*, IV, 335.

[27] *KGW*, V, 1, 3 [140]. See also Ch. Menke, "Distanz und Experiment," 73.

Manfred Pütz

Paul de Man and the Postmodern Myth of Nietzsche's Deconstruction of Causality

THERE IS NO doubt that, aside from Derrida's work on Nietzsche, Paul de Man's assessment of the subversive potential of Nietzschean thought has been the most influential in establishing Nietzsche as a central figure of the deconstructionists' self-proclaimed ancestry and as the fountainhead of many claims characteristic for the deconstructionist venture that attempts to invalidate all major tenets of traditional Western philosophy as a concealed metaphysics of presence. But there can also be little doubt that de Man's discussions of Nietzschean texts in part amount to a virtual misrepresentation, if not misappropriation, of crucial arguments and polemic stances which are all too quickly turned into questionable theories of displaced deconstructionist doctrine and, in some cases, lead directly to the invention and perpetuation of a series of highly dubious postmodern myths. In order to substantiate this charge, I would like to take a closer look at de Man's famous essay on "Nietzsche's Theory of Rhetoric" (later reprinted as "Rhetoric of Tropes" in *Allegories of Reading*)[1] in order to challenge its theories about Nietzsche's alleged deconstruction of causality, which appear in the course of the larger and more ambitious project of demonstrating that the inescapable "rhetoricity" or "figurality" of all language undermines any claims of language as a representational medium that guarantees access to referential truth or unambiguous forms of literal, non-figurative meaning.

At the beginning of his essay, which presents itself as an investigation of the controversial relationship between literature and philosophy, de Man turns to Nietzsche's early lecture notes for a course on rhetoric (given in Basel during the winter semester of 1872/3) and underlines Nietzsche's provocative statements that there is "No such thing as an unrhetorical, 'natural' language . . . that could be used as a point of reference," and that "Tropes are not something that can be added or subtracted from language at will . . . . There is no such thing as a proper meaning . . . ." (105/6). De Man then summarizes the results of this pronounced rhetorical view of language, which he later identifies as "the key to Nietzsche's critique of metaphysics" (109), by stating: "It marks a full reversal of the established priorities which traditionally root the authority of the language in its adequation to an extralinguistic referent or meaning, rather than in the intralinguistic resources of figures" (106).

Once such fundamental propositions have been established — which seem to make Nietzsche's theory of rhetoric a model of de Man's own view that all aberrations of traditional metaphysics are grounded "in the rhetorical model of the trope or, if one prefers to call it that way, in literature as the language most explicitly grounded in rhetoric" (109) — de Man proceeds to search for further corroboration of his claims in the later works of Nietzsche and singles out a by now famous passage of the *Nachlaß* that deals with "the phenomenalism of the inner world." In the passage in question Nietzsche writes:

> The *chronological reversal* which makes the cause reach consciousness later than the effect. — We have seen how pain is projected in a part of the body without having its origin there; we have seen that the perceptions which one naively considers as determined by the outside world are much rather determined from the inside; that the actual impact of the outside world is never a *conscious* one . . . The fragment of outside world of which we are conscious is a correlative of the effect that has reached us from outside and that is then projected, *a posteriori* as its "cause" . . . . [2]

De Man's commentary emphasizes that the binary oppositions of Nietzsche's scheme at first seem to hold nothing unusual, until one notices that the priority of the two poles of the causal relationship, interconnected with the appearance of outer and inner world, seems to be paradoxically reversed. He comments on the result of this apparent reversal in the following way:

> The outer, objective event in the world was supposed to determine the inner, conscious event as cause determines effect. It turns out however that what was assumed to be the objective, external cause is itself the result of an internal effect. What had been considered to be a cause, is, in fact, the effect of an effect, and what had been considered to be an effect can in its turn seem to function as the cause of its own cause. (107)

What is more, de Man goes on to stress that a curious new constellation can now be seen to arise as a consequence of the attested reversal of priorities:

> The two sets of polarities, inside/outside and cause/effect, which seemed to make up a closed and coherent system (outside causes producing inside effects) has now been scrambled into an arbitrary, open system in which the attributes of causality and of location can be deceptively exchanged, substituted for each other at will. As a consequence, our confidence in the original, binary model that was used as a starting point is bound to be shaken. (107–8)

Finally, as de Man draws Nietzsche's observations and his own commentaries on the status of traditional assumptions about causality together, he calls them the "deconstruction of the classical cause/effect, subject/object scheme" (108), and then launches into what he explicitly marks as "the main point" of his argument, namely that the subsequent endless process of arbitrary reversals and substitutions "without regard for the truth-value of these structures" (108) becomes for Nietzsche a purely linguistic event.

If we set aside for a moment the last and probably most far-reaching claim about the arbitrary substitutions and reversals as linguistically generated events, de Man's presentation of Nietzsche's celebrated deconstruction of causality boils down to two interrelated claims that, first, in a given causal relation the cause can be seen as an effect of its effect, whereas the effect can be understood as the cause of its own cause, and second, that this constellation necessarily entails that causes and effects can be freely reversed, interchanged, and substituted for each other without further restrictions. It is in one or the other form, and frequently in both, that de Man's interpretation of Nietzsche's invalidation of causality has entered the mainstream of deconstructionist theory and provided the unchallenged basis for a plethora of self-confident deconstructionist readings of a variety of philosophical and literary texts.

In providing evidence for this observation, I shall restrict myself to three quick references to noted examples in deconstructionist criticism and theory, of which at least two document the rapid transformation of de Man's questionable readings from provocative challenge to authoritative doctrine and hallowed canonization. In her well-known article on George Eliot's *Daniel Deronda*, Cynthia Chase bases her "double-reading" of the novel on the proposition that a letter by one of the characters that points to "present causes of past effects" clearly deconstructs the category of causality, and thus functions as a deconstruction of the novel as a whole.[3] Her central formula of the cause that can be seen as an effect of its effects, and the effects as the cause of their cause, as much as her whole terminological apparatus (reversal, chiasmus, metalepsis) and her references to de Man's Nietzsche interpretation in two notes, clearly show that she is familiar with de Man's argument on the deconstruction of causality and confidently bases her own readings of Eliot's novel on the incontestable certainty of his propositions. In his influential book, *On Deconstruction*, Jonathan Culler, our second example, follows in broad outline de Man's argumentation, enriches it with his own demonstrations of what he calls "the Nietzschean deconstruction of causality," and generally transmits the impression that the latter can be regarded as a canonical example for the revolutionary disruptions of deconstructionist thought and practice.[4] Finally, Christopher Norris, in *Deconstruction: Theory and Practice*, treats the so-called deconstruction of causality as a strategy indicative of recent tendencies in interpretation (he mentions Nietzsche, de Man, Chase, and Culler in this context), though he also leaves no doubt that, in such matters, he greatly prefers "the vigour and sheer argumentative power of Derrida or de Man" to the "routine ingenuity" of their followers and canonizers.[5]

II

If de Man thus seems to have firmly established in poststructuralist circles that an unrefutable deconstruction of causality has been secured by Nietzsche, it remains to be seen how responsible his reading of Nietzschean texts is and how stringent his extensive conclusions are in the given case.[6] As far as Nietzsche's approach to the relationship of cause and effect is concerned, internal as much as external evidence shows that the case de Man presents is weak. In the passage on "the phenomenalism of the inner world," Nietzsche notices a chronological inversion in the process of identifying cause and effect and pairs it with a locational relation (inside and outside). In this operation, he emphasizes the priority of effect over cause on the *perceptual* level of identification, which runs counter to the logical order of priority on either the *explanatory* or an assumed *material* level in the succession of events. Clearly, this (uncontested) observation cannot be translated into de Man's sweeping proposition that now the cause figures as an effect of its effect and, vice versa, the effect becomes the cause of its own cause. All that can be safely concluded from the observed constellation is that the perceived effect now figures as the cause of *searching* for and eventually projecting a cause explaining the initially noted effect. Analogously, the cause of Nietzsche's reversed scheme cannot be seen as the effect of its own effect; it is rather the process of *explanatory identification* of the cause that becomes a function of the event which rests in the initial perception and interpretation of the effect *as* an effect. In other words, what de Man's twisted argument implies is a confusion between two orders of events which, logically, must be kept separate: the order of the *perception* of events and the order of *explanation* regarding those events.[7] In the course of the conceptual confusion instigated by de Man's argument, it is he himself who creates the alleged metonymical relationship between cause and effect, which he then claims as the basis of the actual relationship itself.

The false twist de Man gives to Nietzsche's arguments and observations has far-reaching consequences for the whole case he presents. A first consequence lies in the fact that if de Man's claims that a cause can also be seen as an effect of its own effect, and an effect as the cause of its own cause, are not supported by Nietzsche's text, then his further conclusion that Nietzsche's questioning of the succession of cause and effect leads to an unrestricted reversal between the two poles is equally unwarranted. I would like to pursue the problems involved here in two different directions. To begin with, there is a considerable body of external evidence that Nietzsche has pondered the problem of the reversibility between causes and effects on various other occasions and that in all such cases he has come to results diametrically opposed to what de Man wants to read into the passage he has selected. Perhaps the most dramatic instance of such a consideration on Nietzsche's part comes in a central passage of *Twilight of the Idols*, which was written between late June and early September of 1888 (published in 1889), and thus presumably postdates the passages on "the phenomenalism of the inner world." In a chapter entitled "The Four Great Errors," Nietzsche dedicates eight sections of compact argumentation to the problem of the most pernicious and consequential errors mankind has ever perpetrated, and they all center on cases of misunderstood or misapplied causality. In the opening paragraph of the first section Nietzsche writes:

> *The error of confusing cause and consequence* [Ursache und Folge]. — There is no more dangerous error than that of *mistaking the consequence for the cause*: I call it reason's intrinsic form of corruption. None the less, this error is among the most ancient and most recent habits of mankind: it is even sanctified among us, it bears the names 'religion' and 'morality'.[8]

Nietzsche goes on to castigate three other errors in regard to the concept of causality, which he terms in sequence, "The error of a false causality," "The error of imaginary causes," and "The error of free will." All of these errors involve false derivations and/or applications of the principle of causality which, by the same token, presupposes that there are also correct derivations and applications of this principle. However, since this will be in part the topic of the next section of our discussion, it may here suffice to notice that Nietzsche's extended polemics of "The Four Great Errors" are directed precisely against the idea of the free reversibility and the practice of substituting causes for effects and effects for causes — a practice he summarily calls the great *"psychology of error"* (*TI*, VI, 6) — and hence bear witness against de Man's allegation that in Nietzsche cause and effect become freely permutable elements of an arbitrary, open scheme that is mostly dependent on the figurality of language. Indeed, the gist of the "Four Errors" passages seems to be that, in criticizing false applications of the principle of causality, the concept as such is not radically deconstructed but rather accepted and affirmed in its conventional form. In particular, Nietzsche strongly turns against the *error* of reversing cause and effect, and moreover, does not tie the mistake of confusing them, when it occurs, to any form of rhetorical predetermination, as de Man would have us believe in his reading of the given passage. Consequently, even if one were to regard Nietzsche's critical stance on the pervasive misapplication of the concept of causality as a deconstructive act, it would obviously constitute a form of deconstruction totally different from, if not directly opposed to, what de Man celebrates as the Nietzschean deconstruction of causality in his chosen paradigm.

We arrive at similar conclusions about Nietzsche's skeptical dealings with the concept of causality when we turn to the question of what they have in common with Hume's classical investigation of its validity. Contrary to what some defenders of de Man's case have claimed in this context,[9] the critical thrust of both Hume's and Nietzsche's analysis of the problem is largely the same. Hume had noted, in his *Treatise of Human Nature*, that two essential features of our notion of causality rest on the observable relation of contiguity and temporal succession between separate events which we call cause and effect.[10] However, though contiguity and succession are necessary features of any assumed causal relationship, they are not at all *sufficient* conditions to define the range of the idea in its entirety and alleged universal validity. What is still missing for the full range of the concept is, according to Hume, the notion of a "necessary connexion" between the two poles of the causal scheme. In his subsequent analysis, Hume concentrates precisely on the nature and extent of this idea of "necessary connexion" and finds that it is neither grounded in direct perception nor in logic — and consequently cannot be demonstrated — but rather that it derives from inferences which are themselves tied to such shaky foundations as memory and habit (custom).[11]

In a similar fashion, Nietzsche starts his analysis of the relationship between cause and effect in the "phenomenalism" passage with an observation on temporal succession which — considering an angle different from Hume's for the moment — he finds curiously inverted. In the second paragraph of the passage Nietzsche summarizes his prior observations: "In the phenomenalism of the 'inner world' we invert the chronological order of cause and effect. The fundamental fact of 'inner experience' is that the cause is imagined after the effect has taken place."[12] Although the observation on the inversion of chronological order is not a point Hume was directly concerned with, the whole argument Nietzsche pursues still hinges on the role of temporal succession for the identification of causal relationships,

just as Hume had described it.[13] And since Hume had already noted
that the validity of the notion of causality does not exclusively depend on the establishment of a temporal relation (a point one can
hardly contradict), it follows that the idea of causality cannot be effectively deconstructed by referring only to this subordinate element
of temporality, regardless of whether the temporal scheme in question is seen as predictive (inference from cause to later effect) or in
its inverted retrodictive form (inference from effect to prior cause).[14]
Any convincing deconstruction of causality would necessarily have to
go beyond an attack on subordinate elements of the concept, such as
temporal succession, and address itself to the invalidation of those
elements that make up the core of the concept's claims to universal
acceptance and truth.

As we have seen earlier, the most essential claim constitutive of
the idea of causality rests on the assumption of a necessary connection between cause and effect, which secures the legitimacy of inferences from the one pole to the other in a causal scheme. For both
Hume and Nietzsche, the assumption of a necessary connection becomes highly problematical because it cannot be supported by either
experiental or logical evidence. That causal explanations are not
firmly grounded in any law of causality, which pertains to actual occurrences in the world, but are rather functions of the human mind,
which constantly projects causes and effects on a world of alleged
"things" without noticing that it is merely dealing with inventions of
its own creation, is a standard charge in Nietzsche's recurrent challenges of an "objective" reading of causality. In the passages on the
"phenomenalism of the inner world," Nietzsche first points to the
dubious act of subsequent projection which is here involved, and
later elaborates on the whole procedure leading to our belief in the
existence of actual outer causes for experienced inner effects:

> The whole of "inner experience" rests upon the fact that a cause for
> an excitement of the nerve centers is sought and imagined — and
> that only a cause thus discovered enters consciousness: this cause in
> no way corresponds to the real cause — it is a groping on the basis
> of previous "inner experiences," i.e., of memory. But memory also
> maintains the habit of the old interpretations, i.e., of erroneous
> causality — so that the "inner experience" has to contain within it
> the consequences of all previous false causal fictions. Our "outer
> world" as we project it every moment is indissolubly tied to the old

error of the ground: we interpret it by means of the schematism of "things," etc. (*WP*, 479)

The passage not only stresses that explanations of causal relationships thus derived are "false causal fictions," but it also introduces in the terms "memory" and "habit" two crucial concepts that further underline the similarity between Nietzsche's critique of causality and Hume's skeptical analysis of the same complex. Hume finally held habit (custom) responsible for our inclination to postulate a reliable connection between the separately experienced phenomena of cause and effect, and he thus transformed the problematics of our belief in legitimate inferences into a psychological problem deeply rooted in the human need for familiarity and constancy in an otherwise chaotic and destabilizing flux of experience. In like manner, Nietzsche often radically psychologizes our pervasive search for corresponding causes and effects and attempts to trace it back to its genealogical roots in habit, conscious or unconscious repetition, and fear of the unfamiliar. As we have seen above, the Humean twist of motivational analysis is already apparent in those passages of the "phenomenalism of the inner world" which suddenly evoke memory and habit as crucial categories in our pursuit of causal explanations. It becomes even more apparent, and at the same time enriched by Nietzsche's own motivational speculations, in a note of roughly the same period which, under the heading "Critique of the concept 'cause'," offers the following proposition: "As soon as we are shown something old in the new, we are calmed. The supposed instinct for causality is only fear of the unfamiliar and the attempt to discover something familiar in it — a search, not for causes, but for the familiar" (*WP*, 551).

The argument on habit and familiarity through regularity seems well rehearsed in Nietzsche since it can be discovered in certain variations all over his writings of the later period. In *Twilight of the Idols*, for instance, two longer sections are dedicated to "The error of imaginary causes" and a "psychological explanation" thereof, and both passages emphasize that "memory," "habituation," the reduction of "something unknown" to "something known," as well as a "feeling of fear" (of the unfamiliar) play a crucial role in the rise of the human "cause-creating drive [Ursachen-Trieb]" as a dominant force (*TI*, VI, 4 and 5). With a similar thrust Nietzsche holds in an earlier note (from 1884): "The most strongly believed a priori "truths" are for me — *provisional assumptions*, e.g., the law of causality, a very well acquired habit of belief, so much a part of us that not to believe in it would destroy the race. But are they for that reason truths?" (*WP*, 497). Moreover, Nietzsche seems to be aware that at least part of his argument overlaps with Hume's classical critique of the concept, and consequently he gives credit to his skeptical predecessor for certain crucial aspects of the matter: "We have no 'sense for the *causa efficiens*': here Hume was right; habit (but not only that of the individual!) makes us expect that a certain often-observed occurrence will follow another: nothing more!" (*WP*, 550).

But what does all this mean for our discussion of Nietzsche's alleged deconstruction of causality as it takes shape in de Man's controversial presentation? I think that a close reading of Nietzsche's recurrent quarrels with causality clearly shows that he was not so much concerned with an actual chronological reversal of cause and effect within the phenomenalism of the inner world — a point de Man attempts to stretch to its limits — but that he was rather worried about the undisclosed inferences on which we customarily and uncritically rely when we move between the two poles of the cause/effect scheme as if it formed a universally applicable law. His suspicion against the validity of these inferences is expressed in different ways at different stages of his critical pursuit. In his earlier works, such as *The Birth of Tragedy* and *Daybreak*, Nietzsche predominantly concentrates on false *applications* of the concept of causality. In *The Birth of Tragedy*, for instance, he castigates "the unshakable faith that thought, using the thread of causality, can penetrate the deepest abysses of being," a faith which he explicitly calls a "sublime metaphysical illusion" ["Dieser erhabene metaphysische Wahn"], and in a following passage he insists that the concept, according to Kant, should always be restricted to the realm of appearances instead of aspiring to apprehend and to fathom the depth of the innermost truth and essence of things.[15] Moreover, in *Daybreak* he criticizes forms of *"imaginary causalities* [phantastische Kausalitäten]" which all too often revert to "demonic" causes, and he counters them with the assumption of "real natural causes" and "real natural *consequences*" which seemingly find his full approval (*D*, I, 10 and 33). In his later works, on the other hand, Nietzsche shifts the focus of his critique to charges that perhaps *all* causes are imaginary projections after the fact and that "we invent all causes after the schema of the effect" (*WP*, 551; cf. also *TI*, VI, 4), from which he eventually draws the radical conclusions: "There is no such thing as 'cause'" and: "There are neither causes nor effects" (*WP*, 551). In their overall development, then, Nietzsche's critical dealings with an assumed law of causality can clearly be seen to extend from a pointed attack on particular cases of misapplication to a general questioning of the principle as such, which is exposed as a pervasive fiction that would force any critical observer to the radical verdict: "Interpretation by causality a deception" (*WP*, 551).

However, what Nietzsche tends to overlook in his all-out attacks on the general validity of the category of causality — and de Man should have noticed this weakness in his proclaimed principal witness — is that Kant's epistemology had long given a good answer to the very questions Nietzsche can still be seen grappling with. The revolutionary turn of Kant's transcendental philosophy consisted of an approach that no longer derived categories from experience but rather established them as *a priori* concepts of understanding, which in themselves *constitute* the possibility of experience; that is to say, the general concept of causality was no longer seen by Kant as a result of concrete experiences, but rather the possibility of experience as a result of the general concept in application to the realm of appearance. Nietzsche himself shows an awareness of the change of orientation embodied in Kant's transcendental perspective when he holds in *Beyond Good and Evil*:

> One ought not to make 'cause' and 'effect' *into material things*, as natural scientists do . . . ; one ought to employ 'cause' and 'effect' only as pure *concepts*, that is to say as conventional fictions for the purpose of designation, mutual understanding, *not* explanation. In the 'in itself' there is nothing of 'causal connection', of 'necessity', of 'psychological unfreedom'; there 'the effect' *does not* 'follow the cause', there no 'law' rules. It is *we* alone who have fabricated causes, succession, reciprocity, relativity, compulsion, number, law, freedom, motive, purpose; and when we falsely introduce this world of symbols into things and mingle it with them as though this symbol-world were an 'in itself', we once more behave as we have always behaved, namely *mythologically*.[16]

This is mostly Kantian epistemology in the form of ornate Nietzschean discourse. However, Nietzsche then goes on to misrepresent central aspects of the Kantian approach in an alarming manner,[17] and moreover, aggressively distances himself from Kant by repeatedly attacking the basic differentiation between *noumena* and *phenomena* as untenable, and by exposing what he calls the "sore spot [der faule Fleck] of Kant's critical philosophy" which, for him, rests in Kant's having gone beyond the "purely intra-phenomenal validity" of concepts such as causality in an indefensible act of transgression.[18] And it is this specific turn of Nietzsche's critique that results in a frequent mix-up between the final repeal of the concept of causality and its mere critical restriction, a turn which makes the critic fall behind the achievements of Kantian epistemology in a major way.

III

At this point in the discussion I would like to return to de Man's allegedly new reading of Nietzsche's "phenomenalism" passages, and take up his far-reaching claims that the deconstruction of causality embodied in these passages is rooted in a Nietzschean view of language as defined by its inevitable figurality and the predominance of the rhetorical model of the trope. In support of his encompassing allegations, de Man quotes the following passage from the end of Nietzsche's note:

> The whole notion of an "inner experience" enters our consciousness only after it has found a language that the individual *understands* — i.e., a translation of a situation into a *familiar* situation — : 'to understand,' naively put merely means: to be able to express something old and familiar.[19]

De Man proceeds to elaborate on certain passages from Nietzsche's already mentioned course on rhetoric, which single out the trope of metonymy or metalepsis as a key example for the pervasive "exchange or substitution of cause and effect" (108f), and then switches to the discussion of Nietzsche's early essay "On Truth and Lie in an Extra-Moral Sense" as the prime source of documentary evidence for his general propositions that in Nietzsche there is no escape from "the pitfalls of rhetoric," and that "the necessary subversion of truth by rhetoric as the distinctive feature of all language" must remain the last word in these matters (110).

However, unlike the essay "On Truth and Lie," which indeed almost parades *in extenso* Nietzschean views that support de Man's general hypothesis of the necessary subversion of truth by rhetoric,[20]

other sources of evidence do not work half as favorably in support of
the case de Man tries to make. In fact, they rather expose the weakness of his argument in several respects. For one, the passage from
"the phenomenalism of the inner world" quoted above underlines
that language only serves as a *translator* of notions of our "inner experience" that we constantly struggle to understand, which is to say
that the alleged illusions activated in this context are not really *generated* by language but rather point back to a *pre-linguistic* sphere
that conspicuously makes its influence felt.[21] In the given case, this
sphere is explicitly associated with the idea of the "familiar," and
consequently refers back to a non-linguistic, psychological dimension
of the problem that we have already identified in our treatment of
the parallels between Hume and Nietzsche. Moreover, the metonymy example in de Man's further references to Nietzsche's views on
the rhetoricity of all language becomes counterproductive for the
whole argument when we consider how a metonymy or metalepsis
involving the exchange of cause and effect actually works. De Man
himself selects as an allegedly revealing example for the workings of
this trope the metonymical substitution of "tongue" for language
(108), but it does not follow at all in this example that the playful
exchange between the two terms constitutes an arbitrary reversal of
assumed cause and effect, as de Man would have us believe. What
rather happens in this trope is that one relational term can be substituted for the other precisely because the fundamental conceptual
framework of cause implying effect is envisioned as fully intact, so
that when you mention the one element of the scheme you have
implicitly already referred to the other as its necessary correlative. In
other words, the trope of metonymy posits nothing more than a
rhetorical shorthand device allowing its user to refer from one concept to the other on the basis of the assumption that their inherent
inferential relationship is considered intact instead of questionable or
even reversible at will. If it were otherwise, we could never recognize
a metonymy when we encounter one.

If this is internal evidence against de Man's forced reading of the
passages in question, then external evidence of a serious reductionism in his presentation of Nietzsche's views on language, truth, and
causality is equally close at hand. Granted, de Man is right when he
emphasizes that to a great extent Nietzsche's early philosophy takes
shape as a radical reflection upon the pitfalls of language and that

Nietzsche's theory of rhetoric is indicative of his attempts to expose language as the medium productive of some of the worst errors of philosophy about a world that is traditionally regarded as lying beyond language. After all, it was Nietzsche himself who had, quite early already, insisted that "The deepest philosophical insights lie ready-made in language"[22] and that "The philosopher [is] caught in the nets of language."[23] This point has often been made by critics,[24] and it has also been observed that such a perspective adumbrates the paradigmatic shift in modern philosophy from problems of metaphysics, ontology, and classical epistemology to the project of a critical philosophy of language that, in its most radical form, sees language as the source of all philosophical deceptions which, in turn, will self-destruct when exposed to a rigid critique of the linguistic mechanisms behind them. In this context, de Man has become one of the leading proponents of the argument that the key to Nietzsche's critique of language, which at the same time figures as the key to his dismantling of metaphysics, lies in the recognition of the ineradicable figurality or rhetoricity of all language — a view which provocatively negates the traditional representational model of language and substitutes an encompassing rhetorical model for it.[25] Specifically, the model of the trope is identified by de Man as the fundamental paradigm of Nietzsche's linguistic analysis, and he dedicates an important part of his further investigation to the role of the exemplary tropes of metaphor and metonymy.

One would have to admit that this tropological view of language ascribed to Nietzsche indeed finds ample support in his early (unpublished) writings, and consequently de Man mostly turns for his further argumentation to texts of that period, e.g. the essay "On Truth and Lie," as well as other parts from Nietzsche's unpublished *Philosophenbuch*. However, the case is quite different when we turn to further documents, in which Nietzsche reflects upon properties of language that he holds responsible for the creation and perpetuation of the perennial philosophical illusions, errors, and deceptions generated by language. In particular documents much closer to the note which de Man uses for the opening gambit of his essay present a shift of focus that concentrates on the *grammaticality* of language instead of its figurality as the central feature accountable for its deceptive powers. In a series of passages ranging from *Beyond Good and Evil* to *Twilight of the Idols* and the late notes of the *Nachlaß*, the property of language causing a plethora of decisive philosophical errors is identified as its inherent grammaticality. Thus Nietzsche holds, in *Beyond Good and Evil*, that "The singular family resemblance between all Indian, Greek and German philosophizing" is rooted in a "common philosophy of grammar," which "thanks to unconscious domination and directing by similar grammatical functions" makes "a similar evolution and succession of philosophical systems" unavoidable (*BGE*, I, 20). He further emphasizes, in *Twilight of the Idols*, that the very error which "compels us to posit unity, identity, duration, substance, cause, materiality, being" is grounded in "basic presuppositions of the metaphysics of language" which have reason and grammar for their perpetual advocates, and he closes his argument with the famous dictum: "I fear we are not getting rid of God because we still believe in grammar . . . ."[26] Finally, several notes of the late period underline similar ideas in a slightly different context that brings Nietzsche to reflect on the concept of substance associated with that of the subject in its interrelated metaphysical, psychological, and grammatical senses. Thus he proposes in two consecutive notes of the year 1887: "our belief in the concept of substance — that when there is thought there has to be something 'that thinks' is simply a formulation of our grammatical custom that adds a doer to every deed"; and immediately following: "The concept of substance is a consequence of the concept of the subject: not the reverse!" (*WP*, 484 and 485). In like manner, he had earlier stated, and this time in explicit reference to the problem of our unshakable belief in causality, that

> The separation of the 'deed' from the 'doer,' of the event from someone who produces events, of the process from a something that is not process but enduring, substance, thing, body, soul, etc. — the attempt to comprehend an event as a sort of shifting and place-changing on the part of a 'being,' of something constant: this ancient mythology established the belief in 'cause and effect' after it had found a firm form in the functions of language and grammar. (*WP*, 631)

All of the above quotations make it clear that Nietzsche frequently does not hold the tropological nature of language responsible for inherent metaphysical errors, but rather blames its fundamental grammaticality for the inescapable predisposition to produce a network of errors and illusions among which the notion of causality is only one.

Seen from this perspective, Nietzsche's far-ranging attack on practically all major concepts of traditional Western philosophy reveals itself as a skeptical demolition that constantly plays the idea of (actual) eternal becoming against the idea of an (illusionary) permanent being, and frequently ends up blaming grammar for generating the illusions of logic and knowledge inextricably tied to it:

> In order to think and infer it is necessary to assume beings: logic handles only formulas for what remains the same . . . . The character of the world in a state of becoming as incapable of formulation, as 'false,' as 'self-contradictory.' Knowledge and becoming exclude one another. (*WP*, 517)

Obviously, such passages do not support de Man's narrow interpretation of Nietzsche's charges against causality as derived from his allegedly revolutionary rhetorical model of language, but rather point an accusing finger at other properties of language that constantly become the advocate of major errors of logic and assumed knowledge expressed in this very medium. What is more, beside this line of argumentation — which at least ties the problem of causality to some form of critical questioning of language — there are also decidedly different forms of exposing the deceptions of causality in Nietzsche, which go far beyond the dimension of a critique of language and are all radically suppressed in de Man's hypothesis on the interrelation of rhetoricity and the deconstruction of causality in Nietzsche. In the following section, I would like to turn to such suppressed lines of argumentation and show what light they shed on the questions at issue.

IV

Nietzsche's favorite genealogical method — in itself an approach that involves an affirmation of valid causal linkage between phenomena[27] — is defined by the intention of not seeking for logical or rational solutions to given metaphysical problems, but rather of analyzing the prehistory of their rise as seemingly decisive problems for an individual, a culture, or a specific way of thinking. Thus metaphysical problems are downgraded by Nietzsche to the status of pseudo-problems, while the genealogical explanation of their origin is upgraded to the real effort a philosopher should pursue.[28] In response to this call for genealogical explanation, Nietzsche himself frequently encircles a given problem with a whole array of answers pertaining to the central question of its derivation *as* a problem.

In the case of causality as a reigning concept, Nietzsche's main line of attack is predominantly not directed against its dependence on language, but rather against a false analogy that gives rise to the idea. Central to his argument is the recurrent observation that the origin of the cause/effect scheme is closely related to the conviction that human beings are creatures of free will, and that the will actually causes effects to arise. In Nietzsche's own words: "The popular belief in cause and effect is founded on the presupposition that free will is the cause of every effect: it is only from this that we derive the feeling of causality" (*WP*, 667), and in another compact genealogical formula: "We have believed in the will as cause to such an extent that we have from our personal experience introduced a cause into events in general . . ." (*WP*, 478).[29] As can be seen from a wide range of similar propositions, Nietzsche time and again stresses the questionable interactions of concepts such as "subject," "will," "intention," "doer" and "deed" for the eventual formation of an expanding complex of ideas constitutive of our belief in causality. Consider the following samples:

> We have always believed we know what a cause is: but whence did we derive our knowledge, more precisely our belief we possessed this knowledge? From the realm of the celebrated 'inner facts', none of which has up till now been shown to be factual. We believed ourselves to be causal agents in the act of willing; we at least thought we were there *catching causality in the act.* (*TI*, VI, 3)

> Every thoughtless person supposes that will alone is effective; that willing is something simple, a brute datum, underivable, and intelligible by itself . . . . He does not see any problem here; the feeling of *will* seems sufficient to him not only for the assumption of cause and effect but also for the faith that he *understands* their relationship . . . . The propositions, 'no effect without a cause,' 'every effect in turn a cause' appear generalizations of much more limited propositions: 'no effecting without willing'; 'one can have an effect only on beings that will' . . . . (*GS*, III, 127)

> That which gives the extraordinary firmness to our belief in causality is not the great habit of seeing one occurrence following another but our inability to interpret events otherwise than as events caused by intention. (*WP*, 550)

> We have absolutely no experience of a cause; psychologically con-
> sidered, we derive the entire concept from the subjective conviction
> that *we* are causes . . . . Our 'understanding of an event' has con-
> sisted in our inventing a subject which was made responsible for
> something that happens and for how it happens. We have com-
> bined our feeling of will, our feeling of 'freedom,' our feeling of re-
> sponsibility and our intention to perform an act, into the concept
> 'cause' . . . . The thing, the subject, will, intention — all inherent in
> the conception 'cause.' (*WP*, 551)

In order to see the full range of Nietzsche's genealogical explanations of cause and effect as by-products of the illusions of the will,
one would also have to consider at least three further aspects of the
problem. To begin with, Nietzsche's critique of causality overwhelmingly centers on concepts such as purpose, aim, goal, end, intention,
and thus becomes an all-out attack on the specific notion of *causa
finalis* as constitutive for the teleologicial view of any process under
the guidance of a preconceived end.[30] In the last analysis, all forms of
causality are for him reducible to the incriminated idea of intention
directed towards a final *telos*; an assumption that entails the further
conclusions: "*causa efficiens* and *causa finalis* are fundamentally
one," and: "The belief in *causae* falls with the belief in télē . . . ."[31]
Moreover, Nietzsche sometimes associates the idea of causality with
metaphysical/theological speculations on the origin of the uncondi-
tioned that must necessarily be "causa sui," which again, as "cause in
itself, as *ens realissimum*," becomes the basis of "their stupendous
concept of 'God' . . ." (*TI*, III, 4). Finally, he brings the disruptive
thrust of his argument that the notion of causality is merely a corol-
lary to the idea of the will to a peak, when he denies the idea of the
will any legitimate authority: "But there is no such thing as will"
(*WP*, 488).[32]

Occasionally, Nietzsche draws all his various lines of genealogical
explanation regarding the origin of our belief in universal causality
together and lets them converge in a complex network of cumulative
attacks that variously take the metaphysical, theological, and psychological dimensions of the problem into consideration.[33] But regardless of whether we concentrate on such passages of compact
summary or not, the overall impression of Nietzsche's frequent de-
liberations on the principle of causality as a highly problematic concept remains the same: it is only partly the deceptive workings of

language he blames for the rise and dominance of the concept; and the overwhelming majority of his challenges are developed in contexts which clearly transcend the rhetorical sphere and address themselves to matters of pre-linguistic origin and import.

V

What, then, are we to think of de Man's uncompromising attempt to identify Nietzsche's alleged deconstruction of causality as conjoined with his view of language as a medium of ineluctable rhetoricity and figurality? There is no doubt that de Man is on target when he claims that Nietzsche went to great length in order to discredit the concept of causality as a principle of universal validity within the realm of an allegedly independent being. But given Nietzsche's fundamental proposition that, quite in general, there is no such thing as factual or essential truth but only a proliferation of interpretations bound to an all-pervasive perspectivism of illusionary human "knowledge,"[34] this diagnosis is neither difficult nor very helpful. The key problem of Nietzsche's attempted invalidation of general concepts such as causality becomes rather the question of what instigates and supports the dominance of these principles, or as Nietzsche himself has stated in the specific context of his critique of Kantian philosophy: " . . . it is high time to replace the Kantian question 'how are synthetic judgements *a priori* possible?' with another question: 'why is belief in such judgements *necessary?*'" (*BGE*, I, 11).[35] And it is in respect to this problem that de Man's interpretation seriously misjudges the complexity of answers suggested by Nietzsche. Although language certainly does not figure for Nietzsche as a medium of incontestable problem-solving but rather itself poses a major problem, it is, on the other hand, not the prime instigator of developments which entangle the human mind in the intricate web of self-perpetuating illusions, errors, and deceptions characteristic of its project to grasp the eternal truth of being. Specifically, in the case of causality it is not the pervasive rhetoricity of all language that is deemed responsible by Nietzsche for the decisive errors embodied in this concept, nor is the invalidation of the idea an inescapable result of the deconstructive rhetorical operation de Man wants to ascribe to Nietzsche in the given context. As we have seen, it is rather that Nietzsche points to a whole complex of other interlocking reasons for the origin and dominance of the notion of causality, and it is also clear that he considered crucial inferences of de Man's line of argumentation a serious error.

From a more encompassing perspective, the very questionability of de Man's interpretation in "Rhetoric of Tropes" encloses further questions about the assessment of Nietzsche's own ambiguous and paradoxical discourse, which had to rely on the conceptual apparatus of a language that he himself continuously struggled to discredit as a source of metaphysical errors on the grand scale. In the last analysis, such questions also involve the problem almost ritually battled over between the Heidegger school and the deconstructionist camp of reading Nietzsche, namely whether his philosophy must be seen as the apogee of Western metaphysics in its insurpassable form, or whether we should see it as a philosophy to end all philosophy, effectively exploding the megalomaniac project of metaphysics from the inside in the very act of endlessly repeating its patterns in self-reflexive gestures of ironic allegorization.

However, if this perhaps poses the crucial aporia of Nietzsche interpretation in our time, the immediate problems of de Man's reading of Nietzsche are less puzzling. In "Rhetoric of Tropes," de Man comes dangerously close to playing the role of what Nietzsche himself once called "the worst readers" of texts.[36] In a typically poststructuralist variation of this type of reader, de Man vigorously projects his own convictions about the inevitable subversion of truth by rhetoric into a semi-available Nietzsche in order to regain them triumphantly back from a textual corpus that in many respects fails to support them. Thus de Man the deconstructionist offers us intriguing glimpses of Nietzsche the demythologizer, but in the very process of doing so he also remythologizes — not unlike other deconstructionists have frequently done — the philosophy of his prime witness in a fashion that has far-reaching and apparently lasting results. Maybe this operation encompasses, on de Man's part, merely another exercise of the "blinded vision" which he himself has taught us to recognize in the recurrent aberrant patterns of interpretation, historically arising from specific "interaction[s] between critical blindness and critical insight."[37] At all events, the outcome of what de Man and his followers frequently do with and to Nietzschean texts suspiciously resembles those systematic misreadings of ambivalent statements which de Man ascribes, in his seminal essay on "The

Rhetoric of Blindness," to aberrant readers of Rousseau and other major figures of literature: "The more ambivalent the original utterance, the more uniform and universal the pattern of consistent error in the followers and commentators."[38]

Notes

[1] Paul de Man, *Allegories of Reading* (New Haven/London: Yale UP, 1979), pp. 103–18. Following page references to this source are given in parentheses in the text.

[2] I am quoting the passage in de Man's translation, which refers to the German text of the Schlechta-edition of Nietzsche's works: *Werke in drei Bänden*, ed. Karl Schlechta (Munich: Hanser, 1956), III, p. 804.

[3] Cynthia Chase, "The Decomposition of Elephants: Double-Reading *Daniel Deronda*," *PMLA*, 93 (1978), 215–27. Curiously, Chase uses de Man's terminology and key arguments and also quotes from his article on "Nietzsche's Theory of Rhetoric," however without identifying de Man directly as the source of her assumptions on the deconstruction of causality.

[4] Jonathan Culler, *On Deconstruction: Theory and Criticism after Structuralism* (London: Routledge & Kegan Paul, 1983), pp. 86–88. For an extensive critique of both Chase's and Culler's contributions in the context of a theory of narrative, see Jon-K Adams, "Causality and Narrative," *Journal of Literary Semantics*, 18, 3 (1989), 149–62.

[5] Christopher Norris, *Deconstruction: Theory and Practice* (London/New York: Methuen, 1982), pp. 133–35. One might also add Harold Bloom to the ranks of de Man canonizers when he selects "Rhetoric of Tropes" for his critical anthology *Friedrich Nietzsche* (New York: Chelsea House, 1987), and enthusiastically celebrates it as a "pathbreaking study of Nietzsche's theory of rhetoric" (p. vii).

[6] On de Man reading Nietzsche, cf. Thomas Böning, "Literaturwissenschaft im Zeitalter des Nihilismus? Paul de Mans Nietzsche-Lektüre," *Deutsche Vierteljahresschrift für Literaturwissenschaft und Geistesgeschichte*, 64, 3 (1990), 427–66; Maudemarie Clark, "Language and Deconstruction: Nietzsche, de Man, and Postmodernism," in *Nietzsche as Postmodernist*, ed. Clayton Koelb (New York, 1990), pp. 75–90; Richard H. Weisberg, "De Man Missing Nietzsche: Hinzugedichtet *Revisited*," in *Nietzsche as Postmodernist*, ed. Clayton Koelb (New York, 1990), pp. 111–24; Lutz Ellrich, "Der Ernst des Spiels: Zu drei Versuchen einer dekonstruktiven Nietzsche-Lektüre," in *Nietzsche oder Die Sprache ist Rhetorik*, ed. J. Kopperschmidt and H. Schanze (Munich, 1994), pp. 197–218; Brian Vickers, "Nietzsche im Zerrspiegel de Mans: Rhetorik gegen die Rhetorik," in *Nietzsche oder Die Sprache ist Rhetorik*, pp. 219–40; David B. Allison, "*Destruction/Deconstruction* in the Text of Nietzsche," *Boundary 2*, 8, 1 (1979), 197–222; Philip Buyck, "Oratory against Oratory: Paul de Man on

Nietzsche on Rhetoric," in *(Dis)continuities: Essays on Paul de Man*, ed. Luc Herman *et al.* (Amsterdam: Rodopi, 1989), pp. 149–61. A more general investigation of deconstructionist treatments of Nietzsche is offered in Kenneth Asher, "Deconstruction's Use and Abuse of Nietzsche," *Telos*, 62 (1984/85), 169–78.

[7] Cf. also the critique of Jonathan Culler's presentation of Nietzsche's deconstruction of causality in Adams, "Causality and Narrative," pp. 154ff. I would like to add to this critique that Culler's line of argumentation becomes particularly vulnerable when, in his rehash of Nietzsche's and de Man's argumentation, he repeatedly maintains that in the given case the effect can be seen to *produce* its own cause, or that "the effect is what causes the cause to become a cause" (*On Deconstruction*, pp. 87, 88).

[8] *Twilight of the Idols/The Anti-Christ (TI)*, trans. R. J. Hollingdale (London/New York: Penguin, 1990), VI, 1. All references to this and other translations of Nietzsche's works are identified by abbreviated titles and sections given in parentheses in the text.

[9] Thus Jonathan Culler claims that Nietzsche's "deconstruction of causality is not the same as Hume's skeptical argument . . . ." (*On Deconstruction*, p. 87). Arthur C. Danto, on the other hand, rightly emphasizes that Nietzsche's analysis of the problem is mostly the same as Hume's. See Danto, *Nietzsche as Philosopher* (New York, 1965), pp. 93ff.

[10] Hume, *A Treatise of Human Nature*, book I, part III, section II.

[11] See Hume, book I, part III, sections V to XV.

[12] *The Will to Power (WP)*, trans. Walter Kaufmann and R. J. Hollingdale (New York: Vintage, 1968), 479. In another note Nietzsche had earlier emphasized the same point in a somewhat different context: "The effect always 'unconscious': the inferred and imagined cause is projected, *follows* in time" (*WP*, 490). Further references to this source are given in parentheses in the text.

[13] On the problematical role of succession for the concept of causality, see also Nietzsche's statements in *Daybreak (D)*, trans. R. J. Hollingdale (Cambridge, 1982), II, 121; *The Gay Science (GS)*, trans. Walter Kaufmann (New York: Vintage, 1974), III, 112; and *WP*, 545, 632, 633.

[14] For the terminological oppositon of "predictive" and "retrodictive" in the context of causal explanations, see Adams, "Causality and Narrative," p. 152.

[15] *The Birth of Tragedy* and *The Case of Wagner (BT)*, trans. Walter Kaufmann (New York: Vintage, 1967), 15 and 18.

[16] *Beyond Good and Evil (BGE)*, trans. R. J. Hollingdale (London/New York: Penguin, 1990), I, 21. See also Nietzsche's other frequent attacks on the idea of "things-in-themselves" or "facts-in-themselves," for instance in *WP*, 555 and 556.

[17] Cf., for example, the passage in which he claims that Kant had assumed "a sense of causality" (*WP*, 551).

[18] *WP*, 552 and 553. For the decisive question of whether Nietzsche has actually gone beyond Kant by effectively invalidating the distinction between *phenomena* and *noumena*, appearance and thing-in-itself, or whether his own philosophy, in the last analysis, had to rely on this very dichotomy and thus failed to twist free of Kant, see Stephen Houlgate, "Kant, Nietzsche and the 'Thing in Itself'," *Nietzsche-Studien*, 22 (1993), 115–57.

[19] Cf. de Man, *Allegories*, p. 108.

[20] The essay has become one of the favorite sources for deconstructionist readers of Nietzsche precisely because it so obviously supports their own iconoclastic views on language and truth, although Nietzsche himself must not have thought very highly of this early piece because he never published it.

[21] Cf. also Böning, "Paul de Mans Nietzsche-Lektüre," pp. 453f; Maudemarie Clark, "Language and Deconstruction," pp. 85ff.

[22] *Gesammelte Werke* (Musarionausgabe), vol. 5 (Munich, 1922), p. 467 (my translation).

[23] *Kritische Gesamtausgabe* (*KGW*), ed. Georgio Colli and Mazzino Montinari (Berlin/New York, 1967ff), III/4, 19 [135]. Cf. for similar statements *KGW*, IV/1, 6 [39].

[24] For an early example, see Danto, *Nietzsche as Philosopher*, chapter III, section IV. A more recent example is Alan D. Schrift, *Nietzsche and the Question of Interpretation* (London/New York, 1990), chapter V.

[25] For a discussion of other critics dealing with this aspect, see Lutz Ellrich, "Rhetorik und Metaphysik: Nietzsches 'neue' ästhetische Schreibweise," *Nietzsche-Studien*, 23 (1994), 241–72.

[26] *Twilight*, III, 5. On the idea of "a *Verdinglichung* of grammar" in Nietzsche, see Danto, p. 96.

[27] De Man himself approaches this problem, among others, in his essay "Genesis and Genealogy" (*Allegories of Reading*, pp. 79–102) when he discusses the function of the "genetic pattern" in *The Birth of Tragedy*. Predictably, he comes to the conclusion that Nietzsche himself deconstructed all potential claims of validity for the genetic pattern at the same time and in the very process in which he was applying it.

[28] For a discussion of the role of genealogy, origin, and "Ursprung" in Nietzsche, with particular reference to Foucault's controversial essay "Nietzsche, Genealogy, History," see John Pizer, "The Use and Abuse of "Ursprung": On Foucault's Reading of Nietzsche," *Nietzsche-Studien*, 19 (1990), 462–78.

[29] Again, Nietzsche comes close to Hume in this proposition which had been considered and then rejected by Hume as the opinion of others in the general debate on causality. Cf. *Treatise of Human Nature*, book I, part III, section XIV (cf. also the Appendix to book III).

[30] For a sample of passages emphasizing this point, see *Daybreak*, II, 122 and 130; *Gay Science*, V, 360; *Twilight*, VI, 8; *WP*, 550, 552, 645, 666.

[31] See *WP*, 551 and 627. Hume had also denied the justification of a distinction between efficient and final causes though in a somewhat different context and for different reasons (*Treatise*, book I, part III, section XIV).

[32] For similar propositions cf. also *WP*, 671, 692, 715; *Twilight*, VI, 3; *Anti-Christ*, 14. I cannot deal here with the relationship of this statement to other propositions such as, for instance, "we *have* to make the experiment of positing causality of will hypothetically as the only one," followed by the declared intention "to define *all* efficient force unequivocally as: *will to power*" (*Beyond Good and Evil*, II, 36). Discussions of the problems involved in such seemingly contradictory statements are offered in Maudemarie Clark, *Nietzsche on Truth and Philosophy* (Cambridge, 1990), pp. 212–18; and Alexander Nehamas, *Nietzsche: Life as Literature* (Cambridge/London, 1985), pp. 76–80.

[33] In this context, the one chapter most richly imbued with a diversity of arguments developed by Nietzsche is "The Four Great Errors" in *Twilight*, VI. For further pointed remarks on the *psychological* side of the matter, see in particular *WP*, 554, 627, 664, 689.

[34] For one of the most concise statements of this proposition, see *WP*, 481: "I would say: No, facts is precisely what there is not, only interpretations."

[35] Of course, one would also have to keep an eye on the fact that Nietzsche did not always attempt to invalidate universal concepts such as causality but, on the contrary, sometimes *affirmed* their validity when in certain contexts they supplied him with a handy weapon against detested attitudes and world views. Compare, for instance, his diatribe in *The Anti-Christ* against the "psychology of the priest" who "knows only *one* great danger: that is science — the sound conception of cause and effect" (*TI*, 49).

[36] For Nietzsche's view of bad readers, see Hendrik Birus, "Nietzsche's Concept of Interpretation," *Texte: Revue de Critique et Theorie Litteraire*, 3 (1984), 87–102 (in particular p. 90f).

[37] Paul de Man, *Blindness and Insight* (New York, 1971), pp. 106, 111.

[38] *Blindness and Insight*, p. 111.

Hubert Zapf

Elective Affinities and American Differences: Nietzsche and Harold Bloom

A S THE VARIOUS contributions to the present volume amply demonstrate, Nietzsche was a strong presence in American literature
long before the postmodern era, a fact which should not be overlooked in view of the indubitably central role that he plays in postmodern thought. What has changed, however, is that he has become
somewhat of a paradigmatic figure, not only for literature itself, but
for literary theory and criticism. The new Nietzsche of literary theory, who entered America through the mediation of French poststructuralism, mainly of Jacques Derrida, is no longer, or at least no
longer primarily, the Nietzsche of instinctual will to power and the
Dionysian spirit but a more epistemological, metatextual Nietzsche,
whose relevance centers on problems of language rather than existence; on rhetorics rather than poetics; on his deconstruction of the
subject rather than the celebration of the great individual; on the infinite play of linguistic possibilities rather than the tragic paradoxes of
life and death. What has been particularly attractive in Nietzsche to
poststructuralists is his contribution to a global critique of Western
humanist ideology, with its logocentric and anthropocentric assumptions. He has thus become one of the key figures in the more general
politicization of the critical discourse in the past decades, which aims
at exposing and dismantling repressive cultural illusions and har-
monistic ideologies, unmasking them, from a Nietzschean point of
view, as rhetorical strategies which conceal the power structures that
they want to perpetuate. Dominant forms of discourse have been deconstructed to recover the traces of the colonized and marginalized
other which they have long suppressed — non-Western cultures, mi-

norities, women, the body, the material signifier, etc. And Nietzsche, along with Freud, Marx, and others, serves as an important collaborator in this theoretical crusade of universal emancipation.

I

In the landscape of contemporary American literary theory, Harold Bloom occupies a controversial yet indisputedly eminent place. He is certainly one of the most frequently cited American critics, if only because of his role as editor of countless collections of critical essays. But he has also made a significant impact with his own theory of literary influence, which he has expounded in a series of books, notably in his 'tetralogy' *The Anxiety of Influence, A Map of Misreading, Kabbalah and Criticism,* and *Poetry and Repression.*

According to Frank Lentricchia, Bloom is a "true American original," a uniquely individual thinker who belongs to no 'school' of contemporary criticism but is something like a reincarnation of the Emersonian spirit of radical self-reliance in the sphere of theory.[1] I partially agree with this assessment, and I will come back to it later in my essay. But at the same time it seems obvious that Bloom's ideas, like anybody else's, are not original inventions of his own but rather a *mixtum compositum* of various influences that he absorbs and transforms into his unique theoretical model. Among these influences are, most notably, Freud, Northrop Frye, English and American Romanticism, Gnosticism, and the Kabbalah. Also, poststructuralism provides a broader theoretical framework without which his ideas could not have assumed their specific shape. Nevertheless, it seems to me that Nietzsche has been an especially important source of inspiration for Bloom. Indeed, I would like to argue here that Bloom's specific reception of Nietzsche accounts for some of the main differences between his poetics and that of mainstream poststructuralism. For although Bloom shares in the poststructuralist concern with language, text, and reading (or, rather, misreading), his interest is not merely textual but also psychological; and although he shares in the radical criticism of an idealized humanism, he is not a political but an existential critic. While other theorists focus almost exclusively on epistemic or cultural and political aspects of Nietzsche, Bloom revives the more primary concerns of Nietzschean philosophy which have shaped American literature earlier in the century and, interfusing them with the semiological awareness of poststructural-ism, transfers them onto the level of poetic history and theory.

Daniel O'Hara, in a sophisticated argument, has already pointed out the centrality of Nietzsche in Bloom's theory. He analyzes Nietzsche's role in Bloom on the basis of Bloom's own dialectic of influence, interpreting Bloom's important books as illustrating differ-ent stages in the sixfold pattern of revisionism which Bloom devel-oped in *A Map of Misreading*. Yet according to O'Hara, there is a sublime irony at work here which makes Bloom fall victim to Nietzsche's influence at the very point where he claims to have mas-tered it. Nietzsche's "genius of irony" knew about the inescapable fate of being dependent on the forces of history and the past against which one struggles for freedom and self-determination. His answer to this paradox was an open-ended play of continual (self-)parody and endlessly deferred meaning. Bloom, in contrast, celebrates an il-lusory triumph over Nietzsche but becomes in fact merely "another instance" of a "giant shadow's last embellishment."[2] In his heroically staged, antithetical struggle against this overpowering superego of postmodernism, Bloom in the end becomes what he tries to revise; he turns into a figure of reductive self-parody invented by the precur-sor whom he believes to have defeated. However, the play of ironic revisionism of course also applies to O'Hara's own procedure, since he first has to adopt Bloom's model in order to be able to apply it, deconstructively, to Bloom himself. Moreover, to achieve his critical triumph over Bloom, O'Hara has to identify himself with the 'true' Nietzsche, thus claiming, like Bloom, a superior insight and truth-position, while at the same time turning himself, again like Bloom, into another belated version of Nietzsche. This philosophical game of ironic self-contradiction is no doubt a consciously adopted strat-egy, demonstrating that the ironic cycle of parody and self-reflexivity is potentially infinite. But at the same time it shows that the adoption of certain positions of thought, the formulation of identifiable truth-claims, is at least provisionally necessary in order to make that open process of creative-deconstructive self-parody possible in the first place. And this logical 'truth', in my view, applies to O'Hara, to Bloom, and indeed to Nietzsche himself.

As much as I respect the complexity of O'Hara's analysis, I should like to proceed in a different and doubtlessly far simpler way in the present article. My method will be hermeneutic-comparative, focusing not so much on direct or latent influence as on observable affinities and differences. I will first trace the affinities to Nietzsche in some of Bloom's central assumptions; and I will then point out what to me seem to be the crucial differences — differences which, among other things, lead us back to the 'American' element of Bloom's position.

II

If we look at Bloom's theory from the viewpoint of Nietzschean philosophy, we recognize a number of obvious parallels. Indeed, it seems from this angle that Bloom's theory is to a very large extent a condensation of Nietzsche into a theory of poetry and poetic history. This applies first of all to the *tone* and *style* in the two writers. Both Bloom and Nietzsche practice a polemical form of writing, in the original Greek sense of the word *polemos* (= struggle, war), dramatizing their discourse through metaphors of conflict and rhetorical warfare. Their common premise is the conflictive nature of the human mind, whose logical operations are not the agency of a higher truth-impulse but of instinctual drives at war with one another and geared toward survival and self-preservation. Both writers tend to think in extremes rather than in gradations, and tend to use sweeping statements and apodictic, though highly personal generalizations. Both cultivate a rhetoric of high drama, staging their intellectual conflicts in the dramaturgy of world-historical crisis and catastrophe. If Bloom stands out for his 'aggressive personalism', for the blatantly subjective propagation of his idiosyncratic views, something similar could be said about Nietzsche, who has become notorious to mainstream philosophers — and to a host of sceptic admirers — as the 'philosopher with the hammer'. In his antithetical criticism, Bloom like Nietzsche is a cultural iconoclast, a 'critic with the hammer' who mercilessly destroys traditional illusions of meaning, knowledge, and morality, in order to unmask them as comforting anthropocentric fictions.

But the affinities relate to far more than just style. Some of these affinities, Bloom shares with other contemporary critics. Thus, the traditional concepts of *truth* and *reality* are replaced by a field of competing anthropomorphic illusions, whose basis is never any immediate experience but the constantly shifting metaphoric process of cultural self-interpretation. Instead of truth, there are only fictions of truth, as Bloom never tires of insisting, and as Nietzsche formulates in one of his most frequently quoted passages in *On Truth and Lie in an Extra-Moral Sense*, where he describes "truth" as a "mobile army of metaphors, metonyms, and anthropomorphisms."[3] Nietzsche here appears as a crucial source for Bloom's rhetorical-tropological conception of culture, in which poetry gains such a prominent stature because it most strongly and deliberately intervenes with and revisionally subverts the apparently stable world of cultural metaphors. As a consequence of the radical relativization of truth, lie and error are no longer something to be avoided or eliminated but a necessary, indeed productive element of all life and cultural activity. Bloom, closely following Nietzsche, never ceases to emphasize the unavoidability of error and deception, and, in fact, establishes them as an essential element in his theory of poetry and criticism. Any new text is not only the creative misreading of another text but also the rhetorical denial of this fact, an act of illusion which belies its own indebtedness; in a recurrent formula of Bloom's, art is a "lie against time." In Nietzsche, too — at least in his middle period — art is a special, particularly intensive form of lie, a medium in which "the *lie* is sanctified, and the *will to deception* has a good conscience."[4] Art, according to *The Gay Science*, is "the *good* will to appearance," a "cult of the untrue" which offers us such powerful illusions that the insight into delusion and error as a condition of the knowing and sensitive being becomes bearable.[5]

In this revision of humanist-idealist notions of art, traditional *moral* categories of good vs. evil are replaced by transmoral categories such as original vs. derivative, self-reliant vs. dependent, and above all, strong vs. weak. In the emphasis on *biopsychological* rather than on moral or epistemological categories, Bloom's specific profile and difference from the characteristic reception of Nietzsche in contemporary criticism begins to become more clearly visible. "In real life it is only a matter of *strong* and *weak* wills," says Nietzsche in *Beyond Good and Evil*.[6] Bloom, more than any other critic, stresses the will to power as the fundamental driving force of cultural and, especially, of poetic activity. This will to power is not, as in other recent theories, primarily a political or textual but an anthropological phenomenon, a universal motivating force which belongs to life itself, and which becomes personalized in the will of strong individuals. It is here that I think Bloom is farthest away from mainstream post-modern criticism, and also closest to the spirit of Nietzsche's philosophy. For even though Nietzsche deconstructed the subject as a unified transcendental category and questioned the coherent identity of an authentic self in favor of an interplay of various, even contradictory masks and images of the self, he nevertheless retained the notion of individuals as existential centers of experience and sources of creativity.[7] And this notion is emphatically shared by Bloom, who in fact bases his whole poetic theory on it.

What this entails is a concept of *textuality* totally different from poststructuralist views. The text, to Bloom, is not a mere semiotic structure or material signifier but the concretization of psychic forces, of a linguistically articulated will to power, which is the will of life itself as expressed and intensified through the agency of individual personalities. Bloom makes this difference clear at the beginning of *Poetry and Repression*, when he reverses Derrida's question: "What is a text, and what must the psyche be if it can be represented by a text?" to: "What is a psyche, and what must a text be if it can be represented by a psyche?"[8] He thus replaces the priority of textual by the priority of psychic realities, which nevertheless remain dependent on language and rhetoric for their self-expression. Bloom etymologically traces 'psyche' to its original meaning of 'to breathe', so that poems become verbal representations of the living 'breath' of an individual will, even though this will can only be realized in rhetorical, tropological form, that is to say, in a broken and self-conflictive form. Nevertheless, the act of poetic troping brings life and text together, linking existential reality and creative structure: "Figuration turns out to be our only link between breathing and making."[9]

But the will to textual life continually encounters resistance, the resistance of other wills, of tradition and authority, of the past and its paralyzing compulsions of repetition. Most of all, it encounters the resistance of great, internalized models of anterior texts which have become idealized norms and thus exert a silencing pressure of conformity on the new writer. If one would venture a generalization from here, one could say that the most fundamental and also most Nietzschean assumption of Bloom is that texts are allegories of the never-ceasing struggle of *life against death*. This struggle, according to the perspective from which we look at it, assumes various shapes, but throughout retains its basic form. On the level of language and textuality, it occurs in the conflict between troping and fixed concepts, between figuration and literal meaning. To Bloom, as to Nietzsche, language is not a static system but a dynamic process of individual utterances. It is word-as-act rather than word-as-meaning. And if to Nietzsche literal speech is figurative speech which has forgotten that it is figurative speech and is thus trapped in a prison-house of 'dead metaphors', Bloom pushes this point even further by equating figuration with textual 'life', and literal meaning with textual 'death'. The act of troping becomes a central means of manifesting the will's desire for life and linguistic survival against the pressures of conformity enacted by established systems of meaning.

On the level of the psyche, the symbolic conflict of life and death appears as the conflict between the desire for original (self-)creation and the anxiety of influence. This idea of an overpowering influence of tradition, of the burden of a cultural past which threatens to paralyze the present, is also an important motif in Nietzsche. His whole cultural critique can be said to be directed against the tradition of a life-negating asceticism, the depressing weight of history, and the exaggerated authority of ancestors which overshadows modern self-definitions. A more direct parallel to Bloom's theory of influence can be seen in *The Genealogy of Morals*, II, 19, where Nietzsche explores the strange guilt complex that characterizes the relationship of later to earlier generations, the deep-rooted anxiety of indebtedness to their cultural achievements which demands continual sacrifices. Fear of the ancestor and his power is inevitably involved in the achievements of the new generation, and the recognition of anteriority and belatedness is the price which has to be paid for new success.[10] Bloom clearly shares this premise, for in his view new creativity also exacts a high price, involving partially sinister rites of sacrifice and symbolic repayment.

Another, even more explicit parallel to Bloom is contained in *Beyond Good and Evil*, where Nietzsche shows in his description of the relationship between Epicurus and Plato how Epicurus uses vicious polemical irony to unmask the superior truth-claims of Platonic philosophy as a particularly effective form of public self-fashioning, but how he also, in his rhetorical 'triumph' over Plato, perhaps disguises ulterior motives of competitive envy and ambition towards this prominent predecessor. Nietzsche demonstrates this ambiguous attitude in what Bloom would call an act of troping by Epicurus, who

calls the Platonists "Dionysiokolakes," meaning "flatterers of Di-
onysios" (the tyrant of Syracuse), thus presenting them as sycophants
of tyrants and also as mere actors or impostors without any authenticity. We have here an example in miniature of the workings of the
revisionary imagination via the act of troping as Bloom describes it in
his theory.

> How malicious philosophers can be! I know of nothing more ven-
> omous than the joke Epicurus permitted himself against Plato and
> the Platonists; he called them *Dionysiokolakes*. That means liter-
> ally — and this is the foreground meaning — "flatterers of Di-
> onysius," in other words, tyrant's baggage and lickspittles; but in
> addition to this he also wants to say, "they are all *actors*, there is
> nothing genuine about them" (for *Dionysokolax* was a popular
> name for an actor). And the latter is really the malice that Epicurus
> aimed at Plato: he was peeved by the grandiose manner, the *mise en
> scène* at which Plato and his disciples were so expert — at which
> Epicurus was not an expert — he, that old schoolmaster from
> Samos, who sat, hidden away, in his little garden at Athens and
> wrote three hundred books — who knows? perhaps from rage and
> ambition against Plato? . . . It took a hundred years until Greece
> found out who this garden god, Epicurus, had been. — Did they
> find out? —[11]

This Nietzschean notion of aggressive-creative competition is clearly
reflected in Bloom's concept of the power struggle between the
ephebe and the precursor, which is the central drama in his story of
poetic influence. We see how the allegorical battle of 'life against
death' is here displaced and symbolically re-enacted in the sense that
the precursor has already successfully performed that battle and that
the whole energy of the ephebe is directed towards absorbing,
through destructive but also self-sacrificial appropriation, the precursor's strength. In this intertextual psychodrama, the deeper structures of texts *are* structures of 'real life', that is of aggression, strife,
envy, distortion, deceit, and indeed violence, even while they disguise themselves in humanist idealizations. *Defence*, according to
Bloom, originally means 'to strike, to hurt,' while *troping* means 'to
turn',[12] so that tropes become weapons in a poetic warfare: "The
strong imagination comes to its painful birth through savagery and
misrepresentation."[13]

What the poet above all needs in this battle is courage (one of the
most frequently occurring words in Bloom), the courage to attack

one's internal enemies, and thereby to confront the risk of self-annihilation, to confront pain and suffering, to confront the fear of the abyss — and, finally, to confront the fear of death. The successful battle against the precursor ultimately becomes a symbolic victory over death itself, and it is here that Bloom locates the deepest motive for poetic creation. Poetry is only the most condensed, intensive, and individualized form of language and rhetoric, because like all human sense systems it is a manifestation of "the will's revulsion against time,"[14] of its revenge upon time and mortality. Indeed, the victory of the strong poet is only complete when he has also reversed the dictatorial law of time itself, the law of earliness and belatedness, of cause and effect, so that in his successful transumption of the precursor poem he no longer appears to have been 'influenced' by it, but, in a sublime revisionary irony, to have "written the precursor's characteristic work" himself. The great poem is thus a victory over time's assertion 'It was!' or, to remain in our allegorical drama, a triumph of life over death.[15]

Once more, the parallels to Nietzsche are striking, most obviously in *Thus Spoke Zarathustra*. In the chapter "Of Redemption," Zarathustra speaks of the will as the great liberator, who however is not finally free, because he remains a prisoner of time, wherein consists his greatest melancholy: "Willing liberates: but what is it that fastens in fetters even the liberator?/ 'It was': that is what the will's teeth-gnashing and most lonely affliction is called. Powerless against that which has been done, the will is an angry spectator of all things past." Therefore: "To redeem the past and to transform every 'It was' into an 'I wanted it thus!' — that alone do I call redemption!" And in the chapter "Of the Vision and the Riddle," Zarathustra speaks of the courage which enables him to overcome his melancholy:

> For courage is the best destroyer — courage that *attacks*: for in every attack there is triumphant music./ Man, however, is the most courageous animal: with his courage he has overcome every animal. With triumphant music he has even overcome every pain; human pain, however, is the deepest pain./ Courage also destroys giddiness at abysses: and where does man not stand at an abyss? Is seeing itself not — seeing abysses?/ . . . Courage, however, is the best destroyer, courage that attacks: it destroys even death, for it says: 'Was *that* life? Well then! Once more!'[16]

As in Bloom, the redemption of the self from the weight of the past, from the paralyzing grip of its own fears, is not a mere matter of re-flection and consciousness but the result of an internal battle, of a *symbolic action* which is also radically existential and which in its "triumphant music" produces its own, irresistable motivation and Dionysian appeal; that is to say, it produces its own art, which is the art of life itself.

Bloom's strong poet is the incarnation of this power of conflictive self-production. He is the transference into literature of Nietzsche's Overman, whom Nietzsche envisages as a Utopian figure in *Zarathustra*, and who is able to face and live with the abyss of exis-tence, and through his 'art' of active self-production helps to stimu-late life, to intensify and enhance it against the deadly forces of tradition and conformity. The Overman is — as yet — an exceptional individual, an aristocrat of the mind, whose capability for creative freedom Nietzsche sets off against the slave mentality of the 'mass man' (*Herdenmensch*). Nietzsche compares the latter to a camel, who patiently bears the yoke of historical morality, while the Overman is like the lion who oversteps historical limitations and courageously fights against the dragon of conventional values, the monstrous, life-denying superego of cultural tradition. He is a Promethean rebel against authority, who is always in the process of becoming himself by constantly remaking himself, without ever 'having' himself. In his famous poem from *The Gay Science*, entitled "Ecce Homo," Nietzsche links the Overman to the element of fire as a metaphor of the unconditional intensity and self-consuming power of his creative urge. Zarathustra himself, the ancient Iranian religious figure who served as Nietzsche's model, had in his radical reforms retained the ancient cult of fire as a mythic center of his spiritual aims, building a Temple of Fire in honor of this elemental destructive-creative force. In Bloom, too, fire is one of the most conspicuous and recurring tropes in which the strong poets express their antithetical imagina-tion.

Beyond the radical critique of cultural idealizations, Bloom and Nietzsche share a prophetic, parareligious attitude which oscillates between rationality and mysticism, between radical scepticism and new mythography. As Bloom points out, his intention is to decon-struct "over-spiritualized" cultural attitudes, but at the same time to oppose the total "despiritualization" of contemporary culture. His strong poet is like Nietzsche's Overman-as-spiritual-leader, through whom the act of creation itself, the 'making' of world and self, become the new, supreme value that emerges after the transvaluation of all values. Art is the central paradigm of this activity, which is also the activity of life itself.[17] It seems to me that it is this privileging of art as the quasi-metaphysical paradigm of all cultural creativity which Bloom shares with Nietzsche, and which significantly distinguishes him from other contemporary theorists.

III

The preceding comparative assessment has shown that the affinities between Bloom and Nietzsche are not restricted to isolated concepts but affect the very substance and texture of Bloom's writings. At the same time, it would be unjustified to reduce Bloom to a mere postmodern variant of Nietzsche, as O'Hara has tried to do. On the contrary, if we examine some of their crucial differences, we become aware how these two writers, in their apparent congeniality, are also quite distinct.

One of the differences is that Bloom, in his methodology, is far more of a *structuralist* and *systematic theorist* than the arcane eccentricities of his style might suggest. Instead of Nietzsche's non-systematic, protean philosophy with its fluid, constantly shifting arguments and improvised perspectives, we find in Bloom a clearly identifiable structural model which, in its virtuoso application to a stunning variety of texts from all possible cultures and historical periods, nevertheless basically remains the same. This is the model which Bloom calls his Map of Misreading and which, though its content always changes, invariably recurs in its principal features. The individual text is like a surface structure which can be deciphered as the transformation of a deep structure of poetic creation which is universally applicable: "In studying poetry," Bloom says, "we are studying a kind of labor that has its own latent principles, principles that can be uncovered and then taught systematically."[18] The act of poetic creation may be a processual and conflictive event, but the psychodramatic logic it follows can be described as a patterned sequence of dialectic stages which, like a transhistorical law of poetics, underlies the apparently arbitrary, subjective misreadings performed by strong poets. When Bloom in his Map of Misreading sets up a classificatory system of analogies between poetic imagery, rhetorical tropes, psychic defenses, and revisionary ratios, which undergo a parallel process of transumption in three successive stages that in themselves follow a recurring triadic pattern, this is clearly un-Nietzschean in its obsessive systematizing. Instead, it strongly reminds one of the charts of structuralists who have tried to uncover the "unconscious laws of the symbolic mind" (Lévi-Strauss) beneath the conscious manifestations of textual surface structures. Bloom here displays an epistemological optimism which is strangely at odds with his stylistic self-fashioning as a postmodern sceptic and ironic nihilist. In his confident universalizations, he betrays his belief in a, however cryptically, structured order of the world, in a truth which can be captured in those conceptual abstractions of the human mind from which Nietzsche wanted to liberate his gay science. This is a paradox not restricted to Bloom but, as pointed out at the beginning, a characteristic self-contradiction of much of postmodern theory which has yet to be discussed in its far-reaching implications.

Closely interrelated with this difference is another difference that has to do with the attitudes of these two writers to *time and the past*. Nietzsche frequently polemicized against an exaggerated preoccupation with history, because it paralyzed the creative will and distracted from the tasks of the present and the future. In the name of this spirit, he proclaimed a radical break with the tradition of occidental philosophy. In Bloom, what T. S. Eliot called the "historical sense," remains particularly strong, even though it is more sinister and antagonistic than in Eliot. Bloom does not write against or outside of tradition, but rewrites it from within. Even his strong poet cannot escape the cultural past, however viciously he attacks it, for only by confronting it will he be able to express his creative will to power in the first place. The past is omnipresent, it sets the inescapable conditions for whatever claims to be 'new'.[19] Even though the final aim of creativity, epitomized in poetry, is to transcend the tyranny of time, it is nevertheless situated in an irreversible historical process which defines the terms of every new creation. Bloom is thus retrospective where Nietzsche is prospective; he labors in the prisonhouse of history, where Nietzsche shatters its very foundations in order to rebuild it into a playground for his envisioned Overman of the future.

There is, then, a sense of determinism in Bloom's position, a sense of overpowering forces outside the self by which the psyche is constantly threatened to be overwhelmed or annihilated. The emphasis is on structures of compulsion, of repetition, of repression, of anxiety, of guilt, of revenge and defence — in other words on negative, reactionary and self-alienating categories implying the melancholic assumption that the past irrevocably delimits and indeed deforms the possibilities of the present, and that the great, decisive things in cultural history have already happened before the appearance of the modern self, whose only means of spiritual survival is therefore to come to terms with its own belatedness. This melancholy of belatedness seems to be rooted in a more generally *negative* view of man and the world. For Bloom, the world in which we live is a hostile place, constantly alienating us from ourselves, always preventing us from becoming ourselves. It is a place of error and deception, a structure of illusions built on abysmal nothingness, empty of meaning. Nietzsche, of course, shared this view of radical negativity; indeed, he made it the necessary basis of any new beginning. Yet the decisive step of his Overman is to face the abyss in order to transcend it towards an affirmation of all existence, including its negativity. To be sure, Bloom's poetic Overman shows clear parallels to this concept: the courage of confronting the abyss in the deadly fight with his own deepest fears is his only way of becoming a truly strong poet. But the aim and redemptive outcome of this fight is quite different. In the case of Nietzsche, there is a transcending of suffering and alienation towards tragic acceptance, an overcoming of the *horror vacui* by an *amor fati*, a Dionysian celebration of eternal becoming as an inseparable unity of creation *and* destruction. This affirmation includes temporality and death, and thus includes the disappearance of the individual in the larger process of Life from which it has temporarily emerged. In Bloom, the transcendent impulse and the redemptive struggle are directed *against* time and death, and towards the symbolic immortality of the individual self.

Indeed, it seems as if the dualism between material and spiritual world, between body and soul, which Nietzsche set out to abolish, reappears in Bloom in poetological form. This may be due, at least in part, to the continuing influence of Romantic ideas in Bloom's theory. Bloom began his academic work as a scholar of Romanticism, and the visionary aspects of that movement, in the sense of an aspiring of the finite self towards the infinite, of the desire to immortalize oneself by becoming the creator of one's own world, can still be noticed, although in a more broken and paradoxical way, in Bloom. Nanette Altevers, in fact, has argued that Bloom's oeuvre, rather than dealing with matters of history and rhetorics, follows instead the pattern of the Romantic quest for the autonomous self as exemplified, above all, in Wordsworth's *Prelude*.[20] Altevers points out the "transcendental" conception of the sovereign self which has more and more clearly reasserted itself in Bloom's more recent writings. But here it is essential to add that Bloom's is a *negative transcendentalism*, which must be seen as the reverse side of his rather deterministic view of history and of an alien world hostile to the self. If the self is unfree in this world, it follows that it can achieve its freedom only through the act of negating the world. As mentioned above, Bloom's poetic transcendentalism is as much akin to the satanic school of Romantic poetry as to Wordsworth, sharing with it the spirit of rebellion against all authority outside the self, as is exemplified in Milton's Satan, in Blake, or indeed in Shelley, on whom Bloom published his first book.

There is, however, still another source for Bloom's negative transcendentalism, which as yet has attracted little attention but which should be mentioned in this context, and that is the role of *gnosis* as a speculative framework which has become increasingly important in the development of Bloom's thought. In *Agon*, Bloom explicitly defines his position as that of a "Jewish gnostic," and goes on to argue that his theory of poetry centers on the idea that poetry is itself essentially a form of gnosis.[21] Gnosis means 'knowledge of God', not however in a positive, direct sense but again *ex negativo*, as a form of knowing which must strive through and beyond the falseness of creation, although it is imprisoned in it. This world is a fallen world, and the body is only a temporary vessel for the migrating soul, for the primeval self which is at once demonic and potentially divine, and which precedes and outlives the empirical self, constantly struggling for its return to the higher sphere of the *pleroma* or state of original fullness from which it has fallen. For this ascension to higher aeons and spheres, the self must fight against the forces of alienation, the angels of spiritual death who threaten to take away its light, the 'spark' or 'pneuma' which is the original creative potency of the self. As we have seen, texts are the prime medium of this gnostic struggle for regaining one's pneuma or 'breath', that is to say one's deeper self, through the fight with the angel of death into whom the idealized precursor turns.

As becomes clear at this point, the power which the poet gains in his battle is in the end quite different from the will to power in a Nietzschean sense, because the gnostic "inmost self is absolutely alien to the cosmos, to everything natural,"[22] involving ascetic sublimation of bodily drives rather than being, as in Nietzsche, a manifestation of them. The asceticism which Nietzsche castigated as a symptom of Western civilization's aberration from natural life thus re-enters Bloom's discourse, and with it the dualism between the physical and the metaphysical world, which Bloom describes in the opposition between the *psychic* or worldly self and the *pneumatic* or transmundane self. Gnosis originated from a rebellion against mainstream Judaeo-Christian beliefs, rejecting the presence of God in the historical world, and claiming paradoxical knowledge of the divine Creator precisely through the recognition of His final unknowability. Gnostic knowledge is thus antithetical, paradoxical knowledge, a form of 'negative theology' characterized by mystic radicalism but opposed to any fixed system of belief, as Bloom asserts. And it is here that he sees the affinity, indeed the identity between gnosis and poetry, as distinguished from rational, philosophical knowledge. Poetry becomes a form of gnostic knowledge, in the act of writing as well as in the act of reading, and in this it is itself a negative theology, a paradoxical quest for absolute self-knowledge which is authenticated in the self's discovery of its ultimate unknowability. It is a "performative" kind of knowledge which achieves a momentary victory of the *pneuma* over the *psyche*, and can transmit to the reader its power to lift itself "beyond experience."[23]

We can see here how Bloom's position changes towards a more mystical, less historical or rhetorical stance in his later works. But we can also see how assumptions of his previous works are preserved and gain an additional dimension. For the poetic presence of the gnostic self is only there in its absence: "our essence is immortal only because it is evasive."[24] And therefore the act of troping, of a constant "turning" which is a "flowing, a becoming, an Orphic metamorphosis," is the only form of true poetic self-presentation, still containing the revisionary notion of intertextual strife, but at the same time yielding, through its very *aporias*, "a joyful sense of freedom."[25]

This last quotation is from Ralph Waldo Emerson's *The Poet*, and brings us to a final and, to my mind, crucial difference between Bloom and Nietzsche that Bloom himself likes to call the *American difference*. Emerson is Bloom's prime example not only for this difference, but for his theory of poetry-as-gnosis in general. He is the archetypal poet who turns the multiple influences that he absorbs into the medium of a troping which, in its radical fluidity and transitoriness, actualizes the living 'pneuma' of that deeper, aboriginal self which would be buried in any fixations of meaning or rhetorical figuration.[26] This is not the postmodern literary pragmatism which Richard Poirier ascribes to Emerson, also locating the American difference in the paradigmatic role of Emerson and his individualization of texts into self-presentational, discontinuous speech-acts. Rather, it involves a more existential or spiritual pragmatism in which the poet again performs the drama of creation by catastrophe, which is the original drama of creation itself, following his demonic revisionary drive to turn his own belatedness into a continual earliness, into ever new beginnings. All poetic energies are mobilized against the mystical strength of the past in order for the self to reclaim its aboriginal freedom. Emerson's texts are characterized by a fusion or paradoxical coexistence of the most advanced and most regressive stages of self and culture, by a radical openness which brings together the modern and the archaic, the civilized and the barbarous or "shamanistic" aspects of the self: "Emerson . . . is at once our sweetest and most civilized writer and our wildest and most primitivistic."[27] In this audacity of unlimited self-acceptance, the world is humanized in the poetic act to the point where the poet-as-maker himself becomes divine, a "liberating god," as Emerson calls him.

Unlike Nietzsche's Overman, this Emersonian poet is not a "heroic vitalist,"[28] a tragic affirmer of Life against the individual self, but rather an existential humanist affirming the individual self against the apparently superior force of fate. By achieving the liberation of the transcendental self from the boundaries of all traditions and external authorities, Emerson has founded what Bloom calls the *"American Religion."* And the decisive difference from European forms of religion, including Nietzsche's nihilist reversal, is that this is no longer a religion of *"God*-reliance" but of pure *"self*-reliance."[29] "God" in this context means all authority or primary power outside the self to which the self is only secondary, to which it is a subordinate function or element. In Nietzsche, this power beyond the self would be life as that larger process of growth and decay, of creation and destruction, to which the individual self, like all of existence, is subjected, and in which it can triumph only by accepting its own disappearance. In Emerson, and the American Religion that Bloom extracts from him, the self returns from the bondage of the temporal, material, or textual world to its original freedom and creative power, which is a spiritual power that knows it is finally removed from time and history, solely reliant on itself. The only form in which this religion is adequately expressed is literature, for only in literature can the paradoxical act of gnostic self-knowledge be performed, in which the self, by always going beyond itself, discovers itself as the creator of its world. This creative power of strong poets is quite real to Bloom. Emerson, the strongest of all 'modern poets', becomes nothing less than the demiurge of American culture who, with his religion of self-reliance, has inescapably set the terms for all later American consciousness and writing. "The mind of Emerson is the mind of America, for worse and for glory," states Bloom.[30] And by aligning himself with Emerson, and claiming him as prime witness and inspiring precursor of his own theories, Bloom can repeat Emerson's gesture of cultural independence, placing himself within the frame of a distinctly American tradition which he can set off against Continental types of contemporary literary theory.

Nietzsche is an exemplary touchstone for Bloom's American difference, because he is both so close to and yet so far removed from Emerson and Bloom. Nietzsche's Overman, who clearly has inspired Bloom's idea of the strong poet, finds the ultimate test of disillusioned truthfulness in the laughing recognition of the law: "die Art ist alles, Einer ist immer Keiner" — that the life of the single individual, for all his suffering and self-importance, is of no weight in the greater life of the species.[31] In contrast, the core of the American Religion, which is also the core of Bloom's theory, is the apotheosis of the individual self. In spite of all its negativity and revisionary anger, then, Bloom's position is in the end a humanist position. For all its iconoclastic rhetoric of deconstruction and cultural radicalism, it offers not so much a contribution to a new form of literary history or literary anthropology but to a new metaphysics of literature which is indistinguishably interfused with a central American myth, the myth of the sovereign self.

Notes

[1] Frank Lentricchia, "Series Editor's Foreword," in Harold Bloom, *The Breaking of the Vessels* (Chicago/London: U of Chicago P, 1982), p. x.

[2] Daniel O'Hara, "The Genius of Irony: Nietzsche in Bloom," in Jonathan Arac et al. (eds.), *The Yale Critics: Deconstruction in America* (Minneapolis: U of Minnesota P, 1983), p. 123.

[3] "On Truth and Lie in an Extra-Moral Sense," in *The Portable Nietzsche*, trans. Walter Kaufmann (New York: Penguin, 1976), p. 46.

[4] *On the Genealogy of Morals*, trans. Walter Kaufmann and R. J. Hollingdale (New York: Random House, 1967), III, 25.

[5] *The Gay Science*, trans. Walter Kaufmann (New York: Random House, 1974), II, 107.

[6] *Beyond Good and Evil*, trans. Walter Kaufmann (New York: Random House, 1989), I, 21.

[7] See, for example, the following passage from his posthumous papers: "The individual both *is* and *produces* what is wholly *new*; he is absolute, all acts wholly *his own*." Quoted from Werner Hamacher, "Disgregation of the Will: Nietzsche on the Individual and Individuality," in *Friedrich Nietzsche*, ed. and intr. Harold Bloom (New York: Chelsea House, 1987), p. 172.

[8] *Poetry and Repression* (New Haven: Yale UP, 1976), p. 1.

[9] *Poetry and Repression*, p. 2.

[10] *Genealogy of Morals*, II, 19.

[11] *Beyond Good and Evil*, I, 7.

[12] *Poetry and Repression*, p. 10.

[13] Harold Bloom, *The Anxiety of Influence: A Theory of Poetry* (New York/Oxford: Oxford UP, 1973), p. 86.

[14] *Poetry and Repression*, p. 10.

[15] *Anxiety of Influence*, p. 16 and passim.

[16] *Thus Spoke Zarathustra*, trans. R. J. Hollingdale (Harmondsworth: Penguin, 1961), pp. 161 and 177–78. I have translated "klingendes Spiel" not as "triumphant shout" but as "triumphant music."

[17] Theo Meyer in *Nietzsche und die Kunst* (Tübingen/Basel: Francke, 1993) points out that this apotheosis of art is characteristic of Nietzsche's later phase, whereas in his middle period he had included art in his critique of cultural illusions.

[18] *Poetry and Repression*, p. 25.

[19] It seems to me that in this respect, Bloom and O'Hara have more in common with each other than with Nietzsche. I take seriously Nietzsche's subtitle to *Beyond Good and Evil* as a "Prelude to a Philosophy of the Future," and I agree with Michel Haar that the notion of the Overman also implies an alternative to the present and a projection into the future: "the philosophy of the Overman unfolds as a philosophy of the Future while yet presenting something quite different from the philosophy of Progress." ("Nietzsche and Metaphysical Language," in *The New Nietzsche*, ed. David B. Allison, Cambridge/London: MIT Press, 1985, p. 24.)

[20] Nanette Altevers, "The Revisionary Company: Harold Bloom's 'Last Romanticism'," *New Literary History*, 23 (1992), 361–82. "Like Wordsworth's *Prelude*, Bloom's 'severe poem'[i.e., *The Anxiety of Influence*] is a psychological autobiography which narrates the history or growth of the poet's own mind" (p. 363). Although I agree with Altevers's general observation that Romantic influences shape Bloom's work in a significant way, her exclusive claim in regard to Bloom's indebtedness to Wordsworth is as one-sided as is O'Hara's equally exclusive claim in regard to his indebtedness to Nietzsche.

[21] Harold Bloom, *Agon: Towards a Theory of Revisionism* (New York/Oxford: Oxford UP, 1982), pp. 1ff.

[22] *Agon*, p. 8.

[23] *Agon*, p. 13.

[24] *Agon*, pp. 34–35.

[25] *Agon*, p. 33.

[26] See *Agon*, "Prelude" and first chapter.

[27] Harold Bloom, *Figures of Capable Imagination* (New York: Seabury, 1976), p. 51.

[28] *Figures of Capable Imagination*, p. 53.

[29] Cf. *Agon*, "Emerson: The American Religion," pp. 145–78.

[30] *Agon*, p. 145.

[31] *The Gay Science*, I, 1: " . . . the species is everything, *one* is always none."

Robert Ackermann

Nietzsche Ground Zero

I ADDRESS THOSE scholars who have experienced feelings of alienation when serving as committee readers on PhD dissertation
committees in the following circumstances. The dissertations in
question advance large but surprising claims about well-known philosophers, claims that are apparently supported in the dissertations by
extensive quotation. These claims nevertheless seem dead wrong
when measured against the reader's automatic intuitions concerning
the philosopher being discussed. At the defense, having raised questions about the claims and the quotations, the reader, with serious
misgivings, and regretting not having more adequately prepared,
yields to the sheer presence of quotation and the implications of col-
legiality, and signs approval.

I confess my own sins. In recent years, I have served as a committee member on dissertation committees where the candidates' dissertations have charged some very well known contemporary
philosophers with major and obvious contradiction. The dissertations
supported their charges of contradiction with showcased quotations.
On the occasion of each defense, and in the absence of a detailed
personal knowledge of the philosopher under attack, I felt that this
philosopher was too good to have held simultaneously the two views
imputed to him in the dissertation. My doubts bolstered by the
overall quality of the discussion, I went on to question whether the
passages supporting one side or the other of the contradiction could
mean what the candidate said they meant, somewhat arbitrarily
picking as the wrong claim the one that seemed sillier to me, but
hampered by an inability to produce matching quotations against the
interpretations offered. Uttering some carefully crafted dark remarks

during the discussion of the candidate's performance, I signed my name as illegibly as possible, and left — depressed.

Crude versions of the hermeneutical circle were called into play to respond to my misgivings on each and every one of the occasions described. It was always suggested that "any" readings whatsoever that are backed by dogged determination and specific quotation are legitimate. This appeal to the hermeneutical circle works in the following way. A reading can be said to be defensible if its large interpretive claims are consistent with sentences of relevant text marshalled in their support. Large claims are given by the reader as *hypotheses* of "interpretation," and the legitimacy of these claims is then established by quoting sentences of text. It doesn't really matter that the large hypotheses can't themselves be quoted as text. Authors don't often admit to inconsistency, and some interpretive claims could not be cited in an author's original text because the relevant ideas and vocabulary in question came into scholarly discourse as a *reaction* to the author's work. Large and novel claims can be advanced as completely new readings of an author, provided that the author's writings hold sentences that support the claims. (Somehow, they always seem to be there.) Where sentences are noticed that do not support the claims, they can be treated as irony, sarcasm, humor, or whatever, that is, as having some tropic meaning consistent with the large interpretive claims being made, or as evidence of slips or minor contradictions, or sometimes as too trivial to be mentioned.

In this form, the hermeneutical circle is vacuously self-confirming. The problem is that the use of the large interpretive claims to select the "serious" supportive sentences, coupled with the play of chosen dismissive tropes, means that the author's text can't really repudiate the interpretation if the interpreter is at all clever.[1] It is not being suggested here that hermeneutics should have as its goal a single "best" reading, nor that completely new and better readings of texts are impossible.[2] Nor is it being suggested that employment of the vacuous hermeneutical circle is essentially linked to dissertation writing. Its described use in dissertations becomes that of many books in philosophy.

Insofar as the hermeneutical circle describes an interplay between textual detail and global textual meanings, it should really be conceived as a hermeneutical spiral, or even as a hermeneutical strange attractor. The reason for this is that a relatively coherent text must always modulate the link between its detail and its major claims through intermediate claims of increasing scope that reduce ambiguity by pruning away careless possibilities latent in mere detail. This modulation, while preserving the importance of detail, places heavy constraints on global meaning. There are *many* intermediate levels of meaning and sensibility modulating between large claims and individual sentences in any important philosophical text. These modulations must be controlled by readers if legitimate readings of philosophical texts are to be developed. As with large interpretive claims, relevant intermediate-level claims are often not succinctly expressed as specific sentences in the text, but their invocation should explain why individual sentences in the author's texts have the detailed construction that they do, as opposed to other possible constructions with very similar meanings. In many cases, sufficiently large passages of text also exhibit distinctive material features, apart from the hypotheses of meaning involved, that interpretation should be able to comment on. When the intermediate levels of interpretation are ignored, and text is taken simply as text, as in the deployment of the logic of the vacuous hermeneutical circle, it may be true that texts can mean anything. Fixing intermediaries to control interpretation cannot force a single defensible interpretation of complex texts completely; that's why interpretation always remains open and interesting, even if not all interpretations are equally legitimate.

Large interpretive claims are often produced by readers who advance these claims *within* an already existing and known set of analytic categories. Such readers are typically slotting their authors into familiar conceptual terrain for polemical purposes. The problem is not merely that familiar interpretive notions are involved. The problem is that their use in vacuous hermeneutical circles allows interpretive hypotheses to be formulated quite independently of particular features of the text under interpretation.

Turning to Nietzsche, one of the distinctive features of his corpus is his widespread use of aphorisms. Vacuous hermeneutics has argued that Nietzsche was too incoherent to mount persuasive arguments, and the aphorisms stand as a tribute to his confusions of thought. This highly abstract argument can then be supported — just by quoting some aphorisms that seem to have little to do with one another. This is not a level of interpretation worth pursuing in any detail, and its practitioners don't bother. They're busy with a global

positioning of Nietzsche for purposes of refutation. Disagree with
Nietzsche or not, Nietzsche took himself to be a philosopher whose
philosophical claims couldn't be captured within the existing philosophical vocabulary. Nietzsche said that he deliberately wrote aphorisms in the service of a philosophical writing strategy designed to
accommodate his perception that what he had to say couldn't be
formulated within existing conceptual frameworks. The aphorisms
were not intended as discursive conceptual development, but as
goads and indicators to new paths of investigation. Philosophers who
feel that careful discursive development can express their views don't
usually write aphorisms. Nietzsche may have been wrong about himself, or trying to fool us, but we can begin by thinking it unlikely —
if Nietzsche is worth reading at all — that he is a positivist, or a
pragmatist, or a Buddhist,[3] or anything that can be so easily set
down. When he is interpreted vacuously, however, Nietzsche is often
presented as holding extreme views with respect to those held by his
interpreter. The intuition that his views are extreme is correct.

I want to illustrate some severe misreadings of Nietzsche through
the use of the vacuous hermeneutical circle by considering contemporary Nietzsche interpretation in the United States insofar as it occurs apart from the detailed scholarship of Nietzsche specialists, and
is used to slot Nietzsche into some already accepted philosophical
category for the purpose of arguing a philosophical thesis. The writers who use Nietzsche in this way believe that they can easily express
his global views, and that their readings can be grounded (if necessary) in short passages from Nietzsche's texts. Readers may assume
that this kind of secondary scholarly use of Nietzsche is not important, or that it is a phenomenon most clearly marked in the writings
of authors who are not philosophically trained. But the problem is
more serious. The use of the vacuous hermeneutical circle allows
Nietzsche to be badly misread no matter what the background sophistication of the argumentative text in which he is situated. To illustrate this, I will here consider four interpretations of Nietzsche
that are used in the service of larger argumentative projects. These
four are offered by an unknown graduate student, by two established
academic authors writing outside professional philosophy
(psychology and political theory), and by a very well known contemporary philosopher. There is surprisingly little to choose between
these four in terms of misreading. It would be pointlessly utopian to

suggest censorship or sanctions for misreading. Most sophisticated readers recognize that quotation in the service of polemics is likely to truncate the sophistication of an author's views. So what is the harm? The harm is that genuinely original positions can get so relentlessly trivialized by mechanical labelling that they are simply lost as intellectual possibilities. This, I think, is what has happened frequently to Nietzsche. He *is* original, because he *isn't* at all any of the philosophers he is taken to be when the vacuous hermeneutical circle is invoked.

Nietzsche is frequently read as some kind of an interpretive relativist, and then taken as a convenient icon for a relativism to be "refuted" by the main thrust of the argument in which he is mentioned. Writers who do this allude to passages that suggest Nietzsche took truth to be a metaphor, that he believed in the play of interpretations, that he believed in masks behind masks, etc. But wait! No careful reader of the *Untimely Meditation* on David Strauss could accept that Nietzsche thought there were defensible readings of Strauss as a "serious" philosopher (although praise by others of Strauss as a serious philosopher is quoted by Nietzsche). Among those who can read, Nietzsche thinks, Strauss can't be taken seriously. The close examination of specific sentences from Strauss's writings in the relevant *Untimely Meditation* shows in detail their literal incoherence. Nietzsche is coherently arguing that Strauss has nothing coherent to say *because his grammar is too confused to permit intelligible expression.*[4] Similarly, no careful reader of Nietzsche on philological and genealogical methods could imagine that Nietzsche thought that just any old reading of Homer, or Socrates, or Plato, was possible. Nietzsche's notion of reading (*not* to be confused with the everyday notion of "reading") is highly normative, and it depends on a close and ruminative scrutiny of texts. Not everyone whose eyes move across a page and who then reports what they see in the text is a reader in Nietzsche's terms. The democratic notion of "newspaper" reading may be like that, but it isn't Nietzsche's notion. Nietzsche thought some readings of crucial authors so much better than others that the former could be said to be "right" and the latter "wrong," even if no *best* "right" reading could be attained in the face of the Dionysian flux driving human history. There are few genuine readers in Nietzsche's normative sense. They must see literally everything that is to be seen in a text, including what isn't there. Nietzsche came to feel that his own works had found no readers in this sense. Since Nietzsche's normative and aristocratic scholarship is on plain view in many passages, it is clear that he was no interpretive relativist, and passages that encourage reading Nietzsche as a relativist should be approached with caution.

Nietzsche Ground Zero refers to interpretations of Nietzsche through employment of the vacuous hermeneutical circle. This is the place where he is usually read, and where he is often taken as a relativist. What is not noticed at Ground Zero is the obverse of what Nietzsche noticed as missing in the writings of David Strauss — the notion of a complicated and coherent structure whose intermediate structural linkages could be traced. Nietzsche had very clear views about Strauss. Strauss's works were an eclectic stew of sentences taken from here and there, and simply cobbled together. Therefore Strauss could be read vacuously, as holding anything. Strauss was thus a relativist. Nietzsche felt that his own works were not cobbled together, and could not be read as relativistic. Readings of Nietzsche that accuse him of piling up incoherencies, if Nietzsche is right about this, *must* be wrong.

I now turn to the four examples of *Nietzsche Ground Zero* as the topic of my essay. The first instance, an article by an American graduate student completing a dissertation on race and class in American politics, reads Nietzsche as a relativist.[5] If you're tired of Nietzsche's influence on Hitler, the author allows that Nietzsche's opinions were but a minor source of fascism, but, bringing the attack up to date, the author thinks that Nietzsche's opinions are a major source of the "post-modern politics of difference" that defends the cultural legitimacy of the Sex Pistols: "That such an idea [difference], one hundred years later, would become the basis for vaunting the radical "difference" of a gay Black cross-dressing woman of the underclass did not, in all probability, occur to Nietzsche."[6] (I grant the explicitly expressed opinion.) It is then argued (roughly) that a catastrophic economic crisis is being ignored by contemporary intellectuals because their attention is directed to issues of "cultural" difference that are in turn misconstrued by post-modern "radical critics" of "Eurocentrism" who equally accept Eurocentrism without recognizing that they do. The author is a revisionist Marxist universalist concerned to trace what he sees as the emergence of a world culture not noticeable to those locked in the debates over "difference." The charge against Nietzsche is that his relativism of cultural "difference" leads to the vacuous radicalism of Foucault and Derrida, critics of Eurocentrism that do not escape the limits of Eurocentrism.[7]

Richard Shweder, a distinguished psychologist, provides our second example. He mounts an extensive discussion of Nietzsche in which he accuses him of having failed to achieve a satisfactory relativism (the one Shweder is seeking) because Nietzsche was an anti-relativist positivist (!).[8] Here Nietzsche is once again linked to relativism, but this time with reversed polarity. Shweder's positivist Nietzsche refuses all posits of higher cultural realities and all symbolic forms as having no reference. This, Shweder seems to fear, prevents cultural "differences" from being taken seriously, for they cease to exist, and hence a true relativism cannot be suspended between equally viable cultural options. Nietzsche believed neither in a chic politics of "difference" nor in the non-existence of cultures. What he thought was that some cultures were superior to others at particular times in being more life-affirming at that time.[9] What he also thought was that European life was dead (or nearly dead), terminated in a nihilism that had no resources for grounding new attempts at transcendent life-affirming values. Had he known in detail about non-European, non-Christian cultures, he might have found some of them decisively superior to the European Christian culture of his time. What we do know is that he thought some culture beyond "good and evil" (this last his reference to the exhausted value table of Christianity) *had* to be found to replace European culture if Europeans were to avoid annihilation. He did think that a revised version of the ancient Greek noble value table of "good and bad" (a value table with eastern antecedents) could do the job.

Shweder takes Nietzsche's assertion "God is dead" as encoding the absence of transcendent meanings. But at Ground Zero, the assertion that God is dead possesses no tense. Nietzsche meant that God (yes, the Christian God) *had been alive.* Why is this so hard to see from Ground Zero? Because Nietzsche's interpreters who stand there think in terms of timeless reference (if God doesn't exist, then he never really was, since he's eternal by definition) and they miss Nietzsche's quite opposite conclusion that what exists can be said to exist only for the time in which it supports or thwarts will to power. God had been powerful, but now he is dead because all his options have been played out on what is now the lifeless field of nihilism. He has nothing more to say now. God has become irrelevant to life. There is nothing *supernatural*, to be sure, so that the details have to be coded into historical events taking place entirely on Earth, but Gods do exist, as this one did. They exist as creatures that live and then die. Nietzsche might be wrong, but his detractors all too often make him sound stupid by simply abusing his notion of history. Something is wrong when Nietzsche is forced into a conceptual space divided into just two possibilities: skeptical positivism or the possibility of multiple objective worlds. What's wrong is that alleged Nietzschean positivism and Shweder's post-Nietzschean anthropology are both static, frozen in time, non-Nietzschean.

We turn now to the third example, one in which Nietzsche's "relativism" is said to be somehow responsible for the degradation of the morals of American youth, a thesis argued by explicit reference to Nietzsche in Allan Bloom's *The Closing of the American Mind*.[10] Bloom's book works only on the premise that his American readers are just as ignorant as he describes them to be. In a way, the book is a perfectly wild read, filled with such fun maneuvers as blasting Nietzsche for Nietzsche blasting democratic education right after Bloom devotes some number of pages to his own blasting of the ignorance of American students. (Surely Nietzsche should have been on target for Bloom just this one time.) Students are described by Bloom as entering the American university as naive relativists only to be fully convinced of theoretical relativism by reading Nietzsche there.

A book allegedly devoted to the relentless pursuit of truth and to dismissing as irrational any choices of value made in the absence of the crucible of democratic dialogue is in fact filled with gratuitous insult. The view suggested by this irony that makes Bloom a great American humorist is difficult to square with the general tone of the text, which will here be taken to balance the impression of possible levity. Bloom is angry about the subversion of open Greek democratic and progressive values carried out in the American university due to the influence of obscurantist Germans, notably Freud, Nietzsche, Marx, and Weber. No doubt in an effort to keep argumentative lines clear, Bloom neglects to mention Leibniz, ignores Humboldt, and only grazes Kant.

Bloom offers two interpretations quite similar to those we have already met. Nietzsche is accused of relativism, as he was above by the first author (Goldner). On the other hand, Bloom's misreading is linked to Shweder's in his repetition of the well-worn line that Nietzsche denies the existence of God. Indeed, Bloom wears it down even more through repetition. Nietzsche is repeatedly quoted as saying that God is dead: "The quest begun by Odysseus and continued over three millennia has come to an end with the observation that there is nothing to seek. This alleged fact was announced by Nietzsche just over a century ago when he said, 'God is dead'" (143). "'God is dead,' Nietzsche proclaimed . . . Man, who loved and needed God, has lost his Father and Savior without possibility of resurrection. The joy of liberation one finds in Marx has turned into terror at man's unprotectedness" (195). The travel agency is more upscale, but we're still at Ground Zero!

Our fourth example of the use of Nietzsche is offered in the works of Richard Rorty.[11] Surely, by having attained the secure ground of philosophical accomplishment, we will now have avoided Nietzsche Ground Zero. The first thing to notice is that if Nietzsche succeeded in dancing when he wrote — as I believe he did in his exquisitely light use of formidable scholarship — Rorty manages to remain philosophically conversational, just the style he urges as appropriate for philosophy. For example: "Such a Nietzschean line of thought leads to the kind of avant-garde philosophy which Lyotard admires in Deleuze."[12] This remark occurs as a Rortyan developmental aside in a discussion of how a Deweyan attempt to frame a sense of local community splits the difference between Habermas and Lyotard. No heavy scholarship here (or indeed anywhere else in Rorty's *Philosophical Papers*), just suggestive conversation. It would be wrong, then, to expect heavy textual analysis from Rorty. It would also be wrong to tie suggestions down to a dreary insistence on consistency. Nonetheless, when Nietzsche is mentioned, Rorty slots him into a conceptual space that is already available to us. At times, Nietzsche is paired with Dewey, and valorized as a pragmatist: "I see Nietzsche as the figure who did most to convince European intellectuals of the doctrines which were purveyed to Americans by James and Dewey."[13] Elsewhere, Nietzsche is paired with Loyola, both taken as ideological loonies who exist outside the realm of rational persuasion: Nietzsche and Loyola "are crazy because the limits

of sanity are set by what *we* can take seriously."[14] What links
Nietzsche and Loyola here is the notion that truth is a matter of
solidarity or agreement (not reference). On this occasion, one of very
few, Rorty stops chatting for a moment, takes a book down from the
shelf, and quotes (or does he quote from memory?):

> He [Nietzsche] wanted us to be able to think of truth as: "a mobile
> army of metaphors, metonymns, and anthropomorphisms — in
> short a sum of human relations, which have been enhanced, trans-
> posed, and embellished poetically and rhetorically and which after
> long use seem firm, canonical and obligatory to a people."[15]

Now, are we making progress? Rorty's approach makes Nietzsche
redundant in the history of philosophy. If we start with Loyola and
Dewey, each of them resonating with one of the two different
Nietzsches, we can place Nietzsche's views in terms of already existing conceptual resources. But can these two Nietzsches be grounded
in relevant passages of text? While pragmatism may be more flexible
than positivism, attaching Nietzsche to pragmatism seems to repeat
the problems of attaching him to positivism, whether or not one
shields him from thinking that truth is a matter of convergence over
time.[16] The basic problem is Nietzsche's very low opinion of science
(in the sense in which science is commonly taken, as physics, chemis-
try, etc.). Nietzsche saw science as the utilitarian manufacture of facts
already anticipated in a grounding value table that had pretty well
exhausted itself. Pragmatists, to make short work of it, must respect
science, and Nietzsche does not (in terms of his own version of what
science is commonly taken to be).[17] If I may be conversational for a
moment, Nietzsche's view of science, in common with that of nearly
all nineteenth-century philosophers, was almost certainly wrong. If
Nietzsche had thought of science as grounded in Kuhnian paradigms, and hence in value tables of a kind, he might have had a different philosophy of science, he might have valorized science, and he
might indeed have been a precursor of pragmatism. But he didn't.

Now let us turn back to Rorty's anti-metaphysical, anti-referential
Nietzsche, who has already made two earlier appearances. Is it true
that Nietzsche denies the coherence of representation or reference?
Isn't it clear that he does so only when representation or reference
are taken as *timeless* links between language and the world in an
epistemology that takes an atemporal notion of *truth* as its basic
category? When Nietzsche gives up reference or representation as

timeless, he doesn't lapse into incoherence except for those who must think reference is timeless. He is stating that specific values make "references" that are life-serving (and hence *exist* in his historical sense) for certain periods of human history. These references are not the timeless references of standard analytic semantic theory. For Nietzsche, there is only the world of becoming in which we exist as animals, but as animals capable of defeating or tricking change for a period of time (overcoming or transcending nature) through value posits that must eventually run back down into Dionysian chaos. Life-serving posits simply run back more slowly. Nietzsche's opposition to metaphysics was not coded into a (silly) claim that reference is irrelevant (there *is* Dionysian chaos!), but into a denial that there is a "world of Being" that can serve as the address of reference (as in all of the Platonisms that darkened metaphysics). He didn't simply reverse polarities within metaphysical space, he tried to wipe out the essential category of an explanatory world *behind* this world, or the necessity for thinking large textual structures as the bearers of meaning. In this way, he can be regarded as having overcome metaphysics more decisively than those who have followed him.

Rorty's quotation about truth as an army of metaphors, etc., is often quoted as representing Nietzsche's "theory" of truth. This quotation occurs in an early (and unpublished) text, and it is not substantially developed in Nietzsche's later work — because it is not Nietzsche's theory of truth; it is rather his account of what ordinary truth is when you strip away its supposed reference to a world of (timeless) meanings. What are ordinarily considered truths have *histories*. They *become* firm and obligatory over time. So the quotation is not a "theory" of truth, but the observation that truths may grow and then die, becoming life-denying as they ossify. Readers who miss this historicity, as they so often do in the imputed quotation about the death of God, fail to hear the Nietzschean beat. They are reading as though Nietzsche replaced one notion of reference with another, in other words, they are misreading from an assumption that objectivity and relativism exhaust the possibilities. Nietzsche's *are* dangerous thoughts for such readers. They are *neither* positivist/pragmatist (one logic for all) *nor* relativist (to each his own logic). They are dangerous because they require *new* thinking about cultural superiority, and they require new concepts with which to express that thinking.

Nietzsche isn't available for inspection at Ground Zero. He had a feeling and a need for heights, for the heights of real mountains, not the heights of mountainous logical abstractions. At the very least, one needs to *look up* from Ground Zero to see where he was standing.

Notes

[1] The hermeneutical circle seems often to be conceived as though its legitimacy was related to the hypothetical-deductive method in science, global claims corresponding to hypotheses, and individual sentences providing the data for possible confirmation. The problem with the parallel is that good scientific hypotheses don't typically arrive as candidates for confirmation out of the blue, but arise from analogy to previously successful hypotheses. In this case, something like a hermeneutical spiral out of previously successful interpretation is at work. Using the vacuous hermeneutical circle is like positing "useless" theoretical entities, arguing that nothing in the data proves that they don't exist, and that they can be invoked in "explanations," without weighing the costs of their postulation against rival hypotheses.

[2] New readings of value generally result from bringing new concepts to bear on the interpretation of texts, not from generating "new" authorial positions in terms of existing critical vocabulary. Deleuze's "new" readings of Bergson, Hume, Leibniz, Spinoza and others are exemplary instances of this mechanism.

[3] Nietzsche's "Buddhism" has been seriously proposed. All you need is a few obscure passages and the notion that Nietzsche looked to the east to get started. Lester H. Hunt's *Nietzsche and the Origin of Virtue* (London: Routledge, 1991) reads Nietzsche as urging all individuals to find their own virtues by experimenting with life in whatever locations they find themselves in. Hunt suggests among other things that Nietzsche can be used by philosophers, tycoons, farmers and spot-welders (!) in order to each find their own virtues (p. 178). Portraits of Nietzsche as the patron saint of spot-welders at your local garage? Why not? Nietzsche was clearly impressed by graceful, integrated movement.

[4] See the conclusion of the first *Untimely Meditation*, the one titled "David Strauss, the confessor and the writer." Nietzsche gives many examples of specific sentences from Strauss, commenting extensively on their internal incoherence. Curiously, these examples and the commentary are missing from Hollingdale's English translation, which seems to diminish or ignore their importance for Nietzsche's argument (see the note on pp. 54–55 of *Untimely Meditations*, trans. R. J. Hollingdale (Cambridge: Cambridge UP, 1983). There is a brief discussion of this complex in my *Nietzsche: A Frenzied Look* (Amherst: U of Massachusetts Press, 1990), pp. 36–7.

[5] See Loren Goldner, "Postmodernism Versus World History," *Against the Current*, 8, 3 (July/August, 1993), 26–35. Goldner is described as a graduate stu-

dent living in Cambridge, Mass., currently completing a dissertation on race and class in American politics.

[6] Goldner, p. 27. Is it really possible to imagine Nietzsche reading *Mein Kampf* or listening to the lyrics of the Sex Pistols without vomiting, in view of his precise fussiness about style as exhibited whenever he talks about the craft of writing?

[7] Accusing Nietzsche of relativism is not the only sign that in Goldner we are at Ground Zero: "This is the real Eurocentric view. And what do the ostensibly radical multicultural postmodernists tell us about all this? Precisely nothing. And why? Because, through Nietzsche and Heidegger, Foucault and Derrida, they have swallowed the Hellenophile romance whole, except to change the plus and minus signs" (Goldner, p. 33). Hello? Nietzsche gave the Hellenes a plus sign and never looked outside of Greece? But from whence came Zarathustra? From whence came Dionysus? Why are Dionysus and Apollo *opposed* to each other in the Greece of *The Birth of Tragedy*? There isn't the slightest hint in these remarks that the author is aware that Nietzsche saw sharply "different" Hellenes, the ancient nobles of the good/bad table giving way to the sharply diminished Greek "scientists" of the good/evil table, the historical movement carefully recorded in the *Genealogy*.

[8] Richard A. Shweder, "Post-Nietzschean Anthropology: The Idea of Multiple Objective Worlds," *Relativism: Interpretation and Confrontation*, ed. Michael Krausz (Notre Dame: U of Notre Dame Press, 1989), pp. 99–139. Nietzsche is explicitly said to be a "protopositivist" (p. 111). Shweder's scholarly credentials show that Ground Zero is not just a dissertation writing disease that is cured during a distinguished career trajectory.

[9] There are many, many possible quotations. It might be noted that in the first of the *Untimely Meditations*, Nietzsche discusses at great length how German military victories were misused when they were taken to indicate the superiority of German culture over other cultures. In the *Genealogy*, Nietzsche is at pains to suggest that the victory of Socratic rationalism over the table of bad and good did not show any intrinsic superiority of scientific rationality. Nietzsche's indicators have to do rather with health, which in turn is resonant with what is life-affirming. The question of Nietzsche's own coherence is another matter. Here I am only suggesting that he is being completely misunderstood when he is taken to be the champion of any kind of atemporal cultural relativism.

[10] Allan Bloom, *The Closing of the American Mind* (New York: Simon and Schuster, 1987).

[11] Nietzsche is a frequent point of reference for Rorty. I will consider here only the recent two volume collection of Rorty's *Philosophical Papers* (Cambridge: Cambridge UP, 1991). Volume 1 is titled *Objectivity, Relativism, and Truth*, and volume 2 is titled *Essays on Heidegger and Others*. The two volumes, true to their conscious conversationsal intent, present only indices of names dropped, and no indices of subjects discussed. To judge from the name indices, Nietzsche

is one of the most frequently named philosophers in Rorty's papers, although there are no sustained discussions of Nietzsche's texts.

[12] Rorty, vol. 2, p. 176. This *is* representative of the way in which Nietzsche (and other philosophers) are involved in Rorty's text.

[13] Rorty, vol. 2, p. 2. Nothing in the text explains the peculiar temporal notion involved in the suggestion that Nietzsche was explaining to Europeans the doctrines of James and Dewey. I thought that we thought that James and Dewey (and Peirce) were at least originals.

[14] Rorty, vol. 1, pp. 187–88.

[15] This is Rorty introducing a quotation from Nietzsche in vol. 1, p. 32. The Nietzsche quotation, in turn, is taken from the essay "On Truth and Lie in an Extra-Moral Sense," cited from Walter Kaufmann's translation (pp. 46–47) of *The Portable Nietzsche* (New York: Viking Press, 1954). Rorty seems to like this quotation as capturing the essence of at least one Nietzsche. It is given again on p. 186 of vol. 2, and bits of the quotation are cited elsewhere.

[16] Rorty shields him in this way on p. 32 of volume 1. This provides an opening for Loyola as Nietzsche's *alter ego*, but at the immediate expense of any plausibility for Nietzsche's pragmatism. One might have thought that the last phrase of the "army of metaphors" indicated convergence. Is it possible that the notion of different Nietzsches is a consequence of his internal contradictions, or of his philosophical development? Surely, but then *Nietzsche* shouldn't be such a casual reference point. The "army of metaphors" quotation, taken as a central defining text for Nietzsche's own position, has the awkward feature of appearing only very early on in Nietzsche's production.

[17] Nietzsche's relationship to the natural science of his day was complicated. He read natural science, and at times tried to exploit ideas derived from Darwinism, and from physics. He nonetheless rejected Darwinism as supporting the survival of the "average." At one point, he was intrigued by the possibility of a proof of the eternal return derived from physics, although his attitude here is uncertain. In any event, his *published* works are uniform in condemning the output of the actual natural sciences as a delusion and a fraud where that output was taken as constituting a superior form of knowledge. Therefore, despite the details, Nietzsche lacks the sensibilities associated with pragmatism. Need I observe that any phrase to the effect that truth is what works would have driven Nietzsche into a rage?

Index